PRETRIAL ADVOCACY

Advance Praise for Pretrial Advocacy

Guttman and Lore have distilled decades of litigation experience into this manageable yet indispensable treatise. All too often lawyers fail to develop a litigation game plan at the outset of their case reflective of the relief the complaint purports to seek: a trial. *Pretrial Advocacy* instructs litigators on how to make sound decisions early on that will impact their readiness to bring a case to trial or relatedly to extract maximum value for their clients. This book should be in every serious litigator's library.

Jerry Martin
Former United States Attorney for the Middle District of Tennessee
Partner, Barrett Johnston Martin & Garrison, LLC

Years ago, the concept of "managerial judging" introduced a narrative framework for thinking about patterns of judicial behavior already familiar to any active litigator. In *Pretrial Advocacy*, Guttman and Lore offer an analogous narrative to help situate pretrial litigation processes along the arc from injury to trial. In doing so, they help their readers both better *understand* pretrial advocacy and better *practice* it.

Robert B. Ahdieh
Dean & Anthony G. Buzbee Endowed Dean's Chair
Texas A&M University School of Law

Pretrial Advocacy offers knowledge and guidance to law students interested in civil litigation. This easy-to-read book covers all the major rules—as well as strategy and best practices. Recommended!

Scott Dodson
James Edgar Hervey Chair in Litigation, Geoffrey C. Hazard
Jr. Distinguished Professor of Law, Director, Center for Litigation
and Courts, UC Hastings College of the Law

PRETRIAL ADVOCACY

Reuben A. Guttman

Senior Founding Partner
Guttman, Buschner & Brooks PLLC

J.C. Lore

Distinguished Clinical Professor
Rutgers Law School

NATIONAL INSTITUTE FOR TRIAL ADVOCACY

Address inquiries to:
Reprint Permission
National Institute for Trial Advocacy
325 W. South Boulder RD., Ste. 1
Louisville, CO 80027-1130
Phone: (800) 225-6482
Fax: (720) 890-7069
Email: permissions@nita.org

ISBN 978-1-60156-769-7
FBA 1769
eISBN 978-1-60156-770-3
eFBA 1770

Library of Congress Cataloging-in-Publication Data
Names: Guttman, Reuben A., author. | Lore, J. C., author.
Title: Pretrial advocacy / Reuben A. Guttman, Senior Founding Partner,
    Guttman, Buschner & Brooks; J.C. Lore, Associate Clinical Professor,
    Rutgers Law School.
Description: Louisville, CO : NITA, National Institute for Trial Advocacy,
    [2021] | Includes index.
Identifiers: LCCN 2021022101 (print) | LCCN 2021022102 (ebook) |
    ISBN 9781601567697 (paperback) | ISBN 9781601567703 (ebook)
Subjects: LCSH: Pre-trial procedure–United States.
Classification: LCC KF8900 .G88 2021 (print) | LCC KF8900 (ebook) | DDC
    347.73/72–dc23
LC record available at https://lccn.loc.gov/2021022101
LC ebook record available at https://lccn.loc.gov/2021022102
Printed in the United States.

 Wolters Kluwer

Official co-publisher of NITA.
WKLegaledu.com/NITA

CONTENTS

ACKNOWLEDGMENTS

We are thankful for the thoughtful insights, suggestions and assistance of Evan Benedon, Tom Bienert, Erica Briggs, Justin Brooks, Traci Buschner, Richard Celler, Veronica Finkelstein, Jonathan Freidin, Philip Freidin, Alan Fuchsberg, Cole Garcia, Hon. Nancy Gertner, Dan Guttman, Robert Guttman, Dick Harpootlian, Jason Kanterman, Jon Karmel, Chris Kenney, Jack Kolar, Corey Labrutto, Joseph Lanni, Melissa Lore, Brad Miller, Bill Nettles, Hon. Jack Nevin, Elizabeth Newsome, Dr. Caroline Poplin, Mimi Ramirez, Thomas Reilly, Steven Rogers, Liz Shofner, Anthony Sole, Bob Stropp, Stephanie Sweiling, Whitney Untiedt, Mario Valdivia, Aaron Verosky, Liza Vertinsky, Hon. Matthew W. Williams, and Paul Zwier.

FOREWORD

JUDGE NANCY GERTNER (RETIRED)

I was a trial lawyer for twenty-four years, trying criminal and civil cases, on all levels, trials and appeals, and in all jurisdictions, federal and state. I then had the privilege of becoming a federal judge in the District of Massachusetts, where I served for seventeen years, leaving the bench to join the faculty of the Harvard Law School. This is a book I wish I had had in both roles. And if I did, the pages would have been dog eared and covered in coffee stains from over-use.

Pretrial Advocacy is a book that is both practical and theoretical; it teaches litigation as a process informed by rules and cases, but also by strategic considerations. It instructs lawyers how to engage in pretrial pleading and discovery not for its own sake, but with an ultimate goal in mind—namely, trial. That trial may never come; the case may settle or be dismissed on summary judgment, but the enterprise is a critical one. A lawyer who envisions what a trial looks like, who prepares for it from the moment of the first client interview, is a lawyer who makes informed, strategic judgments about what to do or not do. Better yet, that lawyer has kept all options open, including trial, *because they have prepared for it.*

Changes in the Federal Rules of Civil Procedure have made cases front-loaded; more is required to plead a case and get past the procedural hurdles to trial. And while the purpose of the front loading in the Federal Rules of Civil Procedure was, in part, to save litigation costs by weeding out frivolous cases, too often it does the opposite. It promotes the worst of both worlds: fewer and fewer jury trials *and* high transaction costs.[1]

---

1. Perhaps the biggest casualty is civil rights cases, which are too often dismissed. As Suzette M. Malveaux states: "While the Federal Rules of Civil Procedure are trans-substantive, their impact is not . . . [T]he confluence of Rule 8(a)(2)'s pleading requirements and Rules 12 (b)(6)'s dismissal criteria – as ...interpreted by the Supreme Court in Bell Atlantic Corp. v. Twombly, [127 S. Ct. 1955 (2007)], and Ashcroft v. Iqbal [129 S. Ct. 1937 (2009)] has a distinct detrimental impact on civil rights cases alleging intentional discrimination," Suzette M. Malveau, *Front Loading and Heavy Lifting: How Pre-Dismissal Discovery Can Address the Detrimental Effect of Iqbal on Civil Rights Cases,* 14 LEWIS & CLARK L. REV. 65 (2010).

It is a self-fulfilling prophesy. If the only horizon lawyers see is how to settle the case, or win at pretrial scuffles, they will not learn the rules of evidence, trial strategy, dealing with jurors, or jury-waived trials. Lawyers who do not learn trial strategy are lawyers less and less willing to contemplate what a trial would look like. Worse still, such lawyers lose a strategic tool, a way of prioritizing discovery and pleadings. Pretrial discovery and motion practice becomes willy nilly, lawyers running in place because they believe that is what modern advocacy requires.[2]

Pretrial Advocacy is the antidote to that phenomenon. It fills an important space for litigators. It teaches how to try cases from the moment a client contacts the lawyer through the trial, encouraging lawyers to engage in strategic decisions about pretrial discovery and motion practice. Why depose this witness rather than another? What is the purpose? What are the salient documents—not every single one, not just the few "gotcha" documents, but those that build the narrative.

Do not overlook *Pretrial Advocacy*'s important contribution to the teaching of the Federal Rules. This is the way the rules of civil procedure were intended to be understood: not as dead-end, abstract exercises but as part of a narrative culminating in a trial. They are not just words on a page, to be interpreted linguistically; they are informed by context, animated by certain concerns, and intertwined with other rules.

Pretrial Advocacy encourages the reader to know both the Federal Rules of Civil Procedure and the Federal Rules of Evidence. These two sets of rules cannot be read in isolation. Rules of evidence necessary frame the answers to the questions raised by the rules of civil procedure—about relevance, about privilege, about hearsay. For example:

> Even in applying FRCP 9(b) to fraud pleadings in fraud cases, plaintiffs might consider reminding the court that at trial cases can be made on circumstantial evidence, as FRE 401 makes no distinction between circumstantial and direct evidence. FRCP 9(b) states pleadings alleging fraud or mistake require particularity of allegations. This may confuse some litigants into believing they need to allege direct evidence. Yet, when FRCP 9(b) is read in context with FRE 401, it is clear that requiring a pleading standard more stringent than the evidentiary standard was not intended.[3]

In this book, these are not just abstract points. *Pretrial Advocacy* is filled with practical tips and insights that other judges will surely appreciate. It urges lawyers

---

2. Arthur R. Miller notes that "*Twombly* and *Iqbal* are producing more pleading motions, more delays, more costs, more appeals, and potentially more inappropriate dismissals." Arthur R. Miller, *Simplified Pleading, Meaningful Days in Court, and Trials on the Merits: Reflections on the Deformation of Federal Procedure*, 88 N.Y.U. L. Rev. 286, 346 (2013).
3. Section 10.4

to invoke the court's decision-making authority "strategically, sensitive to the court's limited time."[4] It urges the collegial civility that the Model Rules of Professional Conduct endorses. "While emotion and instinct may counsel an aggressive stance, remember that you *will* have a relationship with your opponent throughout the course of the litigation—you only get to decide its tone. Being firm, yet cordial, will result in a different relationship than being rude or aggressive. Meet-and-confer dialogues, like all contacts with opposing counsel, the court, clients, and the outside world, a place where reputations develop. Be an honest broker and a person who keeps their word."[5]

When I was on the bench, I evaluated discovery disputes, often presented at a decibel level which I frankly could not fathom no matter how hard I worked. I was reminded of the law professor who sent me identical letters about two different potential clerk candidates; he took the time to write on each letter, "I really mean it." Which recommendation, I asked, did he "*really* mean"? Pretrial pleadings are sometimes like that; one party throwing every conceivable motion at the other, and then rushing to court when not satisfied. I would ask, what relief do you "really want"; "all of the above" is not an answer. *Pretrial Advocacy* will guide you in targeting your motions to achieve the best result for your client and avoid wasting the court's time.

This book's advice will not only help you navigate your litigation through the court; it will help you better serve your client: "Be the judge's problem solver, make their life easier, and earn credibility with the judge and your opposition."[6] "Make the brief and the motion self-contained so neither the judge nor his clerks have to revisit either document to fully understand the argument. Repetition is not generally a problem."[7]

Pretrial Advocacy clarifies its excellent advice with scenarios and examples that change abstract principles into concrete action plans. My personal favorite is in the section on taking a deposition, using the game "Battleship" as a metaphor.

Too often books about the law are either/or. Either academic—not intended for the practitioner who needs to know both the rules and the rationale behind the rules—or pragmatic—implying that the text of the rule is all you need to know and ignoring the context into which they fit. This book sits in both worlds—for the lawyer, for the judge, for the teacher, and for the student aspiring to all of the above.

---

4. Section 10.3
5. Section 10.5
6. Section 10.4
7. Section 10.5.1

Preface

Trial lawyers love analogies. Analogies translate complex or unfamiliar concepts into something understandable for those not otherwise immersed in the nuances of the subject matter.

There is no shortage of analogies that can be used to describe the pretrial process: the kitchen of a five-star restaurant; the script development and rehearsals for a Broadway play; or perhaps the first fifty-eight minutes of a football game for those who only want to know the final score.

The above is a shorthand way of saying that the process leading up to trial not only determines the outcome of the trial but also whether a complaint—the handful of raw ingredients a plaintiff brings to their counsel—will get anywhere close to trial. And like the kitchen in a five-star restaurant, pretrial is where all the work gets done, turning those ingredients into a beautifully prepared feast of evidence that the ultimate recipients—the judge or jurors—will consume and appreciate, rendering a favorable verdict.

Television and movies dwell too much on trials, reveling in scorching cross-examinations with "aha" moments and oral arguments that rival the elegance of the Gettysburg address.

Those trial moments are the tip of a massive iceberg, to use another analogy. The iceberg's lowest layer is an aggrieved client or perhaps a public interest lawyer with a vision of change that will address or prevent injury or adverse treatment. The second layer involves case investigation with proceeding layers involving legal research, the application of law to facts, the drafting of a complaint, motions to dismiss, initial disclosures, discovery, expert identification and reports, more motions practice, and then, and only then, trial. At each layer, a diligent attorney will reassess their position; reassess the evidence; recheck the law; continue to discuss matters with their client; and determine what is necessary to keep a case from going to trial (or get a case to trial) and what opportunities exist for resolution.

The pretrial process both readies cases for trial and drives case resolution to avoid trial. Ninety-nine percent of all cases resolve during the pretrial process; they are disposed of through motions practice or—through the necessary fact finding and rulings on motions along the way—the parties gauge their relative risks, factor in the costs of litigation, and decide to create certainty through a settlement that takes resolution out of the hands of a judge or jury.

In sum, the pretrial process is quintessentially American; it recognizes that process itself can dictate a substantive result. It is a process whose backbone is transparency; the type of transparency that gives both the allegedly aggrieved and the accused an opportunity to decide their own fate through settlement.

Anyone who questions the significance of the pretrial process need only appreciate how much of our common law is developed from the pretrial stages of cases. Indeed, many matters come before the Supreme Court without any trial occurring. Service of process, subject matter jurisdiction, pleading standards, summary judgment, class certification, and experts are pretrial matters; they are all outcome determinative; they have all been reviewed by the Supreme Court.

Of course, the pretrial process, the ability to get a trial, and the American Court system itself are part of a branch of government that, on any given day, creates an opportunity for any citizen—without regard to their position in life—to have an issue heard and perhaps even change the trajectory of the Republic. Most certainly, it will change individuals' lives. If there is any doubt about this point, just study the great civil rights cases of the last seventy-five years.

Realizing the significance of pretrial litigation, we wrote this book fully appreciating that too many individuals and families need representation they cannot afford. The court system has become expensive, complicated and—quite simply—difficult for plaintiffs, defendants, and others who are touched by it. Globalization, new employment paradigms, and the technology with which we record, store, and retrieve information has created new challenges for the court system and the litigation process. Indeed, as we finish this book, the world is burdened by a pandemic that challenges a legal process that depends on face-to-face confrontation and communication.

Though the pretrial process is guided by rules, it seeks efficiency and fairness. We write this book to encourage litigators to not just read the rules but also to implement them in ways that accommodate the challenges of a changing world. We write this book to be useful not just to practitioners, but also to jurists and those who teach in law school or continuing legal education programs.

We offer the book as not only a practical manual for the pretrial process but also as a window into the challenges of those who participate in the process. We even hope it is of value to those who have been long-time players or participants.

As a check against our own perspectives or biases, and to provide different perspectives, we have scattered tips from practitioners throughout.

For practitioners, we offer practical advice and useful insight. For those who teach law, we have tried to convey the importance of teaching the rules of procedure and the rules of evidence in some coordinated way. Today's cases are—as we say—"front loaded"—and the rules of evidence simply cannot be left to learn at a later day. We have also sought to convey the culture of litigation, which provides important context for the rules.

For jurists—those looking down from the bench upon a playing field that may be outcome determinative—we hope to offer better insight—almost from a social science perspective—into the politics and emotions of the pretrial world. If this enables jurists to better supervise that world, we will have made an impact.

JC Lore

Reuben Guttman

CHAPTER ONE

PRETRIAL PROCESS

1.1 Introduction

Law is a mixture of substantive and procedural rights. Substantive law without a process of enforcement is tantamount to no substantive law at all.

A fair and transparent process—which includes the pretrial process—promotes confidence in the results. Decisions should flow from a transparent methodology based on the transparency of facts underlying the dispute. Drawing a parallel to mathematics, confidence in the answer is governed by a proof demonstrating how the answer was reached. Remember the grade school math teacher saying, "show your work"?

The pretrial process is critically important—in most cases, it determines the outcome of the trial process.

—Mike Beckwith, Asst. U.S. Attorney, E.D. California

In litigation, the pretrial process is designed so parties themselves can gauge the inevitability of the court's "answer." Often this allows the parties to get the information necessary to resolve the dispute on their own as they know that letting the court do so has some risk. The court or jury may render a favorable or an unfavorable result but in either case the value of the result has to be measured against the costs of litigation and the "time value of money."

Governed by the interplay between written rules, case law, and practice norms, this process requires parties to focus their disputes and survey the facts underpinning each side's claims, while tackling the challenges presented by legal decisions that potentially eliminate claims, validate claims, or determine the issues subject to adjudication. One of the intended consequences of this pretrial advocacy process is forcing the parties to see case strengths and weaknesses so that rational decision-making, based on a review of the evidence, leads to resolution absent a trial. This is precisely why most cases are resolved at the pretrial stage; this is how the process was intended to work, and it is the reason that the pretrial stage of litigation is so significant. Obviously, for those cases that are not resolved before trial, this process serves other important purposes, such as uncovering all the facts that might support or detract from each side's theory of the case or narrowing the issues for trial to focus on what is clearly in dispute.

Understanding the norms of the pretrial advocacy process is critical to zealous representation of a client's interest. Regardless of the strong likelihood the case will be resolved absent a trial, cases should be prepared as if trial were inevitable. If the case does go to trial, that preparation gives the attorney the necessary confidence to pursue all phases of the case from motions practice through discovery, more motions practice, and eventually trial. The opponent recognizes that level of confidence and factors it into settlement evaluation.

1.2 Substance: Knowing the Rules of the Game

To effectively maneuver through the pretrial process, one must generally understand two important sets of rules: the Federal Rules of Civil Procedure (FRCP) and the Federal Rules of Evidence (FRE). Forty-five states have procedural analogues to the Federal Rules of Civil Procedure[1] and thirty-eight states have rules analogue to the Federal Rules of Evidence.[2] Strategic use of these rules can go a long way towards determining litigation outcomes. Carefully negotiated and crafted by rules committees, FRCP and FRE wording has significance even though the phrasing of particular rules may appear incidental. Proper use of the rules requires word-choice analysis, study of the Advisory Committee Notes, and research of case law interpreting the rules. The Federal Judicial Center (FJC) is the educational arm of the federal court system. The FJC website is a valuable resource containing a substantial amount of information including videos featuring sitting judges.[3]

Learn the rules. When you begin to practice law, bring them home and read through them for a little while each evening. Why? Because there really is more than one way to skin a cat. In discovery, at some point, you will make a mistake. You will forget to ask a question or miss asking for a particular category of documents. The important part of making mistakes is learning

---

1. John B. Oakley & Arthur F. Coon, *The Federal Rules in State Courts: A Survey of State Court Systems of Civil Procedure*, 61 WASH. L. REV. 1367 (1986) (of the forty-five states with substantially similar rules to the FRCP, twenty-three states nearly replicate the Federal Rules of Civil Procedure, only six states deviate from them substantially (these numbers predate the E-Discovery Amendment to the FRCP)).
2. UNIF. RULES OF EVID. (UNIF. L. COMM'N. 1999) (thirty-eight states have evidence rules that parallel the Uniform Rules of Evidence. Additionally, the Uniform Rules of Evidence are very comparable to the Federal Rules of Evidence).
3. *See* FED. JUD. CTR., http://www.fjc.gov. The FJC, established in 1967 by an Act of Congress, is the education and research arm of the court system. The FJC's website is loaded with publications and videos providing valuable information on substantive and procedural laws.

how to correct them. In discovery, nearly everything is correctable, but you won't know how unless you know the rules.

—*Janesa Urbano, Senior Counsel, Clark Guldin Attorneys at Law*

Law schools generally teach the FRCP and the FRE in isolation with separate classes on "procedure" and "evidence." Both sets of rules repeatedly reference one another and cannot be fully understood in isolation. Moreover, the notion that the rules of evidence only come into play at the trial phase of litigation is a false one; the goal of the pretrial process is to gather and assimilate evidence that will be used at trial. Thinking about the trial as an abstract event that most likely will not occur is simply a recipe for disaster.

1.2.1 The Federal Rules of Civil Procedure

The FRCP govern lawsuits from the initial filing of a complaint (FRCP 3) through the execution of a judgment (FRCP 69). The FRCP establishes numerous minefields with the potential to eliminate plaintiff claims through motions to dismiss (FRCP 12(b)) or motions for summary judgment (FRCP 56). The FRCP's discovery obligations promote transparency through document sharing, deposition testimony, land inspections, and physical or mental examinations of an injured plaintiff. Different types of motions may induce counsel to assess the integrity of their case and weigh the risks of pursuing a trial. Dispositive motions—motions to dismiss and or for summary judgment—can often prompt settlement discussions. Still, other types of motions can adjust the likelihood of success at trial or make the case less economical to pursue, which also can drive settlement. Included in this list are motions for class certification, motions to exclude evidence, or Daubert motions to limit or exclude expert testimony.

For those students who spend or spent law school mystified by the bevy of rules and their purported complexity, do not despair. Truth be told; procedural and evidentiary rules are a lot about common sense. Rule construction is governed in FRCP 1, which states:

> These rules govern the procedure in all civil actions and proceedings in the United States district courts, except as stated in Rule 81. They should be construed, administered and employed by the court and the parties to secure the just, speedy, and inexpensive determination of every action and the proceeding.[4]

Initially, this wording seems inconsequential. It is, perhaps, the type of language that seems routine; "legalese" that is in the text because the authors had to start somewhere. Yet, FRCP 1 is significant; it gives judges license to apply common

---

4. Fed. R. Civ. P. 1.

sense in pretrial proceedings. Though the phrase "common sense" does not appear in the rule, the words "just, speedy, and inexpensive" are in the rule as is the word "construed." As such, the wording is an arrow in the quiver of counsel who are seeking to explain to a judge why requested relief should be granted.

FRCP 1 is not just a rule about how the court should implement the FRCPs, it is a rule about how the parties should work together to do so. The amendment adding the word "parties" to FRCP 1 went into effect on December 31, 2015.[5] This addition calls for opposing parties' collaboration to construe and implement rules.[6] One might ask if such collaboration conflicts with professional ethics' mandate for zealous and diligent representation.[7] On the contrary, collaboration can favorably position counsel to facilitate and expedite dispute resolution, so long as the situation is not outcome determinative. FRCP 1's language invites the creative lawyer to propose methods aimed at improving court efficiency, unburdening judges with a heavy case load.[8] Think about the impact of FRCP 1; be creative; be efficient; think about the following:

- Stipulations as to facts so as to eliminate the need for certain witnesses and perhaps streamlining discovery and trial.

- Having technical experts confer directly on issues involving collection and retrieval of data for electronic discovery.

---

5. *See* Fed. Jud. Ctr., *Amendments to the Federal Rules of Practice and Procedure 2015—Civil Rules Redline*, https://www.fjc.gov/content/309299/civil-rules-amendments-2015-redline (Dec. 1, 2015). *See also* Practical Law Litigation, *Overview of December 2015 Amendments to the Federal Rules of Civil Procedure*, Thomson Reuters Practical Law, https://us.practicallaw.thomsonreuters.com/w-000-6911.
6. Fed. R. Civ. P. 1 advisory committee's note to 2015 amendment. ("Rule 1 is amended to emphasize that just as the court should construe and administer these rules to secure the just, speedy, and inexpensive determination of every action, *so the parties* share the responsibility to employ the rules in the same way. Most lawyers and parties cooperate to achieve these ends. But discussions of ways to improve the administration of civil justice regularly include pleas to discourage over-use, misuse, and abuse of procedural tools that increase cost and result in delay. Effective advocacy is consistent with—and indeed depends upon—cooperative and proportional use of procedure.") (emphasis added).
7. The American Bar Association's rules used to refer only to the word "zealous" with regard to an attorney's obligation to a client. By way of example, D.C. Rules of Pro. Conduct 1.3(a) states: "A lawyer shall represent a client zealously and diligently within the bounds of the law."
8. Thomas E. Willging et al., *Special Masters' Incidence and Activity: Report to the Judicial Conference's Advisory Committee on Civil Rules and Its Subcommittee on Special Masters* 9 (2000) A study conducted by the Federal Judiciary Center, that surveyed judges and attorneys on the effectiveness of special masters found that "all judges and almost all attorneys thought that the benefits of appointing the masters outweighed any drawbacks and said they would, with the benefit of hindsight, still support the appointments. Attorneys said this regardless of how the special masters' appointments initially came about, and even regardless of whether the masters' involvement benefited their clients. Likewise, almost all special masters we interviewed thought that their appointments were warranted and would not change any terms of their appointments."

- Stipulating to authenticity.

- Bifurcating issues in the case.

- Accomplishing discovery more quickly through the use of remote depositions and hearings.

Consider this example of how FRCP 1 can spur creative problem solving. Suppose the chairman of the board for a Fortune 500 company receives a third-party subpoena for a deposition. The chairman's counsel claims harassment, argues that his client does not have information relevant to the case, and moves to quash the subpoena. At argument on a motion for protective order, the judge appears sympathetic to the chairman's concerns. Although a black letter application of the rules would compel the deposition, the judge is hesitant to mandate the testimony. The colloquy between the parties might go something like this:

> **Judge:** I am quite frankly bothered about requiring the chairman of a *Fortune 500* company to sit for a seven-hour deposition in this case, and I am not persuaded that this woman has any information that will be relevant to this matter.

> **Problem-Solving Counsel:** Your Honor, I appreciate your position and have a proposal that reasonably addresses your concerns. We propose that the chairman be required to truthfully answer six interrogatories regarding the scope of her knowledge. We will agree to limit our deposition to the scope of what she says she knows based on those answers and will limit the testimony to thirty minutes per subject area.

> **Judge:** That seems like a possible solution. Counsel for the chairman, what do you have to say about that?

Notice that the problem-solving approach transforms a hearing into a negotiation where guaranteed relief is now possible instead of an all-or-nothing outcome.

Obviously, FRCP 1 is only the first of 86 rules that comprise the Federal Rules of Civil Procedure. It is not necessary to memorize all 86 procedural rules. However, certain rules arise frequently in the pretrial litigation process and trial lawyers must have a working knowledge of the most commonly used rules.

These key procedural rules are listed below:

- FRCP 1—Scope and Purpose

- FRCP 4—Summons

- FRCP 8—General Rules of Pleading

- FRCP 9—Pleading Special Matters

- FRCP 10—Form of Pleadings

- FRCP 11—Signing Pleadings, Motions, and Other Papers; Representations to the Court; Sanctions

- FRCP 12—Defenses and Objections: When and How Presented; Motion for Judgment on the Pleadings; Consolidating Motions; Waiving Defense; Pretrial Hearing

- FRCP 16—Pretrial Conferences; Scheduling; Management

- FRCP 26—Duty to Disclose; General Provisions Governing Discovery

- FRCP 31—Depositions by Written Questions

- FRCP 32—Using Depositions in Court Proceedings

- FRCP 33—Interrogatories to Parties

- FRCP 34—Producing Documents, Electronically Stored Information, and Tangible Things, or Entering onto Land, for Inspection and Other Purposes

- FRCP 56—Summary Judgment

In addition to the FRCP, specific jurisdictions may have separate local rules and federal judges may also have their own rules. Local rules, meant to increase court efficiency, are typically available on the court's website and judges often provide their own rules once a case is filed or after the exchange of pleadings. They do not override any federal or state rules, but often are more granular than the federal rules. They may concern pleading format, motion presentation, motion timing, and meet and confer requirements. For example, the former chief justice of the United States District Court for the Central District of California, George H. King, required parties to collaborate on motions for summary judgment and file one document containing both sides' arguments. Providing a single, integrated document simplified the court's decision to grant or deny a motion for summary judgment.

Not all local rules pertain to court filings, but instead govern courtroom etiquette. The late S. Arthur Spiegel, of the United States District Court for the Southern District of Ohio, required that all counsel stand behind the podium when addressing the court. Spiegel also mandated all exhibits be pre-marked or provided to the clerk of court before a hearing. When presenting witnesses with exhibits, Spiegel required counsel to ask the clerk of court to present them. While these types of rules may not relate to the substance of your case, not knowing them signals counsel's inattention and might foster adverse court relations.

1.2.2   *The Federal Rules of Evidence*

The FRE governs what evidence courts may consider in making decisions. FRE 102 states "[t]hese rules should be construed so as to administer every proceeding fairly, eliminate unjustifiable expense and delay, and promote the development of evidence law, to the end of ascertaining the truth and securing a just determination." The word "construed" signifies the FRE are not considered black letter mandates, but are instead subject to interpretation. This phrasing forms the lens by which courts and litigants should view the rules. It is what gives judges great flexibility in how they control the flow of evidence.

The FRCP establishes processes for plaintiffs and defendants to obtain information while the FRE determines the admissibility of that information at trial. Proper use of the FRCP's discovery-related rules facilitates counsel securing information in ways that ensure admissibility under the FRE. Some important questions to consider throughout the pretrial process:

- Do I want to use this information at trial?

- Do I want to exclude this information at trial?

During the pretrial process, counsel's primary focus should be acquiring relevant evidence as defined by FRE 401. Relevant evidence "has a tendency to make a fact more or less probable than it would be without the evidence; and the fact is of consequence in determining the action." The FRE does not distinguish direct evidence from circumstantial evidence. Instead, the fact finder is responsible for weighing evidentiary relevance and probative value. During the pretrial process, counsel must collect both direct and circumstantial evidence and concurrently predict its possible usage in dispositive motions and at trial. In closing arguments, it is critical that counsel argue inferences linking the circumstantial evidence to the direct evidence. Since jury discretion dictates the weight of evidence, counsel might also argue against the legitimacy of the circumstantial evidence.

A cursory glance at FRE 401 may give the false impression that all evidence is admissible if it has any probative value. That is certainly not the case, as relevance is just the threshold determination required for evidence to have the possibility of being admissible. If it isn't relevant, then it is "game over" for that piece of evidence. If it is relevant, then you must now look to the other rules to see if they exclude the evidence. Because FRE 401 does not distinguish between direct and circumstantial evidence, the rule has the potential to allow the jury to be burdened with a myriad of evidence that may add little or no value in determining a fact in dispute. The role of FRE 403 is really to create a filter and thus exclude certain types of evidence. FRE 403 states: "the court may exclude evidence if its probative value is substantially outweighed by a danger of one or more of the following: unfair prejudice, confusing the issues, misleading the jury, undue delay, wasting time, or needlessly presenting cumulative evidence."

Some practitioners, and many law students, erroneously forget the importance of these critical qualifying words:

- Substantially

- Unfair

- Undue

- Needlessly

All evidence is prejudicial and is supposed to be prejudicial. We introduce evidence to sway decisionmakers, to prejudice them toward or against one party. It is prejudice which is *unfair* that concerns the court. FRE 403 is a rule of exclusion but when evaluating admissibility through its balancing test, it favors admissibility. FRE excludes *only* evidence that is:

- Substantially outweighed by unfair prejudice

- Substantially outweighed by confusing the issues

- Substantially outweighed by misleading the jury

- Substantially outweighed by undue delay

- Substantially outweighed by wasting time

- Substantially outweighed by needlessly presenting cumulative evidence

1.2.2.1 Authentication

The admissibility of evidence at trial also requires evidence to be authentic with FRE 901 and 902 providing the guidance for how to authenticate evidence. FRE 901(a) defines authentication and FRE 901(b) provides an excellent road map on how the discovery process is used to authenticate nine distinctive evidence types. Additionally, FRE 902 addresses self-authenticating evidence, including electronic discovery.

Simply put, evidence must be what it purports to be. If one party wants to admit the contract in a contract dispute case, they have the burden to prove that this is the actual contract. Sometimes there is no doubt what the item is, and the opposing party does not dispute its authenticity. As you prepare your case, you must plan for the possibility that you will be required to prove the authenticity of the evidence you want the judge and jury to hear. FRCP-facilitated discovery is what secures the information needed to authenticate evidence for trial use.

To take a closer look, suppose a little league pitcher's parents sue the league when a line drive off an aluminum bat hits their daughter in the head, injuring her. The parents maintain the league was negligent by allowing the use of aluminum bats and they seek to introduce the bat into evidence at trial. The bat is relevant because their argument is that the bat caused the injury to the player. Any other bat is not relevant to this case. There are probably hundreds, if not thousands, of the same bat that were manufactured and sold throughout the United States. How does the plaintiff prove that this bat is the actual bat that was used to hit the line drive? Think about the pretrial discovery tools. The parents' counsel could subpoena the batter for a deposition and ask the foundational questions to establish that this is the bat. By introducing the bat as an exhibit at the deposition, the lawyer is securing information to authenticate it for use at trial.

Among the tools of pretrial discovery is FRCP 34 which gives the right to a party to request the production of "tangible things." At deposition and after the production of the bat, one can locate guidance for authenticating the bat at the deposition in FRE 901(a):

> To satisfy the requirement of authenticating or identifying an item of evidence, the proponent must produce evidence sufficient to support a finding that the item is what it purports to be.

FRE 901(b)(4) provides that "distinctive characteristics and the like" may be used to authenticate evidence. This portion of the rule focuses on "[t]he appearance, contents, substance, internal patterns, or other distinctive characteristics of the item, taken together with all the circumstances."

To comply with authentication requirements, the deposition questioning might proceed as follows:

Parents' Counsel: You have in front of you what has been labeled as Exhibit 4; can you identify this item?

Batter: Yes, it is a baseball bat.

Parents' Counsel: Do you know whether this was the bat that you used to hit the line drive that hit the head of Jane Smith on June 1 of this year?

Batter: Yes, it is.

Parents' Counsel: How do you know?

Batter: The bat was a black H&B 34 and was the Roberto Clemente model and had blue tape around the handle and a red spray-painted spot at the top. It is the bat that I have used for two seasons.

By demonstrating the bat's distinct characteristics, the deposition testimony authenticates the bat. However, witnesses may not always be so forthcoming with details. Anticipating this issue, the deposing lawyer should establish the bat's specific branding and markings early in the deposition before ever showing the bat to the witness. Then later, when introducing the bat to the witness, the deposing lawyer reminds the witness of her earlier testimony before asking the necessary authentication questions. This makes it less likely that the witness will deny that it is the bat.

Some items do not require this process because they are self-authenticating. This means that because it is a particular type of evidence, it is presumed to be authentic. The list of these items can be found in FRE 902 and include items such as public documents, public records, and electronically stored information.

It is important to keep in mind that the burden for authentication is very low. The witness does not have to agree or admit that it is a particular piece of evidence. You just need to produce evidence at a sufficient level that a jury could find that the item is what you are claiming it is to satisfy the standard set forth in 901(a). In the previous example, if the witness did not admit the bat was the one used, you would look for other evidence during the pretrial process that would establish its authenticity. There might be a picture of the bat being used. Another witness might be able to identify it as the one used to hit the line drive. There are numerous possibilities and FRE 901(b) does not limit the ways in which you can establish authenticity. The ten examples of ways to authenticate evidence listed in FRE 901(b) are just that—examples. Throughout the pretrial process, you should be thinking creatively about how to use your discovery tools to establish an item's authenticity.

Finally, do not make the mistake of conflating authenticity with admissibility. They are distinct concepts. Authenticity, just like relevance, is something that must be established before admitting into evidence a tangible item. Something that is authentic still must be relevant and not excluded by any of the enumerated concerns in FRE 403. An item, such as an email, text, or contract, might be authentic but it can still be excluded because it is hearsay. Authenticity of evidence is something to think about strategically throughout the pretrial process, but don't forget to keep in mind the other hurdles for admissibility.

1.2.2.2 Hearsay

Although evidence may be relevant under FRE 401, not excludable under FRE 403, and authentic under FRE 901, other rules impacting admissibility must be considered throughout the pretrial process. An important rule impacting the admissibility of documents and statements is FRE 801 and the exclusion of hearsay.

As you discover and think through your own evidence and the evidence of your opponent, you should be thinking about the different issues implicated by a particular type of evidence. Anytime you are dealing with any type of writing such as a letter, statement, contract, email, or text message, you should be thinking about hearsay. Anytime you are dealing with an oral statement about which someone might testify, you should be thinking about hearsay. Once you have discovered or identified this type of evidence, the pretrial process should be used to establish how FRE 801 does or does not exclude it.

Oral and written statements are excluded by FRE 801 unless the rules provide a reason why they should not be. When trying to resolve a hearsay issue through the pretrial process for a piece of evidence you would like to admit, you should consider four different ways that the evidence might not be subject to FRE 801's exclusion:

- It does not meet the definition of hearsay under 801(c).

- It is exempted by the hearsay rule under 801(d).

- It meets the requirements of one of the FRE 803 exceptions where the availability to testify of the person who said or wrote the statement does not matter.

- It meets the requirements of one of the FRE 804 exceptions that requires the speaker or writer of the statement to be unavailable to testify.

By definition, hearsay is an out-of-court oral or written statement "introduced for the truth of the matter asserted." This is one of the most confusing concepts in evidence. In short and to illustrate: a man testifies that he ran out of a theater because "someone yelled the theater was on fire." If the testimony is introduced to show there was indeed a fire, then it is hearsay. You need that statement to be true for it to be relevant. If the testimony is introduced to show why the man ran out of the theater, then the statement that there is a fire does not have to be true to be relevant. Whether there is or is not a fire does not matter. Its relevance is the fact that the statement was said by someone and heard by the man who ran out of the theater. Therefore, it does not have to be true to be relevant and it is not hearsay. If you are not using the statement for the truth of the matter asserted, then it is not hearsay. Therefore, you must evaluate your evidence to determine its relevance because your theory of relevance for an out-of-court statement will often determine its potential admissibility.

Exemptions to hearsay are commonly used in litigation and no rule is more commonly used than FRE 801(d)(2), an opposing party's statement. If one party is trying to use the statement of the opposing party, it is not considered hearsay. This is easy to understand when the parties are individuals, but suppose the defendant is a corporation or a contractor working for a corporation. Securing the admission of an opposing party's statement into evidence may require a determination, through deposition or interrogatory, as to whether the statement was authorized by the corporation or made in a representative capacity. The opposing party exception is broad and thinking about collecting and establishing facts at the pretrial stage will enable you to establish whether evidence will be excluded or admitted at trial.

If the out-of-court statement is hearsay because it is being used for the truth of the matter asserted and it does not fall within the FRE 801(d) exemptions, case discovery should be used to collect evidence that forms the basis for a hearsay rule exception under FRE 803 or 804. Each of these exceptions has elements and requirements that necessitate the discovery of facts in order to persuade the court they are satisfied. The party seeking to utilize a hearsay exception under FRE 803 or 804 has the burden, by a preponderance of the evidence, to convince the court the elements have been met.

Imagine a scenario where a policyholder sues an insurance company for failing to pay a claim on an insured dwelling destroyed by fire. The insurance company argues their coverage excludes fires caused by arson. The fire marshal's report asserts a gasoline spill caused the fire. The insurance company seeks to introduce the city fire marshal's report into evidence. Its counsel argues the report will come into evidence under the "public record" exception to the hearsay rule, FRE 803(8). The insurance company's counsel interviews the fire marshal, who testifies the report represents "factual findings from a legally authorized investigation." (FRE 803(8)(A)(iii)). The insured's counsel seeks to oppose the introduction of the fire marshal's report using FRE 803(8)(B) which states that it is not subject to exclusion as hearsay only if "the opponent does not show that the source of information or other circumstances indicate a lack of trustworthiness." In other words, even if the proponent of the evidence establishes the elements of 803(8)(A) that it is a public record, the opponent can show that the source of the information or other circumstances indicate a lack of trustworthiness and thus, prevent its admission. Zeroing in on the 803(8)(B) language, the insured's counsel deposes the fire marshal and asks the following questions:

> **Insured's Counsel**: Prior to issuing a final draft of the report, you shared a draft with the insurance company?
>
> **Fire Marshal:** Yes.
>
> **Insured's Counsel**: That draft concluded that you did not know the source of the fire?
>
> **Fire Marshal:** Yes.
>
> **Insured's Counsel**: In fact, based on your tests, there was no evidence of gasoline starting the fire.
>
> **Fire Marshal:** Yes
>
> **Insured's Counsel**: The only information that you have about gasoline even being on the premises came from the insurance carrier?
>
> **Fire Marshal:** Right.

1.2.3 Interplay between FRCP and FRE

To reiterate, the FRCP and the FRE cannot be read in isolation. Procedural rules govern many processes involving the collection and use of the same facts, documents, and information regulated by the evidentiary rules.

A primary area of interplay occurs between FRE 702 and FRCP 26. FRE 702 governs expert testimony and FRCP 26 governs mandatory disclosures. Selection of experts and witness preparation occurs during the pretrial process. Through the pretrial motion process, the court determines if an expert may testify and, if so, whether limitations are placed on that testimony. Those decisions are governed by FRE 403, FRE 702, and the Supreme Court decisions in *Daubert v. Merrell Dow Pharmaceuticals*, 509 U.S. 579 (1993), *General Electric Co. v. Joiner*, 522 U.S. 136 (1997), and *Kumho Tire Co. v. Carmichael*, 526 U.S. 137 (1999).

The process of filing pretrial motions begins with meeting FRCP 26's disclosure requirements. FRCP 26(a)(2) states "[i]n addition to the disclosures required by 26(a) (1), a party must disclose to the other parties the identity of any witnesses it may use at trial to present evidence under Federal Rules of Evidence 702, 703, or 705." The rule describes the specific disclosures that are required. These disclosures are foundations for questioning at "expert depositions," and ultimately, a basis for an admissibility challenge of the expert's testimony. In *Daubert*, the Supreme Court declared trial court judges the gatekeepers for determining whether an expert may testify.[9]

Another example of the interplay between the FRE and FRCP is between FRE 612 and FRCP 30(b)(6). Under FRE 612, courts may order disclosure of privileged or work product protected documents that were used to refresh a witness' recollection before testifying. In the context of a FRCP 30(b)(6) witness, however, the corporate witness generally has no recollection of actual events or information, but instead is educated on the corporation's collective knowledge before testifying as the corporate representative. Is it appropriate to require a Rule 30(b)(6) witness to produce every document they reviewed in preparing for the deposition? Or should some type of balancing test be applied given that the individual witness is not having his or her individual recollection refreshed? In *Adidas America, Inc. v. TRB Acquisitions LLC*, the court addressed this issue, considering "an "automatic" waiver under FRE 612" applied by some courts that required Rule 30(b)(6) witnesses to produce every document they reviewed, as well as "a case-by-case balancing test" applied by other courts. The court ultimately adopted its own standard, "a middle-ground approach between the automatic waiver rule and the balancing test."[10] This particular issue is a developing area, with no clear and controlling precedent from the Supreme Court. However, it illustrates how interpretation and application of the two sets of rules can impact a case.

1.3   Substance: Case Law Governing the Litigation Process

Obviously, you will look to case law for guidance on the substantive legal issues in your case. However, it is important to recognize that case law is also relevant

---

9. Daubert v. Merrell Dow Pharms., Inc., 509 U.S. 579 (1993).
10. Adidas Am., Inc., v. TRB Acquisitions LLC, 324 F.R.D. 389, 20-21 (D. Or. 2017).

to the litigation process. To a large extent, the rules governing that process are straightforward; however, there is a large body of interpretative case law. These court interpretations of the rules are critical to success and you should familiarize yourself with them.

1.3.1 *Court Decisions Regarding Pleading*

For decades, law schools trained students that non-fraud-related pleadings[11] need only meet the "notice" pleading requirement established by *Conley v. Gibson*, 355 U.S. 41 (1957). *Conley v. Gibson* interpreted FRCP 8 as requiring only "a short and plain statement of the claim showing that the pleader is entitled to relief." This simply means that for non-fraud-related claims, plaintiffs only have to allege information that sufficiently places the defendant on notice of the claim.

Two cases fundamentally altered the pleading rules, without actually changing their text. In *Bell Atlantic Corp. v. Twombly*, 550 U.S. 544 (2007) and *Ashcroft v. Iqbal*, 556 U.S. 662 (2009), the Supreme Court determined that judges must strip out conclusory allegations to evaluate the sufficiency of a complaint. The Court explained judges should determine a claim's plausibility by evaluating the facts. Though pleadings are discussed later in the book, changes in pleading standards require lawyers to front-load their litigation efforts, conduct deeper investigations, and gather facts they otherwise would have waited until discovery to collect.

1.3.2 *Court Decisions Regarding Summary Judgment*

Assuming your complaint survives a motion to dismiss and discovery is complete, you enter the second minefield called "summary judgment." FRCP 56 states "The Court shall grant summary judgment if the movant shows that there is no genuine dispute as to any material fact and the movement is entitled to a judgment as a matter of law." For years, this rule meant that the movant had two obligations: (1) presenting the court with a set of undisputed facts, and (2) explaining why, based on those undisputed facts, the plaintiff is not entitled to relief as a matter of law. In *Celotex v. Catrett*,[12] the Court tweaked these obligations, imposing an obligation on plaintiffs to, at the very least, present evidence that makes a prima facie case. In *Celotex*, the plaintiff claimed injury from disease caused by exposure to asbestos, the defendant's product. The Court said it is the plaintiff's burden to show that Celotex's product caused the injury and to provide evidence supporting that conclusion at the summary judgment stage. The

---

11. When claims are fraud-related, containing allegations similar to "fraud or mistake," pleadings are subject to FRCP 9(b)'s heightened standard. FRCP 9(b) demands that pleadings "state with particularity the circumstances constituting fraud or mistake." The "particularity" requirement, as interpreted by the courts, requires plaintiffs to plead the "who, what, when, where, and how" of the case.
12. Celotex v. Catrett, 477 U.S. 317 (1986).

National Institute for Trial Advocacy

Celotex case is part of what is known as the "Summary Judgment Trilogy"—three U.S. Supreme Court decisions on summary judgment issued in 1986. The Trilogy also includes *Anderson v. Liberty Lobby Inc.,*[13] and *Matsushita Electrical Industrial Corp. v. Zenith Radio Corp.*[14]

In *Anderson v. Liberty Lobby*, the respondents, a non-profit group of political activists, filed a libel action against a columnist that wrote several articles portraying the respondents as neo-Nazi, anti-Semitic, racist, and fascist.[15] The issue before the Supreme Court was whether the circuit court had erred by failing to consider the plaintiff's heightened evidentiary burden of proof of actual malice, at the summary judgment stage.[16] The Court held that the heightened evidentiary standard from the relevant substantive law applies at the summary judgment stage.[17] Accordingly, the Court noted that there is no genuine issue of material fact "if the evidence presented in the opposing affidavits is of insufficient caliber or quantity to allow a rational finder of fact to find actual malice by clear and convincing evidence."[18]

Similarly, in *Matsushita Electric Industrial Co., Ltd. v. Zenith Radio Corp.,* the plaintiffs, manufacturers, and sellers of consumer electronic products, sued various competitor-manufacturers who were headquartered in Japan.[19] Plaintiffs claimed that the defendant had engaged in a "scheme to raise, fix and maintain artificially high prices for television receivers sold by [defendants] in Japan and, at the same time, to fix and maintain low prices for television receivers exported to and sold in the United States."[20] The Supreme Court affirmed the lower court's holding of summary judgment for the defendant.[21] The Court emphasized that the party opposing summary must do more than simply show that there is some metaphysical doubt as to the material facts in order to establish a genuine issue of fact sufficient to warrant trial.[22] Consequently, "[w]here the record taken as a whole could not lead a rational trier of fact to find for the non-moving party, there is no 'genuine issue for trial.'"[23] The Court, however, recognized that facts and inferences must be viewed in the light most favorable to the party opposing summary judgment.[24]

---

13. Anderson v. Liberty Lobby Inc., 477 U.S. 242 (1985).
14. Matsushita Electrical Industrial Corp. v. Zenith Radio Corp., 475 U.S. 574 (1986).
15. *Anderson*, 477 U.S. at 242, 244–245.
16. *Id.* at 247.
17. *Id.* at 254.
18. *Id.*
19. *Matsushita*, 475 U.S. at 574, 577.
20. *Id.*
21. *Id.* at 593–94.
22. *Id.* at 595–98.
23. *Id.* at 1356.
24. *Id.* at 587.

1.3.3 Court Decisions Regarding Class Certification

Seemingly straightforward, FRCP 23 governs class actions using a four-prong test: 1) the class is so numerous that joinder of all members is impracticable; 2) there are questions of law and fact common to the class; 3) the claims or defenses of the representative parties are typical of the claims of the class; and 4) the representative parties will fairly and adequately protect the interests of the class. However, these criteria are not so precise that they elude court interpretation.

Through a series of Supreme Court decisions, class actions are now a serious point of contention and certification challenges are a minefield for litigants. For example, in *Wal-Mart Stores, Inc. v. Dukes*, the Supreme Court overturned a grant of certification to a nationwide class of 1.5 million female Wal-Mart employees because the plaintiffs did not have enough in common to constitute a class. Their claims were based on numerous independent decisions affecting class members in different ways rather than a single discriminatory policy.[25] The Court emphasized that the class could not meet the FRCP 23(a)(2) "commonality" requirement because their allegedly common question, that is, why they were disfavored relative to other employees, could not produce a common answer across the class, and it urged district courts in other cases to engage in a "rigorous analysis" of the factual record to determine if certification is appropriate. For plaintiffs' attorneys, this decision was seen as significantly undermining the ability to certify a class without undertaking an enormous amount of discovery.

Similarly, in *Comcast Corp. v. Behrend*, the Court reversed the certification of a class of cable television customers alleging that their provider monopolized a local market for cable services.[26] The Court ruled that plaintiffs failed to show that common issues of damages predominated in the action as required by the FRCP 23(b)(3). The plaintiffs' damages model could not sufficiently isolate damages such that they could be attributable to the alleged antitrust activity, and thus were not able to be measured across the entire class. The Court re-emphasized that district courts and courts of appeal should conduct a rigorous analysis of the factual record to determine whether expert methodologies support a finding of certification, even where doing so involves an inquiry into the merits of the damages calculation to determine whether common issues of damages predominated.

The Supreme Court has also permitted consumer contracts to include arbitration provisions that include waivers of the right to participate in class or collective actions. In *American Express Co. v. Italian Colors Restaurant*, the Court held that such waivers are enforceable even where a plaintiff's cost of arbitrating individually would exceed that plaintiff's potential recovery.[27]

---

25. Wal-Mart Stores, Inc. v. Dukes, 564 U.S. 338 (2011).
26. Comcast Corp. v. Behrand, 569 U.S. 27 (2013).
27. Am. Express Co. v. Italian Colors Rest. 570 U.S. 228 (2013).

National Institute for Trial Advocacy

From the plaintiff's perspective, class action cases are economically efficient. From the defendant's perspective, denial of class certification will cause the plaintiff to drop the case. Conversely, when a case is certified as a class action, the defendant's exposure increases exponentially.

1.3.4 *Court Decisions Regarding Experts*

Assume your client shops at the five-dollar store and purchases a pen light that barely provides any light. Since it is not cost efficient to bring a case for five dollars in damages, you decide to bring the case as a class action against the manufacturer.

Bringing your defective pen light case may require expert testimony to support an argument for class certification and verify defendant liability. To certify a class, you must show there are common questions of fact. Your proposed expert testifies that the defendant's manufacturing practice resulted in a uniform defect, common to all 10,000 flashlights, that rendered the pen light nonfunctional after just twenty minutes of use.

Pursuant to FRCP 26(a)(2)(B), you serve opposing counsel with the expert's report. Upon review, the court will determine whether the proposed testimony meets the requirements of FRE 702. As previously mentioned, the Supreme Court's *Daubert* decision declared trial courts the "gatekeeper" to determine whether expert testimony is sufficiently reliable to be heard at trial. Expert testimony that does not meet that standard will be excluded. As a result, if liability, damages, or class certification cannot be determined in the absence of expert testimony, a successful *Daubert* motion can effectively terminate a case.

CHAPTER TWO

MEETING THE CLIENT

2.1 The Beginning

2.1.1 Case Screening

When your office receives a phone call or email about a potential case, you need a process for what comes next. The time between a prospective client's initial contact and your decision to enter into a formal agreement for legal representation is referred to as "case screening." During this stage, you determine whether to represent this person (or entity), and the potential client decides whether they want you to represent them. During the case screening process, you should be looking to answer these threshold questions:

1) Should I engage in the representation?

2) If yes, what is the scope of that representation and can I engage in targeted litigation meeting the client's needs?

During this initial stage, set clear expectations for the relationship and what you can and cannot do. Naturally, what is achievable varies greatly depending on how the facts play out. Clients may ask: "Do I have a case?"[1] or "Isn't it awful what they did to me?" When answering such questions, respond as an advocate, not a cheerleader. The cheerleader creates false confidence and sets high expectations of which you may fall short. A response might be: "Based on what you are telling us, it appears there is a cause of action, but we need to look at all the documents and see the response from the defendant." Many attorneys are reluctant to take this approach, favoring a hard sell tactic. Yet, one can instill confidence by simply stating: "I can best serve you by looking at the case from all angles, advocating the strengths, and addressing the weaknesses, legal or factual."

---

1. Think of the scene from the movie *Philadelphia* where the lawyer played by Denzel Washington is asked by a client if he has a case and the reply is "absolutely." It is, of course, never that simple.

"We are scrupulously honest from the start, about fees, about our chances to succeed, about our qualifications. That honesty must be maintained throughout. If it is, when hard decisions must be made, the client will follow you."

—*Phillip Freidin, Founding Partner, Freidin Brown PA*

2.1.2 How to Initially Screen

2.1.2.1 Should the First Meeting with a Client be in Person?

Meeting with a potential client requires time and resources—your time and your resources. Do not spend too much time on initial consultations without sufficient return. If you run a high-volume practice, you could easily get bogged down in consultations that do not lead to representation. Depending on your business model you may consider charging the client for the initial consultation. Consultation charges are a way to screen for clients not truly interested or able to retain your services.

Sometimes free consultations are a primary way to generate new business, especially if you are just starting your practice. If so, consider that time when computing your overall fee or contingency structure instead. Plan for the time and adjust your fees accordingly.

Initial phone interviews are an effective tool to screen clients. And, of course, the advent of remote technology—including Zoom—has created an additional means of screening clients, including those who cannot break away to meet in person. One thing we learned through the COVID-19 quarantine is that the meetings by Zoom or other methods can almost be as good as having a face-to-face conference with the client.[2]

Of course, not meeting a client in person has its disadvantages. However, if you have a high-volume practice, phone and remote interviews are a great alternative. If you generally screen via phone interview, but think an in-person meeting is necessary, or if a client insists, make an exception and meet with them in person.

Above all else, trust your instincts. You can often get a sense from a quick phone conversation that the person or case is not right for your firm.

You should also consider several other questions before agreeing to meet with a client:

- Is this the type of case that my firm can and should handle?

- Does this case require expertise or resources beyond our capabilities?

---

2. *See* Nat'l Inst. of Trial Advoc. Remote Advocacy: A Guide to Survive and Thrive (2020).

- If the case does not suit our firm, is this a good case for a referral?

- A note on referrals: Referrals can generate referral fees and establish or enhance relationships with other attorneys.[3] Even if your jurisdiction does not permit referral fees, the referral itself can establish goodwill with an attorney who may refer a case back to you.

2.1.2.2 Red Flags and Warning Signs

To find out how a client might behave in an attorney-client relationship, look for red flags:

- Is the client a serial litigator?

- Does the client have a personal axe to grind beyond the four corners of the suit?

- Has the client put their life on hold pending recovery of a "pot of money"?

- When probed on facts, does the client go on tangents of personal animus?

- Does the client respond to factual inquiries with hyperbole?

- Can the client articulate how they have been injured?

- Does the client have their own vision of the law?

- What has the client posted on social media?

- Is the client in serious financial trouble or experiencing problems at home?

All this information can indicate whether a client will be reasonable in dealing with you and the opposing party, and whether the allegations are supported. A difficult client can be a significant detriment to your practice, eating away at both your time and your happiness. Difficult clients can interfere with your representation of other clients. Lawyers sometimes reject new cases because of the extra stress and time spent dealing with existing difficult clients.

---

3. David L. Hudson, Jr., *Sharing Fees With a Lawyer Outside the Firm is OK as Long as Certain Ethics Rules are Followed*, Am. Bar Ass'n J., (July 1, 2016) http://www.abajournal.com/magazine/article/ sharing_fees_with_a_lawyer_outside_the_firm_is_ok_as_long_as_certaic_ethics ("[T]here is a significant amount of variation in state ethics rules governing division of fees. Colorado, for instance, prohibits referral fees outright, while a few others have not incorporated ABA Model Rule 1.5(e) into their ethics codes. Some states, such as California, only require client consent and a total reasonable fee and do not require joint responsibility. Other states require that there always be some form of joint responsibility.").

2.1.3   *The Individual Plaintiff*

Individuals seek representation for a range of matters from basic torts, such as medical malpractice and car accident injuries, to economic injuries, such as causes of action under various state and federal consumer laws, to employment cases brought for wrongful discharge, to breach of contract.

These cases fall into sub-categories: cases brought as stand-alone individual claims, cases that are brought as class actions, or matters swept up into multi-district litigation.

Your goals for initial information inquiries are threefold. Find out: 1) why the client contacted you; 2) what the client hopes to achieve by retaining a lawyer; 3) what facts support the client's claims (or defenses). These types of open-ended questions get the answers:

- How did you find our firm?

- What are you trying to accomplish by contacting a lawyer?

- What would be your ideal outcome?

- Have you met with other lawyers?

- Please explain the sequence of events.

- What documents do you have supporting your claims or defenses?

- Are there witnesses who support your claims or defenses?

- Are there others who have similar claims?

2.1.4   *Individual Defendants and Small Entities*

In contrast to a plaintiff's counsel, the defense counsel interviews clients who have not chosen to engage in litigation; circumstances placed the client in or on the verge of legal action. It is always personal when the defendant is an individual or a small entity, such as a partnership or small, closely held corporation. Where the claim involves discrimination, fraud, a partnership or personal divorce, the matter can be heated. Sometimes, the client schedules an interview because they received a letter threatening litigation or an actual complaint. The client may have an existing relationship with you or may be contacting you just for this litigation.

All litigation interferes with a defendant's business or daily life, in some way. As a starting point, determine whether the client can withstand the tumult of contentious litigation or does the matter necessitate rapid resolution, even if at some cost? Some questions to consider:

- How does the client earn money?

- Is the client a public figure or business leader?

- Does the client have a brand and reputation to protect?

- Will information surface in the litigation that will impact brand and reputation?

- Will litigation publicity be a factor?

- Can the client produce witnesses for deposition and case preparation without disrupting its business?

- Will factfinding and discovery reveal collateral exposure including, e.g., tax liabilities?

- Will potential settlement set a bad precedent for the client's interests?

- Are there other victims?

It is crucial to understand the client dynamic. If it is a small corporation, to whom will the lawyer be reporting? Who has settlement authority? If the defendant is an individual, are there relatives or advisors the client will be looking to for guidance?

The client's perception of their case is also important. Does the client view it as a moral affront, or can this case be dealt with through decisions that are "business-like" in nature? Look for the following red flags:

- "I want to crush the plaintiff; I am outraged."

- "Pull out all the stops, I will spend anything."

- "Let's file counterclaims to pressure them."

For plaintiff's counsel, such red flags may be a reason to reject representation. For defense counsel, these are most likely red flags that must be acknowledged and addressed. Credit the anger but refocus the dialogue. You might say: "I perfectly understand why you want to destroy the plaintiff, but you run a successful and lucrative media corporation, so we need to resolve this suit as simply, or quickly, as possible because you do not make money being in court."

2.1.5 *Corporations as Plaintiffs and Defendants*

Representing corporations is a nuanced business. The decision to even engage in litigation is a matter of corporate law. The state of incorporation, and their laws, along with the bylaws or articles of incorporation, establish the technical process—perhaps a vote of the board of directors or a shareholder's resolution—by which the corporation can engage in affirmative litigation.

There are ethical considerations for both the plaintiff's and defendant's counsel. Will you represent the corporation itself, or individuals associated with the corporation? Can you represent both? If so, what kind of waiver will you need?

There is also the question of who within the corporation will oversee the representation by outside counsel and the constraints on that person. If the general counsel supervises outside counsel, do they report to the board of directors? Does the general counsel have authority to act independently?

Factfinding during the intake interview should cover four areas: 1) which corporate processes govern the litigation; 2) the general business of the corporation; 3) the facts of the case; and 4) expectations for the litigation.

The internet is an excellent resource to gather info regarding the corporation's general business. Do not stop with a Google search though; there may be other questions concerning corporate history, customer base, and the products or services they produce and deliver.

You will obviously need to know the facts, which always boil down to the "who," "what," "where," and "how" questions. The following are going to be important:

- How does the corporation store documents?
- Does the corporation have a document preservation and destruction policy?
- Has the corporation's in-house counsel sent a litigation hold notice?
- Who are the witnesses?
- Are any former employees potential witnesses?

As to the matter of process, retrieve corporation bylaws and information in preparation for the interview. Here are some areas to cover:

- To whom will our firm be reporting?
- What kinds of reporting will you need from our firm?
- Will we need approval on decisions impacting procedure such as extensions of time limits?
- What role will the shareholders or directors play in the litigation including settlement?

2.1.6 *Deferring the Decision*

You will often be unable to fully evaluate a case during the first meeting with a potential client. You want to discuss your time frame for case assessment and the terms of representation. These are some of the things you might say:

> "You have given us enough information to start our investigation. We will look at the law and the facts, but we may have more questions."

> "Can you send us the documents you mentioned? We will need to review them before we can determine whether to take the case."

2.2 Taking the Case: How to Decide?

After the initial meetings and information gathering, you need to decide whether or not to take a case. In general, there are three overarching considerations in making this determination: the client, the claim, and the damages. In addition to the red flags previously mentioned, determine whether you want to work with this client. Are they going to be reasonable? Are they credible? How will they behave in legal proceedings? You want to be comfortable and the client must be comfortable. Keep in mind that taking cases with little or no merit is a failing business model. As plaintiff's counsel, you must have a legitimate claim to move forward; as defense counsel, you must be concerned about asserting defenses that have no merit. This does not mean that there are those who are not entitled to a defense, it just means that lawyers need be concerned about sorting through the range of defenses and asserting those that are grounded in law and fact.

When considering the case from the plaintiff's perspective, look for the potential to recover adequate damages for litigation and additional money to pay the clients and yourself, especially in a contingency fee situation. Great claims with the potential for a sizable damages award are great, but not without a defendant who has the financial means to pay. That is not a way to sustain a business. When defending a matter, or as a plaintiff in a non-contingency fee situation, your concern is whether the defendant can cover the costs of litigation.

Estimating litigation costs helps determine whether or not to accept a case. Such evaluation also helps when advising a potential client. This sample chart catalogues many potential litigation costs. The first step in determining the cost of a case, and usually the most expensive part, is deciding how to staff the case and the hourly rates for each individual working on the case. Second, estimate time needed for the included tasks. Third, add other probable costs and establish a projected budget for the litigation.

Description	S/H #1	Rate	Assoc. #1	Rate	Assoc. #2	Rate	Para #1	Rate	Fee Estimate
Case Assessment, Planning & Strategy									
Initial Fact Investigation									$___
Research									$___
Experts									$___
Negotiations & Potential ADR									$___
File & Document Management									$___
Settlement									$___
Other Activities									$___
								Subtotal:	$___
Pleadings & Motions									
Preliminary Injunctions/ Remedies									$___
Conferences									$___
Pretrial Motion									$___
Court Appearances									$___
Hearing Preparation/ Attendance									$___
Other Motions									$___
							Pleadings/Motions Expenses:		$___
Discovery									$___
Depositions • Plaintiff Representatives • Defendant Representatives • Third Party #1 • Third Party #2 • Etc.									$___
Expert Discovery									$___
Discovery Motions									$___
Other Motions									$___
Interrogatories									$___
Admissions									$___
							Discovery Total Expenses:		$___

(*continued*)

Description	S/H #1	Rate	Assoc. #1	Rate	Assoc. #2	Rate	Para #1	Rate	Fee Estimate
Trial Preparation & Trial									$___
Mediation Expenses									$___
Pre-trial Statement Prep									$___
Witness List Preparation									$___
Exhibit List Preparation									$___
Fact Witnesses									$___
Expert Witnesses									$___
Written Motions & Submissions									$___
Trial/Hearing Attendance									$___
Post-Trial Motions									$___
							Total Trial Expenses:		$___
Appeal									$___
Appellate Motions & Submissions									$___
Appellate Briefs									$___
Oral Argument									$___
							Total Appeal Expenses:		$___
Other Expenses									$___
Travel time									$___
Transcripts									$___
Copying, etc.									$___
Total Other Expenses:									$___
TOTAL EXPENSES									$___

2.3   Do I Have the Skills to Take the Case?

After meeting with your client, you will have a good understanding of the relevant legal issues. Ask yourself if this is the type of case you can and should be handling.

Model Rules of Professional Conduct (MRPC) 1.1 addresses the issue of competence and provides initial guidance. "A lawyer shall provide competent representation to a client. Competent representation requires the legal knowledge, skill, thoroughness and preparation reasonably necessary for the representation."

What standard of representation is needed and what qualifications or background experience are required? You must have the competence or be capable of securing the competence, meaning that your current skill set places you in the orbit of being able to do the work required by a particular case. Lacking the skill is not necessarily a bar to representing the client, because you may be able to associate other counsel who have particular expertise or experience.

If your prep and research require significant time commitment, your client may be billed for many hours for which another lawyer would not need to bill. Comment 1 to MRPC 1.1 says that you are allowed to spend time getting caught up: "[a] lawyer need not necessarily have special training or prior experience to handle legal problems of a type with which the lawyer is unfamiliar . . . . A lawyer can provide adequate representation in a wholly novel field through necessary study."[4]

You do not have to be the best at what you do, you only need to be competent. Early in your career, you might be more willing to accept diverse cases that help to establish your practice and cover the overhead costs associated with running a law practice. But honestly assess your ability to learn this new area of law. It is risky to accept cases too far out of your comfort zone. You will want to consider:

- Do I want to spend the time to get up to speed?

- If I get up to speed in a case, will I learn something that can help me in future cases?

- If I struggle with this area of the law, do I run the risk of damaging my reputation in the community or with this client?

2.4 Is There a Conflict?

2.4.1 Conflict Checks

Before accepting representation, consider this threshold question: are you certain that you can be loyal to this new client's interest while remaining loyal to your current and former clients? "Loyalty and independent judgment are essential elements in the lawyer's relationship to a client."[5] The success of our adversarial legal system depends on each party having a lawyer loyal to him. This rationale is the foundation of the rules requiring conflict checks before undertaking representation of a new client.[6] Comment 1 to Model Rule 1.16 explicitly states, "A lawyer should not

---

4. MODEL RULES OF PRO. CONDUCT r. 1.1 cmt. 2 (AM. BAR ASS'N 1983).
5. MODEL RULES OF PRO. CONDUCT r. 1.7 cmt. 1 (AM. BAR ASS'N 1983).
6. "To determine whether a *conflict of interest* exists, a lawyer should adopt reasonable *procedures*, appropriate for the size and type of firm and practice, to determine in both litigation and non-litigation matters the persons and issues involved." MODEL RULES OF PRO. CONDUCT r. 1.7 cmt. 3 (AM. BAR ASS'N 1983). "A partner in a law firm . . . shall make reasonable efforts to ensure that

accept representation in a matter unless it can be performed competently, promptly, without improper conflict of interest and to completion."[7]

To assess the existence of an impermissible conflict, review the rules that ensure your loyalty to current, former, and prospective clients. These model rules provide the primary guidance for determining whether a conflict exists:

Potential Conflicts

MRPC 1.7 and 1.8	Current Clients
MRPC 1.9	Former Clients
MRPC 1.18	Prospective Clients
MRPC 1.10 and 1.9(c)	Firm-Based Conflicts[8]

2.4.2 Current Clients

MRPC 1.7 contains two parts. Section (a) tests whether a conflict exists. Section (b) lists possibilities for representing a client even if a conflict of interest exists.

---

the firm has in effect measures giving reasonable assurance that all lawyers in the firm conform to the Rules of Professional Conduct." MODEL RULES OF PRO. CONDUCT r. 5.1(a) (AM. BAR ASS'N 1983). Comment 2 to Rule 5.1 explicitly notes that: Paragraph (a) requires lawyers with managerial authority within a firm to make reasonable efforts to establish internal policies and *procedures* designed to provide reasonable assurance that all lawyers in the firm will conform to the Rules of Professional Conduct. Such policies and *procedures* include those designed to detect and resolve conflicts of interest . . .
MODEL RULES OF PRO. CONDUCT r. 5.1 cmt. 2 (AM. BAR ASS'N 1983). Note that while Comment 3 to Rule 1.7 states only that a lawyer "should" adopt such *procedures,* the Comment further states that "ignorance caused by a failure to institute such *procedures* will not excuse a lawyer's violation of this Rule," and Rule 5.1 uses the mandatory language "shall." *See* Eli Wald, *Lawyer Mobility and Legal Ethics: Resolving the Tension Between Confidentiality Requirements and Contemporary Lawyers' Career Paths,* 31 J. LEGAL PROF. 199, 208.
7. MODEL RULES OF PRO. CONDUCT r. 1.16 cmt. 1 (AM. BAR ASS'N 1983).
8. MODEL RULES OF PRO. CONDUCT r. 1.10(b) (AM. BAR ASS'N 1983) (provides guidelines for when a lawyer leaves a firm, what can the firm do with future clients that conflict with the attorney who left). Comment 5 to Rule 1.10 notes how Rule 1.10(b) "operates to permit a law firm, under certain circumstances, to represent a person with interests directly adverse to those of a client represented by a lawyer who formerly was associated with the firm. The Rule applies regardless of when the formerly associated lawyer represented the client. However, the law firm may not represent a person with interests adverse to those of a present client of the firm, which would violate Rule 1.7. Moreover, the firm may not represent the person where the matter is the same or substantially related to that in which the formerly associated lawyer represented the client and any other lawyer currently in the firm has material information protected by Rules 1.6 and 1.9(c)." Comment 8 to Rule 1.9 notes that section (b) "provides that information acquired by the lawyer in the course of representing a client may not subsequently be used or revealed by the lawyer to the disadvantage of the client. However, the fact that a lawyer has once served a client does not preclude the lawyer from using generally known information about the client when later representing another client."

Under section (a), a concurrent conflict exists in two instances: 1) if your representation of the prospective client would be directly adverse to a current client (an example of directly adverse would be those on opposite sides of the litigation); or 2) if your representation were materially limited by your responsibilities to another client, former client, third person, or by your own personal interest. For example, you cannot represent a client who is trying to demolish the condominium building that you currently live in. In this situation, your personal interest might be opposite the interest of the potential client.

Section (b) states that even when conflicts exist under section (a), you may represent the prospective client if you believe it will not adversely affect the other relationship, **and** each client consents in writing after consultation. There is no representation waiver prohibited by law[9] or in matters involving opposing parties.

Once representation begins, MRPC 1.8 provides guidance concerning what client transactions and interactions are permissible. Note that some of these may be consented to while others cannot. For example, engaging in certain business transactions with the clients requires the client's informed consent. However, sexual relations with a client are never permitted, unless that relationship began before the representation, even with consent. As MRPC 1.8(k) explicitly states, if an action is individually prohibited, the entire firm is also prohibited.

2.4.3   Former Clients

When determining whether to represent a current client, be aware of your loyalty to former clients. MRPC 1.9 addresses what duties you have to former clients. Section (a) explains personal restrictions concerning former clients. Section (b) describes what you can and cannot do after leaving a firm. In other words, if you had a conflict at your old firm, that conflict may travel with you to the new firm.

First, you are prohibited from representing a prospective client in the same or substantially-related matter if the person's interests are materially adverse. For example, a lawyer who assisted a client in establishing a revocable trust for the benefit of the client's spouse and issue may not later represent another party in an attempt to satisfy the new client's claims against the trust by invading the assets of the trust.[10]

---

9. MODEL RULES OF PRO. CONDUCT r. 1.7 cmt. 16 ("Paragraph (b)(2) describes conflicts that are nonconsentable because the representation is prohibited by applicable law. For example, in some states substantive law provides that the same lawyer may not represent more than one defendant in a capital case, even with the consent of the clients, and under federal criminal statutes certain representations by a former government lawyer are prohibited, despite the informed consent of the former client. In addition, decisional law in some states limits the ability of a governmental client, such as a municipality, to consent to a conflict of interest.").
10. Joy M. Miyasaki, *Advanced Estate Planning Techniques: Avoiding Ethical Dilemmas*, ALI-ABA COURSE OF STUDY MATERIALS, SL073 ALI-ABA 431 (Feb. 2006).

However, with the former client's informed consent and written confirmation, this can be waived. MRPC 1.9 (b) prohibits representing clients at a new firm in the same or a substantially-related matter that was handled at your prior firm. This can also be waived with informed written consent.

2.4.4 Prospective Clients

Lawyers commonly meet with potential clients but decide not to represent them. Despite never establishing a formal relationship, you now have certain responsibilities towards that former prospective client. Most importantly, the information you learned during that meeting remains confidential. If you receive information during those initial interviews, information that could seriously harm the former prospective client, you cannot represent another party in the same or substantially-related matter. MRPC 1.18(d) allows this conflict to be waived under two circumstances. First, it can be waived by both parties' written informed consent. It can also be overcome if the lawyer who learned the information was properly screened and walled off from the rest of the firm. In this latter scenario, other members of the firm can engage the representation.

MRPC 1.2(c) provides that "a lawyer may limit the scope of representation if the limitation is reasonable under the circumstances and the client gives informed consent." This is generally a bad option for very complicated litigation, but you can consider it under some circumstances. A common way to limit the scope of representation is to restrict representation to trial court proceedings. If there is an appeal, a separate agreement is required.

Limited representation can also assist a client unable to afford representation at every stage of the proceeding. With civil legal services being less available due to dramatic budget cuts, sometimes limited representation might be the only option for a client who would otherwise proceed pro se. You could provide initial legal advice, draft pleadings, or do some other form of legal coaching.[11]

2.4.5 Setting Up a Conflict Check System

Conflict of interest issues are the most common claim in malpractice suits.[12] Every attorney's office, whether a solo practitioner or a large firm, must set up a

---

11. Lawyers should be very careful about the ethical dangers of partial representation. Many jurisdictions require lawyers who prepare documents for *pro se* litigants to clearly identify that it was the lawyer who drafted the document. Courts may also require lawyers to appear at court or do work beyond their initial agreement if fairness and justice require. We recommend that whenever possible to forgo partial representation and commit to representing through an entire stage of the proceeding.
12. Debra Cassens Weiss, *Why the Increase in Malpractice Risk? Lawyers for Plaintiffs Point to Trial Lawyering, Bill Padding*, ABA JOURNAL (Feb. 12, 2020), https://www.abajournal.com/news/article/why-the-increase-in-malpractice-claims-lawyers-for-plaintiffs-point-to-trial-lawyering-bill-padding ("The most common alleged malpractice error concerns conflicts of interest….").

system to easily check potential clients. Most law firms use sophisticated programs that require you to capture all relevant information for each case. It then runs new potential clients through the system to assess conflicts. Your initial intake form should include the information needed for your database to check for a conflict. At a minimum, maintain an accurate list of all clients and the attorneys that work on each matter. Gather this information initially from potential clients and continue updating it throughout the case:

- Names of people related to the litigation such as employers, beneficiaries, spouses, children, company names.

- Opposing party.

- Opposing party's counsel.

Once collected, run the above information through your system for any matches. If they exist, do more digging to determine their relationship to your firm and whether they are a current or former client. Apply your jurisdiction's Rules of Professional Conduct to confirm you can proceed with your representation. Gather identifying information about the parties such as phone numbers and addresses.

2.5. Formalizing the Attorney-Client Relationship

2.5.1 *Retainer Agreements*

"Know your state's ethical rules and statutes governing retainer agreements. Different states have very specific requirements for retainer agreements, often with heightened requirements for contingency agreements. Non-compliance can have massive ethical and financial consequences."

—*Michael Williams, Partner, Bienert Katzman Littrell Williams LLP*

A well-drafted retainer agreement prevents disputes and sets client expectations. Because each case is different and each jurisdiction has their own requirements, there is no singular sample of the perfect retainer agreement. However, there are guiding principles and core topics to be addressed in every good retainer agreement. A retainer agreement is a contract. It must comply with contract requirements to be enforceable. A retainer agreement should address these topics:

- Fees, including who is covering what expenses.

- Scope of representation.

2.5.1.1 Fees and Costs

Fee structures can include fixed, contingency, hourly, and blended which involves a lower hourly rate with a small contingency fee or success bonus. Explicitly state the type of fee arrangement. Not only will this set appropriate client expectations; it also becomes your enforcement method for collecting or defending fees, should you have a dispute with the client. Simply explain, but with sufficient detail, the fee arrangement so the client understands. At a minimum, explain the basis for your rate and fee. Consider being explicit about the timing for fee payment. The retainer agreement's fee section should describe who is responsible for what costs. For example, who is responsible for filing costs, experts, and transcripts?

2.5.1.2 Scope of Representation

Your retainer agreement should include a detailed description of the scope of your representation. In some cases, it may be wise to also include what you are not going to do for the client. For example, if representing a client in a civil lawsuit against the police for using excessive force, explain that your representation does not include defending the client in the criminal proceeding arising out of the same incident. Also, be explicit that your agreement only pertains to a certain level of representation—if you are only representing them at the trial court proceeding, explicitly state that it does not include representation at the appellate level. If you choose to continue your representation at another level, you can always draft a new retainer agreement.

During the intake interview, there may be questions regarding your compensation. Depending on the client's response, compensation may be a litmus test for whether representation is even possible. To establish trust and to provide transparency which fosters trust, discuss fees with your client at the outset. Explain them in detail and with clarity. Fees are a frequent source of conflict between client and lawyer. MRPC 1.5 addresses attorney fees. The rule requires that attorney fees be reasonable under the circumstances. MRPC 1.5(a) lists the various factors for consideration, including:

> (1) the time and labor required, the novelty and difficulty of the questions involved, and the skill requisite to perform the legal service properly; (2) the likelihood, if apparent to the client, that the acceptance of the particular employment will preclude other employment by the lawyer; (3) the fee customarily charged in the locality for similar legal services; (4) the amount involved and the results obtained; (5) the time limitations imposed by the client or by the circumstances; (6) the nature and length of the professional relationship with the client; (7) the experience, reputation, and ability of the lawyer or lawyers performing the services; and (8) whether the fee is fixed or contingent.

If you typically only seek clients who can pay an hourly fee and can cover costs, a client seeking contingency representation may be a nonstarter. Clients seeking contingency representation may have a vision about percentages that may be inconsistent with the attorney's economic model.

2.5.2 *Other Considerations*

2.5.2.1 Mandatory Arbitration and Mediation for Fee Disputes and Malpractice Claims

Litigating fee disputes and malpractice claims can be costly and time-consuming for both parties. Some attorneys place arbitration clauses in their agreements with clients while others believe that such clauses—unless they are the product of arm's length negotiation—are fundamentally repugnant to the common-law tradition and a client's Seventh Amendment rights to a jury. Still, a client and an attorney may favor such a clause as a way to resolve a dispute in private so as to avoid publicity. Short of arbitration, mediation is also a mechanism to resolve fee disputes. Each jurisdiction has its own limits on how and when these clauses can be used; however, most states permit their use.

Though mandatory arbitration can be quick and cost-saving, mandatory arbitration clauses generally elicit concern. Is mandatory arbitration just privatizing our judicial system? Should the judiciary and jurors decide these issues? Such questions apply in many legal matters, not just to mandatory arbitration for attorney-client disputes.

2.5.2.2 How Does the Relationship End?

At some point the relationship with your client will end, and that might occur sooner than either of you planned. Manage expectations early. The retainer agreement should explicitly state things that will cause you to withdraw from a case. Retainer agreements are usually signed at the very beginning of the case, when much research and fact gathering still needs to be done. As your investigation progresses, facts may develop differently than anticipated or the law may not provide a pathway to bring a claim. Sometimes you hire experts who cannot support your client's claim. Under such circumstances, you may need to terminate representation. It is always a good idea to both explain it to the client and memorialize it in the retainer agreement.

Also explain the client's right to terminate the representation. This should also be included in the initial retainer agreement.

2.5.2.3 Setting the Expectations for Billing and Beyond

Again, your retainer agreement should outline specifics relating to payment of costs and fees such as who is responsible, the manner of payment, and payment timing. Including those particulars helps avoid conflict and confusion down the road.

The attorney-client relationship functions best when it is symbiotic. Avoid disagreement by establishing timelines for clients to complete tasks such as providing documentation or other information. Consider setting up a communication structure, especially if you anticipate that you will be working with a difficult client. For example, set timetables for return phone calls and email replies to keep the client engaged and the relationship functioning at a sufficient level.

2.6 Fee Arrangements

Helping clients is important but charity begins at home. You must put a roof over your head, feed your family, and pay the expenses necessary to sustain a law practice including rent, staffing, legal research, and malpractice insurance. Though this may sound like a cute way to introduce the issue of client costs, the fact remains that calculating overhead—both personal and professional—is vital to determine client charges.

There are multiple variations of fees-and-costs relationships with clients:

- A straight hourly rate with the client also paying costs.

- A reduced hourly rate with the client paying costs and the attorney receiving a success bonus.

- A straight contingency fee with the client advancing costs.

- A straight contingency fee with the attorney advancing costs.

- Client pays everything except costs under a retainer agreement.

These fee arrangements seem self-explanatory; however, each type of arrangement comes with its own variations. Study local bar rules to learn what requirements apply. Establish the arrangement that makes sense for both client and lawyer. Your business model may be premised on a blend of relationships, so give consideration for the right "blend." For example, can an attorney really focus on contingency cases—where they receive payment at the end of a case (or may not even recover any fees)—while they must work on "hourly" matters to generate income to pay the bills? Why is this an issue? The contingency model is designed to generate a multiplier on the hourly rate to offset the risk of no recovery and the time value of differing payment. Firms that work on contingency often only work on a contingency basis. Firms that blend contingency and hourly work often have a harder time adjusting the mix to create a stable business model,

2.6.1 *A Straight Hourly Rate with a Client Also Paying the Costs*

A straight hourly rate where the client pays the costs is the classic arrangement. The primary question is: what should the rate be? First, keep in mind that there are fees and costs for everything. Partners, associates, paralegals, and those with technical or scientific expertise each have their own rate. Attorneys and firms must calculate rates based on meeting overhead and what the market will pay. The rates should reflect the experience and skills of the attorney and of course their demand; experienced attorneys often charge a higher hourly rate because their knowledge level creates efficiencies. Their learning curve may be less.

Firms should establish rates for administrative items including copying, faxing, and legal research. Travel, expert costs, and deposition expenses also fall within the costs category.

When negotiating the fee and costs provisions in a retainer agreement, consider the overall expenditures and the client's ability to pay. A client's agreement that they will pay a certain rate for your fees is not worth much if the case drags on and the client runs out of money. Problems occur when you are stuck with a case not generating income and court approval is required to resign from the case.

Have a realistic discussion with the client concerning the case's anticipated costs and fees. This approach forces the client to be practical about the litigation and potential strategies. A client being sued for $50,000 may decide offering a settlement of $15,000 is more cost efficient than spending money on a defense that may cost more than the plaintiff's demand.

Requiring a retainer is one way to make the client appreciate that litigation is a rich man's sport. Attorneys can ask clients to deposit a specific sum of money into an escrow account. When the client is billed for fees and costs, the attorney draws down on the account. The client may be required to replenish the account to a certain level. This type of retainer arrangement helps attorneys prevent situations where they must chase down the client for money.

2.6.2   A Reduced Hourly Rate with the Client Paying Costs and the Attorney Getting a Success Bonus

Many firms and clients find blended arrangements to be advantageous. These arrangements allow firms to collect an hourly rate, while the client gets the advantage of solving cash flow problems. One thing that would not change is the client's responsibility for covering the costs as they are incurred.

Rates and bonuses are not set in stone and can be adjusted based on the complexity and length of the case. What is an appropriate rate reduction or bonus increase? Obviously, the greater the reduction in the hourly rate, the higher the bonus.

Blended arrangements require creativity. For example, some statutes allow for damages and the recovery of fees and costs. An attorney may propose a reduced hourly rate and the assignment of fees and costs—as a bonus—while the client keeps all the damages and no contingency fee comes from that portion of the award.

2.6.3   A Straight Contingency with the Client Advancing the Costs

Another variation is the straight contingency fee with the client advancing costs. Contingency fee agreements allow attorneys to share in the recovery. An attorney's share varies depending on how the case is resolved. If resolved before trial, the share might be thirty-three percent. If resolved at verdict, the share might be forty percent. What happens if there is an appeal? Would the contingency share increase?

2.6.4   A Straight Contingency with Attorneys Advancing the Costs

Many contingency arrangements require the attorney to advance costs. Review the special bar rules governing these types of arrangements before you enter into one. Contingency arrangements are well-suited for clients who have little money but excellent cases on both the merits and damages. Attorneys are not concerned about risking the output of costs because they will almost certainly—if their analysis is correct—recover them along with a contingency fee.

When advancing costs, consult accountants for advice concerning taxes and the treatment of costs. Typically, the IRS does not allow for cost deductions at the time they are incurred or when money is spent.

Attorneys also engage in contingency litigation where the only potential recovery of costs and fees result from a fee-shifting statute. Fee-shifting provisions exist in many civil rights and consumer protection statutes.

Attorneys filing a suit for injunctive relief may not recover damages, but may still apply for fees under a fees-shifting statute. With public interest cases, the question remains as to how to set rates. One source of guidance is the "Laffy Matrix," which arose from *Laffy v. Northwest Airlines, Inc.* 572 F. Supp. 354 (D.D.C. 1983).

| Year | Adjustment Factor** | Paralegal/ Law Clerk | 1–3 | Years Out of Law School* | | | |
				4–7	8–10	11–19	20 +
6/01/20 – 5/31/21	1.015894	$206	$378	$465	$672	$759	$914
6/01/19 – 5/31/20	1.0049	$203	$372	$458	$661	$747	$899
6/01/18 – 5/31/19	1.0350	$202	$371	$455	$658	$742	$894
6/01/17 – 5/31/18	1.0463	$196	$359	$440	$636	$717	$864
6/01/16 – 5/31/17	1.0369	$187	$343	$421	$608	$685	$826
6/01/15 – 5/31/16	1.0089	$180	$331	$406	$586	$661	$796
6/01/14 – 5/31/15	1.0235	$179	$328	$402	$581	$655	$789
6/01/13 – 5/31/14	1.0244	$175	$320	$393	$567	$640	$771
6/01/12 – 5/31/13	1.0258	$170	$312	$383	$554	$625	$753
6/01/11 – 5/31/12	1.0352	$166	$305	$374	$540	$609	$734
6/01/10 – 5/31/11	1.0337	$161	$294	$361	$522	$589	$709
6/01/09 – 5/31/10	1.0220	$155	$285	$349	$505	$569	$686

(continued)

	Adjustment	Paralegal/		Years Out of Law School*			
Year	Factor**	Law Clerk	1–3	4–7	8–10	11–19	20 +
6/01/08 – 5/31/09	1.0399	$152	$279	$342	$494	$557	$671
6/01/07 – 5/31/08	1.0516	$146	$268	$329	$475	$536	$645
6/01/06 – 5/31/07	1.0256	$139	$255	$313	$452	$509	$614
6/1/05 – 5/31/06	1.0427	$136	$249	$305	$441	$497	$598
6/1/04 – 5/31/05	1.0455	$130	$239	$293	$423	$476	$574
6/1/03 – 6/1/04	1.0507	$124	$228	$280	$405	$456	$549
6/1/02 – 5/31/03	1.0727	$118	$217	$267	$385	$434	$522
6/1/01 – 5/31/02	1.0407	$110	$203	$249	$359	$404	$487
6/1/00 – 5/31/01	1.0529	$106	$195	$239	$345	$388	$468
6/1/99 – 5/31/00	1.0491	$101	$185	$227	$328	$369	$444
6/1/98 – 5/31/99	1.0439	$96	$176	$216	$312	$352	$424
6/1/97 – 5/31/98	1.0419	$92	$169	$207	$299	$337	$406
6/1/96 – 5/31/97	1.0396	$88	$162	$198	$287	$323	$389
6/1/95 – 5/31/96	1.032	$85	$155	$191	$276	$311	$375
6/1/94 – 5/31/95	1.0237	$82	$151	$185	$267	$301	$363

The methodology of calculation and benchmarking for this Updated Laffey Matrix has been approved in a number of cases. See, e.g., McDowell v. District of Columbia, Civ. A. No. 00-594 (RCL), LEXSEE 2001 U.S. Dist. LEXIS 8114 (D.D.C. June 4, 2001); Salazar v. Dist. of Col., 123 F.Supp.2d 8 (D.D.C. 2000).

* "Years Out of Law School" is calculated from June 1 of each year, when most law students graduate. "1–3" includes an attorney in his 1st, 2nd, and 3rd years of practice, measured from date of graduation (June 1). "4–7" applies to attorneys in their 4th, 5th, 6th, and 7th years of practice. An attorney who graduated in May 1996 would be in tier "1–3" from June 1, 1996 until May 31, 1999, would move into tier "4–7" on June 1, 1999, and tier "8–10" on June 1, 2003.

** The Adjustment Factor refers to the nation-wide Legal Services Component of the Consumer Price Index produced by the Bureau of Labor Statistics of the United States Department of Labor.

2.6.5   The All-Inclusive Retainer

Another option is the all-inclusive retainer, which is a fixed fee (plus costs) to cover a specific area of work. For example, in labor relations, a labor union may negotiate a retainer agreement to pay a fixed monthly fee for a firm to handle all grievances, arbitrations, and court injunctions.

2.6.6   Flat Fee

Flat fee arrangements charge clients a set fee amount for handling a legal matter from beginning to end. Flat fees are common in straightforward matters where costs are not likely to vary much. For example, flat fees are commonly used in municipal court traffic violations or will drafting/estate planning.

2.7   Holding and Disbursing Client Funds

2.7.1   *Maintaining Client Funds*

MRPC 1.15 requires the safekeeping of client's property. Jurisdictions vary on the specific requirements, but attorneys have a professional fiduciary duty and must act accordingly. Client property is an area where attorneys, often unwittingly, encounter disciplinary action for mishandling client funds.

All jurisdictions require that attorneys have client trust accounts (CTA).[13] Those accounts usually come in two forms: a single account for all client fund deposits or individual accounts where only the individual client's funds are kept. Trust accounts are meant to keep your personal funds separate from your client's funds. Attorneys are not permitted to comingle client and personal funds. Accurate trust account records must be kept and maintained for a certain number of years.

Withdrawing funds from a trust account is strictly prohibited until that money has been earned. For example, if you receive a $10,000 retainer, that money should go into a trust account. Retainers are paid for services not yet performed and cannot be withdrawn until earned through providing legal services and the client approves the bill for those services. Trust accounts are usually used for:

- The initial retainer;

- Holding funds from a settlement;

- Holding client funds for later disbursement in circumstances where you are acting as a fiduciary for an estate.

---

13. The American Bar Association's Model Code of Professional Responsibility specifically addresses the issue of trust accounts and commingling of funds. Disciplinary Rule DR 9-102, Preserving Identity of Funds and Property of a Client states:
(A) All funds of clients paid to a lawyer or law firm, other than advances for costs and expenses, shall be deposited in one or more identifiable bank accounts maintained in the state in which the law office is situated and no funds belonging to the lawyer or law firm shall be deposited therein except as follows:
(1) Funds reasonably sufficient to pay bank charges may be deposited therein.
(2) Funds belonging in part to a client and in part presently or potentially to the lawyer or law firm must be deposited therein, but the portion belonging to the lawyer or law firm may be withdrawn when due unless the right of the lawyer or law firm to receive it is disputed by the client, in which event the disputed portion shall not be withdrawn until the dispute is finally resolved.
(B) A lawyer shall:
(1) Promptly notify a client of the receipt of his funds, securities, or other properties.
(2) Identify and label securities and properties of a client promptly upon receipt and place them in a safe deposit box or other place of safekeeping as soon as practicable.
(3) Maintain complete records of all funds, securities, and other properties of a client coming into the possession of the lawyer and render appropriate accounts to his client regarding them.
(4) Promptly pay or deliver to the client as requested by a client the funds, securities, or other properties in the possession of the lawyer which the client is entitled to receive.

There are different types of trust accounts. Trust accounts used for deposits are generally dependent upon the amount to be deposited and the length of time you anticipate holding the client funds. The larger the amount and the longer it is held, the more likely it is that the money should be placed in a CTA where the client receives the interest.

If the deposit amount is small or if you do not plan to hold it for long, all states now offer Interest on Lawyer Trust Accounts (IOLTA). In most states, IOLTA participation is mandatory. These accounts generate minimal interest, but that interest is collected and distributed to help fund legal services throughout the country.[14] Check your individual jurisdiction for guidelines that specify when you are allowed or required to use a certain type of trust account.[15]

2.7.2   Costs and Fees

Who should pay for the costs and fees for litigation? There is no simple answer, but whatever you agree to, it should be part of your representation agreement. These costs can be significant, especially with protracted or complicated litigation. Costs associated with expert witnesses, depositions, filing fees, and others can quickly add up.

Cost and fees are usually the client's responsibility. What happens in a contingency fee arrangement where the client is unable to pay the litigation cost? In those circumstances, you can advance the costs and recover them later from the settlement amount. This approach can be risky since the settlement amount will not exist if you do not prevail. In those circumstances, unless the client is wealthy, as a practical matter, you will not be able to recover them.

---

14. Carole J. Buckner, *IOLTAs and Client Trust Accounts*, GPSOLO MAG. (July 31, 2011), https://www.americanbar.org/groups/gpsolo/publications/gp_solo/2011/july_august/ioltas_client_trust_accounts ("Although lawyers should review individual state procedures for establishing CTAs, there are several important and typical practical considerations. First, many state rules require that you establish the IOLTA account with a financial institution designated from a list of participating institutions. Typically, the account must be established in the state in which the lawyer practices, unless the client designates otherwise.").

15. N.Y. COMP. CODES R. & REGS. tit. 21, § 7000.1:
The fund is authorized to receive funds from any source for disbursement to nonprofit legal services providers for charitable purposes, including the delivery of legal services in civil matters to poor persons. The fund will receive interest or dividends earned by qualified client funds held by attorneys in unsegregated interest-bearing or dividend-bearing accounts at banking institutions to the extent that such institutions choose to offer and receive the benefits of providing IOLA accounts, and will utilize the interest or dividends so received for the above-stated purposes.

2.8 Defining the Representation—What Does the Client Want/Need You to Do?

2.8.1 *What Power Does the Client Retain?*

The MRPC lay out the decision-making power that both you and the client retain. In a civil case, under MRPC 1.2 (a), the client decides the representation's objectives. In other words, what result does the client want from this litigation? Generally, the attorney retains the power to direct strategy. MRPC 1.4 states that you should consult with your client as to the means of their objective. Usually, a client defers to the expertise and skill of the lawyer, but seek the client's input regardless. The client also decides whether or not to settle.

2.8.2 *Opening a File*

After agreeing to representation, and sometimes even before, you need to open a case file. Many law firms now use sophisticated programs to organize their files electronically. Whether you store a file electronically, on paper, or most likely a combination of both, organization is key. An organized file helps you to avoid mistakes, saves time, and allows you to quickly learn and share information. When multiple people are working on the same case, each person must be able to pick up the file, know exactly what another person did, and navigate the file. If you do not maintain an organized file, mistakes that can impact your case and your credibility can easily happen.

An organized file makes you more prepared for court and to confer with opposing counsel. You always hope to be prepared for things you may have to argue, but the ability to respond to the unexpected will enhance your advocacy skills. When judges ask about something that happened in the case and you cannot find it in your file, or it takes you an uncomfortably long time to find it, you do not look prepared in front of the court or your client.

There are countless ways to organize files, and it varies based upon your practice area or the individual case. There are three core areas that almost any file should include:

1) Correspondence

2) Pleadings

3) Documents/Evidence

The correspondence folder contains your communications record between you and your client, opposing counsel, witnesses, and other third parties. This section should contain a written record of any verbal and written correspondence. Keep the most recent records on top for efficiency.

The pleadings folder contains any court or administrative agency filings or documents, such as:

- Complaint

- Answer

- Notices of Hearings

- Court Orders

- Court or Agency Opinions

- Discovery Requests and Responses

The documents/evidence folder contains items such as: medical records, bills, police reports, investigator reports, witness statements, diagrams, and photographs. Remember that originals, especially originals you may want to use in court, should not have written notes or be hole punched. When reviewing a document, make a photocopy and save the original in a separate section of the folder.

For your pleadings and documents/evidence folders, an index system helps you easily locate items. A chronological list of the documents will save you a lot of time when navigating large case files.

2.8.3 Initial Fact Gathering

At the initial meeting, gather client information and formulate additional methods to engage in initial fact gathering. Chapter Five discusses fact investigation in more detail, but in this section, we will discuss some of the immediate issues to consider at that first meeting.

2.8.3.1 Preserve Information/Evidence

Evidence can quickly disappear. Corporations have programs that automatically purge documents. Video recordings sometimes get erased or taped over on a set schedule. People empty their deleted emails and text messages. At the initial meeting, make sure the information favorable to your client is preserved.

Inform the potential client of their duty to preserve evidence. Evidence destruction can lead to sanctions and a possible spoliation inference.[16] Find out what

---

16. Fed R. Civ. P. 37(e), Failure to Preserve Electronically Stored Information: If electronically stored information that should have been preserved in the anticipation or conduct of litigation is lost because a party failed to take reasonable steps to preserve it, and it cannot be restored or replaced through additional discovery, the court:
(1) upon finding prejudice to another party from loss of the information, may order measures no greater than necessary to cure the prejudice; or

electronically stored information your client has and where it can be located. A formal complaint filing does not trigger the duty to preserve evidence. A reasonable anticipation of litigation triggers that duty.[17]

Identify emails, text messages, and other documents related to the case. Probing questions are often necessary. Clients may not understand what you are looking for and can overlook something's existence and relevance. For example, you might ask a client:

> Q: Do you have any documents relating to this matter?
>
> A: No.
>
> Q: Do you have a computer?
>
> A: Yes.
>
> Q: Do you have an email account?
>
> A: Yes.
>
> Q: Did you ever email about this incident?
>
> A: Yes.

---

(2) only upon finding that the party acted with the intent to deprive another party of the information's use in the litigation may:

(A) presume that the lost information was unfavorable to the party;

(B) instruct the jury that it may or must presume the information was unfavorable to the party; or

(C) dismiss the action or enter a default judgment.

"One of worst things that can happen in litigation is a finding of spoliation, or a spoliation inference given to a jury. Spoliation is defined generally as the destruction or significant alteration of evidence, or the failure to preserve property for another's use as evidence in pending or reasonably foreseeable litigation." Michael E. Adler, *Avoiding the Hammer of a Spoliation Inference: Preservation of Electronic Communications*, (2005) https://www.americanbar.org/newsletter/publications/law_trends_news_ practice_area_e_newsletter_home/preservationecomm.html.

17. "The new rule applies only if the lost information should have been preserved in the anticipation or conduct of litigation and the party failed to take reasonable steps to preserve it. Many court decisions hold that potential litigants have a duty to preserve relevant information when litigation is reasonably foreseeable. . . In applying the rule, a court may need to decide whether and when a duty to preserve arose. Courts should consider the extent to which a party was on notice that litigation was likely and that the information would be relevant. A variety of events may alert a party to the prospect of litigation. Often these events provide only limited information about that prospective litigation, however, so that the scope of information that should be preserved may remain uncertain. It is important not to be blinded to this reality by hindsight arising from familiarity with an action as it is actually filed." Fed R. Civ. P. 37, advisory committee's note to 2015 amendment.

2.8.3.2 Identification of Relevant Documents for Different Types of Cases

Personal injury	Employment	Breach of contract	Fraud
Police reports	Employment offer letters	The contract	Bank statements
Photographs	Termination letters	Letters and emails explaining or evidencing the contract	Tax returns
Videos	Employment manuals	Documents evidencing damages	Relevant documentation
Cell phone photos and videos	Letters and emails		Insurance policies
Notes			
Medical reports and bills			

Defamation	Divorce	Injunctive relief
Copy of relevant statement/publication, e.g., social media posts	Tax returns	Proof of potential harm
Documentation evidencing damages	Prenuptial agreement	Relevant documentation
	Separation agreement	Information about property or finances
	Pension statements	
	Proof of current income	
	Bank statements	
	Mortgages	
	Insurance policies	
	Lists of personal property	

2.9 Initial Ethical Concerns

2.9.1 *Stolen Documents*

Use of workplace documents often creates issues in employment-related cases. Employees often have documents from the employment setting to support claims for relief. Claims arise under different legal theories, some governed by statutory law and some by common law. What an employee may take from the workplace to support a case may require an analysis of the particular statute or common-law remedy that forms the basis of the claim.[18] Local statutes dictate whether your client may face civil liability, and sometimes even criminal liability, for removing documents. In order to properly advise your client, you want to ask:

---

18. *See* Cafasso v. Gen. Dynamics C4 Sys., 637 F.3d 1047 (9th Cir. 2011) (An employee of a technology company contracted to service the military was fired after alleging her employer was defrauding the government. Prior to leaving the office she copied nearly eleven gigabytes of data from company computers in anticipation of bringing a *qui tam* action against her employer on behalf of the government under the False Claims Act. The data amounted to thousands of internal documents. The company filed suit to recover the removed documents citing a confidentiality agreement signed by the employee when she was hired which stated: "I will not remove any [confidential] materials...without the prior written consent of a corporate officer.... Upon the termination of my employment... I shall promptly deliver to [employer] all such materials and copies thereof in my possession an[d] control." Ultimately the parties entered into an "acrimonious period of discovery" wherein the employee refused to identify which of the documents supported her claim or were privileged. Summary judgment was granted as to the claim by the employer that removal of the documents violated the confidentiality agreement. On appeal, the former employee asked the court to adopt a public policy exception to her admitted violation of the agreement in light of her *qui tam* action. While the appellate court recognized the merits of the proposal, they stopped short of adopting it. Saying that such protection would be limited to particular documents reasonably necessary to bringing an FCA claim and would require balancing confidentiality policies against the public's interest. Here they held that the employee's appropriation of thousands of internal documents was so "vast and indiscriminate" that any public policy exception would fail to provide her relief.); *see also,* Quinlan v. Curtiss-Wright Corp., 204 N.J. 239, 8 A.3d 209 (2010) (Believing she had been passed over for promotion due to widespread gender discrimination, an employee made copies of 1800 internal documents (including a performance evaluation of the male colleague who received the promotion) and filed a sex discrimination suit against her employer. During the discovery phase, the employer became aware of the copied documents and terminated her employment for theft. The now former employee then added a claim of retaliatory discharge to her suit against her ex-employer and the trial jury found in her favor. On appeal the trial court was found to have erred when they charged the jury that plaintiff's use of the documents during depositions was protected. The state supreme court reversed. While they agreed that the wholesale copying and removal of internal documents was in violation of company policy and therefore not protected conduct, the plaintiff's use of the relevant performance evaluation during deposition was, in fact, protected (citing the "strong remedial purposes" of the state's law against discrimination and the impact that the evaluation would have in the limited context of the suit) and upheld the trial jury's finding in favor of the plaintiff.).

1) How did you obtain those documents?

2) What do those documents contain?

3) Do they contain confidential information?

4) Is viewing confidential information part of your job?

5) Do you have permission to view those documents?

6) Have you shared these documents with anyone else?

2.9.2   Taping/Recording of Interview

Client-recorded conversations supporting a case are common. Clients looking to support their claim and convince others of wrongdoing often seek out this type of evidence. You may be confronted with a recording during your first meeting or at any point in the case. Discuss the legal ramifications of recording with your client.

Recording a conversation without the consent of all parties is a crime in some states. About 25 percent of states require two-party consent, meaning that all parties must consent to be recorded. If your client recorded a conversation, they could be subject to both criminal and civil penalties. However, if your client gathered that information to support a discrimination or harassment claim, they may be protected. Jurisdictions are split on this issue.[19]

The remaining states require only one-party consent. If located in such a state, your client likely has no criminal liability since the client making the recording would have consented.

---

19. *See Heller v. Champion Int'l Corp.*, 891 F.2d 432, 437 (2nd Cir. 1989)("[W]e do not accept the proposition that an employee would never be justified in tape-recording conversations with his superiors and discussing a possible lawsuit"); *but see* Argyropoulos v. City of Alton, 539 F.3d 724, 733-734 (7th Cir. 2008) (Even though plaintiff tried to "obtain evidence of discrimination. . . when she secretly recorded the meeting of her superiors," the court held the aggrieved employee did not have "a license to engage in dubious self-help tactics or workplace espionage in order to gather evidence of discrimination.").

CHAPTER THREE

INTERVIEWING

3.1 Case Theory

At trial, a lawyer must present a coherent and believable story to the judge and jurors. From the moment you consider representing a client, you are creating, developing, and testing out case theories. You will develop and test theories during your investigation and throughout the discovery process. Sometimes these theories are slight variations of the same story. Other times, you are considering very different case theories. The process begins at the initial client interview and continues throughout the case.

Case theories can be broken down into two parts: factual theory and legal theory. Your factual theory is simply the story of what triggered your claim or defense. It is the story of what happened *from your client's perspective*. Imagine if you could play a "movie" of the relevant events for the jurors and judge to help them understand what happened. That movie of what happened is your factual theory. At trial, instead of playing a movie, you will create a believable story through witnesses and evidence.

When cases do not settle prior to trial, the reason is typically because you and opposing counsel have different factual theories. You believe the event happened one way and your opponent believes it happened another way. One way to succeed at the pretrial stage is to convince your opponent that your version is what actually happened. Absent settlement, your goal will be to convince the jurors, or judge in a bench trial, that your version of the events is more believable.

The second part of case theory is your legal theory. Your legal theory answers the question, based upon your factual theory, how does the law allow you to prevail? If your factual theory does not support a legal theory that gives you a pathway to prevail it is not a good factual theory. Lack of a factual theory that allows you to prevail based upon the law is a strong indication that your claim or defense is not tenable; seriously consider settling the case.

Case theory development starts at the initial interview but evolves throughout the pretrial process and until trial. From the outset, you are simultaneously gathering the facts and analyzing the law. Although infrequent, your case theory sometimes changes during trial based upon something unexpected happening. Keep your case theory flexible enough to evolve and develop as you learn information, especially at the early stages. At their initial interview, what your client tells you happened will be the primary source for developing that initial theory. It would be bad lawyering, however, to stop there. More interviews, discovery, and research refine your theory throughout the pretrial stage.

Avoid the dangers of becoming overly committed to a case theory at the early stages of litigation. As you investigate your case, what you think happened drives how you interview witnesses, conduct depositions, and gather evidence. If you are only looking to prove one theory, you may miss out on valuable information that could lead to a different, even stronger theory. Over-committing to a case theory can also get in the way of an honest evaluation of your own case. Throughout the pretrial process, evaluate the weaknesses of your own theory and the strengths and weaknesses of your opponent's theory.

Good storytelling is the touchstone of effective advocacy. The development of an engaging story maintains audience interest and helps with their understanding and memory of your position. This is true not just at trial but throughout the litigation process, from complaint, through discovery, motions, and appeal after trial.

— Eric Newman, Chief Litigation Counsel — Antitrust Division,
Washington State Office of the Attorney General

3.2 Purpose

A client's initial interview is one of the most important discovery tools because your client is likely to be your best source for discovery. If the client cannot personally provide you information, they will frequently be able to tell you how and where to find it so that you can focus your other tools of discovery. By the end of the interview you should fully understand the client's problems, begin to understand the client's goals and objectives, and determine what legal issues are involved.

While the initial interview frames your relationship with the client, keep in mind that in any substantive case, a client will be interviewed on multiple occasions. Information obtained through investigation and discovery will result in additional meetings with the client, where new documents and information are made part of the discussion. In Chapter Four, we focus on the process of counseling a client through the decision-making process, which is frequently done in conjunction with the interviewing process.

The best client interviews are planned in advance but remain flexible. When meeting with a client for the first time, or at the early stages of a case, think about three primary goals:

1) Establishing a rapport;

2) Understanding the immediate needs of your client; and

3) Gathering information.

3.3   Should You Interview Every Prospective Client?

The realities of legal practice, especially a high-volume practice, is that you cannot commit to doing a complete in-person interview with every potential client. Even modest numbers of five to ten client interviews per week could quickly consume a legal practice and get in the way of adequately handling the cases of current clients. When confronted with the situation of too many client interviews, consider alternative screening methods that do not involve a full face-to-face interview:

- Create an intake form that is completed by a potential client.

- Have an assistant or paralegal conduct an initial intake interview.

- When appropriate, use videoconference features to conduct the interview.

Of course, meeting with a client and having adequate time to address all of their concerns is ideal. We encourage you to strive for that goal. However, balanced against the realities of legal practice, consider the alternatives listed above.

3.4   Preparation and Establishing Credibility

Being prepared for an interview is one of the best ways to instill confidence in your client. Preparation will vary based upon the stage of the case. The more you know about a client and their case during the first interview, the more confidence they will have in your ability. This confidence makes your client more willing to share information, and in turn, creates a more effective first impression.

Before your initial client interview, be sure to:

- Review the case file, if there is already an active case;

- Review prior client contacts with your office;

- Research areas of the law related to the new matter with which you are unfamiliar;

- Create an interview plan; and

- Arrange for a comfortable meeting location to meet with your client.

3.5 Who Should Be Present at the Interview?

Clients are almost always nervous when meeting with an attorney. The level of anxiety is elevated when it involves a more vulnerable person, such as a child or an elderly person. Clients frequently bring friends or family members to provide support. Almost always, those friends and family members are not the client and should be asked to leave the room before you begin the interview. Most of the time, the presence of a third party waives confidentiality between you and the client.[1] Be sensitive about how you deal with your anxious client in this situation, as well as their companion. Dealing with it abruptly with no explanation can increase your client's anxiety and distrust. When you encounter an anxious client or a reluctant friend or family member, there are three steps that can successfully resolve the situation.

1) Explain to each person the importance of confidentiality and the special relationship between the lawyer and their client.

2) Explain that you would never want the friend or family member to be put in a situation where they would be forced to testify against the client because confidentiality was waived.

3) Take some time with the friend or family member to answer their questions and address concerns before and after the interview.

Confidentiality is not waived in most jurisdictions when someone from your legal team, such as a paralegal or investigator, is present.[2] Keep in mind, however, that too many people in the interview will make it feel like an interrogation and can shut the client down. Jurisdictions have variation in who can be present while maintaining privilege and confidentiality; research the law in your jurisdiction.

3.5.1 Setting the Tone

When you meet with a new client for the first time, set the right tone. The following can help you establish a professional, but not intimidating, tone for your first meeting:

---

1. MODEL RULES OF PRO. CONDUCT r. 1.6 (c)(AM. BAR. ASS'N 1983) ("A lawyer should make reasonable efforts to prevent the inadvertent or unauthorized disclosure of, or unauthorized access to, information relating to the representation of a client."). *See* State v. Shire, 850 S.W.2d 923 (Mo. Ct. App. 1993) (a defendant charged with second degree murder had waived the attorney-client privilege because of a family member's presence at a client-lawyer meeting).

2. "Paralegals, investigators, and secretaries must have ready access to client confidences in order to assist their attorney employers." Williams v. Trans World Airlines, Inc., 588 F. Supp. 1037, 1044. (W. D. Mo. 1984). *See* Jenkins v. Bartlett, 487 F.3d 482, 490-91 (7th Cir. 2007) (a third party's presence does not defeat the attorney-client privilege if the third party's presence is to assist the attorney in rendering legal services); United States v. Kovel, 296 F.2d 918, 922 (2d Cir. 1961) (Second Circuit extended the attorney-client privilege to communications between a client and an accountant hired to assist the attorney in representing the client).

- Be on time for the meeting; do not keep the client waiting. This shows respect, shows that you value their time, and helps establish the trust that is essential in the attorney-client relationship.

- Try to arrange for the meeting to occur in a quiet, private space where you can both speak freely and candidly. If that is not possible, try to choose a location that will allow you to focus on the conversation without major distractions.

- Communicate clearly and avoid using legal terms unless necessary, especially if your client is a layperson unfamiliar with the legal system and laws. Many clients are intimidated by a lawyer peppering their discussion with legal terms the client doesn't understand. Some will be too embarrassed to ask what they mean and will leave the meeting already feeling negative about the relationship.

- Outline your plan for the meeting so they know what to expect. Include your objectives: understanding the facts and events that have resulted in the current dispute; understanding the client's goals for the litigation, including what is most important for them to achieve; identifying next steps to move the case forward.

3.5.2 Creating Rapport

Good rapport with your client will set the foundation for your relationship going forward. Take a few minutes at the beginning of the meeting to engage in small talk, introduce yourself, and let the client introduce themselves. Consider sharing some of your professional background and experience, especially if it is relevant to the matter you will be discussing. It can be helpful to find areas of commonality, such as a shared alma mater or favorite sports team, but be careful not to overstep boundaries, as explained in the next section.

If your client does not trust you, they will hold back information. Take your time building trust and do not expect it at the outset. There is nothing worse than learning something new about your client in the middle of his deposition, hearing, or trial.

— Megan Davies, Executive Director, Innocence Delaware, Inc.

Even if you have formed some initial opinions about the matter based on your preparation for the interview, remain open-minded and flexible. Many clients are turned off by a lawyer who comes into the conversation with a recommendation ready to go before even hearing the client's story and goals for the litigation. As your client shares their story, listen to understand; do not be judgmental or dismissive.

This does not mean that you should not tell them if there are facts that might hurt their case. Be honest and upfront about the potential strengths and weaknesses of their case, but try to deliver that information in a way that is constructive and professional.

3.5.3 Setting Personal and Professional Boundaries

While establishing rapport with your client is important, do not make the mistake of confusing rapport with friendship. It is okay to be friendly towards your clients; you do not have to present a cold and uncaring façade. It is critical, however, to maintain a professional attorney-client relationship and set appropriate personal boundaries with your clients. Too many lawyers have been disciplined for engaging in inappropriate conduct with their clients.

Just as personal boundaries are important, so are professional boundaries. Clearly outline the limits of your representation—which aspects of the problem you can help them with, and which ones you cannot. Consider a client who seeks your help with a family dispute over an inheritance. The client has been estranged from their family for several years and believes the deceased was pressured into removing the client from their will. In addition to challenging the will, the client wants to try to repair their relationship with certain members of the family. Be clear that you can assist your client with the challenge to the will, but you cannot help with the interpersonal family relationship issues.

3.6 Facilitators and Inhibitors[3]

3.6.1 What are They and Why are They Important?

In order to maximize your ability to gather information and build trust with your client, you must be aware of the many factors that increase and decrease the flow of information from the client to the attorney. Anything that enhances the flow is a "facilitator." Anything that is an impediment to or stops the flow of communication is an "inhibitor." Binder and Price, in their groundbreaking book, LEGAL INTERVIEWING AND COUNSELING, coined many of the terms discussed below.[4]

---

3. DAVID A. BINDER & SUSAN C. PRICE, LEGAL INTERVIEWING AND COUNSELING: A CLIENT-CENTERED APPROACH 9 (1977) (discussing common psychological factors that enhance or interfere with client motivation and explaining common psychological factors that affect client motivation). In their seminal work, Binder and Price put forward the psychological principles that motivate or dissuade clients to speak. We encourage you to think more broadly than just the psychological factors, but include a variety of factors that will enhance or inhibit the flow of communication.
4. *Id.*

3.6.2 *Facilitators*

3.6.2.1 Interview Location and Setup

Choose the right location for an interview. When the interview occurs in your office, be sure to find a location that is quiet, where you will not be interrupted. If a previous interview with this client either did not go well or was highly emotional, consider choosing a different space within your office.

Choosing where and how you are seated can help the client feel more at ease, and make the meeting feel less like an interrogation. We do not recommend having a large table between you and the client. If you have a large table, consider having you and your client sit at the corner so that you are partially facing and sitting next to each other.

When you choose a location outside of the office, be considerate of issues that might make a client nervous and try to avoid them. Are the client's issues related to a workplace dispute? If so, the client will likely feel nervous about meeting in a place where coworkers might see them. The same type of concern can apply when interviewing in a client's home. They may be concerned about nosy neighbors or other family members in the house.

3.6.2.2 Empathetic Understanding

There are many interview techniques you can use to increase the flow of information, but empathetic understanding and active listening are two of the most important. Use empathetic understanding[5] to demonstrate that you recognize the emotional impact of the client's case. When a client knows that you understand the emotions they are feeling, they are more likely to feel comfortable and trusting, which leads them to disclose more information. For example, when a client tells you about a severe injury they have sustained and how the injury has adversely impacted their daily life, respond by showing empathy. Strive to identify the emotion or feeling the client is exhibiting and let them know that you understand. In the above example, you might respond with, "of course you are upset; this injury has limited your independence."

The emotion can vary, and you should be looking to identify those emotions during the interview. If you cannot identify the emotion clearly, be careful not to guess. Guessing the wrong emotion can backfire and make the client feel like you do not understand their case. Use the technique strategically. And do not empathize with everything the client says—this looks disingenuous.

---

5. *Id.* at 14; Robert M. Bastress & Joseph D. Harbaugh, Interviewing, Counseling, and Negotiating: Skills for Effective Representation 57 (1990).

3.6.2.3   Active and Passive Listening

Active listening[6] is listening to what the client tells you and responding in a way that demonstrates that you heard and understood what they said. This technique is the primary way in which you can demonstrate empathetic understanding to the client. Active listening is often simply done through explaining back part of what the client says to you. Here is an example:

> Client: "I was standing on the corner of 18th and Main when the car came over the curb and hit me on the right side. I immediately went to the ground after traveling through the air for five to ten feet. The next thing I remember is the paramedics kneeling over me asking if I could hear them."

> Active Listening Response: "You were at the corner of 18th and Main streets, right in the middle of town, when the car came over the curb. That must have been scary [empathetic understanding] to be standing on the corner one minute and then see paramedics kneeling over you the next."

In this example, the lawyer demonstrated that they were listening by repeating back relevant facts such as the accident occurring at 18th and Main. The lawyer also used active listening to show empathetic understanding. The lawyer correctly identified the likely emotion (fear) that the client was feeling when the paramedics were kneeling over them.

The following is a list of commonly used active listening techniques:

- Paraphrasing or summarizing what a client has said.

- Asking questions.

- Requesting clarification.

Active listening requires you to pay attention. This demonstrates that you are interested in what the client says and allows you to more effectively use the techniques listed above.

It makes it easier to understand active listening if you also understand passive listening. Passive listening[7] is listening and not responding or responding in a way that does not demonstrate to the client that you were listening and understood what they said. In the above example for active listening, a passive listening response by

---

6. BINDER & PRICE, *supra* note 3, at 25; STEFAN H. KRIEGER, ET AL, ESSENTIAL LAWYERING SKILLS: INTERVIEWING, NEGOTIATION, COUNSELING, AND PERSUASIVE FACT ANALYSIS 119–123 (6th ed. 2020).
7. BINDER & PRICE, *supra* note 3, at 23–24; DAVID BINDER ET AL, LAWYERS AS COUNSELORS: A CLIENT CENTERED APPROACH 25 (4th ed. 2019).

the lawyer would be something like: "OK"; "hmm . . ."; "interesting"; "really?"; "tell me more." None of these responses require you to understand anything the client said, so they do not clearly demonstrate to the client that you were listening. That said, an effective interview includes both active and passive listening. If you use too much active listening, the client may get frustrated and feel like you are just repeating everything they say and keep interrupting their story. Pay attention to the client's reaction and adjust your techniques accordingly.

3.7   Promising Confidentiality and Its Limits

Lawyers and their clients have a special relationship, and that relationship can be used to make the client feel more comfortable and confident in providing you with information. MRPC 1.6 requires that you keep all information regarding your representation of a client confidential unless they give informed consent or disclosure is impliedly authorized.[8] Attorney-client privilege means confidential conversations between a lawyer and a client cannot be used against a client during litigation. Explaining confidentiality and privilege to the client will encourage them to provide you with more information, even the information they perceive to be damaging or bad, to ultimately help their case. Keep in mind that most clients have little understanding of the law, so spending the time to explain these concepts is what gives the client comfort—not the mere recitation.

3.8   Reward and Recognition[9]

A client will often wonder whether they are providing good information or the correct information. Always encourage your client to tell you everything, but they are understandably nervous and self-conscious. Motivate the client to provide more information by rewarding them with positive comments about how the interview is going. For example, a lawyer might say something such as, "you provided great detail in that description" or "this is exactly the type of information that is helpful." Such encouraging and reassuring statements can motivate the client and put them at ease, which will make them more likely to continue providing more information.

3.9   Distracted or Hyper-Focused Client

Most of the time you are dealing with matters of great importance to your clients. Their stories can be very emotional, and clients have sometimes been waiting days, months, or even years to tell someone who they believe cares and can help them. Emotions such as anger and sadness need to be expressed before a person can be receptive to your questions. Sometimes their long wait to tell their story means

---

8. There are additional exceptions that should be explained to the client.
9. BINDER & PRICE, *supra* note 3, at 16–17.

that you must let them say what *they* need before you can pivot to the information gathering *you* need. In other words, allow the client to vent. Of course, sometimes you must limit such venting, especially when you are dealing with significant time constraints. Use your judgment on the appropriate level of venting.

Other times, the client is not fully engaged in the process and seems distracted. Frequently, the client is distracted by some other issue that is usually case related. The client simply wants to talk about something else and cannot focus. Many clients cannot actively engage in the interview process until they discuss the issue that they feel is pressing. If you sense the client is not engaged, ask if they want to share something. Listen to what your client says at the beginning of the interview because they might give you a clue as to what they want to share.

3.10 Mirroring, Matching, and Body Language

Quickly build good rapport by mirroring the client's behavior and posture. Mirroring[10] and matching make them feel more comfortable and more likely to provide information. If your client is very relaxed and casual, for example, do not be unnecessarily formal in your approach. If a client leans forward to talk to you or leans back and crosses his legs, consider letting some time lapse, but then assume a similar posture.

As an interviewer, be aware of the signals your body language sends. If you fold arms across your chest in a closed position, it might appear that you are angry. Reading through reports or notes while a client is talking shows a lack of interest. Occasionally leaning in and making eye contact, or nodding along as your client speaks, or taking notes after your client has said something important, all signal to your client that you are invested, interested, and engaged. When you appear engaged and interested in the client, they are more likely to disclose information.

3.10.1 Eye Contact

Maintain eye contact during an interview to show that you are interested and that you care. It also encourages the client to keep talking because you are signaling that what they are saying is important and helpful to you. It also shows you are confident.

3.10.2 Limit Writing While Talking and Listening

Notetaking can make a client nervous because they feel as though you are interrogating them or are going to challenge them at a later point. However, gathering

---

10. David Binder et al, Lawyers as Counselors: A Client Centered Approach 29-30 (4th ed. 2019); Robert Dinerstein, et al, *Connection, Capacity and Morality in Lawyer-Client Relationships: Dialogues and Commentary*, 10 Clinical L. Rev. 755, 758 (2003).

accurate and important information is critical to the interviewing process. Notetaking should work for you and not against you. Limit notetaking at the beginning of the interview as you build a rapport with the client. Then, when you find it necessary to take notes, explain to the client why you are taking notes and that no one else, except the legal team, will ever see these. Try to limit notetaking during the interview.

3.11 Inhibitors

Lawyers sometimes become frustrated during initial meetings with clients because they sense that clients are not being truthful or entirely forthcoming. You must manage your expectations and understand that this is the situation with almost every initial client meeting. This is completely normal and expected. Once you understand some of the reasons behind it, you can use effective strategies and techniques to minimize the problem.

3.11.1 Reluctance to Disclose Negative Information

Clients are reluctant to disclose negative information to their lawyer when it makes them look bad. This is commonly referred to as the "ego threat."[11] Clients are also reluctant to disclose information that they perceive to negatively impact their case. This is called the "case threat."[12] This reluctance creates a significant barrier to gathering accurate information at the beginning stages of an attorney-client relationship. Building trust over time and through multiple interviews breaks down the client's hesitancy to disclose bad information.

Clients often incorrectly determine what is most helpful and what is most damaging to their case, and therefore hold back information that is helpful. When confronted with this problem, address both the ego and the case threats. Assure the client that you can do a better job when you know everything. First, you can counsel them better when you know the good, the bad, and the ugly facts. Second, you cannot prepare to deal with something if you do not know it. Being surprised is one of a litigator's biggest problems, and it is your job to avoid these problems.

3.11.2 Role Expectations

Some clients believe that lawyers will know exactly what questions to ask to get exactly the information they need.[13] Especially at the early stages of a case, lawyers

---

11. BINDER & PRICE, *supra* note 3, at 10; DAVID BINDER ET AL, LAWYERS AS COUNSELORS: A CLIENT CENTERED APPROACH 12 (4th ed. 2019) ("Ego threat arises when clients withhold information that they consider threatening to their self-esteem.").

12. BINDER & PRICE, *supra* note 3, at 113; DAVID BINDER ET AL, LAWYERS AS COUNSELORS: A CLIENT CENTERED APPROACH 13 (4th ed. 2019) (case threat occurs when the client withholds information they may feel will "hurt their chances of a satisfactory outcome.").

13. BINDER & PRICE, *supra* note 3, at 11.

do not know all the right questions to ask. That is why it is important to get the client talking, and to listen closely for important information you want to learn more about. Asking open-ended questions and just listening can be an effective tool to encourage the client to talk more so you can discover important information. The following types of questions are examples:

- Why you are here today?

- Why do you think you need the help of a lawyer?

- What happened to you?

- Why do you think this happened?

- Who have you talked to about this incident?

- Who was there when it happened?

3.11.3   *Reluctance to Disclose Sensitive Information*

Many times, clients are reluctant to disclose very private and personal information during the first interview, or until they feel comfortable.[14] Establishing a good relationship with the client is the key to them being willing to disclose sensitive information. As the lawyer, you must be willing to ask difficult questions about sensitive information that relates to the case. Acknowledge that these questions are intrusive, but explain that the alternative can be catastrophic to the client's case. If you do not learn about sensitive information, you could be missing critical information that can support their claim or critical bad information that you will not be prepared to deal with at the pretrial stage, or worse, at trial.

3.11.4   *Trauma*

Whether it is a serious injury, the loss of a business, or a contentious divorce, people are often traumatized by the events for which they are seeking your help. The original incident may still be difficult to talk about and each subsequent telling of the event can be a separate traumatic experience. This trauma will affect your client's ability to convey important information, especially at the early stages of the relationship.[15] The pain caused by repeating a traumatic event makes it important that you are as prepared as much as possible for each interview in order to minimize the unnecessary retelling of the event.

---

14. *Id.* at 12.
15. *Id.* at 13.

3.11.5 Forgetting

As time passes, memories fade. It is hard for clients to remember details, even important ones, as the relevant events recede farther into the past. When faced with a client who does not remember something or you believe is mistaken in the memory, you have a couple of techniques at your disposal. You can utilize other tools of discovery to help refresh a client's memory. For example, discovery such as prior statements, photographs, letters, and documents can help refresh your witness's memory. Be careful, however, how you utilize this information. Instead of refreshing their actual memory, you might just be creating a memory that really does not exist.

3.11.6 Perception

People simply perceive events in different ways. This reality can cause variation and even inconsistency between written statements, oral statements, and the evidence. It does not necessarily mean that one person is lying and the other is telling the truth. Many things that relate to the incident itself may also be impacted by prior life experiences that influence perception.

One person might have perceived the event as traumatic and stressful, influencing their ability to see and remember things precisely. It could be something as simple as two people observed the same event from different angles.

To a certain extent, everyone filters what they see and hear through a lens created by their prior experiences. If someone told you a story about an incident that happened at a movie theater, what would be the first image that came into your mind? Most likely, it would be an image of the movie theater you go to most frequently or maybe a theater from childhood. Therefore, unless you were familiar with the particular theater from the story, you would listen to the rest of that story through the lens of the theater that initially came to mind. That theater might be similar, but it could be very different.

As with forgetting, use other discovery information to help your client tell an accurate story about what happened. Probe the client's recall with questions and even challenge their perception of events when you think it is appropriate. A lawyer may attempt to persuade a witness, even aggressively, that the witness's "initial version of a certain fact situation is not complete or accurate."[16]

---

16. Resol. Trust Corp. v. Bright, 6 F.3d 336, 341 (5th Cir. 1993).

3.12 Questioning and Question Form

3.12.1 Why this is Important

The structure of your questions will impact how much and what type of information you will receive from a client or a witness. There are three general types of questions: open-ended, narrowing, and leading. All three types of questions will be used during every interview. The two general purposes for asking questions during an interview are gathering information and building a relationship with the client. How much of each will depend on a variety of circumstances, which are discussed in the following sections.

3.12.2 Question Type

3.12.2.1 Open-Ended

Open-ended questions seek broad answers. These are the types of questions that journalists are taught to ask of witnesses when gathering information for a story. Open-ended questions frequently start with words or phrases such as who; what; where; when; why; explain; describe; tell me about; help me understand . . . .

Open-ended questions are typically asked at the beginning of the interview when you are trying to get an overview of the client's story. They also help a witness to get comfortable with talking. For example, if you were asking a client about an injury suffered during a car accident, you would ask questions such as:

- What happened on September 1?

- Why were you in the area at that time?

- Tell us how the injuries impact your day-to-day activities.

Asking open-ended questions is important for several reasons. You are going to receive information that you might not learn by asking narrowing and leading type questions. Open-ended questions can also put the witness at ease by letting them tell their story to someone whom they perceive is interested and can help—therefore building the relationship.

One problem that occurs with a nervous client is that in response to your open-ended question, they simply do not provide you with much of a response. For example:

Q: Tell us what happened on September 1.

A: I got hurt.

Q: How did you get hurt?

A: By a car.

In these circumstances, consider transitioning to some more narrowing or leading questions to get the client comfortable speaking.

3.12.2.2 Narrowing

After you have a general sense of what happened, gather more specific details about your client and their legal matter. Narrowing questions gather more detailed information about topics you think are relevant and fill in gaps in the information provided. If you were looking for other potential witnesses to a car accident, for example, you might ask more narrow questions such as:

Q: Who was in the car with you?

Q: Do you have their contact information?

Q: What is their contact information?

Q: Are they all family members?

Narrowing questions are helpful in several ways in addition to getting the client comfortable with speaking. They allow you to focus on topics you believe are most important. While open-ended questions allow the client to answer questions in several different ways, narrowing questions require the witness to focus on a specific topic. This difference is apparent in the following example. Imagine asking a client, *what did you do last Tuesday* versus *what did you have for breakfast last Tuesday*? In answering the first question, the client could talk about anything that happened that day from morning until night. However, the second and more narrowing question specifically wants to know about breakfast on Tuesday. In response to the narrowing question, a witness would not start talking about what they did right before bed.

Another important use of narrowing questions is when you are addressing sensitive topics with your client. Consider this scenario: A lawyer is asking their client about what happened on Tuesday and the client keeps avoiding the topic of dinner. The lawyer suspects it is because the client had dinner with a lover. In order to probe sensitive information, assuming it is relevant, the lawyer may need a narrowing question such as, *who did you have dinner with on Tuesday?*

3.12.2.3 Leading for Details

Leading questions are short declarative statements that you are generally asking the client to confirm or deny. Leading questions are usually responded to by a yes or a no. Use leading questions to fill in gaps of information, to confirm information, and sometimes to challenge your client. Examples of leading questions are:

Q: You were traveling fifty miles per hour, right?

Q: Your car was red?

Q: The police arrived at the scene of the accident within ten minutes?

Just be careful about challenging a client during an initial interview, or early on in the relationship, for fear of losing their trust.

3.13   Structuring the Interview

3.13.1   *The Beginning*

At the beginning of the interview, focus on making the client comfortable. During this initial stage, engage in small talk, as discussed earlier in this chapter. Tell the client what to expect during the interview, such as duration, goals, and breaks. This puts the client at ease by managing expectations. This is also a good time to explain confidentiality to the client.

3.13.2   *The Middle*

The middle stage of the interview is the most substantive part and the stage where you gather information to begin understanding the client's issues and goals. Begin with open-ended questions, allowing the client to tell you an overview of what happened and why they are seeking your help. Initially, some clients might not be able to give a narration of the problem. If that is the case, you may need to move quickly to narrowing and leading questions to get the client comfortable with talking or to focus them on the issue that led them to contact you. As the witness becomes more comfortable, revert back to open-ended questions to continue getting an overview of the issues.

After getting an overview, probe for more specific information. This is where you start to use narrowing and probing questions. As the lawyer, you will have a sense of what information is the most relevant and what requires you to get more detail. As you gather more details, transition to leading questions to confirm the information you think you know or want to know.

These three question types do not have to be used in this order in every situation. What is important is to understand the type of information elicited by each type of question. The open-ended question will get the witness talking, usually in the context of a broad overview of a topic. Narrowing questions will focus on something specific, which usually results in the client talking less. The leading question often will be answered with a yes or no, so that should generally be used for confirmation and details. The type of information you are in search of should determine which type of question to ask.

3.13.3   *Ending the Interview*

At the conclusion of your interview there are several things to consider that ease client anxiety, set clear expectations, and prevent your client from getting into trouble. First, make clear whether a decision to represent the client has been made. If you have decided to represent the client, confirm this and discuss the next steps. If you are uncertain about whether you are going to represent them, inform the client about what still needs to be done before a final decision is made. If you are certain that you will not be representing the client, make that clear; best practice is to send a follow-up letter to the client confirming that you are not going to handle their legal matter.

After you have made the decision to represent the client, provide them with guidance to avoid some common problems. Make it clear that they should not discuss the case with anyone else. Those discussions with other people will not be confidential or privileged and can easily be used against them during the pretrial stage and at trial. The other potential problem is post-interview client behavior. Emotion and passion can run high in litigation. When emotional, clients tend to do inappropriate things; remind your client to refrain from action that could reflect negatively on their case, such as contacting witnesses, making statements to witnesses, or doing inappropriate investigation on their own. This guidance can help to avoid the headaches caused by clients acting against their own interests.

3.14   Engaging Professionals After the Interview

Cases and clients present complex problems that frequently need coordinated responses by more than just a lawyer. During the interview you may see an immediate need for an outside professional who can assist you and the client. This type of help can come in many forms and can occur within the context of the legal relationship or outside of it. An expert can be consulted to help understand complicated issues beyond your knowledge. Alternatively, you may notice that a family member is struggling emotionally or mentally and can benefit from working with some type of counseling services. If you are handling a family law matter, you may determine that a social worker can assist in the preparation of your case, in addition to addressing the well-being of the client and their family. The social worker can help secure services or help to develop a plan for resolving family disputes such as child custody.

At the outset of the case, strongly consider engaging outside professionals who can help achieve the client's goals and get better outcomes.

—Professor Zelda Harris, Loyola University Chicago School of Law

---

Another situation might arise if your representation involves something that is drawing significant media attention. Engaging with a crisis communication and reputation management professional can help your client to quickly improve, and sometimes completely change, the narrative of the case. This is very common in the context of corporate clients who are being accused of bad behavior, but also happens to individuals. While many larger companies have communication professionals, some companies and most individuals do not. Lawyers don't have experience managing the 24-hour news cycle, and momentum can quickly and unfairly build against their clients. A communications specialist can get the right messaging, at the right time, to the best platforms. The impact of messaging can affect the case itself by influencing how your client is perceived by the opposing party, but also mitigate ongoing damage while the litigation plays out and beyond.

The best results come when the lawyer anticipates the negative messaging and engages with a crisis communication specialist as early as possible.

—Andrew Bourke, Director of Communications, ChaudhryLaw PLLC

Outside professionals can play an important role in the development and outcome of a case and the well-being of a client. Great lawyers understand when they are needed and don't hesitate to use their help early in the process.

CHAPTER FOUR

COUNSELING

4.1 Introduction to Counseling

4.1.1. Importance

In their time of greatest distress and hardship, clients need your counsel and advice for what very likely is one of the most important issues in their life. It might be advice about initiating a claim, responding to a claim against them, settling a case, or going to trial. Beyond the important impact these matters have in the lives of clients, your ability to counsel your client will be one of the primary ways in which you are judged by your client. More than your legal acumen, clients judge the quality of their lawyer by how they perceive their relationship with you and how well you communicate.[1]

Clients deserve and appreciate your respect. After all, your clients had the good judgment to retain you. You should respect their time, their opinions, and their feelings. If you do not display respect for them, they will likely view you as arrogant and/or disinterested in their case. They will likely become disgruntled and difficult. If you cannot demonstrate respect to a particular client, you have no business being their attorney.

—Jim Griffin, Partner, Griffin & Davis L.L.C.

A good counselor isn't the lawyer who always digs into and reinforces his client's position. Great counselors remain as objective as possible, providing clients with the counseling that they need to hear, not necessarily what they want to hear. Direct and honest advice might not always make the client happy, but in the long run, it will gain their respect. Clients may not react well to your advice, but your role as a professional requires honest and clear analysis. While rare, an unfortunate

---

1. *See generally* Stephen Feldman & Kent Wilson, *The Value of Interpersonal Skills in Lawyering,* 5 Law & Hum. Behav. 311, 320-21 (1981) (discussing the often overlooked importance of interpersonal skills in the lawyer-client relationship).

consequence of this is that you or your client may decide that the relationship is over.

4.1.2 *What is Counselling?*

Television shows and movies love to depict the life of a lawyer as courtroom drama, but modern legal practice looks quite different. Very few cases, especially civil matters, ever get to trial. This chapter discusses the essence of modern-day lawyering—counseling a client through the decision-making process. Most cases resolve before a decision is handed down at trial and sometimes much earlier in the discovery process. The lawyer plays a central role in this decision-making process while ultimately helping the client resolve the case. Although resolution most often happens before the trial, counseling also involves making the decision to proceed to trial.

David Binder and Susan Price, describe the process as follows:

> Counseling . . . refers to the process in which lawyers help clients reach decisions. Specifically, counseling refers to a process in which potential solutions, with their probable and positive and negative consequences, are identified and then weighed in order to decide which alternative is most appropriate.[2]

Your role as a lawyer is that of a problem solver and counseling is the process you must use. Many law students and lawyers let what they believe to be zealous advocacy get in the way of helping the client reach a resolution. Nowhere is there a rule that says you must win at all costs, even if it means being uncivil. Nowhere is there a rule that requires lawyers to maximize every possible monetary gain for their client and pursue every possible legal avenue without regard to personal, emotional, societal, or monetary costs. The broad role of lawyers, which explicitly includes the role of counselor, is promulgated in the MRPC.

> As a representative of clients, a lawyer performs various functions. As advisor, a lawyer provides a client with an informed understanding of the client's legal rights and obligations and explains their practical implications. As advocate, a lawyer zealously asserts the client's position under the rules of the adversary system. As negotiator, a lawyer seeks a result advantageous to the client but consistent with requirements of honest dealings with others. As an evaluator, a lawyer acts by examining a client's legal affairs and reporting about them to the client or to others.[3]

---

2. David A. Binder & Susan C. Price, Legal Interviewing and Counseling: A Client-Centered Approach 5 (1977).
3. Model Rules of Pro. Conduct pmbl. §2 (Am. Bar Ass'n 2020).

Counseling is the foundation of what a lawyer does. Good counseling earns the respect and admiration of your client and many times, opposing counsel.

4.2 Counseling Styles

What does client counseling look like and how is it done? This is not an easy question to answer and there is no single, right way to counsel a client. You must understand the different methods for counseling a client and when you might use part or all of one method. Most lawyers vary their approach depending on many factors including their own preference, client preference, and the specific situation.

There are three threshold questions that need to be considered for those entering any client counseling situation:

- What style of counseling makes the client most comfortable and meets their expectations?

- What style of counseling is most comfortable for the lawyer?

- What style of counseling is best for this specific case type or situation?

Three types of counseling have a long history. In fact, without even knowing the names of these techniques, it is likely that you have used them in your everyday life when giving advice to a friend, family member, or a client. The three methods of counseling are sometimes referred to by slightly different names but fall into these three categories:

- Lawyer-centered[4]

- Client-centered

- Collaborative decision-making[5]

These methods of counseling can be viewed as three points on a spectrum; they are primarily defined by the level of control exerted by or deference given to the lawyer in the decision-making process. Lawyer-centered counseling, sometimes referred to as recommendation, authoritarian, or traditional counseling, is at the opposite end of the spectrum. In this style, the lawyer takes more control and direct influence over the decision-making process by directly recommending the course of action to the client. Client-centered counseling, at one end of the spectrum, is a method developed and put forth by Binder and Price.[6] The client-centered approach places the decision-making process primarily in the hands of the client.

---

4. This type of counseling has also been referred to as authoritarian or traditional. *See* Douglas E. Rosenthal, Lawyer and Client: Who's in Charge? 172-74, 174 n.54 (1974).

5. This type of counseling has also been referred to as participatory. *Id.* at 154.

6. Binder & Price, *supra* note 2.

In between those models on the spectrum is collaborative decision making, which has some characteristics of each model but strives to find a balance between the two extremes of the attorney's role in the decision-making process. The collaborative approach was put forward by Robert Cochran.[7]

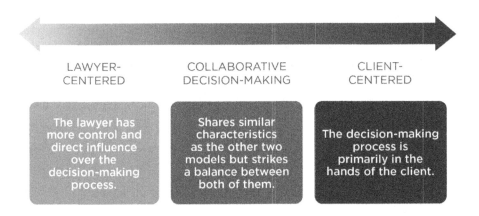

LAWYER-CENTERED	COLLABORATIVE DECISION-MAKING	CLIENT-CENTERED
The lawyer has more control and direct influence over the decision-making process.	Shares similar characteristics as the other two models but strikes a balance between both of them.	The decision-making process is primarily in the hands of the client.

4.2.1   Lawyer-Centered Counseling

Lawyer-centered counseling was the dominant method of counseling prior to the 1970s.[8] In a 1974 study, Douglas Rosenthal concluded that many, if not most, lawyers counseled by dominating the problem-solving.[9] Rosenthal originally referred to this as the traditional model of counseling.[10] Although this study was limited in size, Rosenthal concluded that clients achieved better outcomes when they were more engaged in problem-solving; he advocated increasing client participation.[11]

There are several characteristics of lawyer-centered counseling:

- The client is very passive in the decision making.

- The lawyer dominates the problem solving by providing a recommendation.

- The lawyer makes this recommendation based upon what the lawyer perceives as the best option for the client.

Imagine a plaintiff who is considering settling a wrongful termination of employment case. The defense offers to settle the matter for $50,000 without an admission

---

7. *See generally* ROBERT F. COCHRAN, JR. ET AL., THE COUNSELOR-AT-LAW: A COLLABORATIVE APPROACH TO CLIENT INTERVIEWING AND COUNSELING § 1-4 (3d ed. 2014).
8. *Id.* at §§ 1-2, 1-3.
9. *See* Rosenthal, *supra* note 4, at 174.
10. *Id.* at 7-28.
11. *Id.* at 29-62.

of liability. The plaintiff's attorney analyzes whether that is an acceptable offer by considering factors such as the likelihood of success at trial, the potential amount of recovery, and the cost of litigation. The attorney might conclude that there is only a 60 percent chance of success at trial, and the maximum recovery is likely to be $90,000 with an additional $10,000 in litigation costs if proceeding to trial. Therefore, the lawyer believes the settlement offer is a good offer and recommends that the client take it based upon the lawyer's own analysis.

In its purest form, lawyer-centered counseling lacks client involvement in the decision-making process. One of the traits, and the weakness, of this type of counseling is that decisions about what is best for the clients are primarily evaluated through a filter of the lawyer's beliefs and values. This type of counseling only succeeds, however, if the lawyer and the client have the same values. This is frequently not the case, and therein lies the problem. What if money is not the most important issue for the client? The client might be upset about the way they were treated by the company and wants the company to admit to the wrongful behavior. Therefore, accepting a $50,000 settlement without the admission of wrongdoing would not be the best decision for the client because what the client values is different from what the lawyer values.

4.2.2   Client-Centered Counseling

In the 1970s, as a response to a dominant culture where professionals saw their role as controlling the decision-making process—not just in the legal profession, but all professions—Binder and Price put forward a new model of client counseling that occupies the other side of the counseling spectrum.[12] The model resists the notion that professionals should be controlling their clients and was developed to provide more client control and autonomy in the relationship.

The model of client-centered counseling involves full participation of the client in the decision-making process with the lawyer giving deference throughout the process. As described above, what seemed inadequate about lawyer-centered counseling to many people was the assumption that lawyers and clients valued things in the same way.[13] This new model allowed the lawyer an opportunity to ensure that the client's values and objectives are considered in the decision-making process.

Client-centered counseling focuses on understanding the client's goals and priorities. The lawyer acts as a neutral guide who helps the client assess options, benefits, and consequences while allowing the client to reach a decision. An important aspect of this model is that the lawyer should be careful not to unduly influence the client's decision. Although there is variation, the general steps of client-centered counseling are:

---

12. BINDER & PRICE, *supra* note 2.
13. *Id.*

- Identify the legal and non-legal problems.

- Identify from the client's perspective what is most important.

- Help the client to identify the different potential options.

- Help the client identify the pros and cons of each decision.

- Guide the client's decision making based upon the values and beliefs of the client.

In its purest form, client-centered counseling maximizes client autonomy in the decision-making process. Although the lawyer strives to maintain a neutral role, this does not diminish the importance of the role. The lawyer's professional expertise is necessary to understanding the legal issues and identifying the possible options; something that would be difficult, if not impossible for the layperson to determine on their own. There is a reason you were hired.

4.2.3 *Collaborative Counseling*

It's the client's decision, but they want us to lead.

— *Philip Freidin, Founding Partner, Freidin Brown PA*

Very few lawyers are at the extreme ends of the spectrum, utilizing only client-centered or lawyer-centered counseling techniques. In the middle is the collaborative decision-making model and the form most commonly used in the modern lawyer-client relationship. This model developed because of the belief that, "the authoritarian [lawyer-centered] model provides too small a role for clients, the client-centered approach provides too small a role for lawyers, and that clients will be best served when lawyers and clients resolve problems in the law office through collaborative decision making."[14]

The core goal of counseling is problem-solving. The client has a problem, and the lawyer is expected to help resolve this problem. In the collaborative model, the lawyer and client function more as equals, while one party plays a more dominant role in the other two models.

4.3 Factors that Influence Counseling Style Choice

Few lawyers utilize the same style for all situations. What follows is a list of common factors that will influence which counseling style you employ in a given situation:

---

14. COCHRAN ET AL., *supra* note 7, at § 1-4.

- *Client Preference:* Your client may feel more comfortable with the lawyer taking the lead role. For example, the immigration or asylum-seeking client who is not familiar with the American legal system and scared about the process may want your direct recommendation. The indecisive client may explicitly ask you for a recommendation. The CEO of a large corporation may want to defer to the lawyer because they do not want to spend the time working through the decision-making process. Another CEO client might want to have a greater role in the decision-making process because they are used to controlling the situation. In short, what your client wants is going to influence where on the spectrum of counseling you will fall.

- *Type of Issue:* As a lawyer, you will feel more or less comfortable providing a recommendation based upon the type of case. In a case with large financial or human consequences, a lawyer will want more client involvement in the decision-making process. Imagine a scenario where a lawyer recommends going to trial, with little involvement from the client in coming to that decision. Then, the case is lost at trial. If the client does not feel they were part of the decision-making process, they could feel angry towards the lawyer—with potentially catastrophic consequences for the lawyer-client relationship. The client is more likely to accept a bad outcome if they were involved in the decision-making process and ultimately made the call to proceed to trial.

- *Level of Confidence:* The more confidence a lawyer feels in what they are recommending, the more comfortable they will be taking a dominant role in the decision-making process. Of course, the opposite is true. In a case with great uncertainty, such as when a lawyer believes that there is a 50 percent chance of prevailing at trial, the lawyer is more likely to involve the client in the decision-making process. Several other factors can impact your confidence in your recommendation. Your level of experience with a case type might also impact where you fall on the counseling spectrum. If you are in your second year of legal practice, your case experience is likely to be limited, especially when it comes to the resolution of a case through settlement or trial. The lack of confidence created by your limited experience will make you more inclined to involve the client in the decision-making process. Additionally, if the case involves a new practice area where you have minimal or no prior experience, you may also be inclined to move on the spectrum in the direction of more client-centered counseling.

- *Imperfect Knowledge:* This is related to the issue of level of confidence but specifically considers what level of knowledge the lawyer has about the case. This could be impacted by the stage of the case. At earlier stages of the case when all the facts are not known, the lawyer may lack confidence in controlling the decision-making process. No matter what the stage, even with robust discovery, there will always be a level of imperfect knowledge. There is always more information disclosed at trial, witnesses will testify better or worse than expected, judges and jurors will react to information differently. That lack of complete and perfect knowledge makes some lawyers uncomfortable in dominating the decision-making. For almost all attorneys, the level of knowledge moves the lawyer toward one end of the spectrum or the other.

- *Lawyer's Practice Type:* It goes without saying that a lawyer's time is not limitless. Alas, client-centered counseling takes more time, which some lawyers just don't have. Imagine a lawyer who primarily handles landlord-tenant cases for one of the many legal service agencies. That lawyer may have a caseload in the hundreds and average ten to fifteen court appearances per day. If that lawyer tried to engage in pure client-centered counseling, the practice would be untenable. On the opposite side, the lawyer who handles a small number of high-impact cases at a time will have more time to engage in the process of client-centered counseling.

- *Personal Preference:* What type of lawyer are you? Are you a more directive person to whom making recommendations comes naturally? Or are you someone who prefers to talk through all the options with someone else without offering your position? Clients can usually tell when you are not genuine, and this can be apparent when adopting a counseling model that is outside of your comfort zone. Although lawyers should always strive to improve their lawyering skills, at the foundation of every lawyer is their own individual personality. A lawyer's comfort level with a specific style will cause them to move towards that end of the spectrum.

- *How You Feel:* Do not underestimate the impact of fatigue, frustration, and energy level on the process of counseling. There are days and cases which take more of a physical and emotional toll on the individual lawyer than others. Because the client-centered counseling model is a more time-intensive process, there are simply days where you move the other way on the spectrum because you just do not have the same level of energy. Try to be aware of these situations when they occur to ensure you are not leading your clients to make a decision they will later feel they were pressured into. On the other hand, you may struggle to maintain the client-centered counseling model when dealing with a client who is very indecisive or with whom you have discussed the same issue multiple times without resolution. When this happens, it may make sense to take a more dominant position on this one issue to move the case along. You then can return to a more client-centered approach for subsequent decisions.

4.4   Building Confidence

The foundation of client counseling begins at the outset of the lawyer-client relationship. The client must have confidence and trust in the lawyer. How the client feels about the lawyer is not primarily dependent on any individual technique or method used for counseling. Trust and confidence are developed throughout the representation of the client. The client who sees the lawyer as unprepared, lacking knowledge, or disinterested in the client's goals will be less likely to feel comfortable with a lawyer's advice regardless of which model you are using.

4.4.1   Not One Moment in Time

Counseling a client is not a single event in the life of a case. Counseling is intertwined with the process of interviewing, fact-gathering, and case preparation because it happens at all stages of a case. At the early stage, you may counsel a client about whether to file a complaint. In the middle of a case, you may counsel a client about how to manage discovery issues. Towards the end, you will counsel your client about whether to settle the case or go to trial.

4.4.2   Who Has the Power to Make the Decisions?

Who has the ultimate power to make each decision? It depends. The counseling process presents many decisions throughout the course of the litigation. Much of the guidance about the allocation of authority between the client and lawyers is laid out in MRPC 1.2 and its comment, which is mirrored by almost every state.[15]

> (a) Subject to paragraphs (c) and (d), a lawyer shall abide by a client's decisions concerning the objectives of representation and, as required by Rule 1.4, shall consult with the client as to the means by which they are to be pursued. A lawyer may take such action on behalf of the client as is impliedly authorized to carry out the representation. A lawyer shall abide by a client's decision whether to settle a matter.[16]

The comments to the rule give some additional clarity.

> [1] Paragraph (a) confers upon the client the ultimate authority to determine the purposes to be served by legal representation, within the limits imposed by law and the lawyer's professional obligations. The decisions specified in paragraph (a), such as whether to settle a civil matter, must also be made by the client. See Rule 1.4(a)(1) for the

---

15. MODEL RULES OF PRO. CONDUCT r. 1.2 cmt. 1 (AM. BAR ASS'N 2020); *see also, e.g.,* CAL. RULES OF PRO. RESP. r. 1.2 cmt. 1 (2018); TEX. DISCIPLINARY RULES OF PRO. CONDUCT r. 1.02 (2019); FLA. RULES OF PRO. CONDUCT r. 4-1.2 cmt. (2019); N.J. RULES OF PRO. CONDUCT r. 1.2 (2015); COLO. RULES OF PRO. CONDUCT r. 1.2 (2020).
16. MODEL RULES OF PRO. CONDUCT r. 1.2 (AM. BAR. ASS'N 2018).

lawyer's duty to communicate with the client about such decisions. With respect to the means by which the client's objectives are to be pursued, the lawyer shall consult with the client as required by Rule 1.4(a)(2) and may take such action as is impliedly authorized to carry out the representation.[17]

As MRPC 1.2 dictates, the client has the ultimate authority to make a decision about the objectives and goals of the representation. These are the important decisions in the case and are frequently dispositive. Examples include:

- Whether to proceed and file a complaint

- Who are the defendants

- Whether or not to settle the case

- How much to offer for settlement

- Whether to proceed to trial

- What type of defenses to present

Generally, if it is a decision about tactics or procedures, or, in other words, decisions about the "means" by which the client's objectives are to be pursued, the lawyer shall consult with the client, but the decisions are frequently left to the lawyer because of their expertise and knowledge. Examples include:

- Whether to file a motion

- Which witnesses to depose

- What questions to ask during a deposition

While it would be nice to assume that lawyer and client will agree on every decision, this is not practical. Though infrequent, situations may arise where the client and lawyer disagree about how to proceed. The comments to MRPC 1.2 make clear that there is no prescribed way to resolve such disagreements and that they may in fact lead to the termination of the representation:

> [2] On occasion, however, a lawyer and a client may disagree about the means to be used to accomplish the client's objectives. Clients normally defer to the special knowledge and skill of their lawyer with respect to the means to be used to accomplish their objectives, particularly with respect to technical, legal and tactical matters. Conversely, lawyers usually defer to the client regarding such questions as the expense to be incurred and concern for third persons who

---

17. MODEL RULES OF PRO. CONDUCT r. 1.2. cmt. 1 (AM. BAR ASS'N 2020).

might be adversely affected. Because of the varied nature of the matters about which a lawyer and client might disagree and because the actions in question may implicate the interests of a tribunal or other persons, this Rule does not prescribe how such disagreements are to be resolved. Other law, however, may be applicable and should be consulted by the lawyer. The lawyer should also consult with the client and seek a mutually acceptable resolution of the disagreement. If such efforts are unavailing and the lawyer has a fundamental disagreement with the client, the lawyer may withdraw from the representation. See Rule 1.16(b)(4). Conversely, the client may resolve the disagreement by discharging the lawyer. See Rule 1.16(a)(3).[18]

4.5   The Counseling Process

Once initial information has been gathered, decisions will have to be made. The framework and fundamentals for what is required for counseling a client remain the same for almost any type of situation at different stages of the case. Of course, there will be some variation. The lawyer's goal remains the same when counseling a client: help the client make a choice. Because of the complexity and important consequences of even the simplest legal matters, there are almost always going to be several options from which to choose.

4.5.1   *What are the Steps for Counseling the Client?*

- How involved does your client want to be?

One of the first things to determine is how involved in the process your client wants to be. Do they want to be involved in all aspects of the case? Do they want only to make major decisions and leave all the details up to you? How familiar with the legal system and litigation are they?

- Who makes what decisions in litigation?

Throughout the life of the case there are countless decisions to be made. It is not practical to consult your client on every decision, which means that you need to determine which decisions must or should be made in consultation with the client. As previously discussed, there is very little guidance and a generally broad rule to guide the lawyer. Discuss this with your client at the beginning of representation. That conversation will look very different depending on whether your client is a company and you are dealing with in-house counsel or if your client is someone who has no legal training or knowledge. If your client is generally unfamiliar with litigation, you will need to provide more background information about the process

---

18. Model Rules of Pro. Conduct r. 1.2. cmt. 2 (Am. Bar Ass'n 2020).

so that your client can make an informed decision about their level of involvement in decision-making. Always keep in mind that the decision made at the outset of the litigation can be revisited and adjusted as needed. A client who asked to be involved in every decision may realize that they underestimated the number of decisions to be made and want to have you handle some of the minutiae. On the other hand, a client who asked only to be involved in major decisions might decide they want more involvement as the case progresses.

4.5.1.1   The Lawyer Must Understand the Client's Goals and Objectives

This is a process that each lawyer must engage in with their client. Only lawyers at the far extreme end of the spectrum utilizing lawyer-centered counseling would skip or minimize this step. In the purely lawyer-centered model, the lawyer would only gather information, identify the issues, and recommend a course of action based on his own values and beliefs. The group of lawyers who counsel by that method is small, and we do not recommend taking that approach. Clients are typically less satisfied with their representation and tend to get less than ideal results. There are exceptions, such as the client who requests the lawyer to play the dominant role in decision-making because they are too busy or not interested in being engaged. Other clients might be so overwhelmed and lacking confidence that they want the lawyer to dominate the relationship.

The goals and objectives of the client may take multiple meetings to fully understand and may change during the representation. Imagine a divorce and child custody case where a client meets with a lawyer right after the separation and has just moved to a nearby town. During the initial meeting, the client identifies as his primary goal that he wants the children to live with him during the week and attend school in his area. Over the course of the case, the client sees that the children are thriving in their current school, and the children have asked your client if they can remain in their present living situation during the week to stay enrolled in their current school. Additionally, the client would prefer to have more weekend time with the children. Or consider a businessman who believes that a former employee who went to a competitor stole confidential business information before leaving. Initially, his primary objective was to fight the case before a jury to ensure that the alleged wrongful conduct of his former employee and competitor are made public. He is not concerned about the cost of the litigation; he is focused on the principle of the matter. During the course of the litigation, his spouse becomes ill and he no longer wants to spend time and money on the litigation, preferring to focus on his spouse. He now wants to reach a settlement. These are just examples, but they illustrate the need to check in with your client regularly (even if there have not been major developments in the case).

The client can have far-ranging and diverse goals that require you to listen closely and ask questions to accurately identify the goals and objectives of the representation, as well as to prioritize when there are multiple goals. Financial relief is often a priority, but stopping there is a huge mistake for any lawyer. Possible long-term goals and objectives are: resolving the case as quickly as possible; getting someone to admit to wrongful conduct; making wrongful conduct public through a trial; deterring others who might engage in the same conduct by demonstrating that action will be taken against them; and protecting co-defendants.

The lawyer's role as counselor is not simply to accept the client's goals, but to help them evaluate those goals to determine if they are in their own best interest and the best interest of others. Legal disputes are accompanied by passion and emotion; these often cloud the client's judgment. A client can feel hurt, pain, and anger and want to retaliate or litigate the case to the point of trial. Helping the client to process the impact of emotion on their goals sometimes helps them to change their goals to something more realistic or even more beneficial. Explaining the financial and emotional cost of prolonged litigation might change the goals and objectives of the client, which will influence the options you present to your client.

4.5.1.2 Create and Evaluate a List of Options

The ease of creating and evaluating options will vary based upon the experience level of the lawyer. The inexperienced attorney will find this process challenging, while the seasoned lawyer will have years of experience to draw upon. Additionally, the more familiarity a lawyer has with a particular type of case, the easier it will be to understand and evaluate options because they have seen similar cases before. No lawyer has discovered a way to precisely value a case or predict the likelihood of success or defeat. This can make the process of evaluating a case daunting, especially for less experienced lawyers. Yet, clients will routinely ask for this information and are not satisfied with a response of, "I don't know" or, "It's really hard to say." Therefore, you must figure out how to assess a case so that you can provide better answers to your client.

Consider getting help with this process from an experienced and objective source. Less experienced lawyers will always benefit from the knowledge of someone who has handled similar legal matters. All lawyers, including practiced veterans, will benefit from someone objective giving feedback and perspective. Even experienced lawyers become immersed in a case and sometimes are unable to objectively judge issues such as likelihood of success. Despite their best efforts to the contrary, lawyers become personally invested in their cases and clients, which can cloud their judgment. In addition, a lawyer well-versed in similar cases can overlook differences in a new case and assume it will be the same as previous cases they have handled. Getting objective feedback in these situations is useful.

Seek out other lawyers in your office who can spend time brainstorming and evaluating options. You must always be aware of not disclosing confidential information[19] but a layperson can help you understand the strengths and weaknesses of a case and how jurors or judge might perceive your proposed approach. A layperson unfamiliar with the legal system can uncover what does and does not sound right with your case, frequently pointing out things that you may have overlooked.

The process of creating and evaluating options happens throughout the life of the case, not just at the end when the lawyer and client are deciding to settle or proceed to trial. Other common examples of decisions you will make with your client include: should you send a demand letter; should you file a complaint; where should the complaint be filed; should you seek injunctive relief and if so, should it be a temporary restraining order or a preliminary injunction; should you file a motion to dismiss; do you have any counterclaims that should be made; should other parties be joined in the lawsuit; should you demand a jury or are there reasons a bench trial would be preferable; what level of discovery should you conduct; should you file a motion for summary judgment; and should you consider mediation.

Make this assessment within the context of the client's goals and objectives. Each decision is likely to have a time and financial cost that the client may or may not be interested in assuming. For example, some clients may want to keep discovery cost to a minimum, so they may not want to take video depositions, which are more costly than a traditional deposition with only a court reporter.

4.5.1.3   Discuss Options with the Client

Depending on the type of counseling used, the client is more or less likely to be involved in the process of generating options. If the lawyer utilizes client-centered counseling in its purest form, the lawyer may wait to generate options until meeting with the client. Most lawyers do not counsel in this manner because it is time-consuming and inefficient. Additionally, the lawyer will appear better prepared if they have generated and evaluated the options prior to meeting with the client. Most clients expect the lawyer to prepare options to discuss with them.

I recall advising my domestic violence clinic students to work with outside professionals (i.e. social workers, victim-witness advocates, rape crisis advocates) to secure a safety plan for the client and not rely solely on court ordered relief through an order of protection or temporary detention/ incarceration of the abuser.

—Professor Zelda Harris, Loyola University Chicago School of Law

---

19. Model Rules of Pro. Conduct r. 1.6 (Am. Bar Ass'n 2020).

Even when you have created your own list of options prior to meeting with the client, remain open to new ideas generated in consultation with the client. Other factors can also impact your evaluation of the case as it progresses, such as new information discovered during the course of the case or court decisions on motions or discovery issues in the case. Another common occurrence during representation is that a client's circumstances change, therefore, influencing their goals and objectives. A client may have underestimated the toll litigation can take and, feeling exhausted and emotionally drained by the process, want to settle the case more quickly. The client's financial situation may have changed so that a protracted and costly discovery process is no longer a possibility.

How you present options to your client can strongly influence the client's decision. Be aware of your tone and enthusiasm for a particular option. Clients will recognize when you are more excited and confident about an option. For the client looking for comfort and reassurance that they are making the right decision, tone can be a powerful influencer. Sometimes that is intentional, but other times it might not be. We are not recommending to always present options in a neutral way, but be aware that how the client perceives your confidence will impact their decision-making. This can be a problem when you have chosen a more client-centered approach or when the client misreads your enthusiasm for a particular option.

The selective choice of facts when presenting options also can lead to a client's misperception about the strength of the case. Never deceive a client by withholding facts. Be aware, however, that the choice to remind them only of certain facts or the way those facts are organized will influence how the client views the strengths and weaknesses of a case.

4.5.1.4 Whenever Possible, Identify the Risks, Costs, and Likelihood of Success for Each Option

Provide the client with some information about how you determined this information, particularly if it is based on any assumptions. For instance, if you assumed that there would be no motion practice in one of the options, make that clear to your client. While you and your client can control whether you file any motions, you cannot control whether the opposing party does—you will still need to respond to those motions. You might find yourself in a situation where your client shares a version of events that is based on what they know but they acknowledge that they do not have all the information. Be sure your client understands that your assessment of the case could change significantly if evidence comes to light that contradicts your client's version of events.

4.6   Important Issues to Consider When Evaluating a Case and Discussing Options with the Client

4.6.1   Discovery Process

When you are generating and evaluating the options, risks, and costs, consider and explain the discovery process. Depending on your client's prior experience with litigation and whether they are a company—likely to have a substantial volume of electronic records—or an individual—who may have far fewer electronic records—be prepared to educate your client on what the discovery process is likely to entail and the associated costs. In today's electronic world, much of the discovery process involves hiring vendors to search through hundreds of thousands of documents and emails using keywords. It is not always practical or affordable to have a lawyer review each and every document before turning it over in the discovery process. Clients must understand both the cost of hiring a vendor to perform searches, copy, and provide access to electronic records (if needed) and the possibility that information that is not relevant to the case will be turned over to their opponent. Many people lack any sense of the volume of electronic records that must be searched—even in the corporate environment. Individuals with no experience in the legal system tend often to not understand that you may have to search all their personal emails, text messages, social media posts, or documents on their computer for information relevant to the case. Some people might consider this an intrusion; counsel them at the outset about what they should expect in the discovery process.

By the same token, ensure that your client understands what it means to include certain claims in their case and that there will be discovery about those claims. Clients sometimes do not comprehend the extent to which they will be required to provide information to support a claim and that this information, barring a confidentiality order (which many courts frown upon), could be made public. Consider the personal injury lawyer whose standard procedure is to include claims for loss of consortium and describes this claim to his client as "the injury having an impact on your relationship with your spouse." Loss of consortium is actually broader than that and can include the loss of any of the following: love, companionship, comfort, care, assistance, protection, affection, society, moral support—and enjoyment of sexual relations. A client who does not realize the extent of this claim might be surprised or even offended at their deposition when asked questions about intimate details of their relationship. Had they been counseled at the outset that including such a claim would likely mean that they would have to provide such information when asked, they may have decided not to include the claim.

This can also occur in business cases. Consider a closely-held, private company that wants to bring suit and include a claim to recover lost profits. Counsel the client that proving lost profits will require producing financial records showing profit and loss for multiple periods. Some private companies that have no duty to publicly disclose such information prefer to keep it confidential. They would need to weigh their desire to bring the claim against their desire to keep such information secret.

Of course, your client's level of knowledge and prior involvement in the legal system will dictate how much detail you need to provide while counseling on these issues. A business client who has been involved in litigation before likely knows what is involved in proving lost profits, but a business client who owns a small business and has never sued or been sued before may not. A client who has no prior involvement in legal disputes and is unfamiliar with legal terminology may require you to spend more time explaining potential claims and what will be needed to prove them.

4.6.2 External Factors

It is important to always take into account external factors when assessing case options and be sure to discuss them with your client.

4.6.2.1 Reputation of and Experience with Opposing Counsel

As all lawyers eventually learn, opposing counsel come in many different types. Once you know who opposing counsel will be in a case, find out as much information about the law firm and the actual lawyer(s) as you can. Other lawyers, either in your office or colleagues in the legal community, are good sources of information. Any information is helpful, but determine as much of the following as possible: What experience do they have with the type of case at issue? Are they considered an expert in this type of litigation? What is their approach to litigation: Do they typically take a reasonable, measured approach or do they pursue scorched-earth litigation? How do they approach discovery: Are they reasonable in settling disputes or are you likely to have to seek resolution from the court for discovery issues (which will likely cost your client more money)? Do they have a reputation for repeatedly seeking extensions of deadlines (again something that can draw out the resolution of the case and increase your client's cost)? Do they put forward cogent arguments or make baseless, unsupported assertions?[20]

Sometimes the opponent's selection of a particular lawyer or law firm can tell you a great deal about how they intend to approach the case. For instance, if the opponent hires a megafirm with a national reputation for this type of case, you can assume they are very serious about the litigation. They might be trying to send a

---

20. While it might seem counterintuitive to want an opponent who puts forward coherent arguments, it is much easier to respond to such arguments than to someone who is unprepared or makes fanciful arguments. This is especially noticeable in motion practice where having to parse out your opponent's argument, restate it cogently, and then respond to it can take a significant amount of time and cost your client more money.

message that they are willing to spare no expense on the case. This information can be useful to share with your client.

4.6.2.2   Reputation of and Experience with Assigned Judge

Similar to your efforts to gather information about opposing counsel, seek insights into the judge assigned to your case. Personal experiences from lawyers who have had cases before that judge can be the most useful, although a review of the judge's relevant opinions and orders should also be done. Information such as how the judge treats plaintiffs versus defendants or corporate parties versus individuals is important. How does the judge manage their trial calendar: Are they working on a significant delay such that any trial may be years away? Does the judge have a reputation for applying pressure to settle cases? Does the judge regularly refer cases to, or strongly encourage the parties to engage in, mediation? Does the judge have a reputation for being able to work through complex fact patterns and legal issues? What was the judge's background before taking the bench? Do they have any experience relevant to the issues or parties in your case? Is it possible that this experience could make the judge more or less inclined to understand and/or appreciate your position?

4.6.2.3   Current Political and Social Climate

Often it is important to understand the current political and social climate and how that might impact your client's case. At various times throughout history, different industries are viewed more or less favorably, depending on what is going on in the world. Negative publicity for some industries will make the public, and therefore the jury pool, less likely to trust a company. For example, the subprime mortgage crisis in the United States that led to 2008's recession diminished the public's view of the banking industry considerably. Companies in that industry needed to factor this diminished trust into their potential risks of litigation. Accordingly, be aware of such issues so that you can counsel your client about them.

Other social and political issues might not be related to a specific industry but rather a particular type of case. For example, after the #MeToo movement went viral in 2017, many companies opted not to litigate sexual harassment or discrimination claims for fear generally of the public backlash, but also more specifically of strong feelings about the issue impacting a jury in their decision-making process.

4.6.2.4   Potential Jury Pool in the Court System Where the Case is Being Litigated

For any litigation that will be decided by a jury, it is critical to understand the pool of potential jurors who may decide your case. Certain geographic locations have reputations for certain outcomes. There are locations where the jurors have a reputation for siding with local parties over parties from out of state. There are also locations where the jurors tend to favor individuals over corporate parties. Depending on your case, demographics may also be important. A location where the majority of the jury pool has completed higher education might result in a better outcome if the facts and issues in your case are particularly complex. This information can be useful in making decisions at the outset, such as where to initiate litigation if you are the plaintiff. However, it also can be useful in assessing the likelihood of success as the case progresses.

4.6.2.5 Presenting Settlement Offers

While it is generally prudent to always present your client with all settlement offers, no matter how ridiculous or egregious you might think they are, some jurisdictions require that you share all offers, even if you are certain you know how they will respond.[21] If you and your client have agreed to the acceptable parameters of settlement, you are generally not required to inform them of the offer.[22] Even if that is the case, you may choose to discuss the offer with the client for a variety of reasons such as your belief that it is the opponent's final offer or if you want to convey to the client that your opponent is negotiating in good faith.

4.7 Common Issues in Counseling

4.7.1 *Staying within Your Role*

In dealing with clients, certain practices raise red flags.

First, you are counsel to the client; you are not the client. What do we mean? In seeking out legal advice, some clients are looking for representation, empathy, and vindication. Representation is the easy part. As to empathy, attorneys can empathize with their client's plight without drawing themselves into the dispute as co-victims or aggressors. Your job as an attorney is to look at a claim from all sides, credit all positions, evaluate the law, weigh the equities, and then represent a position. Getting drawn into the client's emotional plight may cloud your judgment.

None of this means that you cannot feel passion for your case; on the contrary, doing so is a good thing. But passionate representation does not mean blind representation. It means evaluating the totality of the client's plight and counseling the best course of action.

Many cases are emotional for both the lawyer and the client. Although you are a counselor, protect against crossing over that line where you become the therapist, confidant, or friend. For most lawyers, providing therapy is not what we are trained

---

21. MODEL RULES OF PRO. CONDUCT r. 1.4 (AM. BAR ASS'N 2020).
22. MODEL RULES OF PRO. CONDUCT r. 1.4 cmt. 2 (AM. BAR ASS'N 2020).

to do. Acting as a therapist will not only drain your time and energy resources, but it will cloud your objectivity. In those circumstances where therapy is needed, consider making the appropriate referral to a professional. A trend in public interest work is to have social workers on staff who can assist with areas of support beyond the range of the lawyer. However, outside referral is always available and you should see your role of a counselor as guiding clients to seek that help.

Sometimes clients, particularly those who have no experience with the legal system and are looking for representation regarding a personal issue, will confuse your role of lawyer and start to think of you as a confidant or friend. They might share personal information unrelated to the case you are handling or ask you to participate in social events or engagements with them. Learn to recognize these situations early and make clear to your client the limits of your professional relationship.

4.7.2 *Being Honest with Your Client*

You are not a cheerleader and all news is not good news. Predictions of victory and a constant positive spin can not only create an undue expectation, but can also cloud the client's ability to think objectively about the case. Consider, for example, when a defendant-client asks about the merits of their case and is promised initially, and through the course of the litigation, that they will win. Then, the defendant loses motions to dismiss and for summary judgment. On the eve of trial, his counsel—for the first time—recommends settlement. The client responds, "if I knew I had to pay money, I would have settled this thing sooner and avoided legal fees."

If a client asks about the merits of their case, respond as a lawyer should; this instills client confidence. What does this mean? The following responses fall into the lawyer-like category:

> "I am comfortable with where we are right now in the litigation, but the one thing I know about litigation is that there will be good days and bad days."

> "If the facts are as you have recited them, I am comfortable with our position now."

> "I would have preferred that we won the motion, but litigation is a journey and we have a ways to go."

> "I think this is a case that should settle; it does not make sense to litigate it and it is one that can be resolved."

> "It is possible for you to litigate this matter but there are a number of obstacles including . . . ."

CHAPTER FIVE

CASE INVESTIGATION

5.1 Introduction

The past three decades have seen a shift toward front-loaded litigation. The era where litigants wrote cursory complaints in anticipation of filling in the details through discovery is over. Instead, lawyers prepare complaints that survive the stringent fact pleading and plausibility standards.[1] These claims must also pass the summary judgment gauntlet and still be alive after motions in limine and *Daubert* motions. Of course, if the matter is a class action, the plaintiff must meet the FRCP 23's class certification criteria. This often requires the presentation of evidence and perhaps even expert testimony.

Once a complaint is filed, it progresses on a court-established schedule that sets periods for fact discovery, expert discovery, and dispositive motions. Once the schedule is in place and the clock starts running, parties are often pressed to meet deadlines.

When putting a case together, complete as much work on the case as possible (including investigation) before filing the complaint and before timelines start to run. This is called front-loading the investigation process. For those bringing a case, defense—anticipating potential attacks on your case—is the best offense. Gathering facts, developing legal theories, and plotting out legal and factual defenses is easier before the court imposes deadlines. Such an approach is imperative, especially with newer pleading standards requiring fact pleading. Courts look at factual allegations and sustain a complaint if—based on the factual and non-conclusory allegations—it states a plausible theory of recovery.

---

1. *See, e.g.*, Ashcroft v. Iqbal, 556 U.S. 662 (2009); Bell Atlantic v. Twombly, 550 U.S. 554 (2007). In his article, Professor Miller does a marvelous job of outlining the changes to the pleading standards. Arthur Miller, *From Conley to Twombly to Iqbal: A Double Play on the Federal Rules of Civil Procedure*, 60 DUKE L. J. 1 (2010).

5.2   A Word About the Rules of Evidence

In the new front-loaded world of litigation, you must understand the Federal Rules of Evidence. The rules frame how you think about the case at its earliest stages, will guide what is admissible, and set your trajectory to trial.

FRE 401 provides the basic two-part test in determining whether evidence is relevant:

> Evidence is relevant if:
>
> (a) It has a tendency to make a fact more or less probable than it would be without the evidence.
>
> (b) The fact is of consequence in determining the action.

The rule does not use the words "circumstantial" or "direct." Circumstantial evidence allows the advocate to argue the inference that something transpired. Often this occurs when advocates piece together the "circumstantial evidence." Consider this fact pattern:

- There was a plate of cookies.

- There was a dog who was left in the room.

- The cookies were gone when the baker returned.[2]

While no one saw the dog eat the cookies—i.e., no direct evidence—these factoids point to the logical conclusion that the dog ate the cookies. If the cookies contained chocolate and the dog got sick, an expert for the prosecution could testify that dogs are allergic to chocolate. Alternatively, if the dog did not get sick, the dog's court-appointed counsel might use an expert to testify the dog could not have eaten the cookies because the dog did not get sick.

As you go through the investigation process, appreciate how factoids of circumstantial evidence can be pieced together to allow for argument of very powerful inferences.

Knowing the rules of evidence is not something that can be left until the time of trial. The rules detail the mechanics of processing information for presentation or excluding information from litigation and trial.

In addition to Rule 401, there are at least three other rules you must understand when investigating a case:

---

2. The authors credit NITA faculty member and Michigan prosecutor Barbara Morrison for this example.

Rule	Title	Excerpt
801	Definitions That Apply to This Article; Exclusions from Hearsay	"(c) . . . 'Hearsay' means a statement that: (1) the declarant does not make while testifying at the current trial or hearing; and
		(2) a party offers in evidence to prove the truth of the matter asserted in the statement."
901	Authenticating or Identifying Evidence	"(a) In General. To satisfy the requirement of authenticating or identifying an item of evidence, the proponent must produce evidence sufficient to support a finding that the item is what the proponent claims it is."
902	Evidence That Is Self-Authenticating	"The following items of evidence are self-authenticating; they require no extrinsic evidence of authenticity in order to be admitted . . . ."

Take time to appreciate the rules of hearsay—specifically what is <u>not</u> hearsay. FRE 801 defines hearsay and excludes from that definition the opposing party's statements and those from an opposing party's agents where the agent makes the statement within the scope of the relationship:

(d) **Statements That Are Not Hearsay.** A statement that meets the following conditions is not hearsay:

(1) *A Declarant-Witness's Prior Statement.* The declarant testifies and is subject to cross-examination about a prior statement, and the statement:

(A) is consistent with the declarant's testimony and was given under penalty of perjury at trial hearing, or other proceeding or in a deposition;

(B) is consistent with the declarant's testimony and is offered:

(i) to rebut an express or implied charge that the declarant recently fabricated it or acted from a recent improper influence or motive in so testifying; or

(ii) to rehabilitate the declarant's credibility as a witness when attacked on another ground; or

(C) identifies a person as someone the declarant perceived earlier.

(2) *An Opposing Party's Statement.* The statement is offered against an opposing party and:

(A) was made by the party in an individual or representative capacity;

(B) is one the party manifested that it adopted or believed to be true;

(C) was made by a person whom the party authorized to make a statement on the subject;

(D) was made by the party's agent or employee on a matter within the scope of that relationship and while it existed or

(E) was made by the party's coconspirator during and in furtherance of the conspiracy.

FRE 801(d)(2) excludes from hearsay letters, emails, and documents authored or authorized by your opposition. Of course, with any piece of evidence authenticity must also be established under FRE 901 or 902.

Keep in mind that evidence is a broad-based concept including:

- Written materials

- Photographs

- Videos

- Mechanical things like guns, cars, and parts

- Test results

- Zip drives

- Computer hard drives

- Metadata

- Statements of witnesses

- Testimony of witnesses

This list could go on and on; and, of course, each of the above categories includes all kinds of items.

In addition to 801's exclusions, FRE 803 outlines twenty-three exceptions to the hearsay rule and FRE 807 creates a catch-all residual exception for evidence that is otherwise reliable. The following FRE 803 exceptions is a checklist for those investigating a case:

FRE 803 Exceptions

803(3)	Then-Existing Mental, Emotional, or Physical Condition
803(4)	Statement Made for Medical Diagnosis or Treatment
803(5)	Recorded Recollection
803(6)	Records of a Regularly Conducted Activity
803(7)	Absence of a Record of a Regularly Conducted Activity
803(8)	Public Record
803(9)	Public Records of Vital Statistics
803(10)	Absence of a Public Record
803(11)	Records of Religious Organizations Concerning Personal or Family History
803(12)	Certificates of Marriage, Baptism, and Similar Ceremonies
803(13)	Family Records
803(14)	Records of Documents That Affect an Interest in Property
803(15)	Statements in Documents That Affect an Interest in Property
803(16)	Statements in Ancient Documents
803(17)	Market Reports and Similar Commercial Publications
803(18)	Statements in Learned Treatises, Periodicals, or Pamphlets
803(19)	Reputation Concerning Personal or Family History
803 (20)	Reputation Concerning Boundaries or General History
803(21)	Reputation Concerning Character
803(22)	Judgment of a Previous Conviction
803(23)	Judgments Involving Personal, Family, or General History, or a Boundary

FRE 803 is a great resource for fact investigation. First, FRE 803 outlines all the places to gather admissible evidence, many of which do not involve discovery or contact with your opposing party. Second, it makes you consider whether evidence you gather is either not hearsay or fits into an FRE 803 exception.[3] Fitting something into an FRE 803 exception may require its own investigation. Consider FRE 803(6), known as the "business records exception":

> (6) Records of a Regularly Conducted Activity. A record of an act, event, condition, opinion, or diagnosis if:

---

3. Only use the residual exception as a last resort because it is rarely successful. With the many hearsay objections available, the residual exception is rarely needed.

(A) the record was made at or near the time by—or from information transmitted by—someone with knowledge;

(B) the record was kept in the course of a regularly conducted activity of a business, organization, occupation, or calling, whether or not for profit;

(C) making the record was a regular practice of that activity;

(D) all these conditions are shown by the testimony of the custodian or another qualified witness, or by a certification that complies with Rule 902(11) or (12) or with a statute permitting certification; and

(E) the opponent does not show that the source of information or the method or circumstances of preparation indicate a lack of trustworthiness.

To utilize this exception, collect the necessary information to meet FRE 803(6) (A)–(E)'s requirements. If the relevant information is not excluded under the hearsay rules, it must be authenticated.

FRE 901 governs documents that must be authenticated and FRE 902 governs documents that are self-authenticating (a live witness is not necessary to authenticate the document). The authenticity of evidence simply means that the evidence is what it purports to be. For example, if you want to use an email that was sent by Person A as evidence, you need to establish evidence sufficient to support a finding that it is the actual email Person A sent. If it is a forgery or an email sent by Person B it would not be authentic if you claim it was sent by Person A.

All types of evidence are subject to authentication.[4] During the investigation process, refer back to FRE 901. It provides specific guidance on the information necessary to authenticate particular types of evidence. In addition, FRE 902 and its newest subparts detail authentication of electronically stored information.[5]

Finally, consider FRE 201 on "Judicial Notice of Adjudicative Facts" during your investigation. That rule states:

Rule 201. Judicial Notice of Adjudicative Facts

(a) Scope. This rule governs judicial notice of an adjudicative fact only, not a legislative fact.

(b) Kinds of Facts That May Be Judicially Noticed. The court may judicially notice a fact that is not subject to reasonable dispute because it:

---

4. And even though something is deemed authentic it can still be excluded on other grounds, such as hearsay and relevance.
5. FED. R. EVID. 902.

(1) is generally known within the trial court's territorial jurisdiction; or

(2) can be accurately and readily determined from sources whose accuracy cannot reasonably be questioned.

(c) Taking Notice. The court:

(1) may take judicial notice on its own; or

(2) must take judicial notice if a party requests it and the court is supplied with the necessary information.

(d) Timing. The court may take judicial notice at any stage of the proceeding.

(e) Opportunity to Be Heard. On timely request, a party is entitled to be heard on the propriety of taking judicial notice and the nature of the fact to be noticed. If the court takes judicial notice before notifying a party, the party, on request, is still entitled to be heard.

(f) Instructing the Jury. In a civil case, the court must instruct the jury to accept the noticed fact as conclusive. In a criminal case, the court must instruct the jury that it may or may not accept the noticed fact as conclusive.

FRE 201 opens up a body of information available in government reading rooms[6] and through the Internet for you to consider when deciding what evidence or expert testimony is necessary to prove the case. For example, in a medical malpractice case against a hospital, consider using FRE 201 to enter into evidence hospital or medical standards set forth by the Joint Commission on Accreditation of Hospitals. Or consider a case involving eyewitness testimony where an issue for impeachment is whether it was dark at 6 p.m. A website like timeanddate.com can provide the sunrise and sunset times for the day in question. Weather reports from the National Weather Service could also provide useful information.

FRE 201 is invaluable as a means to get foundational information before the court; using FRE 201 may also alleviate the need for, or cut down on, costly experts whose use may prompt a fight over exclusion of the testimony. Suppose the case involves an employee alleging hearing loss after prolonged exposure to excessive noise in the workplace. Is there a document—perhaps even a government standard—that explains how excessive noise can cause hearing loss?

---

6. The U.S. government maintains various reading rooms, some of which are electronic, where documents released in response to Freedom of Information Act requests are housed. These documents are made available to the public.

5.2.1   A Word About Work Product and Privileges

The attorney-client privilege protects "confidential communications by a client to an attorney made in order to obtain legal assistance."[7] The "mere fact that an attorney was involved in a communication does not automatically render the communication subject to the attorney-client privilege,"[8] rather, the "communication between a lawyer and client must relate to the legal advice or strategy sought by the client."[9]

Proposed Rule of Evidence 503, also known as Supreme Court Standard 503 (PR 503), establishes a benchmark for determining the scope of the attorney-client privilege under federal common law:

> A client has a privilege to refuse to disclose and to prevent any other person from disclosing confidential communications made for the purpose of facilitating the rendition of professional legal services to the client, (1) between himself or his representative and his lawyer or his lawyer's representative, or (2) between his lawyer and his lawyer's representative, or (3) by him or his lawyer to a lawyer representing another in a matter of common interest, or (4) between representatives of the client or between the client and a representative of the client, or (5) between lawyers representing the client.[10]

While PR 503(a)(4) defines representative of the lawyer, it unfortunately does not define what a representative of the client is.

> A communication is "confidential" if not intended to be disclosed to third persons other than those to whom disclosure is in furtherance of the rendition of professional legal services to the client or those reasonably necessary for the transmission of the communication.[11]

The Tenth Circuit has explained that a critical component of the privilege is "whether the communication between the client and the attorney is made in confidence of the relationship and under the circumstances from which it may reasonably be assumed that the communication will remain in confidence."[12]

---

7. *In re* Grand Jury Subpoena Duces Tecum, etc., 697 F.2d 277, 278 (10th Cir. 1983) (quoting Fisher v. United States, 425 U.S. 391, 403 (1976)).

8. Motley v. Marathon Oil Co., 71 F.3d 1547, 1550-51 (10th Cir. 1995).

9. United States v. Johnston, 146 F.3d 785, 794 (10th Cir. 1998).

10. Fed. R. Evid. 503 (Proposed Rule).

11. *Id.* at (a)(4) (Proposed Rule); *See also* United States v. Kovel, 296 F.2d 918, 922 (2d Cir. 1961) ("what is vital to the privilege is that the communication be made in confidence for the purpose of obtaining legal advice from the lawyer.").

12. *In re* Qwest Commc'n Intern. Inc., 450 F.3d 1179, 1185 (10th Cir. 2006) (quoting United States v. Lopez, 777 F.2d 543, 552 (10th Cir. 1985)), *abrogated on other grounds by* Fed. R. Evid. 502.

Significantly, however, the communication must be "made for the purpose of facilitating the rendition of professional legal services ***to the client.***"[13] A "client" is defined by PR 503 as "a person, public officer, or corporation, association, or other organization or entity, either public or private, ***who is rendered professional legal services by a lawyer,*** or who consults a lawyer with a view to obtaining professional legal services from him."[14] In keeping with PR 503, courts have held that the attorney-client privilege protects communications between lawyers and clients where such communications are for the purpose of rendering legal advice.[15]

Generally, relaying a privileged communication to a third party waives the privilege.[16] One exception to this waiver rule is the common interest doctrine.[17] Also known as the joint defense doctrine, it allows separately represented parties with common legal interests to share information with each other and their respective attorneys without destroying the attorney-client privilege.[18] Despite some practitioners referring to it as a "privilege," the common interest doctrine is not a separate privilege, but rather stands as a notable exception to the general rule that the attorney-client privilege does not attach to communications including or subsequently shared with third parties.

The common interest doctrine "protects all communications shared within a proper 'community of interest,' whether the context be criminal or civil."[19] The Tenth Circuit, among others, adopted a so-called "congruence of legal interests" requirement when assessing the existence of a common interest privilege.[20] A congruence of legal interests exists where "different persons or entities 'have an identical

---

13. Fed. R. Evid. 503(b) (Proposed Rule) (emphasis added).
14. *Id.* at (a)(1) (Proposed Rule) (emphasis added).
15. Upjohn Co. v. United States, 449 U.S. 383 (1981); United States v. Schwimmer, 892 F.2d 237, 243 (2d Cir. 1989) (attorney-client privilege protects communications made to agents assisting client); CSC Recovery Corp. v. Daido Steel Co., No. 94 Civ. 9214, 1997 U.S. Dist. LEXIS 16346, 1997 WL 661122 at *1 (S.D.N.Y. Oct. 22, 1997) (attorney-client privilege protects communications between clients and attorneys and agents of both); H.W. Carter & Sons v. William Carter Co., No. 95 Civ. 1274, 1995 U.S. Dist. LEXIS 6578, 1995 WL 301351 at *3 (S.D.N.Y. May 16, 1995) (communications by public relations consultants who assisted attorneys in rendering legal advice protected by the attorney-client privilege).
16. U.S. v. Schlegel, 313 F. Supp. 177, 179 (D. Neb. 1970) (privilege does not apply to information conveyed to third parties); *see also* Teleglobe Commc'ns. Corp. v. BCE, Inc., 493 F.3d 345, 361 (3d Cir. 2007) (explaining that "if a client subsequently shares a privileged communication with a third party, then it is no longer confidential, and the privilege ceases to protect it").
17. Tenth Circuit courts have held that because "[t]he common interest doctrine is an exception to the general rule of waiver, [a] court must determine that a party waived a privilege before it can consider whether the exception applies." *See* Beltran v. InterExchange, Inc., Civil Action No. 14-cv-03074-CMA-CBS, 2018 U.S. Dist. LEXIS 22564, 2018 WL 839927 at *4 (D. Colo. Feb. 12, 2018).
18. Teleglobe Commc'ns. Corp., 493 F.3d at 363-64 & n.18.
19. *Id.* at 364.
20. Beltran, Civil Action No. 14-cv-03074-CMA-CBS, 2018 U.S. Dist. LEXIS 22564, 2018 WL 839927 at *4.

legal interest with respect to the subject matter of a communication between an attorney and a client concerning legal advice. . . . The key consideration is that the nature of the interest be identical, not similar."[21] Notably, in order to be protected under the common interest doctrine the communications must be intrinsically privileged. A communication that is not privileged on its own does not suddenly become privileged simply because one common interest participant shares it with another.

5.3   Chart Things Out

When first analyzing a case, the names, dates, acronyms, and facts can blur together. Absorb the details by making charts or outlines. Who are the key players or witnesses? What are the key entities? What is the timeline of events? What are the good facts and what are the bad facts?

For key players, who has information about the case? Who can provide direct evidence and who can provide circumstantial evidence? If the case involves a business dispute, be sure to consider former employees. For each employee, make notes concerning what information and documents they may possess.

For entities, list the key entities; chart the ownership structure and the chain of command. Note their principal place of business and place of incorporation. Consider how they can be served; do they have a registered agent? For publicly owned companies, some of this information can be found in the company's 10K filings.

Understanding timelines is essential for case investigation and development. Many people store and retrieve information based on time sequence. Charting out a timeline is an efficient way to see where facts fit and where gaps in the narrative exist. Timelines—like witness lists—are litigation tools. Add to it, subtract from it, and annotate it with references to documents, including emails, PowerPoints, and other charts.

---

21. Frontier Refin. v. Gorman-Rupp Co., 136 F.3d 695, 705 (10th Cir. 1998) (quoting NL Indus., Inc. v. Commercial Union Ins. Co., 144 F.R.D. 225, 230-31 (D.N.J. 1992)); United States ex rel. [Redacted] v. [Redacted], 209 F.R.D. 475, 479 (D. Utah 2001) (relying on *Frontier Refin.* and the same principle applies in False Claims Act cases); *see also* Duplan Corp. v. Deering Milliken, Inc., 397 F. Supp. 1146, 1172 (D.S.C. 1974) (a seminal case on the issue, which requires that "the nature of the interest be identical, not similar, and be legal, not solely commercial"); ServiceMaster of Salina, Inc. v. United States, No. 11-1168-KHV-GLR, 2012 U.S. Dist. LEXIS 53399, 2012 WL 1327812, at *3 (D. Kan. April 17, 2012) ("The doctrine does not apply when the parties merely have similar legal interests or when the interests are solely commercial or business in nature."); *but see Teleglobe* at 365 (noting the Restatement's more flexible approach wherein "'the common interest . . . may be either legal, factual, or strategic in character [and t]he interests of the separately represented clients need not be entirely congruent.'") (quoting RESTATEMENT (THIRD) OF THE LAW GOVERNING LAWYERS § 76).

Develop a list of good facts and a list of bad facts. In doing so, remember to distinguish between a fact and a conclusion. Facts form the basis for conclusions. The phrase "John Smith is very intelligent" is a conclusion based on factual predicates. The facts supporting that conclusion may be: 1) John Smith was tested and has an IQ of 160; 2) John Smith has a PhD in chemical engineering; and 3) John Smith holds twenty-seven patents. When investigating a case and gathering evidence, gather facts that can be repackaged into conclusions. This approach is particularly important when interviewing witnesses more likely to dodge or evade questions that elicit conclusions as opposed to questions that seek facts.

5.4   Where Do I Start?

Imagine receiving an email from a potential client. Whether the client is an individual or an entity, you want to know something about the client. Do you even want to represent the client? Are they someone with whom you can work? Your investigation begins with your potential client and it starts with an Internet search encompassing the following:

- News items

- Facebook

- LinkedIn

- Twitter

- YouTube

- Websites

- Filings with government agencies

- Court filings

- Agency—FDA, EPA, SEC—records.

A quick search may reveal that you have a conflict and cannot take the case. Instead of calling the number provided in the potential client's email, a return email declining representation will often suffice.

If you decide to meet with the client, this background information helps you absorb the narrative the client relays during the initial meeting. If the client is an entity, background information provides a better understanding of the client's business, its leadership, and any public disputes. If the client is an individual, know the client's work history and educational background. Does the educational background and work history posted on social media line up with the client's resume or oral representations? Until very recently, many depositions began with a series of questions about work history and educational background. Now, for many individuals, much of that information is available on LinkedIn, Facebook, and other forms of social media.

Client research can also familiarize attorneys with client personalities. Reading tweets, for example, can provide practical insight. Are the tweets angry? Do they reveal personal information? Does the potential client have certain pet peeves? Does the potential client make public statements in the tweets that will become an issue in the case? Do the potential client's habits on social media reflect an individual who will be hard to manage during the course of litigation?

5.4.1 *Investigation to Determine Whether to Take the Case*

After the client meeting and conflicts check, determine whether the client has an action you want to bring or whether the client has a case you want to defend. If it is a plaintiff's case, and you are working on contingency, tell the client you want to investigate before deciding to invest time and costs in the case. For a defense case, tell the client you need time to assess the matter to determine if you are suited for their defense. When considering a defense case, analyze the facts and think about experts you may need to litigate the case. Contemplate whether you have the staff necessary to do the work or whether additional attorneys and/or firms may be required.

You also must determine—upfront—when the statute of limitations or statute of repose will run. If you are plaintiff's counsel and you determine that in five weeks the litigation will be barred, you need to determine quickly whether you will have enough time to gather information to file the cause of action within the limitations period. In such situations, consider the challenge presented by investigating a stale case—some information may be unobtainable due to missing documents and weakened memories. Determine whether any damages are barred by the limitations period. Of course, if you are defending the case the statute of limitations and the statutes of repose can work in your favor. Your investigation may reveal the potential to dispose of the matter early on through motions practice. More particularly, the issue of limitations will focus your investigation; what documents or testimony will be needed to show that the potential plaintiff knew of the cause of action but failed to bring suit within the limitations period? The analysis will require the application of law to fact and—as a preliminary matter—require research on what law applies. It may even require predicate research into what jurisdiction's laws govern the case. If the case is brought in federal court, will there be an "Erie" issue with regard to the potential application of state law?[22]

---

22. Erie R.R. v. Tompkins, 304 U.S. 64 (1938) (holding district courts sitting in diversity applied to state law in which they sit).

National Institute for Trial Advocacy

Consider, for example, a case involving an explosion of a polymer plant resulting in an employee death. The deceased's family contacts you to bring a wrongful death action. You have brought wrongful death actions before, but you know little about the mechanics of a polymer plant. Being candid with the client is always the best approach. Express your desire to thoroughly examine the matter before deciding whether this is a case you can handle. First, read the accident reports. Was there an OSHA investigation? Was there an investigation by the U.S. Chemical Safety and Hazard Investigation Board (CSB)?[23] If the investigations are incomplete, perhaps the local police or fire department has an incident report. Learn investigators' names from each investigative agency and contact them to gather information.

Look at the potential defendants when conducting your preliminary investigation. What are their product lines, safety records, revenue streams, and market capitalizations? Does the defendant company have the ability to pay a judgment? Is there a parent company? Maybe there are multiple defendants? Is there insurance?

Dig deep. Search OSHA citations and prior lawsuits. If the company is publicly traded, examine Securities and Exchange Commission filings for disclosures about government investigations and civil suits.

Research cases containing similar facts. What were the settlements? Keep in mind that many settlements will be confidential. What happened at trial? What mistakes were made during the litigation phase? In other words, if there was a result that established a problematic precedent for your case, are there steps you can take in your case to get a better result? Perhaps you can do a better job of fact collection. Maybe you need to include more facts in the complaint. You may need to use a different damage model.

During your preliminary investigation process, explore relevant experts for this type of case. Are there lawyers specializing in catastrophic injury involving polymer plants? Are these lawyers whom you might consider teaming up with to bring the case? Are there experts in the design and safety of polymer plants? What costs are associated with these experts and must you immediately retain them, so they are not retained by your opponent?

"Clients often wait too long for cost concerns, but hiring an expert early and having them up to speed and available early on in the case can pay substantial dividends. Just because you hire an expert, doesn't mean they have to start voluminous amounts of work right away—get them on board and use them for an hour here and an hour there early on."

—Josh Johnston, Senior Managing Director, Ankura Consulting Group

---

23. *See, e.g.,* CHEM. SAFETY BD., https://www.csb.gov.

Part of this process may require you to go back to the client with more questions. Clients often appreciate that their counsel is trying to "get it right." At the same time, however, clients may end up sharing irrelevant information that may delay or sidetrack your investigation. For this reason, when you go back to the client with questions, do so with focus and purpose. This keeps the client focused and, if you proceed with the litigation, the process will begin to establish the boundaries of your relationship with the client. Keeping the client focused is a balance between being firm and being polite. You can say: "hold that thought; here is what I need to know." Just make sure to ask your client about the other subject at some later point to ensure that you do not miss any information that might be helpful once the case is underway.

You must also determine whether there is an efficient way to bring or defend the case. If the matter involves small damages, is it susceptible to class treatment? Can the requirements of FRCP 23 be met? If you are defending the case, what will be the procedural battle grounds other than matters like class certification, statute of limitations, and perhaps standing?

5.5   You Have Decided to Take the Case; Now What?

Your post retention investigation will be a lot different depending on whether you are defending the case or pursuing the case as plaintiff's counsel. If you are plaintiff's counsel, your investigation has three areas of focus: 1) preparing a complaint, 2) getting to trial, and 3) winning at trial. Assuming that there is no rush to the courthouse because of a limitations problem or because you are filing a class action and want to stake out your position before other filers, you will have an opportunity to carefully gather the facts, and perhaps talk to witnesses, before your opponent has even remotely contemplated a defense.

Your efforts will take you from where your preliminary investigation left off to a deeper dive into the information. Your goal will be to assemble facts that can meet the pleading standards. This means that if it is a non-fraud case, you must assemble the facts—not merely conclusions—that demonstrate a plausible cause of action. If you are pleading a fraud case, FRCP 9(b) requires that the case be plead with particularity. FRCP 9(b) specifically states:

> FRAUD OR MISTAKE; CONDITIONS OF MIND. In alleging fraud or mistake, a party must state with particularity the circumstances constituting fraud or mistake. Malice, intent, knowledge, and other conditions of a person's mind may be alleged generally.

To meet the FRCP 9(b) pleading standards, you must plead the particularities of "who, what, when, where, and how." This is important guidance because it means that the golden nuggets of your investigation will be information about times, dates, meetings, those present at meetings, emails or correspondence, and the times and dates of their transmission or receipt and the names of the recipients and/or transmitters.

Naturally, your investigation starts with your client and this checklist:

- What documents does your client have?

- What other evidence does your client have, including videos, photos, and non-documentary evidence like damaged products or devices that caused injury?

- What is your client's narrative regarding the events?

- Who are the witnesses and what is their background?

Collect this information to fill in the blanks on your complaint, including allegations about the parties. For allegations about your client's background the easiest way to write this section is to work from their resume if they have one. If your client is a business—or if you are making a claim against a business—you can likely find this information on the website.

The information you get from your client may include emails, calendars, and texts. From these, piece together substantive allegations that include times, dates, and references to individuals. As you go through the information you are collecting, use the timeline of events you created during your preliminary investigation; as you collect more information, you can fill in the timeline with more details and outline the narrative for your complaint and for trial. By the way, there is nothing wrong with putting a graphic of your timeline in the complaint. This may help the judge and law clerks as they immerse themselves in your cause of action. Along these lines, keep in mind that you may collect evidence that can be put directly into the complaint in the form of an allegation or graphic. This may include photographs, screen shots of emails, even PowerPoint presentations, if they illuminate or strengthen the case.

As the client identifies witnesses, use social media to find out more about these people, including their work history, educational background, and social relations. By looking at their Tweets, you can even get a feel for how they communicate, whether they are likely to be forthcoming, and whether you and the witness share any commonalities that can be a catalyst for a dialogue with the witness. Significantly, LinkedIn may be a valuable source for admissions about what a person did or did not do during their tenure at a specific job.

As you collect your list of witnesses and research their backgrounds, determine which ones are friendly witnesses, which ones will not be helpful, and which ones—for ethical reasons—you cannot talk to without going through counsel.

5.5.1 *Witness Interviews*

Witness interviews vary depending on the type of case, the witness' relationship to your client and/or the other party, and the personal costs that cooperation may impose on the witnesses. The "personal costs" can include the witness's concern that they will be "drawn into" something that may require time in the form of depositions or court appearances. Or the witness may have concerns about personal exposure in the form of retaliation or counter suits. The witness may even have signed a confidentiality or non-disparagement agreement.

Internet investigations of each witness and information garnered from your client can reveal not only whether a witness will cooperate with your investigation, but also the most effective means for approaching the witness. If the client knows the witness, ask the client to arrange a meeting. You can also retain an investigator or reach out yourself. Each of these approaches has benefits and drawbacks. In each case, remember that anything said to the potential witness is not protected by privilege.

If the client reaches out to a witness, carefully orchestrate the communication. Anything the client tells the witness is discoverable. Obviously, the client cannot make promises such as vowing to share the benefits of the litigation. The message can be simple: "As you know, I am involved in litigation over the car accident. Would you mind sharing what you witnessed with my lawyer?" If the witness has questions, the client might say: "I am sure my lawyer can answer these questions better than I can and would be pleased to do so."

When arranging communication, decide whether the contact will be by phone or in person, and if in person, the location for the meeting. Although an in-person interview is preferred, a witness may favor the comfort of a phone interview, or an initial phone call before the in-person meeting. Ask the witness, "What is most convenient for you?" and let them decide the meeting's format.

Initiating contact yourself may risk establishing a colder connection than if the client made the preliminary call. Think about the message's medium. Options include text, email, letter, or a phone call to their home, work, or cell phone. Consider the information you learned about the witness to assist your decision making. Contacting a witness at work or via email is less intrusive, but if the matter involves the employment setting, doing so may create anxiety for the witness.

As a third option, retain a private investigator to conduct the outreach. If your client is paying an hourly rate for your services, the investigator may save the client money. If the case is handled on contingency, the investigator may increase out-of-pocket case costs. If the investigator lacks expertise, however, you may not get all the necessary information for the case and will lose the ability to spontaneously follow up on answers. When determining the form of outreach, consider that some witnesses are more comfortable speaking with a non-lawyer.

In addition to determining a method of witness outreach, determine what information you need from each witness. Consider the following checklists:

- Information that fills gaps in your theory of the case.

- Information that supports any affirmative defenses.

- Information that undermines case theory or case defenses.

- Information that can be used for impeachment.

- Tangible evidence including documents, emails, photos, videos, and text messages.

Get a read on each witness you meet. Ascertain their willingness to cooperate. Do they exhibit any hesitancy, withhold information, appear dishonest, or simply tell you what you want to hear? What is their motivation? What are their proclivities? Observe everything from their body language to speech pattern.

Decide whether to start with a dialogue about a neutral subject, perhaps not even tied to the case. "My client tells me you are a big baseball fan; did you see the game yesterday?" Or "my client tells me you're from Rochester; my wife grew up there."

Ask the witness if they have any time restrictions for the interview. If they only have thirty minutes, delving into unrelated subjects for the sake of connection may be wasting valuable time.

Learn what kind of evidence—whether emails, photographs, or videos—the witness has in their possession. Asking for too much may seem extremely intrusive, causing the witness to backpedal in fear. Instead try, "Would it be a problem to retrieve the email?" or "That email would be helpful if you don't mind finding it."

Throughout the interview, remember that anything you say to the witness is not covered by attorney-client privilege and that the conversation will also be discoverable. Hence, it is important to remind the witness you are only interested in the truth.

Sometimes witnesses respond to questions with conclusory answers. This occurs because we—as humans—take in many facts, storing them in our head wrapped up as conclusions. We remember events as happy, sad, good, bad, boring, exciting, funny, or even embarrassing. These are all conclusions. Unpacking the facts that support these conclusions is key to any witness interview. You may learn the conclusions are unsupported by fact or that the supporting facts are more compelling than the conclusion. Consider these two scenarios:

A: Your client is a horrible driver.

Q: Can you list all the facts that support your understanding that Jon is a horrible driver?

A: That's just what people say.

Q: Well, what have you personally observed about his driving?

A: I've never seen him drive.

Or consider a line of questioning where the facts are more powerful than the conclusion:

A: Your client's former boss is an awful person, and your client should not feel bad about being fired by her.

Q: You use the phrase "awful person." Why do you say that?

A: She was convicted of fraud and spent time in prison. A jury ruled against her in a sexual harassment case, and she is a registered sex offender.

These two scenarios demonstrate how to cull out the facts. The second scenario illustrates how a factual narrative can be more compelling than the conclusory term a witness chooses to summarize the facts.

Your investigation and witness interviews are necessary for all phases of the litigation from complaint preparation to trial. Think about how you are going to record and present the information that becomes the fruit of your investigation. For motions practice, affidavits or declarations may suffice. You may also decide to take the witness' deposition or call the witness at trial. If, in the case of a third-party witness, you have concerns about the witness appearing for deposition, you can serve a subpoena. Sometimes witnesses are more comfortable being subpoenaed; it allows them to take the position that they had no choice but to testify.

5.5.2 *Document Investigation*

Your investigation will naturally include a search for documents. Documents may come from the client, witnesses, public records, and the Internet. You will need a repository to store these documents. We discuss document handling in Chapter Eight.

Attorneys use documents to draft the complaint, as deposition exhibits, as summary judgment exhibits, and also at trial. As you conduct witness interviews, use documents to prompt a witness's memory or ask witnesses about ambiguities in the documents. Look for direct evidence and circumstantial evidence. Always look for documents that provide information concerning the case's subject area(s) such as witnesses, companies involved, or scientific or technical aspects of the case.

Going back to the chemical plant explosion example, assume your Internet research uncovered a polymer manufacturing flow chart. The flow chart's source may even have the indicia of reliability to be admissible under FRE 201. You also might discover public documents including government corporate integrity agreements, OSHA citations, or criminal pleas revealing all the various players' conduct. When examining the documents, think broadly about their potential value to the case or their admissibility as evidence. Refer to the evidentiary rules while pondering your document collection. Challenge yourself—look at the rules of relevance, hearsay, and documentation about prior bad conduct.

Remember to search for "catalyst" documents. Catalyst documents have circumstantial value because they place witnesses or parties in certain places at certain times. Such documents may show that parties or witnesses interacted with one another. They can also demonstrate whether the parties or witnesses have knowledge about subjects related to showing intent. Consider again the polymer or chemical plant explosion. At deposition, suppose the plant manager testifies that they are unfamiliar with OSHA standards. Of course, indifference itself could show intent. However, if you have attendance records from the defendant company's OSHA training sessions, you may be able —at deposition or at trial—to use the records as an impeachment exhibit when the plant manager denies knowledge of the OSHA safety requirements. Alternatively, the attendance records can be a catalyst, provoking the witness to be truthful during deposition testimony. Consider this line of questioning:

> A: I really have no knowledge of the OSHA requirements. You need to talk with our OSHA coordinator.
>
> Q: I want to show you Exhibit 21, a document produced by your counsel and originating from your files. Can you identify the signature at the bottom of the first page?
>
> A: Yes, it is my signature.
>
> Q: And can you tell me why you signed this document?
>
> A: I signed it to confirm that I attended the OSHA training session.
>
> Q: And does the document accurately reflect the list of all the areas that you confirmed that you learned?
>
> A: Yes.

5.5.3 Investigating the Technical Side of a Case

Some cases have technical aspects and require your acquaintance with areas ranging from mechanics to accounting. Consider again the polymer plant example. You intuitively know that explosions do not occur but for some negligence. Therefore, something went wrong, but what? Although you are not the person to determine the "what," you must locate the person able to provide those answers. During the investigation stage identify both nontestifying experts and experts capable of testifying. The nontestifying, or consulting, expert's job is to answer all your questions. Their purpose is to teach you and they should appreciate that there is no stupid question. These people may not present well at trial or do not have the degrees that are indicia of credibility or reliability. However, they know the area well enough to educate you, review your complaint for technical accuracy, and keep you informed so you can work with the testifying experts.

Focus on locating experts in the prefiling stage. If your case requires technical expertise, have an expert review the complaint before filing. To the extent that you are able, lock in your experts before the other side retains them. An Internet search will quickly identify those who have written, studied, or specialize in particular areas. College and university faculties are excellent sources for identifying those with expertise. Research cases to learn which experts testified in particular areas. Contact other members of the bar—whose practices align with yours—for expert recommendations. But do not omit the obvious. Our everyday lives expose us to people with specific areas of expertise such as accountants, auto mechanics, computer, and software experts. Talk to the people you know, get recommendations, continue your discussions. In the digital age, attorneys too often become captive to the keyboard, limiting investigation to information gathered from the Internet. Although the Internet is a major asset, personal contact is essential. Use the Internet to track down email addresses, arrange phone calls, or schedule personal interviews.

Having some knowledge of the specific subject area is vital to effective expert identification and collaboration. Utilize published articles and books to familiarize yourself with the subject area. When accessible, video lectures by college and university professors can be extraordinarily helpful.

5.5.4   *Legal Research*

Investigations do not end with a single examination of the law. It is a continuing effort. As you learn more about the case your legal theories may change, or you may see legal defenses that were not obvious to you at first glance. Keep a binder of key cases. Expand upon the binder. Reread the cases; every time you do so, you may find passages or wording that becomes more relevant to you as you learn the facts of your case.

Never stop investigating.

—Mike Beckwith, Asst. U.S. Attorney, E.D. California

The starting point for legal research is determining what causes of action provide redress and the elements of those causes of action. Pattern jury instructions or jury instructions from similar cases offer quick introductions to the elements. In addition to studying jury instructions, read verdict forms for the actual questions the jury must answer. Consider a case brought under the federal False Claims Act, a statute providing civil penalties and damages resulting from frauds on the government. The essence of this cause of action involves a false or fraudulent claim, for payment or approval, of a bill or request for payment, transmitted to the government. Once instructed on the elements of false or fraudulent claims, jurors are presented with the following interrogatory:

1. How many false or fraudulent claims were presented to the government?

_____

If you understand how the question is going to be presented to the jury, it is easier to strategize—as in a false claims case—about gathering the necessary information to determine claim numbers and how to present the information to the jury so it can fill in the number. Will you use a witness to testify to the number? Will it be an expert or a lay witness? Or will you use a data compilation as prescribed by FRE 1006?[24]

For each element of the claim, think about whether your investigation provides the necessary evidence to prove each element. Conduct research to determine whether your evidence is admissible or how it can become admissible. Do you expect hearsay or authenticity challenges? Do you anticipate any other efforts to exclude the evidence, particularly under FRE 403?

Unless a plaintiff's cause of action is solely for injunctive relief, the case on the merits will have a damage component. Locate the jury instructions on damages. How is the jury asked the question and how will it record its findings? Always remember to study the verdict forms.

For matters of liability and damages, are experts needed to bridge the gap on proof? Imagine handling a race discrimination case where you assert an employer excluded black applicants from employment. Is there hard evidence to make the claim? Or might you use a statistician to testify that the dearth of black employees in a workplace is not a random occurrence? Research case law for insight into how others met this proof challenge and the legal challenges you will likely encounter. If choosing to use an expert, case law reveals important criteria for selecting experts who can survive *Daubert* challenges.

Similarly, damage questions are always complicated. Law schools offer courses on "remedies" taught by professors who think about remedies and write treatises on the subject. Legal research provides insight into how damages are measured. Suppose your client claims their termination was based on gender. Their salary was $50,000 a year, but one day after the termination, they began a new job paying

_____

24. FRE 1006 allows summaries of information, in lieu of large amounts of documents, to be admitted into evidence if the summary meets certain conditions. The underlying documents must be voluminous. The underlying documents must be admissible. Lastly, the opposing party has the right to inspect the originals.

$60,000 a year. On paper, they had no economic harm. Perhaps they had other harm, maybe emotional harm. Is expert testimony required as to emotional harm or can the plaintiff testify regarding the humiliation and pain suffered? Legal research not only informs whether expert testimony is needed, it also advises on the documents and testimony needed to support your causes of action.

Your claims will undoubtedly be met with a motion to dismiss. Reverse engineer the case. Research opposing counsel's likely arguments to support their motion to dismiss. Areas to consider:

- Pleading standards under FRCP 8 and 9.

- Statute of limitations.

- Standing under Article III and or the statute governing the cause of action.

- Statute of repose.

- Laches.

- Unclean hands.

- Accord and satisfaction.

Legal research determines if you gathered the necessary facts to plead the causes of action that would be sustained on a motion to dismiss. Legal research also guides your discovery process as a whole—what discovery is crucial to survive a motion to dismiss, get past summary judgment, and meet the elements of proof at trial.

Legal research also answers ethical questions. Consider the client with a whistle-blower case under the False Claims Act. They claim their employer—who makes battle tanks for the Army—violated manufacturing specifications and they have the documents to prove it. Can they remove the documents from their workplace? Suppose the documents are not in their possession and they need to access company computers? Suppose some documents memorialize communications between company lawyers and your client? These issues require research. The answers are not all black letter law and may vary from circuit to circuit or state to state. They also depend on the particular facts.

CHAPTER SIX

PREPARING TO LITIGATE

6.1   Introduction

Lawyers are in the business of dispute resolution. The process leading up to filing a complaint, and pursuit of the case through jury verdict and appeal, are all parts of the dispute resolution process. The process is a reality check. The parties will learn the relative strengths and weaknesses of their cases. The process incentivizes the parties to find a resolution; if they cannot resolve their differences, a court will do it for them—and that result may not be one they can live with.

If our goal as attorneys is to "secure a just, speedy, and inexpensive de-termination of every action,"[1] then apologies and lunch should be promi-nent strategic options. Without apologies and lunch, the battle begins with pleadings, letters, emails, and one-way phone missives that intentionally convey uncompromising dominance, self-interest, and separate visions of the past—all matters that are difficult to reconcile. With self-deprecating apologies and "small talk" at lunch, the credibility and believability of each side is given a chance to take root, ears and minds are opened, and trust can be nurtured and developed. My best pretrial practice tip is to have lunch with your opponent at the very beginning and even before filing a complaint if you can.

—Sidney Kanazawa, Mediator/Arbitrator, Alternative Resolution Centers

---

Deciding to move forward with a lawsuit is a big step. It requires at least the com-mitment of time and money. As the lawyer signing a complaint you are assuring the court that you investigated the facts, researched the law, and consider the case to be meritorious. More specifically, FRCP 11(b) states the following:

(b) Representations to the Court. By presenting to the court a pleading, written motion, or other paper—whether by signing, filing,

---

1. Fed. R. Civ. P. 1.

submitting, or later advocating it—an attorney or unrepresented party certifies that to the best of the person's knowledge, information, and belief, formed after an inquiry reasonable under the circumstances:

(1) it is not being presented for any improper purpose, such as to harass, cause unnecessary delay, or needlessly increase the cost of litigation;

(2) the claims, defenses, and other legal contentions are warranted by existing law or by a nonfrivolous argument for extending, modifying, or reversing existing law or for establishing new law;

(3) the factual contentions have evidentiary support or, if specifically so identified, will likely have evidentiary support after a reasonable opportunity for further investigation or discovery; and

(4) the denials of factual contentions are warranted on the evidence or, if specifically so identified, are reasonably based on belief or a lack of information.

Though courts seem reluctant to impose FRCP 11 sanctions, good lawyers are always concerned about their imposition, a concern that drives diligence.[2] More important than avoiding sanctions, diligence and integrity are the foundation of your reputation. A good reputation means credibility with your opposition and the court. It means that when you have a tough case or a case with new applications for existing law, your chances of being heard by the court—and given some deference—are increased. There is—of course—no rule that says this; it is simply a matter of common sense. Indeed, everything you do as a lawyer is not only about your credibility in the current litigation; it is about your reputation and credibility going forward.[3]

---

2. Do not be mistaken though, many courts have been pushed to limit where they do impose sanctions.

3. *See In re* Pearson, 228 A.3d 417 (D.C. 2020) (imposing a ninety-day suspension for violating MRPC 3.1, prohibiting frivolous actions, and MRPC 8.4(d), prohibiting "conduct that seriously interferes with the administration of justice"). The disciplinary proceeding involved lawyer conduct during a lawsuit brought against dry cleaners for allegedly losing a pair of pants. *Id.* at 420. The court departed from the Hearing Committee's recommendation of a thirty-day suspension because Pearson mischaracterized facts, filed frivolous claims impacting court resources, used frivolous legal theories, showed no remorse, failed to acknowledge his misconduct, subjected defendants to years of litigation-related stress, and asserted unfounded allegations against judiciary and disciplinary members. *Id.* at 427-29. *See also* MODEL RULES OF PROF. CONDUCT r. 3.1 & 8.4 (AM. BAR ASS'N 2020).

6.2 The Talk with the Client

Filing a complaint also means the plaintiff and their lawyer(s) are committed to a lengthy process that could take years to resolve, requires document production, depositions, briefings, court appearances, and trial. It is, as we have said, a commitment of both time and money.[4] Clearly inform the client of the obligations associated with filing a suit and what to expect in litigation. From the lawyer's vantage point, this is not merely one discussion but a dialogue that must be repeated with the client. Uncooperative clients can lead to case delays, including the failure to meet discovery deadlines or court schedules. In the end, this is not just a problem for this client's case; it could be a problem that will impact your reputation beyond the scope of this representation.

A client should not, for example, learn for the first time about depositions when you call to tell them you have received a notice and want to discuss the deposition process. Deposition preparation, along with preparation requiring client involvement, should be an ongoing occurrence with refresher sessions prior to the event requiring client participation. Deposition preparation and preparation for trial testimony should really begin as soon as the retention agreement is signed. Every communication with the client should be done with an eye toward that client eventually testifying,

Keep in mind that "communication" is both a practical and an ethical obligation. MRPC 1.4 specifically addresses "Communications." Read the rule and its local or state analogue in entirety. Model Rule 1.4(a)(2) makes clear that a lawyer shall "reasonably consult with the client about the means by which the client's objectives are to be accomplished." As a practical matter, this consultation begins at the first attorney-client meeting, involves substance disclosure and dialogue prior to the retention, and is an ongoing process throughout the litigation. To be clear, the biggest mistake that lawyers can make is not communicating with their clients. Consistent client communication is one of the most important factors impacting client satisfaction.

Discuss the obligations your client will assume as a plaintiff in a lawsuit. If you are entering into an agreement to defend a client, the same type of discussion should occur. Here is a quick checklist:

---

4. One of Atlanta's most respected trial lawyers, Henry R. Bauer, Jr. was fond of saying "litigation is a rich man's sport."

The obligation to read the complaint before it is filed.

The obligation to be available to answer questions and attend meetings.

Any costs and fees that will be associated with the case at each stage of the litigation.

The obligation to submit to a deposition and sit with counsel to prepare for the deposition.

The obligation to read the deposition once it is given.

The obligation to help answer interrogatories and search for documents.

The obligation to preserve documents and produce those that are sought unless there is a protective order.

In sum, advise the client of their responsibilities, including the requirement to preserve documents, produce documents, answer interrogatories, respond to requests for admission, submit to a deposition, appear in court, and testify at trial.

When independent psychological evaluations or medical examinations are at issue, the client needs to know in advance. Though it is helpful to include all of these obligations in the retainer agreement, discuss these matters and do all you can to ensure the client comprehends the obligations, including any financial responsibilities which must be bolted into the retainer agreement. If you think we—the authors—repeat ourselves on these points, you are correct. They are important messages for all lawyers who are about to file or defend a lawsuit.

Your client expects and deserves a prompt response to every contact, inquiry, or comment. Your response should include a realistic evaluation of your client's prospects for time, fees, and results. Your evaluation may well change as circumstances change, and you should promptly advise your client about any significant change. You must exercise great care to avoid unharnessed optimism without discouraging your client's confidence in his own version of events.

—Judge Richard Markus (Ret.), Founding Member, National Institute for Trial Advocacy

---

6.3 Demand Letters

For a plaintiff client, the first step in the process—before even filing a complaint—may be a demand letter. Demand letters lay out the facts, the applicable law, and a proposed remedy. The decision on whether to send a demand letter is a tactical one. On the one hand, it may open up a dialogue that allows you to understand your opponent's defenses and perception of the facts. By the same token, it allows your opponent to preview the support for your claims. The key to a demand letter is making it a catalyst for dialogue. If parties can talk, resolution is more likely. In drafting the letter, think carefully about what will prompt dialogue and what will turn off dialogue. Personal attacks and hyperbole are turnoffs. Stick to the facts and provide evidence where appropriate. In addition, never make threats that are beyond the four corners of your potential suit. For example, never mention the possibility of criminal sanctions. You are not a prosecutor; the right to pursue criminal or regulatory sanctions rests with the government. For you to make such threats raises ethical, if not criminal, exposure for you and your client.

Finally, be aware of FRE 408, which relates to communications made during negotiations. In order to encourage communications and settlement, FRE 408, with narrow exceptions, excludes both offers and the statements made in conjunction with negotiation from being used to prove liability. Therefore, when communicating a settlement demand, clearly indicate that this letter is part of an attempt to settle the dispute. This encourages parties to disclose information through demand letters and conversations without the fear of those letters being used against a party at a later date.

If you are the attorney for the defendant, responding to a demand letter is also a tactical decision. Start from the premise that dialogue is a good thing; discussion is always informative. You can learn more about the claims, the abilities of the lawyer pursuing them, and how much the opposing lawyer understands the case. If the case does not settle at the demand letter stage and litigation is pursued, counsel will work with each other through the pre-litigation process and through trial. Failed settlement negotiations can be frustrating, but keep your cool, remain professional, and do not poison relationships through personal attacks and hyperbolic invective. The discussions prompted by a demand letter mark the beginning of a relationship between counsel that may ultimately—if not immediately—benefit the client. If nothing else, agree to keep the dialogue going or agree to work together to streamline the litigation. Also discuss approaches that may lead to resolution, including mediation, arbitration, and agreement on certain facts, so the litigation is less costly and time consuming.

Assume that you have sent a demand letter informing your client's adversary of the dispute while inviting a resolution. Your demand letter might state an amount of money that will resolve the dispute or nonmonetary terms that would settle the potential claim. Nonmonetary terms may include such items as a letter of reference for a discharged employee, a retraction letter or an apology for a defamation claim, or an agreement to stay away or not trespass on property.

The checklist for your prelitigation resolution efforts might include the following:

- Demand letter outlining the claims and proposing a settlement;

- Responses to counteroffers; and

- Proposals for alternative dispute resolution including mediation and arbitration.

6.4   Filing the Complaint

Many times none of these efforts or mechanisms resolve the case; yet perhaps they have—as discussed above—streamlined the case by agreement or enlightened you as to the viability of certain causes of action.

Unless you have agreed to mediate or arbitrate, the only remaining recourse is filing a complaint. Now it is time for the "attorney-client reality check." Meet with the client and remind them of the litigation obligations, including costs and time commitment. Impress upon the client that discovery can be an intrusive process. Walk the client through the steps of litigation so they understand how time-consuming, protracted, and tedious the process can become. Explain that both sides may need extensions to respond to motions and that such delays must be dealt with in a professional manner. Describe your litigation style to the client, advise them that unnecessarily personalizing the lawsuit may prolong litigation, increase litigation costs, and impede resolution.

In addition, explain to the client the risks, if any, of countersuits, anti-SLAPP motions, contractually mandated fee-shifting provisions, and compulsory arbitration obligations. Undoubtedly, as to the question of compulsory arbitration, this will be an issue that receives significant attention and client dialogue.[5] Compulsory arbitration obligations are routinely enforced by the courts.[6]

Remind the client that lawsuits often divide parties. Defendants may resist immediate settlement, believing it is a sign of weakness. Sometimes the complaint's allegations cause a defendant to dig their heels in, leverage motions to dismiss, or

---

5. Compulsory arbitration is a major challenge to the rule of law. It precludes the right to a jury trial, impedes the development of the common law, and is often a process devoid of transparency. It is of major policy concern that such arbitration agreements are imposed on public interest litigation including civil rights and consumer matters.

6. *See generally* Gilmer v. Interstate/Johnson Lane Corp., 500 U.S. 20 (1991); Am. Express Co. v. Italian Colors Rest., 570 U.S. 228 (2013); Bender v. A.G. Edwards & Sons Inc., 971 F.2d 698 (11th Cir. 1992); Bender v. Smith Barney, Harris Upham & Co., 789 F. Supp. 155 (D.N.J. 1992).

use aggressive discovery tactics in an attempt to drive settlement. In sum, the client should not expect the defendant to surrender once a suit is filed.

Explain that lawsuits have their ups and downs. There are good days and bad days. Lawsuits are a process. One day in a lawsuit is the equivalent of one weather forecast, where the entire trajectory of the suit is comparable to climate. Perhaps this analogy will not resonate with your client but get to know your client and think of ones that will work.

For some clients, particularly individuals, the lawsuit becomes the most important part of their life and consumes them. Explain to the client that they should go on with life as the litigation proceeds, yet not neglect their responsibilities to the case. What does this mean in practical terms? Consider the client who seeks counsel for a wrongful discharge from employment. They have not only lost a regular stream of income; the emotional toll also may be considerable. The client feels humiliated and wants recourse that punishes the defendant. The emotional toll becomes so consuming that the client refrains from seeking new employment. They send you emails every day inquiring about the case and routinely repeat information that has already been relayed to you. As the case drags on, the client—who has not found employment—becomes more emotionally distraught. This situation is not healthy for the client or the attorney-client relationship; and it is not conducive to a full recovery in court. First, the law often requires that plaintiffs mitigate their damages. This means that in an employment case, a client must make real efforts to find work. Second, a client making the lawsuit their sole focus becomes a more difficult client because they want to move the case at a faster pace than the process will allow. Moreover, they become less objective about the case's value. This poses problems for settling the case, negotiating or agreeing to extensions, and making decisions regarding when to be aggressive in enforcing discovery obligations.

A demand letter and its response are a reality check. After this attorney-client reality check, clients may reconsider settlement or decide not to go forward at all. If the client chooses to proceed, the ground rules established at the reality-check session will promote a smooth attorney-client relationship where the informed client is prepared and not plagued by anxiety.

6.4.1 Is the Attorney Prepared?

An attorney must be prepared for the litigation process, and financial considerations are fundamental to preparation. For a case taken on a contingency basis, can the lawyer afford to litigate through trial without being paid? If the lawyer advances costs, have all costs been anticipated? Here is a checklist:

- Filing fees

- Deposition transcripts

- Videographer fees (if the depositions have been recorded)

- Travel expenses

- Costs for storing electronic information

- Copying costs

- Costs of extra support staff including overtime

Carefully evaluate the cost of each line item. Discovery that produces electronic information, depending on the size of the production, can result in document storage fees well into the thousands of dollars each month. If you are going to use a vendor for electronic discovery, consult with the vendor and project the costs. Plot out the number of depositions, anticipate travel if the case requires it, and formulate a realistic budget.[7]

Lawyers doing contingency work find it useful to estimate the costs of a case. At the end of the day, the client is responsible for those expenses; cost projections help determine whether the case is even worth bringing. For example, will the costs exceed the recovery? If the litigation is brought under a fee-shifting statute, determine whether the anticipated expenses can be recovered and at what rate.[8]

For cases where the attorney expects to recover attorney's fees, make sure that a system exists to record fees and costs. Time entries for particular tasks should be kept in increments that are fractions of an hour. Many lawyers keep their time in minimums of a tenth or two-tenths of an hour. Avoid block billing (billing a large increment of time for many activities). Look at the local case law to determine what rules judges apply when fees are sought. Once you draw a judge, look at the rules that judge imposes when determining the propriety of fees and costs. By "rules," we mean that you should study the opinions the judge authored in deciding fee and cost petitions.

When charging an hourly rate, assess the client's ability to pay all lawsuit fees and costs. For example, consider a client who earned $75,000 a year, with a family to support, hiring you to file a lawsuit alleging their employment dismissal was racially motivated. You may enter into an hourly agreement but be aware that if the litigation progresses into discovery and your client remains unemployed, there will be no money to pay legal bills. Conversely, if the client does secure employment, damages are mitigated, and it may no longer be worth bringing the suit. In sum, be concerned not only with the type of agreement—whether hourly or

---

7. You can also look for ways to reduce the budget by perhaps avoiding travel and taking depositions by remote means.
8. The Laffey Matrix, which applies to litigation in the District of Columbia in fee shifting cases, is one means of eyeballing the rates that may be recovered when the court is awarding fees. *See, e.g.,* Laffey Matrix, http://www.laffeymatrix.com/.

contingency—the client agreed to, but also whether that agreement makes sense and will survive the life of the contract.

Whether an attorney possesses the skills necessary to bring a case is a primary concern. Lawyers should be comfortable drafting papers, appearing in court, taking depositions, and trying a case. Lawyers new to the profession simply do not have this experience. Sometimes, small cases present opportunities for new lawyers to gain experience; however, if the case is complicated and beyond the lawyer's level of experience and comfort, bringing in co-counsel is an appropriate solution. A co-counsel provides assistance and helps to bridge the experience gap, but sometimes (often in contingency cases), they can contribute to the costs of litigation.

Even experienced litigation attorneys bring in co-counsel. Matters sometimes involve a technical area of the law such as intellectual property, tax, environmental law, or perhaps labor and employment law. Attorneys must assemble, and be confident in, a solid team for the litigation. Putting together a team for a case is particularly apt in contingency litigation where the attorney is advancing costs and needs to decrease their litigation risks. "Cutting" other counsel into the case—giving them percentages of the recovery and requiring them to advance costs—can hedge the risk and increase the odds of recovery by bringing in forces that know the area of law, the defendant, or who have solid litigation and or trial skills.

Part of assembling the right team means advance consideration regarding experts. Primary considerations:

- Are experts needed to testify to the merits of a case such as causation?

- Are experts needed to quantify damages?

- Are experts needed to help the trier of fact understand the evidence?

What do we mean here? First, after you gather and put into evidence all of the necessary facts, is an expert needed to interpret the facts? Will the facts alone show causation or liability, or will an expert be needed to bridge the gap? Suppose you want to prove that your friend's dog ate your chocolate chip cookies. You can put on witnesses who will testify that one minute the cookies were on the plate and the next minute they were gone and there was a dog in the room. This is called circumstantial evidence because no witness actually saw the dog eat the cookies. But suppose the dog got sick. You could have an expert testify that dogs are allergic to chocolate to explain the malady. The same is true of damages. Experts are used to quantify damages in all sorts of cases ranging from claims for emotional distress to claims alleging violations of the antitrust and securities laws.

In choosing experts, look at the case law and determine how other counsel have used experts in similar circumstances. More importantly, determine what type of expert testimony has been accepted by the courts, particularly the courts in your jurisdiction. This is essential research because if your case hangs on the testimony of an expert for liability or damages, you may burn up a lot of time and money in the litigation process only to find—shortly before trial—that the legs have been knocked out of your case because the court will not allow the expert testimony.

It is crucial to retain your experts early because: 1) the other side may contact them first; and 2) experts can provide insight regarding what information they will need to render an opinion, so counsel knows what to secure during the discovery process.[9]

6.4.2 *Where Do I File?*

There are often many choices when selecting an adjudication forum, including state court or many federal circuit courts where one can assert jurisdiction. State and federal systems have courts with varied jurisdictions. In the federal court system, most litigation is brought in United States' district courts instead of other federal courts with more limited jurisdictions such as the court of claims, the bankruptcy courts, or the court of international trade.

The threshold question is whether three requirements have been met for a trial court to entertain a plaintiff's claim. The three requirements are: 1) jurisdiction over the parties or things (usually referred to as personal jurisdiction); 2) jurisdiction over the subject matter; and 3) proper venue. Regardless of what type of claim it is, whether it is a claim brought by a plaintiff, a counterclaim brought by a defendant, or a cross claim brought by a co-defendant, the court must have jurisdiction over both the parties or things and over the subject matter of the claim in order to properly exercise its authority over the case. If the court does not have jurisdiction over the parties or things, the court must dismiss the case unless the party submits to the jurisdiction or waives personal jurisdiction.[10] For example, a party may submit to the jurisdiction and waive a jurisdictional challenge by answering a complaint and, thus, proceeding with the litigation.[11]

6.4.2.1 Personal Jurisdiction

Personal jurisdiction refers to the court's authority to require a party to appear in the forum and its power to make a decision affecting that party. Personal jurisdiction can generally be waived (contrast this with subject matter jurisdiction, which cannot be waived). Thus, if the party being sued appears in a court without

---

9. You may also consider hiring a consulting expert. A consulting expert is someone who becomes part of your legal team that help you to understand the scientific or technical issues in a case. The consulting expert does not testify, and communications between the lawyer and the consulting expert are privileged. In contrast, if you hire a testifying expert to render an opinion and testify, those communications between the lawyer and the expert are not privileged.

10. *See* Fed. R. Civ. P. 12(b). *See also* Swaim v. Moltan Co., 73 F.3d 711, 718 (7th Cir. 1996).

11. *See, e.g.,* Gilmore v. Palestinian Interim Self-Gov't Auth., 843 F.3d 958, 963–65 (D.C. Cir. 2016).

objecting to the court's lack of personal jurisdiction over it, then the court will assume that the defendant is waiving any challenge to personal jurisdiction.[12]

There are three types of personal jurisdiction: 1) jurisdiction over the person; 2) in rem jurisdiction; and 3) quasi in rem jurisdiction. Jurisdiction over the person (also sometimes referred to using the overarching term personal jurisdiction) gives a court the authority to determine the rights and liabilities of a person or entity, such as a corporation or partnership. In rem jurisdiction is implicated when an object or real property, such as a piece of land, is the subject of the legal action. Most often applicable when the possible claimants are unknown, it gives a court the authority to determine title to that object or real property. Quasi in rem jurisdiction is utilized for the purpose of forcing a person or entity to submit itself to the jurisdiction of the court by asserting jurisdiction over the property of that person. Like in rem jurisdiction, it also gives a court the authority to determine title to property, but it is used when the claimants are known.

6.4.2.2 Subject Matter Jurisdiction

Subject matter jurisdiction, or the court's authority to hear a specific kind of claim, comes into play when deciding whether the case will be filed in a federal or state court. To determine this, lawyers must analyze whether a federal court will have the basis to assert subject matter jurisdiction. The U.S. Constitution, Article III, Section 2, outlines the basic framework for federal court jurisdiction.

The two bases for federal subject matter jurisdiction are: 1) diversity of citizenship and the amount in controversy; and 2) federal question jurisdiction. Congress codified federal question jurisdiction in 28 U.S.C. §1331, stating, "The district courts shall have original jurisdiction of all civil actions arising under the Constitution, laws, or treaties of the United States." Diversity of citizenship and amount in controversy jurisdiction, codified in 28 U.S.C. §1332, provides, with some exceptions such as class actions (discussed later in this chapter), that the federal "district courts shall have original jurisdiction of all civil actions where the matter in controversy exceeds the sum or value of $75,000, exclusive of interest and costs, and is between . . . citizens of different States" or citizens of a State and those of a foreign state.[13]

6.4.2.2.1 *Class Action Litigation*

A class action is a representative suit on behalf of a group of people similarly situated. Class action suits aim to promote judicial economy and efficiency, protect defendants from inconsistent findings, protect the interests of absentees, and amplify the means of attorneys to deter wrongdoing by defendants. Class action suits also have far-reaching effects, bringing about institutional and government change and forcing companies to disgorge significant profits if wrongdoing is found. However,

---

12. *See* FED. R. CIV. P. 12(b)(2), (h)(1).
13. 28 U.S.C. § 1332.

before the 2005 enactment of the Class Action Fairness Act (CAFA), class action suits were severely criticized by lobbyists as benefiting attorneys rather than class members and encouraging attorneys to bring unsupported claims against innocent parties, knowing that defendants would rather settle than risk a large judgment against them. Whether or not these concerns were fully or partially legitimate, Congress sought to correct these concerns with the passing of CAFA, with opponents of the legislation arguing that it was merely an attempt to push class actions into federal court where the courts were potentially less amenable to these actions.

CAFA amended the subject matter jurisdiction requirements for certain class actions in several ways that enabled federal courts to exercise diversity jurisdiction in cases that were previously filed in state courts.

First, CAFA gives federal courts original subject matter jurisdiction over class actions in which the aggregated amount in controversy exceeds $5 million, where any member of the plaintiff class is a citizen of a different state than any defendant, and the class includes at least one hundred members.[14]

Second, CAFA permits removal from state to federal court of actions that satisfy the diversity requirement. CAFA also made three major modifications to general removal provisions: 1) it eliminated the one-year time limit on removing cases; 2) it made a defendant's citizenship in the forum state irrelevant; and 3) it allowed for any defendant to remove.

CAFA gives a federal court the discretion to decline jurisdiction if it finds that one-third to two-thirds of the plaintiff class members are from the same state as the primary defendants and the action has various claims that directly link it with a particular state. When exercising this discretion, courts consider whether the claims asserted involved matters of national or interstate interest, whether the claims asserted will be governed by the laws of the state where the action was originally filed or by the laws of other states, and if the class action has been pleaded in a manner that seeks to avoid federal jurisdiction.

6.4.2.3   Venue

Now that we have discussed the first two threshold requirements, personal jurisdiction and subject matter jurisdiction, we will address the third threshold requirement for a court to hear a plaintiff's case: proper venue.[15] Venue refers to the specific court (and the location) in which a case is brought. For a given claim, there is not always a single venue that is appropriate. In each city, county, state, or country, there may be many courts in which a case may be brought, though one specific court may be more appropriate or proper than another. Notably, all other

---

14. 28 U.S.C. § 1332(d).
15. Unlike personal jurisdiction, however, there is no constitutional requirement for proper venue in order to have a valid judgment.

jurisdictional requirements must be satisfied before venue can even be considered. It should be the final part of your assessment after you have determined which courts would have jurisdiction over your claims. In other words, for a court to be a proper venue, it first must have jurisdiction to hear the case. However, even when personal jurisdiction exists, venue may still be inappropriate.

Determining proper venue is essentially a question of convenience and justice. The federal venue rules seek to ensure that the case takes place in a forum that is convenient for the parties, and that the plaintiff does not choose a court that is unfair to the defendant. The federal venue statute, 28 U.S.C. §1391, provides venue is appropriate in a federal court, based on: 1) where the defendants reside; 2) where the underlying events occurred or relevant property is located; or 3) in the rare situation where neither of the above two options will work, wherever a defendant is subject to personal jurisdiction.[16]

6.4.2.3.1   *Choosing a Venue*

Whether or not a case may be filed in federal or state court is not mutually exclusive because jurisdiction often overlaps. When there is a choice, how does one decide where to file? Some considerations:

- Where will the case move to trial quicker?

- Which forum(s) is most familiar with the law?

- Which procedural and evidentiary rules are most favorable to the case?

- Which court is more likely to certify a class, grant an injunction, and/or allow an expert?

- Where is the attorney more comfortable?

- Is removal to federal court a possibility?

- Where will a judge or jurors be most sympathetic to the lawsuit?

Additionally, if your case is a contract dispute, be sure to examine the contract for a forum selection clause. If the parties agreed on a particular court or forum in their contract, you must file in that forum or be prepared to establish why the clause should not be honored.

As noted above, venue is often appropriate in more than one judicial district and in some cases a court will transfer a case to a more suitable district.[17] While transfer

---

16. 28 U.S.C. § 1391.
17. *See* 28 U.S.C. § 1404 (governing the transfer of venue in the federal court system). It should be noted that a federal court cannot transfer a case to a state court or a court in another country, only to another federal court.

of venue is outside the scope of this chapter, the federal venue transfer statute can be instructive on important considerations for determining the most appropriate forum. Because these requests are made on the basis of "convenience" or "in the interest of justice," the court will apply both public and private factors to determine whether to transfer a case. The private factors include: 1) ease of access to evidence; 2) availability of compulsory process to cause witnesses to participate in the case; 3) cost for willing witnesses to participate; and 4) other practical considerations that would make a trial easy, speedy, and inexpensive. The public factors include: 1) administrative difficulties resulting from court congestion; 2) local interest in having the case decided in the original forum; 3) familiarity of the forum with the law that governs the case; and 4) avoidance of difficulties in conflicts of law or the application of foreign law. If you anticipate the defendant will object to your selected venue, be prepared to address the factors above if they seek to transfer venue to another court.

If it seems like we are reciting rules or statutory provisions in this chapter, you are not mistaken. Too often lawyers, particularly new lawyers, seeking a career in litigation believe much of what they need to know can only be acquired through experience. It is true that experience hones the skills of many good lawyers. However, a new lawyer driven by fear of failure, who painstakingly parses through procedural and evidentiary rules, can often outmaneuver experienced lawyers who abandon reliance on the letter of the rules.

Experienced lawyers must revisit these rules and keep updated copies. The rule of law is dynamic, not static. As modes of travel and communication change, the rules of jurisdiction and venue also change. Similarly, pleading standards and discovery requirements are also subject to modifications.

These considerations apply not only to the plaintiff, but also are relevant to defense counsel contemplating a petition to remove the case from state court to federal court. Forum decisions require due consideration. Lawyers who are familiar with the local venues are a valuable resource for advice.

6.5   *Choosing a Partner or Local Counsel*

Litigation is always about choosing the right team. This is a rule for lawyers, in-house counsel, and clients. A lawyer may know the client and their business well, but do they know the jurisdiction where the litigation will occur, the technical area of the case, or the science required to translate expert knowledge to usable testimony? A solo practitioner just needing extra help with a case might consider teaming with a partner who can advance some of the costs.

Assembling a litigation team is critical for both plaintiffs and defendants. If primary counsel is not admitted in the jurisdiction where litigation will occur, securing local counsel is an obvious first step.

Local counsel may assume the following roles:

- File a motion on behalf of the lead or "foreign counsel" for pro hac vice admission.

- Conform pleadings to local standards.

- File pleadings.

- Provide advice on local rules.

- Provide guidance regarding the proclivities of local judges.

Local counsel can contribute significantly by revealing the proclivities of local judges. Lead counsel can make strategic decisions once they know how a court may approach various issues, ranging from substantive areas of the law to discovery disputes to the handling of exhibits in court. Local counsel can also warn against courtroom conduct that may agitate the judge. While some judges are indifferent to counsel wandering around the courtroom, others detest it and demand that counsel remains behind the podium. Some judges allow counsel to hand exhibits directly to a witness and others require clerks to hand the witness an exhibit. Local counsel can also provide guidance on courtroom capabilities such as screens to show PowerPoint presentations.

The best way to "know your judge" is to go to that judge's courtroom and watch. You would have a clear picture of how to approach issues after observing my courtroom for only thirty minutes. I'm surprised that only a few lawyers do this.

—Justin Victor, Of Counsel, Greenberg Traurig LLP

Knowledgeable local counsel can advise on whether a case should even be brought in their venue. Perhaps a local law presents issues or maybe the case will not resonate with the local jury pool.

Even when a lawyer is admitted in a particular jurisdiction, finding local counsel can still be beneficial. Suppose a Manhattan attorney intends to bring a case in Rochester. Hiring a Rochester local counsel, who knows both the court system and the lawyers who may be your local opposition, can be very advantageous. Suppose you need a deadline extension, want to negotiate a discovery schedule, or have procedural issues suitable for negotiation. Having someone in the local community familiar with opposing counsel can help resolve those issues. Even having local counsel say to their local counterpart, "Judge Jones will not want to hear this dispute and will want us to work it out," can be a very powerful message.

Whether finding local counsel or adding to your litigation team, selecting lawyers for the case should not be a haphazard endeavor. Talk to other lawyers and former judges; concentrate on candidates based on their litigation experience and results. Ask whether they have time for the case or will they give the work to a partner or associate? Evaluate their work history. Was their knowledge of the court system gained through a clerkship, as a former judge, as a prosecutor, or public defender?

Although most cases are resolved before trial, have someone on the team that can either try the case or guide the attorney through trial (if the attorney lacks trial experience). Consider adding lawyers with considerable trial experience or those with both trial experience and knowledge of the case subject area. Consider litigation of a ground water contamination case: someone with environmental law experience, who worked with hydrogeologists, or collaborated with the type of experts who may eventually testify would be a valuable addition to the legal team.

CHAPTER SEVEN

INITIATING THE LITIGATION

7.1 Introduction

You and your client decide the dispute cannot be resolved absent filing a lawsuit. The lawsuit alleges key facts from your investigation, including those relayed to you orally by your client and other witnesses. Key facts also originate from client documents and Internet-sourced public documents including newspapers, magazines, filed lawsuits, and government reports and statements.

Before advising a client to embark on a civil lawsuit, you must explain that no matter if they win or lose, they will commit the next several years to this ordeal emotionally, psychologically, and financially. Being a party to a lawsuit is all-encompassing and often becomes an identity. At the end, they will never get those years back. A client must understand this before making an informed choice.

—Priya Chaudhry, Founding Partner, ChaudhryLaw PLLC

The complaint marks a seminal point in the litigation process. Once on the path to trial, you are subject to motions to dismiss, motions for summary judgment, and motions in limine. These motions can eliminate some, or all, of your claims. Moreover, even if your case proceeds to trial, some or all of the claims may be untenable, depending on the court's rulings relating to evidentiary matters. If you are the plaintiff, some or all of your claims may be dismissed on a directed verdict, which can occur before the defense puts on its case. And finally, the jury could rule for or against you on some or all of the claims. Post-trial motions may also set aside some or all of the claims—and then there are appeals. It may sound like the risks are all one-sided; however, they are not. Every pretrial procedural loss for the plaintiff alters the odds and perhaps makes settlement more costly.

7.2 Strategic Drafting

Along the litigation path, settlement opportunities will arise. After all, the process is designed to prompt settlement. Yet, just as the process drives settlement, it also elicits emotion. Details in complaints, answers, motions, and judicial hearings often become obsessions for the parties. The process provokes anger and the abandonment of objectivity. Of course, emotions vary depending on the parties and the issue at hand. Is the dispute between individuals or companies? Is there an insurance carrier involved or will the defendant pay the bill? Was there a breach of contract? Does the matter involve divorce, discrimination, or fraud? Does the complaint prompt parties to talk resolution or does it cause the defendant to dig in their heels and fight to vindicate their reputation? Does it matter how the complaint styles the allegations or whether the causes of action insinuate attacks on the defendant's character? Does fraud, when added as a second cause of action to a breach of contract claim, make settlement more difficult or does it add leverage, driving a quicker settlement?

How you draft the complaint and select legal causes of action (or theories) can impact settlement windows. In all cases, the plaintiff's goal is surviving dispositive motions and getting to a jury. Focus on these objectives. Such a strategy opens settlement windows along the way. Some legal theories, however, trigger reactions from defendants that foreclose settlement opportunities. When faced with a complaint, defendants consider the following:

- Is my reputation impugned and should I aggressively defend it?

- Will settlement set a bad precedent, encouraging others to sue me?

- Will settlement arouse suspicion of guilt from regulators or criminal prosecutors?

- Will my insurance cover litigation costs?

- Will my insurance pay for a settlement?

- Will discovery make information public that could impact my reputation or my brand, or cause regulatory problems?

- Will defending the action divert resources?

Given these considerations, different legal theories elicit different reactions from the defendant. The chart below separates theories into four categories.

The Four Categories of Civil Disputes

(I) Complaints with "personal" claims that are initially polarizing	(II) Complaints with potential regulatory or criminal implications that are initially polarizing and can have settlement complexities	(III) Claims involving "vanilla" business disputes that tend to trigger negotiations	(IV) Claims that may be personal but involve insurance are more likely to settle
Fraud	Antitrust	Breach of Contract	Negligence
Discrimination	Securities	Debt Collection	Breach of Fiduciary Duty
Breach of Fiduciary Duty	Environmental		Legal Malpractice
Family Law			Defamation
Breach of Employment Contract			
Business Interference			

In every dispute, apply legal theories that can lead to resolution. Consider, for example, a situation where a hotel owner advertises that his hotel's amenities include an indoor pool, three restaurants, and a daily maid service. Aaron Verosky reads the advertisement, books a five-hour flight, and arrives at the hotel only to find the indoor pool without water, all three restaurants closed for renovation, and the maid service is on strike. Aaron retains counsel. His counsel sends several demand letters to the hotel owner requesting damages but receives no response. Aaron and his lawyer decide to file suit. The facts provide several legal theories for recovery. First, he can sue for breach of contract, claiming the hotel brochure and its advertisements created a contract. However, this theory has limitations. The defendant may argue that there was no express contract. In addition, even if Aaron were to win a contract case, he might not recover consequential damages including the airfare costs.[1] On the other hand, Aaron could plead a fraud case and allege the defendant knowingly misrepresented the hotel's offerings. The fraud case might allow Aaron to recover the airfare along with punitive damages and perhaps even emotional distress. The fraud case is not without flaws either. Defendant will argue he placed the

---

1. *See, e.g.*, Hadley v. Baxendale, 156 Eng. Rep. 145 (1854) (holding no consequential damages are awarded when the breaching party is unaware of the special circumstances causing the damage).

advertisement many months ago, when the hotel was in full operation, and did not intend to deceive Aaron. A fraud claim may require intent to deceive at the time the misrepresentation or fraudulent omission occurs. Alternatively, Aaron could plead a cause of action for negligence. Under this theory, Aaron would argue the hotel owner owed a duty to review advertising for accuracy of content and failed to do so.

Each theory for contract, fraud, and negligence has pros and cons. A fraud claim may require proof by clear and convincing evidence, whereas claims for breach of contract might only require proof by a preponderance of the evidence. Fraud or breach of contract claims may not be insured, whereas a claim for negligence is more likely to be insured. Pleading an insured claim often involves a carrier who views the cause of action objectively and may be more inclined to settle. This is important because each of these claims generate different emotional impacts. For example, a breach of contract accusation is less an attack on someone's integrity than is a claim for fraud. Moreover, a negligence claim speaks more to a mistake or error than even a breach of contract case.

Finally, when it comes to selecting the cause(s) of action, theory selection is not a zero-sum game. Plaintiffs often choose multiple causes of action; there is a rationale for doing so. Some causes are easy to prove, other causes expand potential damages, and combining causes may force a defendant to defend one cause of action by admitting to another. The hotel owner's defense of the fraud claim may generate an admission of facts that sets up a negligence claim. Unfortunately, there is no perfect choice. An insurance carrier may provide an objective party, and a deep pocket, to resolve the dispute. However, insurance carriers may decline to defend altogether, or defend under reservation of a right to back out if it deems the cause of action is not covered by the policy.

Which "counts" should be pled is dependent on the client's goals, the client's resources, and their tolerance for protracted litigation, as well as whether an insurance carrier is involved and the particularities of the defendant. The combination of legal theories that you will choose is unique to every fact pattern and set of defendants and plaintiffs. Once you choose the theories, reverse engineer the case and determine whether those theories make the defenses easier or more difficult. You are, in essence, playing chess. There are basic considerations in terms of moves, and maybe even some established moves, but every game is different and every opponent is different.

7.3 Theory Selection

In addition to causes of action, the word "theory," often used in litigation, conveys a number of things. Theory involves applying facts to a point of law. Cases consist of theories on many different points. There are liability theories, damages theories, and sub-theories about causation and mitigation.

Lawyers do not have a real-time, bird's-eye view of the events giving rise to a claim. Lawyers instead have theories about what happened. Theories are supported by facts organized in a particular way. When juxtaposed against a legal cause of action, theories formulate claims or defenses.

Lawyers choose theories to create efficiencies in litigation, streamline or enable proof, or disable defenses. Theory selection can complicate or simplify a case. A theory of what happened can lead to more than one legal cause of action. Consider the following example:

Defendant enters into a contract to pay $10,000 for his daughter's wedding. The third installment of $3,000 is due two days after the wedding. The defendant does not make the payment. One cause of action, or theory of liability, is the defendant breached the contract by not making the final payment. In this scenario, the damages are $3,000 and may include interest. A second cause of action is a fraud claim. Fraud presents an opportunity to secure punitive damages. However, proving fraud is difficult, requiring both an intent to deceive and actual reliance on what was or was not said i.e., a "fraudulent omission."

But are we interested in a clever application of the law, or a theory that hangs together; one that at the end of the day is believable? Do we believe the defendant entered into the contract never intending to fulfill its terms or do we believe the defendant just ran out of money? What are the facts? Does our claim rely on far-fetched inferences or do hard facts exist to support the fraud claim?

Consider where the client wants to be at the end of the day. A vanilla breach of contract claim for $3,000 is not a personal attack. In contrast, a fraud claim may immediately polarize the parties and impede an expeditious, amicable resolution. Though a fraud claim elevates the potential for higher recovery, the litigation's incremental costs may outweigh the risk of no resolution or a resolution difficult to achieve. Moreover, a fraud claim may communicate the plaintiff "overreached," indicating to the court that the plaintiff's credibility is questionable.

Selecting the causes of action and theory development about different facets of the case requires client discussions. It is not just the lawyer who has the burden of dealing with certain theories. Suppose, for example, the client says, "do whatever you can do to get me the biggest recovery."[2] The case proceeds to discovery and the defendant serves a document request for the plaintiff's psychiatric and medical records along with a request for the plaintiff to undergo an independent psychiatric examination. Upon learning of these requests, the client accuses the lawyer of failing to communicate that the additional claim for emotional distress invited expansive personal discovery. The client threatens termination and demands the

---

2. The lawyer pleads actual damages and emotional distress. Actual damages are those damages directly related to the alleged wrongdoing; damages attributable to emotional distress is compensation for the impact of the wrongful conduct on the plaintiff's mental state.

emotional distress claim be dropped. The end result is a weakened litigation position and a delay of potential case resolution.

7.4   The Complaint: The Process Begins with Factual Allegations

All civil cases begin with a complaint. The complaint puts your vision of the case on paper. Complaints set forth allegations, supported by legal theories. They are filed with the court and then served on the defendant. The complaint has two primary audiences: the judge and the defendant. Depending on the complaint's nature, it may be discovered by media with easy access to court filings stored in electronic format. To be clear, a complaint filed in court is generally a matter of public record and reporters routinely review public filings.

The judge evaluates the allegations' sufficiency and determines whether the action proceeds to the next stage of litigation: discovery. The complaint may be the first time the defendant and his counsel see the specific factual allegations matched to legal theories.

In federal court, and in states with analogous rules, the pleading standard is fully governed by FRCP 8. FRCP 8 states the following:

> **(a) Claim for Relief.** A pleading that states a claim for relief must contain:
>
> > **(1)** a short and plain statement of the grounds for the court's jurisdiction, unless the court already has jurisdiction and the claim needs no new jurisdictional support;
> >
> > **(2)** a short and plain statement of the claim showing that the pleader is entitled to relief; and
> >
> > **(3)** a demand for the relief sought, which may include relief in the alternative or different types of relief.[3]

A plaintiff alleging fraud or mistake must also meet the requirements of FRCP 9(b). That section states:

> **(b) Fraud or Mistake; Conditions of Mind.** In alleging fraud or mistake, a party must state with particularity the circumstances constituting fraud or mistake. Malice, intent, knowledge, and other conditions of a person's mind may be alleged generally.[4]

---

3. Fed. R. Civ. P. 8.
4. Fed. R. Civ. P. 9(b).

7.4.1 Evolution of the Pleading Standard

In 1957, the Supreme Court adopted a standard long-referred to as the "notice pleading" standard. In *Conley v. Gibson*, the plaintiff alleged discrimination claims and the defendant argued "the complaint failed to set forth specific facts to support its general allegations of discrimination, and that its dismissal is therefore proper."[5] Writing for the majority, Justice Black opined:

> The decisive answer to this is that the Federal Rules of Civil Procedure do not require a claimant to set out in detail the facts upon which he bases his claim. To the contrary, all the Rules require is "a short and plain statement of the claim" that will give the defendant fair notice of what the plaintiff's claim is and the grounds upon which it rests.[6]

The Court also noted:

> . . .[t]he Federal Rules reject the approach that pleading is a game of skill in which one misstep by counsel may be decisive to the outcome, and accept the principle that the purpose of pleading is to facilitate a proper decision on the merits.[7]

For a half-century, law schools taught, and lawyers practiced, the *Conley* notice pleading standard. In 2007, the unthinkable happened. The Supreme Court overturned its own notice pleading standard in *Bell Atlantic v. Twombly*.[8] The Court cemented the new standard two years later in *Ashcroft v. Iqbal*,[9] a case more factually consistent with *Conley*. In *Twombly*, the Court grappled with an antitrust case involving allegations of parallel pricing. The Court opined:

> Federal Rule of Civil Procedure 8(a)(2) requires only "a short and plain statement of the claim showing that the pleader is entitled to relief," in order to "give the defendant fair notice of what the . . . claim is and the grounds upon which it rests," *Conley v. Gibson*, 355 U.S. 41. While a complaint attacked by a Rule 12(b)(6) motion to dismiss does not need detailed factual allegations, *ibid.*, a plaintiff's obligation to provide the "grounds" of his "entitle[ment] to relief" requires more than labels and conclusions, and a formulaic recitation of a cause of action's elements will not do. Factual allegations must be enough to raise a right to relief above the speculative level on the assumption that all of the complaint's allegations are true.[10]

---

5. Conley v. Gibson, 355 U.S. 41, 47 (1957).
6. *Id.*
7. *Id.* at 48.
8. Bell Atl. Corp. v. Twombly, 550 U.S. 544 (2007).
9. Ashcroft v. Iqbal, 556 U.S. 662 (2009).
10. *Twombly*, 550 U.S. at 555.

If the *Twombly* decision left any doubt regarding whether the new pleading standard was limited to antitrust cases, *Iqbal* eliminated such doubt. In *Iqbal*, the Court dealt with allegations that a prisoner was denied constitutional rights because of his religious beliefs. The *Iqbal* court, following the logic in *Twombly*, first explained that,

> A pleading that offers "labels and conclusions" or "a formulaic reci-
> tation of the elements of a cause of action will not do." Nor does a
> complaint suffice if it tenders "naked assertion[s]" devoid of "further
> factual enhancement." To survive a motion to dismiss, a complaint
> must contain sufficient factual matter, accepted as true, to "state a
> claim to relief that is plausible on its face." A claim has facial plausi-
> bility when the plaintiff pleads factual content that allows the court
> to draw the reasonable inference that the defendant is liable for the
> misconduct alleged. The plausibility standard is not akin to a "proba-
> bility requirement," but it asks for more than a sheer possibility that a
> defendant has acted unlawfully."[11]

The ultimate logic of both *Iqbal* and *Twombly* is for courts to strip out conclusory allegations, focus solely on the facts, and determine whether a complaint states a plausible claim.

Reception to the new pleading standards was mixed. In professional circles, some practitioners—particularly defense lawyers—welcomed the change and applauded its timeliness, arriving when courts were inundated with lawsuits. In other circles, scholars and plaintiff's lawyers characterized the rulings as a mechanism to cut litigation short, absent full and complete discovery.[12] To a large extent the most salient attack has been to the plausibility standard, which some argue provides a basis for judges to impose a subjective view of the claims. To the extent that this occurs, theorists argue—of course—that the plausibility standard means that judges are given the latitude to do more than "call balls and strikes"; rather they have leeway to define the strike zone.

In an Iqbal/Twombly world, attorneys must distinguish between facts and conclusions, collect those facts, and assemble them to plead cases according to the new plausibility standard. Regardless of whether one agrees with the new standard, it

---

11. *Iqbal*, 556 U.S. at 678 (citations omitted).
12. *E.g.*, Arthur Miller, *From Conley to Twombly to Iqbal: A Double Play on the Federal Rules of Civil Procedure*, 60 Duke L. J. 1 (2010); A. Benjamin Spencer, *Pleading Conditions of the Mind Under Rule 9(b): Repairing the Damage Wrought by Iqbal*, 41 Cardozo L. Rev. 1015 (2020). Law professor A. Benjamin Spencer argues *Iqbal*'s majority opinion advanced an erroneous interpretation of FRCP 9(b) when it held that FRCP 8(a)(2)'s plausibility pleading standard applied to FRCP 9(b)'s second sentence, "Malice, intent, knowledge, and other conditions of a person's mind may be alleged generally." Spencer alleges this interpretation is inconsistent with the original understanding of Rule 9(b) and resulted in many adverse consequences.

forces counsel to begin the litigation process by boiling a case down to the facts. How does one distinguish a fact from a conclusion? Consider this statement: "Joe Smith was terminated from employment because of his religion." Under the Iqbal standard, this is arguably a conclusion. Counsel must find facts supporting this conclusion. "While legal conclusions can provide the framework of a complaint, they must be supported by factual allegations."[13]

IQBAL/TWOMBLY Analysis
Complaint = Facts and Conclusions
Court only looks at the facts
Court determines if factual allegations create plausible claims
If claims are plausible, then the complaint is sustained

From the judge's vantage point, let's dissect the core allegations of two complaints alleging discrimination.

Core allegations of complaint 1:

1) Plaintiff, who is Jewish, was employed by Roxy Trucking, Inc. until his termination on December 21, 2019.

2) Despite performing his job well, Roxy Trucking, Inc. terminated plaintiff based on his religion.

3) Defendant's conduct was outrageous and violated Title VII of the Civil Rights Act of 1964, 42 U.S.C. § 2000e.

Core allegations of complaint 2:

1) Plaintiff Jerry Cole, who is Jewish, was employed as a financial analyst for Roxy Trucking, Inc. from 2004 until December 21, 2019.

2) On or about December 15, 2018, the Piper Group purchased Roxy Trucking, Inc. Subsequent to the purchase, the Piper Group appointed Joseph Orange as the supervisor over the financial analysts at Roxy.

3) On December 24, 2018, Orange emailed plaintiff inquiring: "What will you be doing for Christmas?" Plaintiff responded: "We are Jewish, we do not celebrate Christmas."

4) On December 26, 2018, Orange emailed plaintiff stating: "I have been thinking about it, and I don't understand why you do not celebrate Christmas, do you not celebrate the birth of Jesus?"

5) On April 16, 2019, Orange emailed all ten analysts at the Piper Group

---

13. *Iqbal*, 556 U.S. at 679.

wishing them a "Happy Easter," noting that: "Of course this goes to everyone except Cole."

6) On or about September 21, 2019, Orange emailed plaintiff stating: "I hear there is another Jewish holiday, don't tell me you are taking time off."

7) On or about November 1, 2019, Orange gave plaintiff his performance review which contained the following comments:

- Attendance not acceptable; took too many days off claiming religious holidays.

- Will only work on Sundays and needs to be available on Saturdays for work.

- Needs to fit in more, not sure if this is possible.

8) As a result of his performance evaluation, plaintiff was put on probation.

9) On December 21, 2019, Orange emailed plaintiff and stated: "You are being terminated. You do not fit in. I wish you the best."

For a defense lawyer, the first complaint is a softball pitch and presents an opportunity to move for dismissal citing the *Iqbal/Twombly* standard. The first core allegation relating to the plaintiff's religion and place of employment is factual; however, the remaining allegations are conclusory. Therefore, the judge is left with three usable facts: the plaintiff is Jewish, he was employed by the defendant, and the plaintiff was terminated. The judge must leap to conclude the termination was plausibly related to religion.

The second complaint presents a challenge for a defense lawyer. The nine core allegations are purely factual. None of the allegations contain direct evidence. However, the totality of the circumstantial evidence allows for an argument of inference that the termination was at least, in part, based on religion. Even if no direct evidence of the impropriety exists, causes of action can be based on circumstantial evidence. Indeed FRE 401 does not use the words "circumstantial" or "direct." Evidence is evidence and it is for jurors weigh or value its worth.

The attorney must piece the circumstantial evidence together in a narrative form and then argue the inference. Of course, if the circumstantial evidence is properly organized and presented, the facts will make the argument. What do we mean by this? Often facts laid out in the form of a narrative lead the listener or decision maker to reach a conclusion on their own. Imagine, for example, a puzzle of the United States. If you in place twenty pieces in the right place, you may not need to tell someone watching that it is a map of the United States; that conclusion will be evident.

Changes to the pleading standard arguably affected complaints, making them longer. Two reasons explain why this happened. First, conclusions by definition are encapsulations of multiple facts. The *Iqbal/Twombly* pleading standard forces lawyers to unpack simple conclusions and allege the multiple facts supporting the conclusions. Second, because the plausibility standard gave judges latitude to evaluate the sufficiency of a complaint, plaintiff attorneys sometimes feel compelled to over-plead so they have ample information to cite to when opposing a motion to dismiss and arguing the plausibility of the causes of action. Recall the first complaint contained three core allegations while the lengthier second complaint contained nine allegations.

7.4.2   FRCP 9(b)

When pleading fraud or mistake, plaintiffs must pay special attention to FRCP 9(b) which requires a party to "state with particularity the circumstances constituting fraud or mistake. Malice, intent, knowledge, and other conditions of a person's mind may be alleged generally."[14]

The 9(b) requirement applies to all common-law fraud claims, RICO statute claims, state false claims, and federal and state FCA claims. To some degree, the heightened pleading standard imposed by *Iqbal/Twombly* under FRPC 8(a) made FRCP 9(b) superfluous. Still, defense lawyers brief FRCP 9(b) in motions to dismiss, arguing a common law of FRCP 9(b), which creates requirements particular to certain claims that fall within its orbit.[15] When contemplating a fraud claim, anticipate pleading your complaint with particularity.[16]

7.4.3   Standing

Plaintiffs have the burden of demonstrating subject matter jurisdiction. FRCP 12(b) sets forth seven defenses:

---

14. FED. R. CIV. P. 9(b).

15. *See, e.g.*, United States ex rel. Wollman v. Gen. Hosp. Corp., 394 F. Supp. 3d 174, 187 (D. Mass. 2019) (explaining that in a False Claims Act action, FRCP 9(b)'s heightened pleading standard requires a relator to "provide details that identify particular false claims for payment that were submitted to the government." "[M]erely alleging facts related to a defendant's alleged *misconduct* is not enough . . . Rather, a [FCA complaint] must 'sufficiently establish that false claims were submitted for government payment' as a result of the defendant's alleged misconduct." (citations omitted)).

16. *Id.* at 188-189 (The district court judge denied defendant's motion to dismiss for failure to state a claim and held the relator pled fraud with sufficient particularity. "She provides notable detail with respect to the commonplace occurrence of overlapping surgeries at MGH, including the date, surgeon, start time, location, duration, and type of surgery for numerous procedures." The relator also "provided specific . . . identification numbers, amounts billed . . . and amounts paid for several claims . . ." In addition, the judge confirmed the relator adequately pled scienter "by identifying specific allegedly false claims and alleging a broader scheme to defraud Medicare and Medicaid that was supported by active concealment of concurrent surgeries from patients and intentionally restricted record-keeping practices designed to avoid government detection." (citations omitted)).

(b) How to Present Defenses. Every defense to a claim for relief in any pleading must be asserted in the responsive pleading if one is required. But a party may assert the following defenses by motion:

(1) lack of subject-matter jurisdiction;

(2) lack of personal jurisdiction;

(3) improper venue;

(4) insufficient process;

(5) insufficient service of process;

(6) failure to state a claim upon which relief can be granted; and

(7) failure to join a party under Rule 19.[17]

A FRCP 12(b)(6) motion to dismiss arises from the failure to meet *Iqbal/Twombly* standards: assuming the truth of the facts pled, the case is either implausible or does not state a legal cause of action.

While an FRCP 12(b)(6) motion addresses the merits of the case, a 12(b)(1) motion addresses the court's ability to hear the case. A court cannot hear a case if it lacks subject matter jurisdiction or the plaintiff lacks standing. FRCP 12(b)(1) arguments include constitutional impairments, such as no "injury in fact,"[18] mootness, or ripeness for adjudication. In addition to constitutional standing challenges, another argument is standing under the statute, known as prudential standing. For example, a defendant in an antitrust case may argue the indirectness of the plaintiff's injury prohibits filing suit under federal antitrust laws for treble damages.[19] In *Fair Housing Council of Suburban Philadelphia v. Montgomery Newspapers*, the Third Circuit provided an analysis of the standing requirements.

> The standing inquiry in most cases is two-tiered, involving "both constitutional limitations on federal-court jurisdiction and prudential limitations on its exercise." First, a plaintiff must satisfy the "case" or "controversy" requirement of Article III. This requirement has been described as "immutable," and as the "irreducible constitutional minimum." The standing requirements embodied in the "case" or "controversy" provision of Article III mean that in every case, the plaintiff must be able to demonstrate:

---

17. Fed. R. Civ. P. 12(b).
18. Fair Hous. Council v. Montgomery Newspapers, 141 F.3d 71, 74 (3d Cir. 1998).
19. *See, e.g.*, Associated Gen. Contractors v. Cal. State Council of Carpenters, 459 U.S. 519, 541 (1983).

An "injury in fact—an invasion of a judicially cognizable interest which is (a) concrete and particularized and (b) actual or imminent, not conjectural or hypothetical; second, there be a causal connection between the injury and the conduct complained of-the injury has to be "fairly trace[able] to the challenged action of the defendant, and not . . . the result [of] the independent action of some third party not before the court". Third, it must be "likely," as opposed to merely "specula-tive," that the injury will be "redressed by a favorable decision." Each of these elements of Article III standing "must be supported in the same way as any other matter on which the plaintiff bears the burden of proof, i.e., with the manner and degree of evidence required at the successive stages of the litigation."[20]

When drafting a complaint, anticipate a 12(b)(1) challenge. With 12(b)(6) motions, courts judge the sufficiency of the complaint by analyzing the face of the complaint and any documents incorporated by reference. But when a 12(b)(1) motion asserts a jurisdictional issue, extraneous evidence may be offered for the court's consideration. In some cases, jurisdictional questions become a matter for discovery. Remember that jurisdiction cannot be waived and may be introduced and reintroduced at any time.

7.5   Complaint Format

Complaints generally have a basic format including an introduction, allegations of jurisdiction and venue, allegations about the parties, allegations of fact, the counts, and a prayer for relief. Yet, complaints can vary markedly depending on the facts, the novelty of the causes of actions, or the complexity of the area of law. Claims for fraud, injunctive relief, and class actions include additional pleading requirements. As a guiding rule: do not overcomplicate a simple case and do not under plead a complex matter.

---

20. *Fair Hous. Council*, 141 F.3d at 74 (citations omitted). While writing this book, the Supreme Court decided a case regarding whether nominal damages satisfy the redressability requirement of Article III standing. Uzuegbunam v. Preczewski, 592 U.S. ___ (2021). The Court, in an 8-1 decision, held that a request for nominal damages satisfies the redressability element of standing when plaintiff's claim is based on a completed violation of a legal right. *Id.* at 11. Chief Justice Roberts, the lone dissenter, criticized the majority stating that judges would now function as "advice columnists." *Id.* at 3 (Roberts, C.J., dissenting). While it is too early to tell the effect of this decision in the federal courts, it is important not to underestimate the power of a claim of nominal damages to satisfy redressability.

Below are three charts outlining the variations of complaints:

BASIC COMPLAINT		
I.	Introduction	
II.	Jurisdiction and Venue	
III.	Parties	
IV.	Facts	
V.	Counts	
VI.	Prayer for Relief	Wherefore, plaintiff seeks [X].

COMPLAINT FOR INJUNCTION		
I.	Introduction	
II.	Jurisdiction and Venue	
III.	Parties	
IV.	Facts	
V.	Injunction Allegations	a) No adequate remedy at law because [X]. b) Plaintiff will suffer irreparable harm because [X]. c) An injunction serves the public interest better because [X].
VI.	Injunction Pleadings	a) Count for injunctive relief b) Wherefore, plaintiff requests that the court issue an order which restrains the defendant from [X].
VII.	Prayer for Relief	Wherefore, plaintiff seeks [X].

COMPLAINT IN COMPLEX CASE		
I.	Introduction	
II.	Jurisdiction and Venue	
III.	Parties	
IV.	Overview of the Law	

(continued)

V.	Class Action Allegations	a) Class definition. b) Allegations of numerosity. c) Allegations of questions involving commonality of law and fact. d) Allegations that claims or defenses of the representative parties are typical. e) Allegations that the representative parties will fairly and adequately protect the interests of the class. f) Allegations as to whether the class is a FRCP 23(a) or FRCP 23(b) class.
VI.	Facts	
VII.	Counts	
VIII.	Prayer for Relief	Wherefore, plaintiff seeks [X].

As illustrated above, each cause of action may require a different type of complaint. If the case is simple, the goal of the complaint is not to overcomplicate the pleading.

Complaints for injunctive relief fall into two categories; those seeking to prohibit conduct from occurring and those seeking to mandate the occurrence of conduct. In either case, the essence of the cause of action is to secure quick relief. With complaints for injunctive relief, prohibiting conduct that may cause irreparable harm is a simpler hurdle than mandating a defendant to engage in conduct.[21] The two types of injunctions are known as mandatory and prohibitory injunctions. Often, those seeking injunctive relief can cast their claim as one for prohibitory relief in order to decrease the litigation burden. Suppose, for example, a labor union seeks an injunction to mandate that a meat packing company provide face masks and personal protective equipment (PPE) to line workers. That same relief can also be cast as a prohibitory injunction by prohibiting the defendant from violating CDC guidance, which requires the provision of PPE.

Applying a complex set of facts to a complex area of law (particularly class actions) requires a more detailed complaint. A complaint essentially describes a dispute. When formulating this description, be mindful of judges' massive court dockets with thousands of cases covering a broad range of laws and fact patterns.

---

21. *See,* Rural Cmty. Workers All. v. Smithfield Foods, Inc., 45 F.Supp. 3d 1228 (W.D. Mo. 2020) (Preliminary injunctive relief "is an 'extraordinary and drastic remedy, one that should not be granted unless the movant, by a clear showing, carries the burden of persuasion.'"); North Dakota v. U.S. Army Corps of Eng'rs, 264 F. Supp. 2d 871, 878 (D. N.D. 2003) ("This burden is particularly great where, as here, plaintiffs seek a preliminary injunction requiring an affirmative act.").

How can you make their job easier? How can you make them care about your dispute? What will get their attention?

7.5.1   The Role of the Introduction

Always start complaints with an introduction. The introduction is an executive summary, articulating the theories and establishing a theme for the causes of action. The theme is "why people care about this case." It has an emotional impact on the decision maker. Use it to inoculate them against counter themes, which may include an argument that the plaintiff's victory will have broad sweeping negative ramifications.

When drafting the introduction, keep in mind that courts are overburdened. It is possible the judge and/or his clerks will only read the introduction. Perhaps they read the entire complaint but glance at the introduction on the day of argument to remind themselves of the facts. Or, maybe the clerks draft a bench memo for the judge, using the introduction as a quick way to get their heads around the case.

In a simple breach of contract case the introduction can be short, as in this example:

> This matter arises out of contract to fabricate a roof, with a twenty-year unlimited warranty, for a domestic dwelling. Plaintiff John Smith paid $10,000 to defendant, "Roofs are Great, Inc." Within one year of the roof's fabrication, it collapsed. Plaintiff Smith seeks recovery in contract and negligence and seeks the recovery of $10,000 and damages attributable to collapse.

If the judge or his clerks read nothing else, they glean the essence of the case from these four sentences.

In complex cases, the introduction is much longer. An introduction should convey a theme, present the theories, and inoculate against defenses. The example below is the first paragraph of a complicated nine-page introduction to a 109-page complaint:

Case 1:07-cv-00081-JPJ-PMS   Document 54   Filed 06/15/10
Page 6 Or 68   Page id#: 269

**Filed Under Seal Pursuant
To 31 U.S.C. § 3730(b)(2)**

1.   INTRODUCTION
   1.   One of the most frightening and devasting disease of our time is Alzheimer's. It is simultaneously terrifying and heartbreaking. It renders its victims powerless, requiring them to rely upon the conscientiousness of those charged with their care. This case is about a company—Abbott Laboratories—that methodically and recklessly

---

(continued)

> endangered this vulnerable population—those with Alzheimer's and other forms of dementia—through the illegal marketing of a drug that Abbott knew was unapproved for the treatment of Alzheimer's, did not work to treat the disease, and was actually dangerous for use by the elderly. Incredibly, Abbott did not limit its wrongful conduct to preying upon the elderly; it also unlawfully marketed its drug, Depakote, to an array of patient populations, including children, placing them at risk for life altering injury or illness. Abbotts's scheme, motivated by money as opposed to a legitimate medical rationale, worked. Sales of Depakote rocketed to over $1.4 billion per year and compensation for senior executives soared as well.

Let's look at these two examples and analyze the logic behind each. The introduction to the simple case tells the court what the case is about in a nutshell. It describes the facts in a way that conveys empathy for the plaintiff, and it does so absent hyperbole. The judge or the decider of fact may quickly grasp the case.

The second introduction is from a False Claims Act (FCA) suit, *United States ex rel. McCoyd v. Abbott Lab'ys*.[22] The FCA involves false or fraudulent claims for payment submitted to the government. The statute only allows monetary recovery. *McCoyd* involved the off-label marketing of the drug Depakote. "Off-label" refers to marketing a drug for purposes not approved by the Food and Drug Administration (FDA). The introduction was designed to convey that although the case was—at its core—about money—the unlawful scheme placed vulnerable humans in harm's way. It was an introduction designed not only to get the court's attention but also the attention of regulatory agencies and the Department of Justice who have the option to participate in false claims cases brought by a whistleblower—known as a "relator." In addition, the introduction was designed to show the "materiality" of the misconduct. Materiality is an element of a claim under the FCA. Was the strategy successful? The case settled for $1.6 billion dollars, including a guilty plea in a parallel proceeding generated from the *McCoyd* case.

Sometimes, you want to use the introduction to inoculate the decision maker against a defense. In another FCA case, *United States ex rel. Brown v. Celgene*,[23] the whistleblower alleged that the defendant drug company off-label marketed two cancer drugs. Though not a technical defense, there was concern the defendant would argue that companies should have latitude in promoting drugs to treat cancer

---

22. United States *ex rel.* McCoyd v. Abbott Lab'ys., Case No. 07-cv-00081 (W.D. Va.).
23. United States *ex rel.* Brown v. Celgene Corp., 2014 U.S. Dist. LEXIS 194471 (C.D. Cal. Mar. 21, 2014).

even if the FDA had not explicitly approved those drugs as cancer treatments. The introduction to the *Celgene* case addresses this concern by arguing that what cancer patients really need is honest information during their window of opportunity to decide upon treatment. Hence the following introduction:

I. **INTRODUCTION**

With sometimes no more than a narrow window of opportunity to make critical decisions about medical treatment, doctors and their patients must have honest information about treatment options including appropriate drug regimes. Patients ravaged by cancer, and often on the edge of life, have no choice but to trust their healthcare providers and the pharmaceutical manufacturers are providing information based on solid evidence, and that independent scientists at the Food and Drug Administration ("FDA") have reviewed their drugs for safety and efficacy.

Crafting an introduction is not only an art, it is an exercise forcing you to reflect on the case, analyze potential flaws in your theory, create a theme, and encapsulate it in a nutshell. One way to think about the introduction is by analogy to the old "inverted pyramid" style of writing that news reporters and sportswriters used, particularly when copy had to fit the printed page. The inverted pyramid's goal is to tell the entire story in the first sentence. Every succeeding sentence just adds more detail to the story. When newspaper editors received a story via a wire service, they would cut from the bottom up to fill a particular space in the paper. No matter where they cut, the story still made sense. Consider this example:

> NEW YORK, NEW YORK—Mickey Mantle drove in 6 runs, including 4 homers, as the New York Yankees beat the Boston Red Sox 10-4.
>
> Whitey Ford struggled through seven innings, allowing a runner on base in each of those innings but held on for the win.
>
> It was the Yankees seventh win in their last nine games.

As illustrated in the above example, the story makes sense as long as the editor cuts from the bottom up. But most significantly, under the inverted pyramid style, the first sentence captures the guts of the story. A complaint's introduction should capture the guts of the complaint. Introductions need not be limited to one paragraph. Regardless of whether it is one paragraph or ten paragraphs, as in the case of a complex complaint, use the introduction to summarize the guts of the case.

Drafting the introduction helps you formulate a short summary for court appearances. It is an opportunity to examine the facts, strengths and weaknesses, and how the law applies in the case. Obviously, if a single judge presides over the case in its entirety, including motions and trial, the judge learns the nuances of the case. Sometimes, however, cases are broken up with procedural matters assigned to magistrates and/or motions assigned to motions court judges. In these situations, it is extremely useful to have at hand a nutshell summary of the case.

7.5.2   The Role of a Legal Section

When considering the complaint's plausibility, the court only looks at the factual allegations. "[T]he Federal Rules do not require courts to credit a complaint's conclusory statements without reference to its factual context."[24] Does this mean there is no value in pleading allegations that might be conclusory or just statements about the law? No. If the claim involves fraud or mistake, there should be enough facts in the complaint to meet the *Iqbal/Twombly* standard or the FRCP 9(b) requirements. But courts sometimes need legal context, especially if the claim involves the application of facts to a complex set of laws or regulations. Consider a whistleblower's claim under the FCA, alleging the defendant cheated the government by submitting Medicare claims for noncompensable services. The whistleblower's counsel is well-served by explaining the FCA and the Medicare regulations to the court. Consider this example from *U.S. ex rel. Graves v. Humana*:

THE MEDICARE PROGRAM

15. Title XVIII of the Social Security Act, 42 U.S.C. §§ 1395 – 1395ggg, establishes the Health Insurance for the Aged and Disabled Program, popularly known as the Medicare Program. The Medicare Program is composed of four parts, Medicare Parts A, B and D are not directly at issue in this case. Medicare Part C authorizes payment for physician and ancillary services, including laboratory and diagnostic tests and procedures.

16. Part C is the part of Medicare policy that allows private health insurance companies, including Humana, in this case, to act as administrators for the United States government in the provision of Medicare benefits. These Medicare private health plans, such as HMOs and PPOs, are known as Medicare Advantage plans, and the private health insurance companies that run these plans are known as Medicare Advantage Organizations.

17. Medicare Advantage, otherwise known as Medicare "Part C," authorizes qualified individuals to opt out of traditional fee-for-service coverage under Medicare Parts A and B and enroll in privately-run managed care plans that provide coverage for both inpatient and outpatient services. 42 U.S.C. §§ 1395w-21, 1395w-28.

18. Part C allows Medicare beneficiaries to receive all Medicare benefits through private insurance plans, instead of directly from CMS. Under Medicare Advantage, the government pays the private insurer – here, Humana – a monthly "capitation" amount per enrolled beneficiary, which is based on the patient's medical conditions. Thus, every month, CMS pays Humana a pre-determined capitated amount for each beneficiary who is enrolled in one of its Part C Plans based on, among other things, the diagnosis codes that Humana submits for these patients, regardless of whether or not the beneficiary receives medical treatment or otherwise utilizes the Plan's services that month. Humana, as the responsible Medicare Advantage Organization (MAO), then pays the capitation payment, less a percentage fee for administration, to the participating doctor or medical practice. This is the only way Medicare Part C payments are made: Participating physicians and medical practices like Dr. Cavanaugh and Plaza Medical cause the medical claims to be presented by providing patient data to the MAO, here Humana, which then makes the actual claim for payment with CMS. CMS's payment to Humana and Humana's resulting payment to Plaza Medical and Cavanaugh is proof the claim was actually made.

---

24. *Iqbal*, 556 U.S. at 686.

19. CMS determines the per-patient capitation amount using actuarial tables based primarily on the patient's medical diagnoses and adjusted for the patient's county of residence and over 70 factors such as age, sex, severity of illness, etc. This is known as "Risk Adjustment." CMS adjusts the capitation rates for each patient monthly, taking into account each patient's previous diagnoses and treatments, which are submitted by the patient's physicians to Humana and by Humana to CMS.

20. Beneficiaries with more diseases or more serious conditions and more frequent medical treatments would rate a higher monthly capitation payment than healthier beneficiaries, whether or not they are treated on a particular month, and Humana is required to submit that data to CMS. *See* 42 C.F.R. §§ 422.308(c) and 422.310. In this case, Plaza Medical Centers, based on Dr. Cavanaugh's diagnoses, submitted monthly treatment, diagnosis, billing information for each of its Medicare Part C patients to Humana which then submitted them in turn to CMS so CMS could determine an accurate capitation rate. CMS then made payments to Humana based on the patient information provided by Plaza Medical/Cavanaugh and Humana.

21. CMS has specifically notified Humana and its Part C providers (including Plaza Medical and Cavanaugh) that it relies on the data they submit to make accurate payments: "Accurate risk-adjusted payments rely on the diagnosis coding derived from the member's medical record". (*See, e.g., CMS 2013 National Technical Assistance Risk Adjustment 101 Participant Guide* at p.13). Put simply, Medicare relies on the patient diagnosis codes and data submitted by Plaza Medical, Cavanaugh, and Humana to determine the capitation payment per patient.

22. Based on this data, CMS issued monthly capitation payments for each Plaza Medical/Cavanaugh Medicare Part C patient to Humana. The payments were electronically transferred from CMS to specific Part C accounts designated by Humana. Humana kept a portion on each Part C payment for itself and then remitted the balance of the capitated payment to Plaza Medical Center for each of its Part C patients. Payments were made by Medicare to Humana and by Humana to Plaza Medical Center each month, every month, in precisely this manner.

23. At least once a month, Humana (like all Part C plans) submits to CMS its updated patient information for its enrolled beneficiaries, including the dates of services and diagnosis codes for all claims submitted by a provider for each enrolled beneficiary. This information was provided to Humana by Plaza Medical Centers and Cavanaugh. This data is submitted using a specific payment form known as a Risk Adjustment Payment System ("RAPS") report.

24. CMS uses this RAPS data to reassess its risk assessment level, and therefore the capitation rates, for each enrolled beneficiary for the following Plan year. Thus, claims submitted in one Plan year would increase the amount of capitation payments for those beneficiaries in subsequent Plan years.

25. Thus, the submission of additional and/or more medically acute diagnoses and treatment codes for a patient will increase the capitated payments received by Humana and Plaza Medical by deceiving CMS into thinking the patients were far sicker and in need of fare more services than they actually were. The practice of falsifying this information to increase payment rates is known as "upcoding." This practice was well-known to providers like Plaza Medical and Humana and of grave concern to CMS.[1]

Obviously, the purpose is to provide the court with a document that encapsulates both the facts and the law. The allegations of law need not be as detailed as a legal brief but should explain the context. The above example may seem lengthy, but it is actually a small portion of a very thick complaint.

7.5.3 *Hyperbole and Adjectives*

Hyperbole uses exaggerated statements or statements not meant to be taken literally in an attempt to elicit empathy. The result is quite the opposite. Judges are too often inundated with hyperbole; it is a distraction that detracts from the litigant's credibility and is draining for judges, whose lives are all about hearing complaints.

When describing a cause of action, use adjectives thoughtfully. Consider whether they provide a more vivid description of the facts or whether they border on exaggerating events. A better approach is to use facts in place of adjectives where possible. Consider these two examples:

> **Example 1**: Plaintiff was brutally battered by defendant, who is a massive man.

> **Example 2**: Plaintiff sustained a fractured eye socket and broken nose when he was hit by defendant, who is 6 foot 4 inches and weighs 260 pounds.

These allegations are not mutually exclusive. In other words, a plaintiff could allege what is written in Example 2 and use Example 1 to summarize the injury for the next allegation. Just take time to think it through: does the added hyperbole detract from the facts that by themselves are powerful? Are you using it as shorthand for a more effective, factual description? Remember the recurring theme throughout this book—make the case with the facts.

7.6 Judging the Complaint

Unless the case involves questions of standing or jurisdiction, the court considers the complaint by looking at the four corners of the allegations. If you refer to a document in the complaint, incorporate the document by reference. Before filing the complaint, think hard about what the motion to dismiss will look like. Reread the complaint, make sure you allege the facts and incorporate by reference the requisite documents you need to respond to a motion to dismiss. It is frustrating to receive the motion to dismiss and wish you had just pled a few more facts. Of course, plaintiffs generally have the right to file an amended complaint before defense counsel files a responsive pleading. An answer is deemed to be a responsive pleading, but a motion to dismiss is technically not a responsive pleading. As a last resort, file an amended complaint clearing up any defects the motion to dismiss highlights. Alternatively, a court can grant the motion to dismiss without prejudice, allowing for the right to file an amended complaint.[25] Of course, whether a court will do this is not something that a plaintiff should count on.

---

25. *See* United States *ex rel* Wollman v. Gen. Hosp. Corp., 2018 U.S. Dist LEXIS 55793, 2018 WL 1586027 (D. Mass. Mar. 30, 2018).

7.7 Summon and Service

FRCP 4 governs summons and service of the complaint. Most states have an analogous rule.[26] The rule details service requirements clearly; there are professional considerations, however, with regard to service. If you know defense counsel, it is courteous to inquire whether counsel will accept service. Service of a complaint can be an emotional experience for the defendant. Counsel are often willing to accept service to spare their client the emotional trauma. Defense counsel for corporations or entities often accept service because it allows them to calculate the precise date for filing an answer or motion to dismiss. When considering accepting service, the defense counsel can request extra time to respond to the complaint. Plaintiff's counsel may similarly ask for additional time to oppose a motion to dismiss. The overarching point is that outreach on the simple matter of service sets the tone for how counsel will deal with each other throughout the case. Outreach on the matter of service also brings the parties together for one last time prior to filing and may prompt settlement discussions.

7.8 Responding to the Complaint

Once you receive a complaint, the single most important task is to calendar a response date. Responses can involve any of the following:

- An FRCP 12(b)(6) motion to dismiss on the merits.

- An FRCP 12(b)(1) motion to dismiss or lack of jurisdiction.

- A motion to dismiss on personal jurisdiction grounds.

- A motion to change venue.

- A removal to federal court.

- An answer to the complaint.

- A motion to compel mediation.

- Settlement.

Each option presents its own strategy and cost considerations. Contemporaneous with calendaring a response date, meet with the client, review the allegations, determine responses to each allegation, and agree on a strategy going forward. Potential strategies may dispose of the case or better position it for litigation.

For example, motions to dismiss for failure to state a claim or for lack of subject matter jurisdiction can dispose of the case. Motions to change venue or dismiss

---

26. *See* FED. R. CIV. P. 4.

for lack of personal jurisdiction may only postpone inevitable litigation. If defense counsel succeeds on a motion to change venue, the case will still proceed, and the persistent plaintiff can file suit where personal jurisdiction exists. Defense counsel should consider changing venue if the dispute is: 1) likely to survive a motion to dismiss; and 2) one where transfer to another jurisdiction and the laws of a different jurisdiction may be outcome determinative. Of course, if the only consideration is to delay the plaintiff's case, changing venue will increase litigation costs for both your client and the plaintiff.

All counsel should game out their cases. As plaintiff's lawyer, think about what is needed to prove the case, hypothesize how the case can be settled, and how to put the case together for trial. As defense lawyer, analyze whether the case can be disposed of through trial motions including summary judgment, what discovery entails, and how to present the case at trial. The defense lawyer should also consider costs, the litigation's impact on the client's reputation, and the client's exposure at trial.

Client strategy discussions will involve some reality checks. Suppose the client owns a small grocery store and has ten employees. One employee files suit claiming disability discrimination. Your client, the grocery store owner, believes they dealt with the employee fairly and wants an aggressive defense. Your projection of defense costs equals approximately half of the client's annual profits. Have a reality check conversation with the client and attempt to resolve the case for a fraction of the litigation costs.

Gaming out the litigation and client reality check conversations prevent both sides from spending an inordinate amount of money on litigation, especially when settlement can save both sides money.

7.9   Arbitration

At the outset of any dispute, plaintiff's counsel should determine whether a case is subject to arbitration. If a contract exists governing the relationship between parties, check it for an "arbitration clause."

Until 1991, there was the perception that the Federal Arbitration Act (FAA) had limited application and did not encompass statutory claims, particularly those involving discrimination. The confusion arose from the Supreme Court's decisions in *Alexander v. Gardner-Denver Co.*[27] and *Barrentine v. Arkansas-Best Freight System.*[28] *Alexander* involved alleged violations of employment discrimination and *Barrentine* involved alleged violations of the Fair Labor Standards Act. In both

---

27. Alexander v. Gardner-Denver Co., 415 U.S. 36 (1974).
28. Barrentine v. Arkansas-Best Freight Sys., 450 U.S. 728 (1981).

cases, the Court refused to compel arbitration where collective bargaining agreements included arbitration clauses.

In *Gilmer v. Interstate/Johnson Lane Corp.*, the Court enforced an arbitration agreement for a claim involving alleged violations of the Americans with Disabilities Act.[29] The Court distinguished collectively-negotiated arbitration agreements from individual agreements. Because the parties made an agreement to arbitrate, the Court explained that unless the substantive law precludes arbitration, then a claim must be arbitrated.[30]

Gilmer opened the floodgates to compulsory arbitration.[31] Arbitration clauses are found in employment agreements, credit card agreements, loan documents, and all types of consumer sales agreements. In some cases, particularly disputes involving sales contracts negotiated between two parties with equal bargaining power, these agreements create efficiencies in dispute resolution without a detrimental impact on the rule of law. In employment discrimination and product defect cases, however, compulsory arbitration requires dispute resolution in proceedings between parties with unequal bargaining power that lack the transparency of the court system. Moreover, arbitration decisions are not always recorded and unlike judges, arbitrators are not bound by the doctrine of stare decisis.[32]

Although there is much debate about the merits of compulsory arbitration, its existence is reality. Where a contractual obligation to arbitrate exists, plaintiffs should be mindful that the complaint will be met with a motion to stay litigation and compel arbitration.

---

29. Gilmer v. Interstate/Johnson Lane Corp., 500 U.S. 20 (1991).

30. *Id.* at 26. *See, e.g.*, MERRICK T. ROSSEIN, 1 EMPLOYMENT DISCRIMINATION LAW AND LITIGATION § 13:14 (Nov. 2019).

31. *See generally*, Am. Exp. Co. v. Italian Colors Rest., 570 U.S. 228 (2013) ("This text reflects the overarching principle that arbitration is a matter of contract....[a]nd consistent with that text, courts must "rigorously enforce" arbitration agreements according to their terms, including terms that "specify *with whom* [the parties] choose to arbitrate their disputes," and "the rules under which that arbitration will be conducted." That holds true for claims that allege a violation of a federal statute, unless the FAA's mandate has been 'overridden by a contrary congressional command.'" (citations omitted)); Bender v. A.G. Edwards & Sons, Inc., 971 F.2d 698, 699, 700 (11th Cir. 1992) ("Since *Gilmer v. Interstate/Johnson Lane Corp.*, it is clear that Title VII claims are subject to compulsory arbitration....Although *Gilmer* involved a claim under the Age Discrimination in Employment Act of 1967 (ADEA), its reasoning is dispositive of the agreement to arbitrate Title VII claims before us....The Supreme Court rejected the employee's contentions that Congress had intended to exclude age discrimination claims from the purview of the FAA and affirmed the Fourth Circuit's judgment that the claims were subject to compulsory arbitration." (citation omitted)); Bender v. Smith Barney, Harris Upham & Co., 789 F. Supp 155 (D. N.J. 1992).

32. Reuben Guttman, *Mourning the Common Law Tradition*, THE GLOB. LEGAL POST (Dec. 19, 2013), https://www.globallegalpost.com/blogs/big-stories/mourning-the-common-law-tradition-22518844/.

If your client receives a complaint whose cause of action is subject to mandatory arbitration, advise plaintiff's counsel and stay the matter pending referral to arbitration. This may be done through correspondence as follows:

Piper & Bingo Attorneys

Re: Thompson v. Jones

Dear Mr. Piper:

We are in receipt of your complaint against our client in the above referenced matter. As you are aware, your client signed a contract that mandates arbitration of the current dispute with Mr. Jones. I refer you to paragraph 6.1 of the enclosed agreement.

We are writing to obtain your consent to a joint motion requesting an order to stay the within action and refer it to arbitration.

We look forward to your prompt response. Naturally, we are available to discuss this matter.

Cordially,

Milo Fordstein

Attorney for John Thompson

If the plaintiff does not agree to refer the matter to arbitration, respond to the complaint by filing a motion to stay the action and refer the matter to arbitration.

7.10   Who to Name as a Defendant

A number of considerations govern who to name as a defendant. Such analysis is easier when case optics indicate a dispute with one wrongdoer. When a case involves more than one wrongdoer, it may be difficult to determine who is the more responsible party. Sometimes, for example, in a medical malpractice case, it is axiomatic that harm would not have occurred but for negligence. Nevertheless, if a patient was under anesthesia, they cannot apportion liability with precision. The patient does not know, for example, whether the attending surgeon, the nurse, or the resident left the sponge in the patient. Hence, everyone is sued and the litigation dynamic forces the defendants to go after each other and apportion liability.

Yet, where liability is not clear, naming multiple defendants may have the opposite effect; they will present a joint defense and increase the plaintiff's litigation burden. Even if the defendants do not join forces, plaintiff counsel risks multiple motions to dismiss, additional depositions, and more dispositive motions. Of course, there are also situations where the damages are so significant that no single defendant can pay for all the damages; multiple defendants may increase potential for a full recovery by opening up more pockets to pay the judgment. The dynamics involving multiple defendants may also result in early settlement or cause defendants to turn on each other. Further, there are situations where the failure to join a necessary party will lead to a motion to dismiss under FRCP 12(b)(7).

As a procedural matter, FRCP 19 "Required Joinder of Parties" governs whether a party is required to be joined and if a failure to do so will lead to the dismissal of the case.[33] As stated earlier, a motion to dismiss pursuant to FRCP 12(b)(7) is the proper means for seeking dismissal where a necessary defendant has not been named, FRCP 19 identifies when a party must be joined as a defendant and lists circumstances that mandate a dismissal when joinder is unfeasible.[34]

7.11 The Answer

When you receive a complaint, remember to calendar the answer date. FRCP 6 explains how to compute time in federal court, including holidays and weekends.

Answers to complaints are governed by FRCP 8 and 12. FRCP 12 provides the exact response time for answers. Response time can vary depending on whether service is waived or whether the defendant is outside all U.S. judicial districts.

---

33. A court has considerable discretion in determining who is an indispensable party. There is no specific formula. Rather, a court must assess the relevant factors surrounding each case. "Joinder under Rule 19 entails a practical two-step inquiry. First, the court must determine whether an absent party should be joined as a 'necessary party' under subsection (a). Second, if the court concludes that the nonparty is necessary and cannot be joined for practical or jurisdictional reasons, the court must then determine under subsection (b) whether in 'equity and good conscience' the action should be dismissed because the nonparty is 'indispensable.' Under Rule 19(a), a party is deemed 'necessary' if complete relief cannot be granted in its absence. In conducting the Rule 19(a) analysis, the court asks whether the absence of the party would preclude the district court from fashioning meaningful relief as between the parties." Hubbard v. Rite Aid Corp., 433 F. Supp. 2d 1150, 1157 (S.D. Cal. 2006) (citation omitted). In Provident Tradesmens Bank & Trust Co. v. Patterson, the Supreme Court identified four 'interests' relevant when determining 'equity and good conscience' under FRCP 19(b). "First, the plaintiff has an interest in having a forum. . . Second, the defendant may properly wish to avoid multiple litigation, or inconsistent relief, or sole responsibility for a liability he shares with another. . . . Third, there is the interest of the outsider whom it would have been desirable to join. ... Fourth, there remains the interest of the courtssss and the public in complete, consistent, and efficient settlement of controversies." CHARLES ALAN WRIGHT, ET AL., FEDERAL PRACTICE & PROCEDURE § 1602 (3d ed. 2020).
34. *See* FED. R. CIV. P. 19.

Though it is important to read the relevant jurisdiction's procedural rules, the general format for an answer includes the following:

ANSWER FORMAT

A RESPONSE TO EACH SPECIFIC ALLEGATION

A LISTING OF AFFIRMATIVE DEFENSES

As previously mentioned, FRCP 8(a) outlines the format for complaints. FRCP 8(b) outlines how a defendant should respond to specific allegations:

(b) Defenses; Admissions and Denials.

(1) *In General.* In responding to a pleading, a party must:

(A) state in short and plain terms its defenses to each claim asserted against it; and

(B) admit or deny the allegations asserted against it by an opposing party.

(2) *Denials—Responding to the Substance.* A denial must fairly respond to the substance of the allegation.

(3) *General and Specific Denials.* A party that intends in good faith to deny all the allegations of a pleading—including the jurisdictional grounds—may do so by a general denial. A party that does not intend to deny all the allegations must either specifically deny designated allegations or generally deny all except those specifically admitted.

(4) *Denying Part of an Allegation.* A party that intends in good faith to deny only part of an allegation must admit the part that is true and deny the rest.

(5) *Lacking Knowledge or Information.* A party that lacks knowledge or information sufficient to form a belief about the truth of an allegation must so state, and the statement has the effect of a denial.

(6) ***Effect of Failing to Deny.*** An allegation—other than one relating to the amount of damages—is admitted if a responsive pleading is required and the allegation is not denied. If a responsive pleading is not required, an allegation is considered denied or avoided.[35]

Note the phrase "lacks knowledge or information sufficient to form a belief about the truth of an allegation" contained in FRCP 8(b)(5). Defense counsel often uses this phrase in response to specific allegations, particularly if they just began acclimating themselves with the facts. Utilizing this phrase allows counsel to deny the allegations even when they are not well-versed enough about the facts to answer so precisely. FRCP 8(c) requires a party to state its affirmative defenses. The rule states the following:

(c) Affirmative Defenses.

(1) ***In General.*** In responding to a pleading, a party must affirmatively state any avoidance or affirmative defense, including:

- accord and satisfaction;
- arbitration and award;
- assumption of risk;
- contributory negligence;
- duress;
- estoppel;
- failure of consideration;
- fraud;
- illegality;
- injury by fellow servant;
- laches;
- license;
- payment;
- release;
- res judicata;

---

35. Fed. R. Civ. P. 8(b).

- statute of frauds;

- statute of limitations; and

- waiver.

(2) *Mistaken Designation.* If a party mistakenly designates a defense as a counterclaim, or a counterclaim as a defense, the court must, if justice requires, treat the pleading as though it were correctly designated, and may impose terms for doing so.[36]

Stating affirmative defenses in the answer is essential. Depending on the law in the jurisdiction, failing to do so may waive the defendant's right to the defense. Asserting the affirmative defense affords the plaintiff adequate notice that the defense will be an issue in the case and provides opportunity for the plaintiff to take discovery on the defense.

7.12 Conclusion

There are many considerations at play when deciding to initiate litigation. The strategy you pursue will impact nearly all facets of the litigation. It can impact the likelihood of settlement or even your potential success on dispositive motions. Think carefully about whether and how to initiate litigation as those decisions will be critical to the outcome of your matter.

---

36. Fed. R. Civ. P. 8(c).

CHAPTER EIGHT

DISCOVERY PLAN AND STRATEGY

8.1 Introduction

The information produced through discovery allows parties to make educated choices when deciding when and whether to resolve a dispute during the litigation process. It is also a means to support or challenge the need for an injunction or to demonstrate whether or not a case is worthy of proceeding as a class action. Decisions by the court during the litigation process may increase or decrease the value of the case; discovery is the window into whether a case will survive summary judgment and how it will present at trial.

The Federal Rules of Civil Procedure (FRCP) provide multiple methods for collecting information that may become evidence at trial or may lead to securing information that will be admissible as evidence at trial. Discovery's primary mechanisms for facilitating information production or the confirmation of information are:

- Initial disclosures[1]
- Request for production of documents[2]
- Interrogatories[3]
- Request for admission[4]
- Depositions[5]

Discovery also involves these secondary mechanisms to acquire information:

- Request to inspect property[6]
- Request for medical or psychiatric examinations[7]

---

1. *See* FED. R. CIV. P. 26(a)(1).
2. *See* FED. R. CIV. P. 34(a).
3. *See* FED. R. CIV. P. 33.
4. *See* FED. R. CIV. P. 36.
5. *See* FED. R. CIV. P. 30 (depositions by oral examination); FED. R. CIV. P. 31 (depositions by written questions); FED. R. CIV. P. 27 (depositions to perpetuate testimony).
6. *See* FED. R. CIV. P. 34(a)(2).
7. *See* FED. R. CIV. P. 35.

All of these tools are available to both plaintiffs and defendants. Parties use them to collect or confirm information from each other and, in some cases, from third parties when accompanied by a subpoena. Choosing which discovery tool to use is a matter of both strategic and economic considerations and dependent on the facts of the case. While each specific discovery mechanism is tied to a specific rule, FRCP 26 provides the overarching framework for discovery.

To paraphrase Stephen Covey, a discovery plan should start with the end in mind. Even as the case is just getting off of the ground, consider outlining the summary judgment or pretrial brief. The exercise will help identify necessary evidence to obtain, develop, or neutralize. Make the document a living one, updating it as discovery proceeds.

—Mary S. Thomas, Pricket Jones & Elliott PA

8.2   The Framework for Discovery: FRCP 26

FRCP 26, entitled "Duty to Disclose; General Provisions Governing Discovery," is the overarching rule outlining the discovery structure and addresses the following:

- Disclosures[8]

- Discovery scope and limits[9]

- Protective orders[10]

- Supplementing disclosures and responses[11]

- Conference of the parties; planning for discovery[12]

- Signing disclosures and discovery requests and responses[13]

Once a suit is filed, the provisions of FRCP 26 guarantee, absent the specific use of the discovery mechanisms outlined above, the exchange of basic information as required in FRCP 26(a)(1)(a):

(a) *In General.* Except as exempted by Rule 26(a)(1)(B) or as otherwise stipulated or ordered by the court, a party must, without awaiting a discovery request, provide to the other parties:

---

8. *See* Fed. R. Civ. P. 26(a).
9. *See* Fed. R. Civ. P. 26(b).
10. *See* Fed. R. Civ. P. 26(c).
11. *See* Fed. R. Civ. P. 26(e).
12. *See* Fed. R. Civ. P. 26(f).
13. *See* Fed. R. Civ. P. 26(g).

(i) the name and, if known, the address and telephone number of each individual likely to have discoverable information—along with the subjects of that information—that the disclosing party may use to support its claims or defenses, unless the use would be solely for impeachment;

(ii) a copy—or a description by category and location—of all documents, electronically stored information, and tangible things that the disclosing party has in its possession, custody, or control and may use to support its claims or defenses, unless the use would be solely for impeachment;

(iii) a computation of each category of damages claimed by the disclosing party—who must also make available for inspection and copying as under Rule 34 the documents or other evidentiary material, unless privileged or protected from disclosure, on which each computation is based, including materials bearing on the nature and extent of injuries suffered; and

(iv) for inspection and copying as under Rule 34, any insurance agreement under which an insurance business may be liable to satisfy all or part of a possible judgment in the action or to indemnify or reimburse for payments made to satisfy the judgment.

Most actions are subject to these required disclosures; however, there are some exceptions set forth in FRCP 26(a)(1)(B). For example, the review of arbitration awards and administrative records are not subject to the FRCP 26 disclosure requirement.

FRCP 26 provides for both mandatory disclosures and a framework for "à la carte" discovery—including depositions, interrogatories and document requests. These are more particularly described by the following rules:

FRCP 30	Establishes proper conduct and procedure for oral depositions by oral examination. This comprehensive rule details everything from proper notification and recording to who is obliged to pay for transcription. Such detailed instructions ensures a fair process for all parties.
FRCP 31	Informs procedure for depositions by written questions.
FRCP 33	Describes the guidelines for serving and answering interrogatories. Questions asked in this format are typically focused and specific.
FRCP 34	Outlines procedures for requesting and obtaining documents and data. It also describes how to request land entry for testing or inspection of property or objects found on the property. The party served with the request "must respond in writing within 30 days after being served."
FRCP 35	Allows parties to submit motions requesting physical or mental examinations. If approved, the court orders the party to comply with the type of examination requested.
FRCP 36	Allows a party to serve the other with written statements that the receiving party must admit or deny. FRCP 36 does not limit the number of statements allowed. Notably, if the receiving party does not respond with an objection or address the matter, the matter is considered admitted.

And while these rules are directly on point, the following rules are also important during the discovery process:

FRCP 27	Governs depositions to perpetuate discovery.
FRCP 28	Governs who depositions may be taken before in the United States and in a foreign country.
FRCP 29	States that unless a court says otherwise, the parties may stipulate that depositions be taken at any time, in any place, in the specified manner, and before any person (may stipulate to the time, place, manner, notice, and audience of depositions). The rule also states that unless a court says otherwise, parties may stipulate that other procedures governing or limiting discovery may be modified as long as the stipulation does not extend time to interfere with the completion of discovery, a hearing, a motion, or trial. Court approval is required in such cases.
FRCP 37	Governs discovery disclosures and responses. When a party fails to respond to a good-faith effort by opposing counsel to obtain discovery or disclosure, the opposing party may make a motion for the court to compel a discovery disclosure or response. Failure to comply with a court order, failure to disclose, failure to attend depositions, and failure to preserve electroni- cally stored information can result in sanctions.

We discuss these rules more in depth later in this chapter.

While the different methods of discovery are governed by separate rules, the
incremental process of discovery feeds on itself. Documents produced in discovery,
interrogatory answers, and responses to requests for admissions can all be used as
deposition exhibits that prompt a witness to answer questions (or otherwise keep
the witness honest). Conversely, interrogatories or requests for admissions may clear
up ambiguities in depositions, authenticate documents, or determine facts that are
not in dispute.

Discovery is premised on the notion that opposing counsel will work amicably to
accomplish the mandates of the rules. FRCP 1 acknowledges the role of the parties
in securing the just, speedy, and inexpensive resolution of cases. This rule—often
overlooked by counsel—states the following:

> The rules govern the procedure in all civil actions and proceedings
> in the United States district courts, except as stated in Rule 81. They
> should be construed, administered, and employed by the court and
> the parties to secure the just, speedy, and inexpensive determination
> of every action.[14]

FRCP 1 is the bedrock of professionalism; it fosters an atmosphere where even
those who oppose each other—and represent their clients vigorously—can agree on

---

14. The rule was amended in 2015 to incorporate the phrase: "and the parties." *See* David G.
Campbell et al., *Amendments to the Federal Rules of Practice and Procedure: Civil Rules 2015*, FED.
JUD. CTR. (DEC. 1, 2015), https://www.fjc.gov/content/309294/rules-amendments-2015-civil
(emphasis added)(discussing the 2015 amendment to FED. R. CIV. P. 1).

the processes to resolve their differences.[15] And, while the drafters of the discovery rules strove for clarity, all rules have areas that are subject to debate; which is why counsel should work to secure agreement on the process.

Naturally, this is sometimes easier said than done. You will face counsel who try to game the rules, seeking interpretations that create an imbalance of power or leverage, or drive up litigation expenses. While these antics are frustrating, for those counsel who are repeat participants in the judicial system, professionalism and attempting to reach agreement on an even-handed application of process is the key to both speedy and efficient litigation and building a positive relationship with the court.

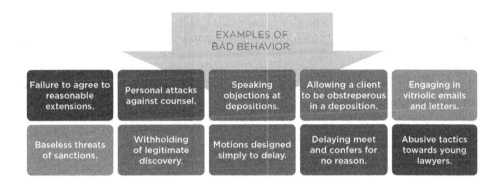

8.3 When Does Discovery Begin?

Filing a complaint does not immediately open the door to discovery. Opposing counsel either answers the complaint or files a motion to dismiss. If answered, the parties engage in discovery, subject to whatever schedule or local court rule—or order—is imposed by the judge assigned to the case.[16]

A complaint that is met with a motion to dismiss, however, may trigger a different approach to discovery, given that the very sufficiency of the claim is being challenged. While nothing in FRCP 12 (which governs motions to dismiss) triggers

---

15. Personal attacks against counsel are deemed as bad behavior and are prohibited in court. *See* Bates v. Bell, 402 F.3d 635, 640-50 (6th Cir. 2005); Thomas v. Tenneco Packaging Co., 293 F.3d 1306 (11th Cir. 2002); Vanderbol v. State Farm Mut. Auto Ins. Co., No. 4:19-cv-119-SDJ-KPJ, 2019 WL 6720524, 2019 U.S. Dist. LEXIS 212463 (E.D. Tex. Nov. 14, 2019). Another common bad behavior is speaking objections at depositions. *See* Hernandez v. Barr, No. EDCV 16-0620-JGB, 2019 WL 4543101, (C.D. Cal. Apr. 12, 2019); Hunter v. GEICO Gen. Ins. Co., No. 17-05070, 2018 WL 4352823, 2018 U.S. Dist. LEXIS 155335 (E.D. La. Sept. 12, 2018).
16. For examples of these local court rules see N.J. Cт. R. 4:24-1(c); Cal. CCP § 2024.060; Mo. Rules Cт. 68.4.6.6.

an automatic stay of discovery,[17] parties can move for discovery stays pending disposition of a motion to dismiss. The results of such motions are mixed. A plaintiff may attempt to press discovery during this period; the defendant will most likely seek a protective order barring discovery until the complaint is sustained in whole or in part. A party seeking discovery during the pendency of a motion to dismiss is more likely to succeed if they can show a legitimate basis to conduct discovery during the pendency of a motion to dismiss, such as preserving evidence or securing evidence for an immediate hearing on an injunction.

Strategically, a plaintiff should consider that holding off on discovery until the motion to dismiss is decided may promote judicial economy. The case may be dismissed, claims may be eliminated, or an opinion may be issued that frames the facts in dispute and provides some focus for factfinding.

If the court sustains the complaint in whole or in part, the defendant must file an answer responding to any remaining causes of action. The parties must then focus on FRCP 26 requirements mandating initial disclosures of information and a joint report to the court providing a basic discovery road map. FRCP 26's process also requires parties to consider whether the case can be resolved, the calculation of damages, and a process for protecting confidential information.

For attorneys who like to procrastinate, FRCP 26 is a dose of cold water. It forces counsel to consider how they will prove their case, what they need to prove it, and how to calculate damages, and to do it all in a relatively short period of time.

8.4 The Culture of Discovery

Judges dislike discovery disputes. While attorneys who deliberately stretch the interpretation of the rules, standing court orders, or judges orders specific to a case—and wait to be accused of a rules violation before changing behavior or engaging in proper compliance—are frustrating, unless the conduct is egregious, try to work out the dispute without involving the court. Judges view resolving discovery disputes as doing little to expedite the resolution of the case on the merits. Moreover, most discovery disputes involve a pattern of conduct that necessitates examining a long trajectory of facts by wading through much hyperbole—it is often hard to determine which party was the instigator of the wrongdoing and hence, which party was at fault or at least more at fault. Judges view this as a distraction from the end game—getting a case to trial or resolution.

---

17. Notably, the Private Securities Litigation Reform Act requires a mandatory stay of discovery while motions to dismiss are pending in actions alleging violations of securities laws, with limited exceptions. *See* 15 U.S.C. § 78u-4(b)(3)(B). Many states, including New York, also have taken this position. *See, e.g.,* N.Y. C.P.L.R. 3211(g)(3) (McKinney 2020); Tex. Civ. Prac. & Rem. §27.003(c). Other states, such as Florida, have laws that specifically do not allow the court to stay discovery solely based on a pending motion to dismiss. *See* Maris Distrib. Co. v. Anheuser-Busch, Inc., 710 So.2d 1022, 1024–25 (Fla. Dist. Ct. App. 1998).

My mother-in-law always says, "you must cut your coat according to your size." While I am unsure of the exact origins of that colloquialism, I have always taken it to mean that one must act or prepare appropriately or proportionally for a task, challenge, undertaking, or moment. In litigation, that concept means that a party interested in a quick resolution must limit discovery and motion practice to topics and issues directly relevant to that goal. Far too often, however, parties will propound volumes of discovery and take overly aggressive positions about unessential issues, allowing their opponent to complicate the litigation, delay trial, and drive up attorneys' fees. To those people, I say, make sure to "cut your coat according to your size."

—*Oderah Nwaeze, Partner, Faegre Drinker*

Therefore, carefully pick which battles to bring before the court. If you believe asking the judge to intervene may be inevitable, create a paper trail of efforts to facilitate a resolution or compromise by documenting the record with emails and letters; be prepared to explain the dispute to the court by showing how the grant or denial of relief will impact the disposition of the case. When creating a paper trail, the goal is to resolve the dispute, look for compromise, and explain why the discovery is necessary for the case. The discovery process rests on consensual relations of the parties and mandates diplomacy; emails and letters should not be threatening, nor should they be written to prove to your client that you are an aggressive lawyer. Anything you write may be shown to the judge and potentially appear in the public record; do not put yourself or your client in a bad light.

Remember that discovery is an imperfect process and the court system lacks the resources to micromanage it. The culture of discovery is cultivated by those who honor the system because they are driven by integrity or simply because doing so creates the type of trust that engenders a good working relationship with opposing counsel. This culture is threatened by those desiring to test the boundaries of the system and game compliance enforcement.

8.5 The Scope of Discovery

In addition to its initial disclosure provisions, FRCP 26 also provides the general framework and scope of discovery. The advent of electronic discovery and the recording of real-time information through emails, texts, and social media, required fundamental revisions to the FRCP. The proportionality requirement reflects the need to set boundaries given the massive volume of documents available today, including electronic communication and data storage. Hence, proportionality questions are boiled down to a common-sense determination of what is needed to get a case to trial and to prove a cause of action.

The scope of discovery itself, whether through deposition or through other means of securing information, is defined as "whether the evidence is calculated to lead to the discovery of admissible evidence."[18] This simply means that, in the discovery process, a party can request information that may likely be inadmissible at trial but will lead to admissible evidence. Examples include:

- Contact information for potential witnesses helps locate those who can provide admissible testimony.

- Details of opponent's document storage methods helps a litigant formulate refined document requests to secure admissible evidence.

- Meeting sign-in sheets help identify those individuals who witnessed an event or can provide testimony about meeting discussions.

- Travel and expense receipts can place witnesses at the time and place of events.

The scope of discoverable information also includes impeachment evidence. Impeachment evidence is used to determine how much weight a decisionmaker should place on evidence introduced to prove the underlying merits of a case. This type of evidence may include:

- Employment records.

- Conviction records.

- Emails, letters, or statements showing bias.

- Inconsistent statements.

- Evidence demonstrating a witness's lack of knowledge regarding a particular event.

- Evidence, such as vision or hearing records, that can show a witness was unable to see or hear a particular event.

When collecting information though discovery, litigants must remember and expect customary pre-trial hurdles, including class certification, summary judgment, and *Daubert* motions. During discovery, defendants look to secure information, including admissions[19] that may eliminate or narrow claims, increase or limit the amount of damages, or make proof harder at trial. Plaintiffs may have opportunities to secure admissions, possibly opening the door to summary judgment on the merits or on a portion of the case—i.e. partial summary judgment. More often than not, plaintiffs simply hope to survive attacks on the claims and advance

---

18. FDIC v. Brudnicki, 291 F.R.D. 669, 678 (N.D. Fla. 2019).
19. *See, e.g*, Fed. R. Evid. 801(d)(2).

to trial. Meanwhile, defendants always look for information to eliminate the case, limit the claims, or position the case for settlement.

When gathering the information necessary to pursue or defend a case, discovery provides transparency so each party may understand their opponent's case and prosecute or defend the case before a judge or jury.[20] It is not necessary to collect every piece of paper or depose every witness. Rather, focus on acquiring the requisite information to convince a judge or twelve jurors to rule in your favor. Proposed discovery must be both relevant and proportional to be within the scope of discovery. The scope of discovery, whether through deposition or through other means of securing information, is defined as "any nonprivileged matter that is relevant to any party's claim or defense and proportional to the needs of the case."[21] Under Rule 26(b)(1), even information that is inadmissible in evidence is within the scope of discovery. Within the discovery process, a party can request such inadmissible information with the expectation that it may lead to admissible evidence.

8.5.1 Proportionality

Rule 26(b)(1) identifies six factors for federal courts to consider and balance in determining proportionality, i.e., whether a discovery request is "proportional to the needs of the case."[22] The way, and the degree to which, any factor applies depends on the facts and circumstances of each case. The 2015 Committee wrote of the 1983 amendments, Rule 26(b)(1) directed courts

> [t]o limit the frequency or extent of use of discovery if it determined that 'the discovery is unduly burdensome or expensive, taking into account the needs of the case, the amount in controversy, limitations on

---

20. FED. R. CIV. P. 26(b) advisory committee's note to 1946 amendment ("The purpose of discovery is to allow a broad search for facts, the names of witnesses, or any other matters which may aid a party in the preparation or presentation of his case." (citation omitted)); *See* FTC v. Sysco Corp., 308 F.R.D. 19, 21–22 (D.D.C. 2015) ("One of the key features of our civil justice system is that parties to a lawsuit are required to exchange information relevant to their dispute before a trial. The reason for this practice is relatively simple—resolving conflicts in a court of law is not a game of 'blind man's bluff,' but 'a fair contest with the basic issues and facts disclosed to the fullest practicable extent.' An open exchange of information prevents trial by ambush. Each side must have the opportunity to fully present its case and to test the other side's evidence through cross-examination of witnesses and presentation of contrary evidence. Such transparency also aids the judge or jury tasked with deciding a case. If the parties are better informed, so too will be the judge or jury who bears the responsibility of deciding which side will prevail." (citation omitted)); *See also* Brannies v. Internet ROI, Inc., 67 F. Supp. 3d 1360, 1362 (S.D. Ga. 2014) ("The discovery rules 'require the disclosure of all relevant information so that ultimate resolution of disputed issues in any civil action may be based on a full and accurate understanding of the true facts.'" (citation omitted)).
21. FED R. CIV. P. 26(b)(1).
22. *Id.* (The six factors are the importance of the issues at stake in the action, the amount in controversy, the parties' relative access to relevant information, the parties' resources, the importance of the discovery in resolving the issues, and whether the burden or expense of the proposed discovery outweighs its likely benefit.).

the parties' resources, and the importance of the issues at stake in the litigation . . . . [T]he rule contemplates greater judicial involvement in the discovery process and "acknowledges the reality that it cannot always operate on a self-regulating basis."[23]

- The first proportionality factor, "importance of the issues at stake," balances case merits against its shortcomings. The 2015 Committee cautioned that the monetary stakes, though only one factor, must be balanced against the other factors.[24] Cases involving substantive issues, "measured in philosophic, social, or institutional terms" are significant considerations that also bear heavily on this factor.[25] The 1983 Committee suggested "many cases in public policy spheres, such as employment practices, free speech, and other matters, may have importance far beyond the monetary amount involved."[26] Such influential legal actions often pursue "small amounts of money, or no money at all," instead seeking "to vindicate vitally important personal or public values."[27]

- The second proportionality factor, the "amount in controversy," denotes the monetary relief plaintiffs request upon filing a complaint.[28] Consideration of this factor generally applies to situations where discovery costs exceed the amount in controversy. Assess those reasonable discovery burdens or expenses and their potential impact on a party's financial gains and losses.[29] According to attorney Max Kennerly, case law related to this factor is sparse.

---

23. Fed. R. Civ. P. 26 advisory committee's note to 2015 amendment.

24. *See id.*

25. *See* Fed. R. Civ. P. 26 advisory committee's note to 1983 amendment.

26. Fed. R. Civ. P. 26(b) advisory committee's note to 1983 amendment.

27. Fed. R. Civ. P. 26 advisory committee's note to 1983 amendment; *see also* Bolch Judicial Institute, Duke Law School, *Guidelines and Best Practices for Implementing the 2015 Discovery Amendments to Achieve Proportionality* 3 (Leah Brenner & Thomas B. Metzloff eds., 2nd ed. 2018) ("An action seeking to enforce constitutional, statutory, or common-law rights, including a case filed under a statute using attorney fee-shifting provisions to encourage enforcement, can serve public and private interests that have an importance beyond any damages sought or other monetary amounts the case may involve.").

28. *See* Bolch Judicial Institute, Duke Law School, *Guidelines and Best Practices for Implementing the 2015 Discovery Amendments to Achieve Proportionality* 3-4 (Leah Brenner & Thomas B. Metzloff eds., 2nd ed. 2018) [hereinafter Implementing the 2015 Amendments] (stating monetary stakes, like the amount in controversy, are only one factor and must be balanced against others).

29. *Id.* ("If a specific amount in controversy is alleged in the pleadings and challenged, or no specific amount is alleged and the pleading is limited to asserting that the amount exceeds the jurisdictional minimum, the issue is how much the plaintiff could recover based on the claims asserted and allegations made. When an injunction or declaration judgment is sought, the amount in controversy includes the pecuniary value of that relief. The amount in controversy calculation can change as the case progresses, the claims and defenses evolve, and the parties and judge learn more about the damages or the value of the equitable relief.").

Few cases have interpreted this factor in depth. The cases that have done so have generally involved a single plaintiff, and the question was whether the cost of the proposed discovery would exceed the amount in controversy. Moreover, courts have been quick to note that discovery in a low-damages case can still be proportionate if the litigation could vindicate other interests.[30]

• The third proportionality factor, "the parties' relative access to relevant information" requires comparing how much access each party has to relevant case information and deciding whether "information asymmetry" exists. Information asymmetry occurs when "one party has or controls significantly more of the relevant information than the other parties."[31] Parties with a lesser amount of, or no access to, information, depend on [formal] discovery to obtain relevant information.[32]

In general, parties who possess or control more relevant information often incur heavier discovery costs and must produce significantly more information in comparison to the amount they request or obtain.[33] Parties who possess minimal discoverable information, or inaccessible information, are often not limited by the amount of discovery they may obtain. When a case involves information asymmetry, proportionality requires permitting all parties access to necessary information, but without the unfairness that can result if the asymmetries are leveraged by any party for tactical advantage. Unfairness can occur when a party with significantly less information imposes unreasonable demands on the party who has voluminous information. Unfairness can also occur when a party with significantly more information takes unreasonably restrictive or dilatory positions in response to the other party's requests.[34]

30. Max Kennerly, *A Plaintiff's Guide to Fed. R. Civ. P. 26 Discovery Proportionality* (July 12, 2017), https://www.litigationandtrial.com/2017/07/articles/attorney/frcp-26-discovery-proportionality/. "It appears that the discovery conducted to date, as well as the discovery requests currently at issue, would certainly not exceed the amount of controversy in this matter." *Id.* at n.15 (quoting *Bell v. Reading Hosp.,* No. CV 13-5927, 2016 WL 162991, at *3 (E.D. Pa. Jan. 14, 2016)). "The court applies the proportionality requirement built into Rule 26, but rejects Sentinel's characterization of the value of Ms. Schultz's case as a $17,000 case that benefits her alone.... If punitive damages are awarded, Ms. Schultz has the potential to affect Sentinel's alleged business practices and to remedy the situation for many insureds, not just herself." *Id.* at n.16 (quoting *Schultz v. Sentinel Ins. Co.,* 2016 WL 3149686, at *7 (D.S.D. June 3, 2016)).
31. Fed. R. Civ. P. 26 advisory committee's note to 2015 amendment; Implementing the 2015 Amendments, *supra* note 28, at 4.
32. *See* Implementing the 2015 Amendments, *supra* note 28, at 4.
33. *See* Fed. R. Civ. P. 26 advisory committee's note to 2015 amendment ("The burden of responding to discovery lies heavier on the party who has more information, and properly so.").
34. *See* Implementing the 2015 Amendments, *supra* note 28, at 4.

- The fourth proportionality factor, "the parties' resources," examines available resources[35] "for gathering, reviewing, and producing information and for requesting, receiving, and reviewing information in discovery."[36] In each case, consider how competing demands of party resources impact the extent or timing of discovery.

  Although more is generally expected of parties with greater resources, this proportionality factor does not require parties to provide all or most of the proposed discovery simply because they are able.[37] The same rationale applies to those with fewer resources. Even though less is expected from those with insufficient resources, parties may not "refuse to provide relevant information simply because doing so would be difficult for financial or other reasons. A party's ability to take discovery is not limited by the resources it has available to provide discovery in return."[38]

- The fifth proportionality factor, "[t]he importance of the discovery in resolving the issues." is "intended to provide the court with broader discretion to impose additional restrictions on the scope and extent of discovery."[39]

  This factor "addresses the likely benefits of proposed discovery based on its importance to resolving issues[40] and the importance of those issues to resolving the case."[41] "Understanding the importance of proposed discovery may involve assessing what the requesting party is realistically able to predict about what added information the proposed discovery will yield and how beneficial it will be."

  "To satisfy the 'importance' factor, the discovery must only be "more than tangentially related to the issues that are actually at stake in the litigation. Even where the cost is considerable, the importance factor is satisfied where "the probative value of the sought-after discovery is potentially substantial because it may be relevant to factual issues at the heart of [plaintiff's claims]."[42]

---

35. *See id.* at 5 ("'Resources' means more than a party's financial resources. It includes the technological, administrative, and human resources needed to perform the discovery tasks.").
36. *Id.*
37. *See id.*
38. *Id.*
39. FED. R. CIV. P. 26(b) advisory committee's note to 1993 amendment.
40. See Implementing the 2015 Amendments, supra note 28, at 6 ("Discovery that is essential to resolving [an] issue is more important than discovery that's cumulative or only tangentially related to that issue.").
41. Id. at 5 ("[W]hat issues or topics are the subject of the proposed discovery and how important those issues and topics are to resolving the overall case. Discovery relating to a central issue is more important than discovery relating to a peripheral issue.").
42. Kennerly, *supra* note 30.

- The sixth, and final proportionality factor, "[w]hether the burden or expense of the proposed discovery outweighs its likely benefit," balance benefits from the acquired discovery against the burden or expense needed to obtain it.[43]

"There is no fixed burden-to-benefit ratio that defines what is or is not proportional."[44] The Duke Law Center for Judicial Studies advises considering the "burden or expense" factor along with the other factors, [addressing and accounting for *the importance of the issues at stake and any resulting societal benefits associated with litigation of those issues.*]

When proportionality disputes arise, the party in the best position to provide information about the burdens, expense, or benefits of the proposed discovery ordinarily will bear the responsibility for doing so. Which party that is depends on the circumstances. In general, the party from whom proposed discovery is sought ordinarily is in a better position to specify and support the burdens and expense of responding,[45] while the party seeking proposed discovery ordinarily is in a better position to specify the likely benefits by explaining why it is seeking and needs the discovery.[46]

These factors give judges a lot of discretion in determining whether a discovery request is "proportional to the needs of the case." When placed in context, the proportionality factors counsel for a commonsense approach. For example, in a breach of contract claim seeking damages of $200,000, a defendant may argue that discovery should be narrowed if the response cost is $300,000. Such contentions involve questions of fact and mandate support from documents or testimony, including affidavits or declarations—challenges based on proportionality cannot be based on a bald assertion.

In larger cases—class actions or multi-million-dollar damage cases—implementing the proportionality requirement has not significantly—if at all—impacted discovery practices. Those cases will always be big enough that the optics of a proportionality argument will be less compelling. Electronic discovery production is proportionally less expensive: documents are not collected from geographically-dispersed filing cabinets and reviewed by individuals searching for hard copies. At least in cases involving large or sophisticated entities, documents are usually kept in electronic form.

---

43. *See* IMPLEMENTING THE 2015 AMENDMENTS, *supra* note 28, at 6. In addition to "[t]he importance of the discovery in resolving the issues," this factor was also a 1993 Committee addition. *See* FED. R. CIV. P. 26(b) advisory committee's note to 2015 amendment.
44. IMPLEMENTING THE 2015 AMENDMENTS, *supra* note 28, at 6.
45. A party requested to provide discovery may have little information about the importance of the discovery in resolving the issues as understood by the requesting party.
46. IMPLEMENTING THE 2015 AMENDMENTS, *supra* note 28, at 9.

Still, the significant proportionality requirement is an arrow in the quiver for lawyers hoping to limit discovery. When seeking discovery, answer the proportionality requirement by articulating a requested document's necessity in proving your case on the merits. Since most discovery requests lead to conferences with opposing counsel, be prepared to answer the central question, "Why are these documents necessary and how can the request be limited?"

8.6 Preserving Documents

Discovery is a two-way street. In addition to securing evidence or information that may lead to the discovery of relevant evidence, parties have an obligation to preserve evidence so that it is available for the opposing party through the disclosure process or affirmative discovery requests. The preservation obligation arises once litigation is pending or reasonably foreseeable. As with many "reasonableness" standards, courts look at the facts of the case to determine whether litigation was reasonably foreseeable. Some courts have cited the Sedona Conference principle, which states that a "reasonable anticipation of litigation" arises only when "an organization is on notice of a credible probability that it will become involved in litigation, seriously contemplates litigation, or when it takes specific actions to commence litigation."[47]

For individual clients who are involved in a discrete personal injury or breach of contract case, document preservation is straightforward. For corporate clients with large databases, countless electronically stored documents, and vast hard copy archives, document holds are more complex. Publicly traded companies subject to federal and state regulation may have existing document retention requirements. Attorneys representing such entities must analyze the situation's particularities and contemplate how those document storage particularities square with existing policies and regulations governing retention. Counsel must then implement a "litigation hold," drafting and disseminating a "document hold" letter directing clients to preserve documents relevant to pending litigation.[48] This letter defines the document hold's subject matter scope and storage method, either electronically or hard copy. Even when clients are already required to preserve documents under an existing policy, a separate hold letter reinforces that obligation. Moreover, with large corporate parties, it may be necessary to work with the client to determine who within the company is likely to have materials relevant to the litigation and ensure those individuals are specifically advised of the requirement to retain relevant documents, including emails and other electronic records.

---

47. *See, e.g., In re* Abilify (Aripiprazole) Prods. Liab. Litig., 2018 WL 4856767, at *3 (N.D. Fla. Oct 5, 2018) (quoting The Sedona Conference Working Group on Electronic Document Retention & Production, *The Sedona Conference Commentary on Legal Holds: The Trigger & The Process*, 11 SEDONA CONF. J. 265, 269 (2010)).
48. Goodman v. Praxair Servs., 632 F. Supp. 2d 494 (D. Md. 2009).

Document hold letters are essential. Counsel should expect witness questions about document preservation efforts to arise during depositions and possibly in interrogatories. It is not only essential to send the letter, but to ensure it is read, understood, and enforced. Therefore, attorneys should meet with their clients, review document retention procedures, and discuss the document hold letter paragraph by paragraph.

The litigation hold obligation applies to both plaintiffs and defendants. Plaintiff attorneys should inform clients of the obligation at the beginning of a representation and defendant attorneys should inform clients once they reasonably anticipate litigation. Although a document hold letter should be an independent document, some litigation attorneys find it useful to include the document hold language in the retainer agreement.

Failing to preserve documents can lead to court-imposed sanctions and litigation under the common-law tort of spoliation, which is recognized in some states.[49] In addition, document destruction may be a basis for a motion to strike claims or defenses.[50]

Spoliation is "[t]he destruction, or the significant and meaningful alteration of a document or instrument."[51] Courts and litigants in the adversary system are increasingly concerned with spoliation of evidence because of its grave consequences.[52] The loss of evidence needed for a fair and just trial can impede the ability of a party in litigation to prove the elements of their claim or defend a claim adequately.[53] Therefore, in an effort to further the goals of deterrence, accurate fact finding, and

---

49. Some jurisdictions recognizing the independent tort of spoliation include: Alabama, Alaska, California, Connecticut, District of Colombia, Florida, Indiana, Louisiana, Montana, New Jersey, New Mexico, Ohio, and West Virginia. *See, e.g.*, Smith v. Atkinson, 771 So. 2d 429 (Ala. 2000) (Alabama); Sweet v. Sisters of Providence, 895 P.2d 484 (Alaska 1995) (Alaska); Smith v. Superior Ct., 151 Cal. App. 3d 491 (1984) (California); Rizzuto v. Davidson Ladders, Inc., 905 A.2d 1165 (Conn. 2006) (Connecticut); Holmes v. Amerex Rent-a-Car, 710 A.2d 846 (D.C. 1998) (District of Columbia); Cont'l Ins. v. Herman, 576 So. 2d 313 (Fla. Dist. Ct. App. 1990) (Florida); Thompson v. Owensby, 704 N.E.2d 134 (Ind. Ct. App. 1998) (Indiana); McCool v. Beauregard Mem. Hosp., 814 So.2d 116 (La. Ct. App. 2002) (Louisiana); Oliver v. Stimson Lumber Co., 993 P.2d 11 (Mont. 1999) (Montana); Tartaglia v. UBS PaineWebber, Inc., 961 A.2d 1167, 1187–91 (N.J. 2008) (New Jersey); Coleman v. Eddy Potash, Inc., 905 P.2d 185 (N.M. 1995) (New Mexico); Smith v. Howard Johnson Co., 615 N.E.2d 1037 (Ohio 1993) (Ohio); Hannah v. Heeter, 584 S.E.2d 560 (W. Va. 2003) (West Virginia).
50. Patterson v. Berrios, No. HHDCV116017657S, 2012 Conn. Super. LEXIS 1434, 2012 WL 2477939, at *3 (Conn. Super. Ct. June 1, 2012); Brookshire Bros., Ltd. v. Aldridge, 438 S.W.3d 9, 21 (Tex. 2014).
51. Napier v. Cinemark USA, Inc., 635 F. Supp. 2d 1248, 1250 (N.D. Okla. 2009) (quoting Patel v. OMH Med. Ctr., 987 P.2d 1185, 1202 (Okla. 1999)).
52. *See* cases cited *supra* note 49.
53. *See Rizzuto*, 905 A.2d at 1173 ("Destroying evidence can destroy fairness and justice, for it increases the risk of an erroneous decision on the merits of the underlying cause of action. Destroying evidence can also increase the costs of litigation as parties attempt to reconstruct the destroyed evidence or to develop other evidence, which may be less accessible, less persuasive, or both." (quoting Cedars-Sinai Med. Ctr. v. Superior Ct., 954 P.2d 511 (Cal. 1998))).

adequately restoring the victim of spoliation in the rightful position, some courts have developed common laws to hold spoliators of evidence liable in tort.

Traditionally, courts have attempted to deal with spoliation in a variety of ways, via jury instruction, exclusion of testimony, dismissal of the case, and other sanctions.[54] However, the oldest method of a spoliation remedy is the spoliation inference, which allows the jury to infer or presume that the evidence that the spoliator destroyed would have been unfavorable to them.[55]

Another way to deal with spoliation during a proceeding is through independent torts. States have recognized several variations of independent torts for spoliation.[56] For instance, some independent torts include first party intentional spoliation, third party intentional spoliation, first party negligent spoliation, and third-party negligent spoliation.[57]

In a criminal context, spoliation in many states is a misdemeanor. For instance, the California Penal Code §135 provides "[a] person, who, knowing that any . . . matter or thing, is about to be produced in evidence upon any trial . . . willfully destroys . . . or conceals the same, with intent thereby to prevent it . . . from being produced, is guilty of a misdemeanor."[58] On the other hand, the New York Penal Law §215.40 establishes that tampering with physical evidence is a class E felony.[59]

In addition to potential criminal liability under an obstruction of justice statute, an attorney who participates, advises, or assists a client in spoliating evidence may also be subject to professional discipline per the Model Rules of Professional Conduct (MRPC).[60] MRPC 3.4(a) provides in pertinent part that an attorney shall not "unlawfully obstruct another party's access to evidence or unlawfully alter, destroy or conceal a document or other material having potential evidentiary value. A lawyer shall not counsel or assist another person to do any such act."[61] Thus, an attorney may be subject to fines or suspension from practicing law when they participate, counsel, or assist a client in spoliating evidence. Lastly, if a client's case is dismissed because of the attorney's unlawful act of spoliation, the attorney could be liable for malpractice.[62]

---

54. *See* Clark v. Alan Vester Auto Grp., Inc., 2009 NCBC 18, 2009 WL 2181675, at ¶80 (N.C. Super. Ct. July 17, 2009); Kelley v. Blue Line Carriers, LLC, 685 S.E.2d 479, 482 (Ga. Ct. App. 2009).
55. *See* Kammerer v. Sewerage & Water Bd., 633 So. 2d 1357, 1360 (La. Ct. App. 1994) (Waltzer, J., concurring).
56. *See Cedars-Sinai Med. Ctr.*, 954 P.2d at 512-18.
57. *Id.*.
58. Cal. Penal Code § 135 (West 2016).
59. N.Y. Penal Law § 215.40 (McKinney 2020).
60. *See* Federated Mut. Ins. v. Litchfield Precision Components, Inc., 456 N.W.2d 434, 437 (Minn. 1990).
61. Model Rules of Pro. Conduct r. 3.4(a) (Am. Bar Ass'n 2020).
62. *See Federated Mut. Ins. Co.*, 456 N.W.2d at 438.

8.7   Confidentiality, Privilege, and Protections

Within discovery, there are three document classes subject to some privilege or protection:

- Confidential documents
- Privileged documents
- Work product documents

The terms "confidential information" and "privileged information" are sometimes confused; they are not the same and hence, not interchangeable.

Confidential documents may be produced, but various restrictions limit their use. Privileged documents are those that should not be produced. Work product documents are sometimes subject to production.

FRCP 26(c) allows courts to restrict access to or use of specific documents or information, including trade secret information.[63] These restrictions are memorialized in protective orders. Protective orders may restrict viewing of materials only by the attorney or by those who sign confidentiality agreements. Some protective orders may even have multiple levels of confidentiality, with the highest level for

---

63. *See* Alexander C. Egilman et al., *Confidentiality Orders and Public Interest in Drug and Medical Device Litigation*, 180 JAMA Internal Med. 292, 292-93 (2020). In complex medical product liability litigation, confidentiality requirements are very extensive. *Id.* at 296. By utilizing overly broad or unwarranted confidentiality agreements and protective orders, medical manufacturers and corporations prevent disclosure of valuable public health information that may contain damaging information related to safety, effectiveness, prohibited practices. *Id.* at 292-93. "[P]arties . . agree to a blanket protective order [accelerating discovery], which allows producing parties to designate discovery materials as confidential without making the requisite document-by-document showing to the court. Instead, the producing party only needs to have a good faith belief that there is good cause to prohibit disclosure. Under such blanket protective orders, companies routinely designate a far broader scope of discovery materials as confidential than what would be permissible under Rule 26(c)." *Id.* at 293. "[C]ourts . . . often improperly . . . impose secrecy without meeting the proper legal standard, thus favoring confidentiality over public access. These prevailing legal practices undermine access to information by patients, clinicians, and the US Food and Drug Administration." *Id.* at 292. "[These practices] also obscure patterns of injury and disease associated with drugs and medical devices." *Id.* at 296. Public access to court records and proceedings is protected by both the United States constitution and common law. *Id.* at 293. Public access can help "physicians reassess the safety of drugs and devices, [lead] medical journals to more closely examine submitted manuscripts for conflicts of interest . . . compel[] companies to reexamine the questionable business practices revealed in lawsuits . . . [and] influence[] regulatory behavior, contributing to subsequent reevaluations of drug and device safety and labeling by the FDA that may lead to additional warnings or other actions. . . Given the strong interests in confidentiality, initiatives from all stakeholders, including attorneys, courts, legislators, and experts, as well as medical professional societies and journals, will likely be necessary to address the issue of unwarranted secrecy." *Id.* at 296. The authors believe advancing access to important public health information is possible through increased involvement across the board, engaged medical experts committed to challenging confidentiality and advocating disclosure, and new legislation or rules imposing stricter burdens to prevent disclosure of information and strengthening existing legal requirements for confidentiality. *Id.* at 294-96.

attorneys only or attorneys and one client representative and a lower level of confidentiality that allows access to a somewhat broader group of individuals.

Protective orders may also require that documents used in court be filed under seal. Such filing requirements create additional burdens on the filing party. Therefore, be mindful of the demands agreed to during the FRCP 26 conference.

When a protective order is in place, disagreements often arise about which documents should be labeled as confidential. Some parties use the label liberally, asserting that all, or nearly all, of the documents they produce are confidential and should be protected. While this strategy may be successful, it may also backfire if opposing counsel brings the question of appropriate labeling before the court. The party asserting its confidentiality bears the burden to establish that a document should be covered by the protective order. Some producing parties will hold up document production until the requesting party provides some modicum of protection for even nonprivileged documents, despite not meeting the burden of demonstrating that its documents merit protection. Such a demand may raise ethical questions if the request protects documents otherwise not entitled to protection under the procedural rules. The ethical issue arises because the producing party is essentially threatening to delay discovery to secure protection to which it is not entitled. Despite the ethics of such behavior, there are—in large litigations—situations where such agreements, to shield otherwise unprotectable documents to avoid discovery delay, are executed. If faced with such a demand, remind opposing counsel that FRCP 26 provides the court with power to dictate the use of documents produced in discovery that do not meet the specific terms of protection.

On the other hand, privileged documents or communications—including those encompassed by the attorney-client privilege—are not subject to production unless the privilege is waived or an exception—including the fraud-tort exception—is demonstrated.[64] For example, privilege is waived when an attorney-client com-

---

64. *See In re* Grand Jury Investigation, 842 F.2d 1223, 1226 (11th Cir. 1987) (applying the two-prong test to determine whether the crime-fraud exception applies, which includes "a prima facie showing that the client was engaged in . . . [or] planning [wrongful] conduct when he sought the advice of counsel, or that he committed a crime or fraud subsequent to receiving the benefit of counsel's advice. . . [and] a showing that the attorney's assistance was obtained in furtherance of the criminal or fraudulent activity or was closely related to it."); Ocean Spray Cranberries, Inc. v. Holt Cargo Sys., Inc., 785 A.2d 955, 959 (N.J. Super. Ct. Law Div. 2000) ("'Fraud' includes civil as well as criminal fraud. There need not be a tortious fraud in the conventional sense. Rather, public policy requires that the term fraud 'be given the broadest interpretation'. It includes virtually all kinds of deception and deceit, even though they might not otherwise warrant criminal or civil sanctions."). Courts have held the crime-fraud exception applies in various circumstances. *See, e.g., In re* Sealed Case, 754 F.2d 395, 401-02 (D.C. Cir. 1985) (with a sufficient showing of client intent, where client is actively planning criminal or fraudulent activity and seeks attorney advice to advance the activity, regardless if the attorney knows they are an instrumentality); *In re* Grand Jury Proceedings, 87 F.3d 377 (9th Cir. 1996) (where client pursues a crime or fraud, even if attorney is unaware, does not take affirmative steps to further it, or even hinders it); U.S. v.

munication is made in the presence of someone not party to the privilege. Consider situations when a client brings a friend or family member to a meeting with counsel. Communications made during that meeting may be waived. Similarly, if a document containing an attorney-client communication is shown to a party outside the privilege, the privilege may be considered waived.[65]

Federal Rule of Evidence 501 states,

The common law—as interpreted by the United States courts in the light of reason and experience—governs the claim of privilege unless any of the following provides otherwise:

- the United States Constitution;

- a federal statute; or

- rules prescribed by the Supreme Court.

But in a civil case, state law governs privilege regarding a claim or defense for which state law supplies the rule of decision.[66]

In diversity of citizenship cases, federal courts look to state law to determine whether a privilege exists. In non-diversity cases, i.e., federal question cases, federal courts apply a federal common law of privilege. In some states, privileges are governed by common law and in some states, privileges are governed by statute.[67]

Chen, 99 F.3d 1495, 1503-04 (9th Cir. 1996) (where lawyer lacked wrongful intent and was unaware services were being used to deceive government agencies; where there is a "prima facie showing" that interactions advanced "intended or present illegality."); Sound Video Unlimited, Inc. v. Video Shack Inc., 661 F. Supp. 1482, 1488-89 (N.D. Ill. 1987) (where client and attorneys discussed using information gained from wire-tapped communications in litigation); U.S. v. Ballard, 779 F.2d 287, 292 (5th Cir. 1986) (to communications with attorney A, who informed client that bankruptcy petitions must include recently sold property; client then used attorney B to file a fraudulent petition); U.S. v. Gorski, 807 F.3d 451, 461 (1st Cir. 2015) (where defendant, to establish eligibility for government contracts, misrepresented his business' ownership and subsequently hired attorneys to restructure the business so it conformed to his misrepresentation); U.S. v. Al-Shahin, 474 F.3d 941, 944-47 (7th Cir. 2007) (where a client requested help in a fraudulent accident claim from an FBI agent, who was also a licensed attorney). *But see, e.g.,* In re Sealed Case, 107 F.3d 46, 49-50 (D.C. Cir. 1997) (closeness in time between communication and crime insufficient to establish exception); *In re* Grand Jury Subpoena, 745 F.3d 681, 691-93 (3d Cir. 2014) (does not apply where client seeks attorney advice about an action but does not form intent to carry out the action until later); U.S. v. Rakes, 136 F.3d 1 (1st Cir. 1998) (does not apply when client was a victim of extortion and not a participant).

65. For a comprehensive discussion of the work-product doctrine, attorney-client privilege, their respective standards of review, and waiver of the attorney-client privilege see United States ex rel. Wollman v. Mass. Gen. Hosp., Inc., No. CV 15-11890-ADB, 2020 U.S. Dist. LEXIS 134542, 2020 WL 4352915 (D. Mass. July 29, 2020).
66. FED. R. EVID. 501.
67. *See, e.g.,* CAL. EVID. CODE §§ 1060-1063 (West 2021).

The following table is a general outline of the privileges about which litigants need be concerned, but it is not an exhaustive list. When determining if one of the

Type of Privilege	Description
Attorney-client privilege	Communications between attorney and the client
Accountant-client privilege	Communications between accountant and the client
Priest-penitent privilege	Communications between clergy and members of their congregation.
Spousal privilege	Private communications, physical or verbal, between spouses during their marriage.
Deliberative process privilege	A common-law privilege that protects communications of a government agency in reaching a decision.
Privilege log	This is a document that details documents and other items excluded from production in a lawsuit due to conflicting privileges protecting the information from being released.
Physician-patient privilege	Communications between a patient and their doctor.
Psychotherapist-patient privilege	Communications between a patient and their psychotherapist.
Public-interest immunity	A common-law principle that prevents litigants from disclosing information would damage public interest.
Reporters' privilege	Protections for reporters that allow them to maintain their confidential sources.
Right to silence	The 5th Amendment right against self-incrimination.
State secrets privilege	Protects communications that the government claims include sensitive information implicating national security.
State secrets privilege—Classified Information Procedures Act	A federal statutory scheme governing the process of discovery for classified materials that arise during the course of a criminal prosecution.
State secrets privilege—Silent witness rule	An evidentiary rule used in connection to references of state secrets in criminal prosecution that shields the information from the public but not the court, parties, or fact finder.

privileges is applicable, be sure to check if the jurisdiction recognizes the privilege and the scope of the privilege recognized.

8.8 Discovery Document Sharing

The federal discovery rules do not generally prevent a party from sharing documents, depositions, or discovery materials with litigants in other cases. "The desire to share information with other litigants and their attorneys is an appropriate goal under the Federal Rules of Civil Procedure, which are intended 'to secure the just, speedy, and inexpensive, determination of every action.'"[68] The caveat is confidentiality. Documents or testimony produced in litigation may be shared with litigants in other cases only if they are not subject to a confidentiality agreement.

If you wish to release discovery materials for use in other cases, then you must modify the confidentiality agreement or protective order.[69] If the materials genuinely merit protection under FRCP 26(c), and are encompassed by protective order, any motion should propose to the court that litigants in other cases agree to the terms of protection.

8.9 Privilege Logs

Once a party anticipates probable litigation, the party should begin determining which documents might fall within the litigation orbit. The party should review those documents and ascertain instances where they can assert the claim that the documents in question are not subject to production because they are: 1) subject to a privilege, 2) attorney work product, or 3) trial preparation materials.

FRCP 26(b)(5) specifically addresses the matter of "privilege logs." The rule states:

> (5) Claiming Privilege or Protecting Trial-Preparation Materials.
>
> **(A)** *Information Withheld.* When a party withholds information otherwise discoverable by claiming that the information is privileged or subject to protection as trial-preparation material, the party must:
>
> **(i)** expressly make the claim; and
>
> **(ii)** describe the nature of the documents, communications, or tangible things not produced or disclosed—and do so in a manner that, without revealing information itself privileged or protected, will enable other parties to assess the claim.[70]

---

68. *Culinary Foods, Inc. v. Raychem Corp.,* 151 F.R.D. 297, 306 (N.D. Ill. 1993) (quoting *Deford v. Schmid Prods., Co.,* 120 F.R.D. 648, 654 (D. Md. 1987)). *See also* Fed. R. Civ. P. 1.
69. Model Rules of Pro. Conduct r. 1.6 (Am. Bar Ass'n 2020); Fed. R. Civ. P. 26.
70. Fed. R. Civ. P. 26(b)(5).

Document descriptions are entered into a privilege log. Below is a sample layout:

Sample Privilege Log

No.	Privilege Log ID	Date	Sender/ Author	Recipient	Record Type	Description	Privilege Type
1	Sample001	2/17/2018	Smith, John	Client, Carol	Email	Email chain reflecting attorney-client communications regarding AC privilege	Attorney-Client
2	Sample002	5/6/2018	Client, Carol	Smith, John	Email	Email requesting legal advice on contract issues	Attorney-Client
3	Sample003	8/1/2018	Smith, John	Client, Carol	Email	Email chain reflecting attorney-client communications regarding fees	Attorney-Client
4	Sample004	10/10/2018	Smith, John	Client, Carol	Attachment	Draft Filing	Work Product
5	Sample005	1/29/2019	Smith, John	Client, Carol	Email	Email chain reflecting attorney-client communications regarding product research	Attorney-Client
6	Sample006	3/14/2019	Smith, John	Client, Carol	Email	Email chain reflecting attorney-client communications regarding litigation strategy	Attorney-Client
7	Sample007	4/3/2019	Client, Carol	Smith, John	Email	Email chain reflecting attorney-client communications regarding fees	Attorney-Client
8	Sample008	9/12/2019	Smith, John	Client, Carol	Attachment	Draft Press Release	Work Product
9	Sample009	11/24/2019	Client, Carol	Smith, John	Email	Email chain reflecting attorney-client communications regarding reimbursement	Attorney-Client
10	Sample0010	1/20/2020	Smith, John	Client, Carol	Attachment	Draft witness list	Work Product

Privilege logs track documents or portions of documents that are withheld from production. When a portion of a document is withheld, the privileged portions are redacted. Review redactions carefully when producing redacted documents. Even when copies are blacked out, one might flip the page over and easily see the underlying copy if proper care is not taken in the redaction effort. When redacting documents in electronic form, it is critical to ensure that the redaction cannot be edited so that the hidden content is revealed or that metadata does not reveal the content that was redacted.

Privilege logs play an important role in depositions and in motions to compel. In depositions, a party challenging an assertion of privilege can use the log as an exhibit to show there is no privilege, no work product protection, or that there is a waiver. When in a deposition, consider this line of questioning on the issue of waiver:

Q: I am showing you what has been marked as deposition Exhibit 22, a privilege log produced by your counsel. I want to direct your attention to line three which is—and I quote: "letter written by John Smith to attorney Jones." It is Bates labeled DEF22223. Do you see this entry?

A· Yes.

Q: I do not want to ask you about the content of this letter: I just want to know who else—other than attorney Jones—received this letter?

A: I sent it to my friend Jim Mayer, and my business advisor Tom Tuttle.

Q: Are they lawyers?

A: No.

Consider this example regarding whether a two-work product doctrine encompasses a document:

Q: I am showing you what has been marked as deposition Exhibit 22, a privilege log produced by your counsel. I want to direct your attention to line four which is an entry that says: "Harmon Report" and the notation is "investigation by Jones Law Firm." It is Bates numbered DEF22435. Do you see this entry?

A: Yes.

Q: Without getting into the content of the report, can you give me a list of all who received the report?

A: Our outside communications firm, in-house legal, and a few others.

Q: What is the name of the "outside communications firm"?

A: Roxbury Associates.

Q: Do you understand why it was sent the report?

A: Yes.

Q: What is your understanding?

A: Roxbury requested the report so it could do damage control with the press.

Using both the privilege log and the deposition testimony generated from questioning the log, the plaintiff may move to compel the production of the documents. With the first line of questioning, the plaintiff would argue waiver. With the second line of questioning, the plaintiff might argue both waiver and the inapplicability of *Upjohn v. United States.*[71] In *Upjohn*, the Supreme Court articulated a limited expansion of the work product doctrine to certain investigations conducted by counsel.

In crafting a motion to compel the production of privileged documents, the party seeking production may ask the court for an in camera review to determine whether the privilege applies. In camera means the judge can review or preview the documents to determine the privilege's applicability. To prompt an in camera review, a party must present evidence supporting a reasonable belief that in camera review will reveal an exception to a privilege.[72]

8.10   The Rules of Discovery

While FRCP 26 provides the framework for discovery, there are also very tailored rules that address the components of the process. Some of these rules, or their provisions, go unnoticed by attorneys.

8.10.1   FRCP 27: Depositions to Perpetuate Testimony

FRCP 27 permits taking depositions 1) before an action is even filed or 2) when a case on appeal may be remanded to the trial court for further proceedings. Under these circumstances, the deposition-seeking party must file a verified petition with the court.[73] The petition asks for an order authorizing a deposition to perpetuate testimony. Courts explained that while FRCP 27 can be used to preserve testimony from an ill witness, "the Federal Rules do not allow early discovery for the purpose of gathering information for future claims against non-parties."[74] When demonstrating the need for pre-complaint discovery, petitioners must establish three elements to prevail on a FRCP 27 petition:

---

71. Upjohn Co. v. United States, 449 U.S. 383 (1981).

72. *See, e.g.* United States v. Zolin, 491 U.S. 554 (1989) (establishing the standard for an in-camera review of documents that are withheld based on the assertion of a privilege).

73. A verified petition is a petition that is made under penalty of perjury.

74. Lloyd v. Whirlpool Corp., No. 19-cv-6225, 2019 U.S. Dist. LEXIS 175668, 2019 WL 5064698, at *2 (N.D. Ill. Oct. 9, 2019). *See also* Pac. Century Int'l, Ltd. v. Doe, 282 F.R.D. 189, 195–96 (N.D. Ill 2012) ("[W]hen the purpose of a discovery request is to gather information for use in proceedings other than the pending suit, discovery is properly denied." (Quoting Oppenheimer Fund, Inc. v. Sanders 437 U.S. 340, 353 (1978)).

1) a focused explanation of what the petitioner anticipates any testimony would demonstrate, and a persuasive explanation of why the testimony will not be used to discover evidence for the purpose of filing a complaint;

2) a good-faith expectation that the petitioner will be a party to an action cognizable in a United States court, but that it cannot currently bring the action or cause the action to be brought; and

3) an objective showing that, without a Rule 27 order, known testimony would otherwise be lost, concealed or destroyed.[75]

Use FRCP 27 when you know a witness is very ill and may be not alive or competent to testify in a deposition or at the time of trial. You may also use the rule to perpetuate the testimony of your own client. Consider, for example, a client with terminal cancer which they believe was caused by asbestos exposure. Draft a FRCP 27 petition requesting a potential defendant's participation in a deposition so the testimony can be used at trial.

8.10.2   FRCP 28: Persons Before Whom Depositions May Be Taken

FRCP 28's provisions regarding who must be present at a deposition are seldom of major significance in the United States. Court reporter services can be located through web advertisements or ads at the back of most bar publications. In addition, once you or your firm launch a website, court reporter services will contact you for business. FRCP 28(c) states "a deposition must not be taken before a person who is any party's relative, employee, or attorney; who is related or employed by any party's attorney; or who is financially interested in the action,"[76] meaning that court reporters cannot work on contingency.

Although the process of taking a domestic deposition may be straight forward, doing so abroad is more complicated. FRCP 26(b) provides a process to take depositions in a foreign country. Those conducting depositions abroad must follow the procedures outlined in the rule.

8.10.3   FRCP 29: Stipulations about Discovery Procedure

FRCP 29 allows parties, by agreement, to modify the procedures governing discovery or the procedures limiting discovery, unless the court orders otherwise. Under FRCP 29(a), parties may stipulate that depositions "may be taken before any person, at any time or place, on any notice, and in the manner specified."[77] FRCP

---

75. *In re* Perpetuate Testimony by Waste Stream, Inc., PRP Grp., No. 520MC0043GTSTWD, 2020 WL 4049944 (N.D.N.Y. July 20, 2020) (citing *In re Petition of Allegretti*, 229 F.R.D. 93 (S.D.N.Y. 2005)).
76. Fed. R. Civ. P. 28(c).
77. Fed. R. Civ. P. 29(a).

29(b) states that a stipulation that extends the time for any method of discovery and interferes "with the time set for completing discovery, for hearing a motion, or for trial"[78] must be approved by the court.

8.10.4 FRCP 30: Depositions by Oral Examination

With fewer and fewer cases going to trial, depositions are often where parties confront each other directly and secure spontaneous information. Here are some highlights from FCRP 30:[79]

- FRCP 30(a)(2)(A)(i) limits parties to ten depositions in federal court. The number can be modified by leave of court. In large cases—particularly class actions and cases consolidated through multidistrict litigation (MDL)—deposition numbers are often expanded beyond this number. Parties seeking to do so usually distinguish between fact depositions and expert depositions, asking the court to allow a certain number of each, with the expert depositions occurring after the fact depositions.

- As specified in FRCP 30(b)(4), depositions may also be taken by "remote means," where attorneys depose a witness by phone or by video conference. The rule is important because it saves time and money when travel would be required to take a deposition. Coordinate arrangements for such depositions through a local court reporter.[80]

- FRCP 30(b)(6) provides a mechanism for taking depositions of an entity or organization by sending a notice that describes "with reasonable particularity the matters for examination." When seeking to depose a party to the lawsuit, counsel directs a deposition notice describing the areas of inquiry. When seeking to depose a non-party, counsel issues a subpoena with the notice attached. The entity must then designate a representative, or representatives, to appear and be deposed. Parties utilize FRCP 30(b)(6) for two reasons. First, a discovery-seeking party may already know who within the corporation or entity knows about the area of inquiry. FRCP 30(b)(6) forces a corporation or entity to produce those person(s) knowledgeable of the area and prepare them for deposition questions within the orbit of the request. Second, testimony that results from a FRCP 30(b)(6) deposition binds the entity. The deponent's testimony is representative, as if the entity were a living being and could testify itself. Importantly, the person produced for the FRCP 30(b)(6) deposition need not have personal knowledge of the events or issues in the case; they can be educated by the documents or other information in the case to speak on behalf of the

---

78. FED. R. CIV. P. 29(b).
79. *See* FED. R. CIV. P. 30.
80. *See* Chapter Nine (discussing remote depositions).

company. An entity may sometimes need to produce multiple individuals in response to a FRCP 30(b)(6) notice if there are several distinct areas of inquiry and there is not a single person at the company who is most knowledgeable about each of the areas of inquiry.

- FRCP 30(d) imposes a time limit on depositions: one day of seven hours. Though not articulated specifically, the rule limits the seven hours to time on the record. Therefore, bathroom and lunch breaks are not included in the seven hours. Work with the court reporter to track time on the record. Where there is significant ground to cover, ask how much deposition time remains.

- FRCP 30(d)(2) provides for sanctions—including reasonable expenses and attorney's fees—where "a person . . . impedes, delays, or frustrates the fair examination of the deponent."[81] Be on alert for this conduct:

  - Deponent's counsel repeatedly interjects "if you know" after every question.

  - Deponent's counsel makes extensive speaking objections.

  - Deponent's counsel either uses hand gestures or puts a hand on the witness to influence testimony.

  - Deponent's counsel speaks on the record in a manner that coaches the witness.

  - Deponent's counsel repeatedly instructs the witness not to answer questions for any reason other than valid attorney-client privilege claims, such as not being "relevant."

- FRCP 30(e) gives witnesses thirty days to review and sign the deposition transcript. Changes may be requested but must be explained. Common adjustments include spelling corrections or other minor modifications of testimony recorded incorrectly. The provision to "read and sign" is not a second bite at the apple; neither attempt nor allow substantive changes to testimony.

8.10.5 *FRCP 31: Depositions by Written Questions*

FRCP 31 allows depositions to be taken by answering written questions. FRCP 30 also grants this right. In such circumstances, counsel delivers written questions to the court reporter, who tenders them to the witness and records the answer. As a practical matter, the rule is rarely, if ever, used.

---

81. Fed. R. Civ. P. 30(d)(2).

8.10.6   FRCP 32: Using Depositions in Court Proceedings

FRCP 32 establishes parameters for using depositions in court proceedings. As a general proposition, depositions may be used against a party if the party received reasonable notice of the deposition, had representation, and the testimony is otherwise admissible under the evidentiary rules. Fundamental uses of a party opponent's deposition include impeachment and admissions. Although FRCP 32(a)(3) does not cite to FRE 801(d)(2)—an opposing party's statement—the rule tracks the language in the evidentiary rules.

FRCP 32 also specifies criteria governing deposition use when the witness is not available at trial and the use of deposition testimony taken in other actions litigating the same matters.

8.10.7   FRCP 33: Interrogatories to Parties

Interrogatories are submitted questions that must be answered under oath. In federal court, in addition to the general provisions of FRCP 26 covering discovery, interrogatories are governed by FRCP 33 "Interrogatories to Parties."[82] FRCP 33 articulates several requirements for answering interrogatories properly and is a relatively simple rule to understand. It specifies that only twenty-five interrogatories (including subparts) may be interposed, and courts may grant leave to serve additional interrogatories under the guidance of Rule 26. Relevant information only needs to be within the scope of discoverable information under FRCP26(b) and does not necessarily have to be admissible as evidence. FRCP 33 provides that "[a]n interrogatory may relate to any matter that may be inquired into under Rule 26(b)."[83]

Under FRCP 33, the interrogatories must be answered by the responding party or by an officer or agent if the party is a corporation, partnership, association, or government agency. Responding parties have a thirty-day response window (calculated in accordance with local rules). Furthermore, the rule dictates that each interrogatory must be answered separately and fully in writing under oath, the ground for objection must be stated with specificity, and that answers, including objections in lieu of an answer, must be signed.

The rule also permits a party to answer an interrogatory by reference to documents in certain circumstances. Under the rule, the responding party may answer an interrogatory by producing business records if the answer may be determined by "examining, auditing, compiling, abstracting" and if the burden of deriving affects both parties to the same degree.[84]

---

82. Fed. R. Civ. P. 33.
83. Fed. R. Civ. P. 33(a)(2).
84. *See* Fed. R. Civ. P. 33(d).

Interrogatories are useful for securing discrete facts and eliminating theories. The identities of event attendees, an accident-victim plaintiff's medication list, or the costs incurred to locate a substitute product for a breach of contract case are discrete facts that can easily be secured through interrogatories.

In contrast, interrogatories are generally less useful when the question seeks a more complex response. First, the answering party often finds such interrogatories objectionable, whether correct or not, and asserts an objection forcing court intervention. Second, using interrogatories that demand complex responses may telegraph a legal theory to the opponent. There is no suggestion to avoid propounding complex interrogatories, but before doing so, consider saving the question for a deposition and reserve interrogatories as the means to identify the best witnesses for the complex questions.

"Contention interrogatories" are interrogatories used to eliminate points of contention. They typically seek a yes or no response. For example, in a negligence case, one might ask:

1) Do you contend that Defendant Smith violated any rule of the American Hospital Association?

If the answer is no, an entire area of inquiry is eliminated from the case, streamlining the litigation. However, contention interrogatories are generally used in conjunction with a follow-up interrogatory:

2) If the answer to Interrogatory is affirmative, identify the rule.

Contention interrogatories pose many problems for lawyers. Their vast impact forces the lawyer to forecast future litigation and assess the impact of answers that take an entire area of potential dispute out of contention. Hence, the process of answering contention interrogatories requires serious consideration of the trajectory of a case; the wrong answer may foreclose a theory or defense that only becomes relevant once additional discovery is done.

For the purposes of summary judgment or trial, interrogatory answers can be:

- cited in the motion or opposition to a motion for summary judgment;

- used to support a statement of undisputed facts or a statement of disputed facts in a summary judgment briefing;

- marked as an exhibit and presented or read to the jurors.

At closing or in a motion for summary judgment, a lawyer is free to argue inferences from the answers. For example, consider a case where the plaintiff sues the defendant, alleging negligence in the fabrication of a stairwell. Consider the following interrogatory directed to the defendant:

How many stairwells has the Jones company been hired to assemble over the past decade?

If the answer is a very small number, the plaintiff can argue the inference that the defendant lacks the requisite experience which ties into a narrative that mistakes were made because defendant is not a highly skilled installer of stairwells.

Interrogatories—like other modes of discovery—may also produce information experts can rely upon in forming their opinions. For this reason, it is often important to consult with the expert—or perhaps non-testifying expert—when preparing the interrogatories.

8.10.8   FRCP 34: Producing Documents, Electronically Stored Information, and Tangible Things, or Entering onto Land, for Inspection and Other Purposes

FRCP 34 governs document requests and production. As a general proposition, document requests are among the first lines of discovery. Structure requests to secure both the good and the bad evidence. Seek documents to support the causes of action, support the affirmative defenses, and attack the reliability of evidence. Document requests may be directed to parties without requiring a subpoena, while requests to non-parties require a subpoena.

As a starting point, FRCP 34(a) provides:

(a) *In General.* A party may serve on any other party a request within the scope of Rule 26(b):

(1) to produce and permit the requesting party or its representative to inspect, copy, test, or sample the following items in the responding party's possession, custody, or control:

(A) any designated documents or electronically stored information—including writings, drawings, graphs, charts, photographs, sound recordings, images, and other data or data compilations—stored in any medium from which information can be obtained either directly or, if necessary, after translation by the responding party into a reasonably usable form; or

(B) any designated tangible things; or

(2) to permit entry onto designated land or other property possessed or controlled by the responding party, so that the requesting party may inspect, measure, survey, photograph, test, or sample the property or any designated object or operation on it.[85]

---

85. Fed. R. Civ. P. 34(a). Requests for entry onto land are particularly useful in environmental cases, trespass or nuisance cases, and environmental cases.

National Institute for Trial Advocacy

Document request procedures are defined by FRCP 34(b).[86] The standard format for document requests includes instructions, a set of definitions, and the actual request setting forth enumerated requests for specific documents or types of documents.

The instructions identify the target of the request, response time, and the production place. Instructions should specify a method of document production. For example, with a small automobile accident case between individuals, production will likely be in paper form. However, even in a case involving individuals and not large entities, contemporary requests still encompass electronic information including emails.

The definitions offer clarity on words or names that may be a matter of dispute. Defining certain words at the beginning of a request ensures that the recipient understands the request's word usage. For example, define the word "document" to include emails, videos, voice recordings, and all electronic information. Or, if the defendant is an entity, a definition might say the "New York Corporation shall include all affiliates and subsidiaries of the Defendant New York Corporation." [87]

When drafting the request's actual language, anticipate how the recipient may interpret your words. Assume their interpretation will work to their advantage. Remember the receiving party is likely to construe any ambiguity as a basis for objections. Be as clear as possible and leave little to no room for ambiguity. To the extent the receiving party claims a misunderstanding with regard to certain words in the request, the requesting party will have definitions to point to.

An underinclusive request may give the recipient a basis to exclude needed documents from production. An overinclusive request may cause a massive document dump and require time-consuming document review yielding little, if any, usable evidence. Overinclusive requests may also lead a recipient to object, predicated on the request being overly broad and not "proportional" to the needs of the case.

Remember that an independently-minded judge viewing the request for the first time will also be the one determining whether the request is ambiguous, seeks privileged information or work product communications, or will lead to proportionality objections.

Parties receiving a document request must either raise specific objections or produce the documents. Typically, a document request is answered with a written response citing objections to the request and specifying which documents will be produced.

---

86. Fed. R. Civ. P. 34(b).
87. *See* Appendix for standard form document request.

The most obvious document request objections include attorney-client privilege and work product doctrine.[88] To some degree, these privileges overlap and are often raised simultaneously.[89] When a party withholds a document based on privilege, the withholding party prepares a "privilege log," as discussed in section 8.9. The party asserting a privilege bears the burden to demonstrate the privilege. Therefore, the log must contain sufficient information to establish the existence of a privilege.[90]

Be careful about asserting the privilege because ultimately the matter may be reviewed by the court. In *United States v. Zolin*,[91] the Supreme Court held that trial courts may review documents in camera to determine whether to sustain an asserted privilege. When challenging a privilege, a party may seek depositions—perhaps pursuant to FRCP 30(b)(6)—to further ascertain the privilege's basis and determine whether the privilege was waived. As the Supreme Court noted in *Upjohn v. United States*, the work product doctrine is not an absolute bar to production.[92] In addition to privilege and work product, other objections may include proportionality, vagueness, ambiguity, and relevancy.

Production requests, particularly in large cases, often begin a negotiation process. The parties discuss what is needed to get the case past the motions process and through trial. Although negotiation requires compromise, that compromise may be a blessing in disguise. When propounding document requests, keep in mind that the larger the production, the more documents there will be to review. Storing documents in electronic form costs money, apart from the additional costs of attorneys or paralegals engaging in document review.

For the purposes of the negotiation, if the documents are to be produced in an electronic form—which makes the most sense for any case of significant size—each party must be proficient in the nuances of electronic information. When produced documents are in electronic form, having internal or outside vendor storage capability is crucial for document review. The requesting party will need to line up a document review platform. Multiple vendor platforms are available. When selecting a platform, consider several variables including cost, system speed, search methods, and the ability to make notations on or to categorize the documents. Prior to the negotiation, the requesting party will inquire about the document delivery method so the documents can be loaded onto the reviewing platform.

When seeking discovery of electronic information, be certain to secure the documents and request their underlying metadata. Metadata is information about the actual documents being produced, data about the data. Metadata can include the following:

---

88. For additional discussion of privilege and privilege logs, *see* §§ 8.7 and 8.9.
89. *See, e.g.*, Upjohn Co. v. United States, 449 U.S. 383 (1981).
90. *See* section 8.9 (sample privilege log).
91. United States v. Zolin, 491 U.S. 554 (1989).
92. *Upjohn*, 449 U.S. at 401-02.

- Whose files the document came from.

- Who edited the document and when.

- Whether the document is authentic.

Why is metadata so essential? Often a party produces a document with no listed authors. A PowerPoint, for example, may contain tons of information but no means of ascertaining a creation date, who created it, to whom it was transmitted, and who made edits. Metadata can provide this information. Prior to the advent of metadata, a deponent often would say, "I have no idea where this came from." Now deposing counsel can introduce an exbibit to the witness as follows:

> **Q:** I would like to show you a document that was produced by your counsel and came from your files, as verified by the metadata. Can you tell me what this is?

> **A:** Yes, it is a PowerPoint presentation given at a meeting I attended. The document was circulated as a pre-read before the meeting.

A discussion of document production cannot occur without a discussion of how electronic information is authenticated for use in court. Documents used at trial as evidence to prove a claim must be: 1) relevant under FRE 401; 2) not excluded under FRE 403; 3) not hearsay or excepted from hearsay under FRE 801, 803, and 807; and 4) authentic under FRE 901 or 902.

"Authentic" means the document is what it purports to be. For example, an email might be relevant in a case. However, it is not relevant if it is fake or was not sent by the person you are claiming it was sent by. The process of authentication is proving to the court that this email was authored and sent by the person you are claiming was the author.

FRE 901 addresses how to authenticate different types of evidence. The rule is easy to understand, and lawyers need only structure their deposition or trial questions so they correspond to the rule's relevant subsections. FRE 902 addresses what is known as "self-authenticating" evidence, including evidence authenticated by declaration. In 2011, the advisory committee amended FRE 902 to include subsections (13) and (14):

> Rule 902. Evidence That Is Self-Authenticating

> The following items of evidence are self-authenticating; they require no extrinsic evidence of authenticity in order to be admitted:

> ***

> **(13)** ***Certified Records Generated by an Electronic Process or System.*** A record generated by an electronic process or system that produces an accurate result, as shown by a certification of a qualified

person that complies with the certification requirements of Rule 902(11) or (12). The proponent must also meet the notice requirements of Rule 902(11).

(14) *Certified Data Copied from an Electronic Device, Storage Medium, or File.* Data copied from an electronic device, storage medium, or file, if authenticated by a process of digital identification, as shown by a certification of a qualified person that complies with the certification requirements of Rule 902(11) or (12). The proponent also must meet the notice requirements of Rule 902 (11).

These provisions allow an affidavit to authenticate documents generated by electronic databases. The rule is particularly useful for documents secured by third-party subpoenas. In lieu of securing deposition testimony to authenticate the production, the document provider need only supply an affidavit in compliance with the rule. This is a matter of negotiation: the requesting party negotiates for such a declaration, proposing that in consideration for the declaration, a deposition to authenticate the documents is unnecessary.

This leads to the final point in our document production discussion: documents may be secured from third parties (individuals or entities who are neither defendants nor plaintiffs) and only require that the discovery propounder attach the document request to a subpoena.

8.10.9 FRCP 35: Physical and Mental Examinations[93]

In contrast to depositions, interrogatories, and requests for admission, no party is entitled—absent an order of court—to secure a physical or mental examination. Physical or mental examinations become relevant—and thus appropriate—only when they are relevant to the proceeding.[94] Such an examination order is dependent upon a showing of good cause and must be conducted by a "suitably licensed or certified examiner.[95]

---

93. *See* FED. R. CIV. P. 35.

94. *See* Schlagenhauf v. Holder, 379 U.S. 104, 114 (1964) (holding that, under Rule 35, a "party" ordered to undergo an examination can be either a plaintiff or defendant). Federal and state courts have approved a variety of examination types including X-rays, blood work, urinalysis, eye exams, stomach content analysis, electroencephalogram, and electrocardiogram. Courts may require a party to establish the procedure's medical acceptance and safety before ruling. *See* RICHARD L. MARCUS, 8 FEDERAL PRACTICE AND PROCEDURE § 2235 (3d. ed. Apr. 2020).

95. FED. R. CIV. P. 35(a)(1). The federal rule does not specify how examiners should be selected. *See* RICHARD L. MARCUS, 8 FEDERAL PRACTICE AND PROCEDURE § 2234.2 (3d. ed. Apr. 2020) ("The usual attitude is that the moving party has no absolute right to the choice of the physician, but that when no serious objection arises, it is probably best for the court to appoint the doctor of the moving party's choice."). *See also* FED. R. CIV. P. 35(a)(1) advisory committee's note to 1991 amendment (stating that the amendment mandating a "suitably licensed or certified" examiner was

Rule 35 requires notice be given to all parties and the person to be examined. The required notice "must specify the time, place, manner, conditions, and scope of the examination"[96] and identify the examiner.

FRCP 35(b)'s provisions govern the various requirements for requests, deliveries, report contents, waiver of privilege, and scope of the examiner's report itself.[97] The party or person examined may request a copy of the examiner's report from the party who moved for the examination. The moving party must deliver the requested report, along with "like reports of all earlier examinations of the same condition" to the requestor. "The request may be made by the party against whom the examination order was issued or by the person examined."[98] FRCP 35(b)(2) requires the examiner to draft a written report detailing "the examiner's findings, including diagnoses, conclusions, and the results of any tests." The party examined waives its privilege if it either: 1) requests and obtains the examiner's report; or 2) deposes the examiner. This waiver applies to the current action or "any other action involving the same controversy—concerning testimony about all examinations of the same condition."[99]

The court may order a party to deliver an examiner's report, and failure to do so, can result in the examiner's testimony being excluded at trial.[100] FRCP 35(b) also applies "to an examination made by the parties' agreement, unless the agreement states otherwise . . . [and] does not preclude obtaining an examiner's report or deposing an examiner under other rules."[101]

As a practical matter in civil litigation, physical and mental health examinations are used primarily in personal injury cases. Where a plaintiff claims a permanent inability to work as a result of the tortious conduct, the defendant is entitled to request that an independent medical examination (IME) be conducted to ascertain the *bona fides* of the plaintiff's claims. Moreover, where the plaintiff is claiming emotional distress as a result of an alleged injury caused by the defendant, an independent mental examination may be requested. In sum, where the plaintiff places physical or mental injury into the case, a physical or mental examination of the plaintiff is reasonable.

Examinations may also be used in other types of common-law matters—including defamation—where the plaintiff is claiming emotional distress damages.

When pleading a plaintiff's case, be aware that seeking damages for physical and/or mental injury may trigger a court order requiring an independent mental

---

a new addition to 35(b) and it is the court's responsibility to assess credentials and "determine the suitability of the examiner's qualifications.").

96. Fed. R. Civ. P. 35(a)(2)(B).
97. *See* Fed. R. Civ. P. 35(b).
98. Fed. R. Civ. P. 35(b)(1).
99. Fed. R. Civ. P. 35(b)(4).
100. Fed. R. Civ. P. 35(b)(5).
101. Fed. R. Civ. P. 35(b)(6).

or physical examination. Alert the client that they may be subject to physical or mental examination. Prepare them during retention discussions and through continuing dialogue as the case proceeds. Never let a client be surprised by a request for physical or mental examination, and do not downplay the potential for such an event.

8.10.10   FRCP 36: Requests for Admission[102]

Admissions are an overlooked asset in discovery. They can be used for mundane things that shortcut trial, like to establish evidentiary foundations for exhibits. They can be used to establish substantive facts as well. Consider using them strategically through the pretrial phase of your case as it begins to take shape. Anything you can do at this stage to make things smoother and easier at trial will work to your benefit in the long run.

— Professor Veronica Finkelstein,
Drexel University Thomas R. Kline School of Law

Any party to a pending action may serve a written request for admission (RFA) on another party. The RFA requires a party to admit or deny the truth or genuineness of any matters or documents relevant to the action. When serving a RFA, each matter must be stated separately.

RFAs are used to find common ground or limit the issues in dispute. RFAs can be considered a discovery device, but only in the sense that they are designed to confirm facts and remove them from contention. The purpose of an RFA is not to discover new information, but to confirm facts are not in dispute.[103] FRCP 36 governs requests for admission:

> A matter is admitted unless, within 30 days after being served, the party to whom the request is directed serves on the requesting party a written answer or objection addressed to the matter and signed by the party or its attorney. A shorter or longer time for responding may be stipulated to under Rule 29 or be ordered by the court.[104]

In a written statement, the responding party may admit the truth of a matter stated, deny the truth, admit parts of the request and deny others, or explain why they cannot truthfully admit or deny. If denying a matter, the denials must be

---

102. FED. R. CIV. P. 36.
103. *See* United States ex rel. Bibby v. Mortg. Invs. Corp., 323 F.R.D. 424, 426-27 (N.D. Ga. 2017) ("'Rule 36 is not a discovery device,' but rather a way 'to facilitate proof with respect to issues that cannot be eliminated from the case, and secondly, to narrow the issues by eliminating those that can be.'" (citations omitted)).
104. *See* FED. R. CIV. P. 36(a)(3).

specific and "fairly respond to the substance of the matter."[105] If a party seeks to admit some parts and deny others, "the answer must specify the part admitted and qualify or deny the rest."[106] If a party cannot truthfully admit or deny a matter, the written answer must provide a detailed explanation as to why. When citing reasons for its failure to admit or deny, a party's lack of knowledge or information is only valid when that party "has made reasonable inquiry and that the information it knows or can readily obtain is insufficient to enable it to admit or deny."[107]

Parties submit written objections when there is a legal basis for not submitting a written answer. All objection grounds must be stated. An objection that a request presents a genuine issue for trial is not, on its own, a valid ground for objection.

One purpose of the rule to authenticate evidence, as in this example:

1) Admit that Exhibit A attached hereto is a true and correct copy of a letter that Defendant John Smith wrote to Clara Jones on August 21, 1976.

Second, RFAs can pin down admissions as to facts, the application of law to facts, or opinions about either.[108] Here are examples:

2) Admit that John Smith was employed by the Smith company from August 21, 1980 until July 1, 2017.

The above is an example of using the RFA to confirm a fact. The next example is where law is being applied to fact:

3) Admit that if John Smith left the company for the sole reason of caring for his grandchildren, he was not constructively discharged.

The next example seeks admission as to opinions:

4) Admit that John Smith has no claim for economic damages if he is not working because he is caring for his grandchildren.

There is undoubtedly an overlap between the second and the third example, but the takeaway is that RFAs can be used expansively.

8.10.11   FRCP 37: Failure to Make Disclosures or to Cooperate in Discovery; Sanctions

In federal court, FRCP 37 addresses discovery derelictions. FRCP 37 is the hammer; it enforces compliance with discovery obligations including document production, interrogatories, requests for admission, deposition questions, requests for

---

105. FED. R. CIV. P. 36(a)(4).
106. *Id.*
107. *Id.*
108. FED. R. CIV. P. 36(a)(1)(A).

mental and physical examinations and requests to inspect property. Pursuant to FRCP 37, a court can compel production, issue remedies that otherwise facilitate the collection of discovery materials, and it may order the recalcitrant party to pay the expenses of pursuing FRCP 37 relief. The rule also authorizes a court to issue relief that can have an outcome determinative effect on the litigation as noted in FRCP 37(b)(2):

> (b) Failure to Comply with a Court Order.
>
> (2) Sanctions Sought in the District Where the Action Is Pending.
>
> (**A**) *For Not Obeying a Discovery Order.* If a party or a party's officer, director, or managing agent—or a witness designated under Rule 30(b)(6) or 31(a)(4)—fails to obey an order to provide or permit discovery, including an order under Rule 26(f), 35, or 37(a), the court where the action is pending may issue further just orders. They may include the following:
>
> (**i**) directing that the matters embraced in the order or other designated facts be taken as established for purposes of the action, as the prevailing party claims;
>
> (**ii**) prohibiting the disobedient party from supporting or opposing designated claims or defenses, or from introducing designated matters in evidence;
>
> (**iii**) striking pleadings in whole or in part;
>
> (**iv**) staying further proceedings until the order is obeyed;
>
> (**v**) dismissing the action or proceeding in whole or in part;
>
> (**vi**) rendering a default judgment against the disobedient party; or
>
> (**vii**) treating as contempt of court the failure to obey any order except an order to submit to a physical or mental examination.[109]

Professional conduct norms require diligent adherence to this obligation. Failure to do so may lead to judges imposing discovery orders, sanctions, and/or jury instructions allowing the assumption that, had the missing or destroyed information been available, it would negatively impact the offending party's case. In this regard, FRCP 37(e) is relevant to the discussion:

> (e) **Failure to Preserve Electronically Stored Information.** If electronically stored information that should have been preserved in the anticipation or conduct of litigation is lost because a party failed to

---

109. FED. R. CIV. P. 37(b).

take reasonable steps to preserve it, and it cannot be restored or replaced through additional discovery, the court:

(1) upon finding prejudice to another party from loss of the information, may order measures no greater than necessary to cure the prejudice; or

(2) only upon finding that the party acted with the intent to deprive another party of the information's use in the litigation may:

(A) presume that the lost information was unfavorable to the party;

(B) instruct the jury that it may or must presume the information was unfavorable to the party; or

(C) dismiss the action or enter a default judgment.

8.11   Supplementing Responses

Once a disclosure or response is made under FRCP 26 be cognizant of any material changes to discovery information. FRCP 26(e) mandates that counsel correct disclosures or responses that are incomplete or incorrect. The disclosure of this new information must be done in a timely manner. Be sure to hand over the additional or corrective information to opposing counsel during discovery or in writing. The court may also order the disclosure of corrective or supplemental information. For expert witnesses, the requirement to disclose additional or incomplete information applies to both the expert's report, which is disclosed under FRCP 26(a)(2)(B), and information given during the expert's deposition. Be sure to disclose additional or incomplete expert information before pretrial disclosures are due under FRCP 26(a)(3).

8.12   The Discovery Plan

Make this your motto: "stay focused and get what is necessary to prove or defend your case." Discovery is time-consuming and costly, regardless of whether you are handling the matter on contingency, on an hourly basis, or through a hybrid of the two.

You used the jury instructions to prepare the complaint; keep looking at those instructions. Focus discovery to secure the necessary evidence to prove or defend the case. Discovery produces an enormous amount of information but only some of that information will actually be used in motions or at trial.

Information gathered or learned through preparing a complaint, answer, or motion to dismiss, plus pretrial disclosures, will guide your discovery plan. Even before or while drafting a complaint, anticipate what disclosures will be required. Anticipating compliance with these disclosure requirements will force you to think or second guess your case theories and refocus the necessary proof. If there is any lesson to be learned in this text, it is to constantly rethink, recheck, second guess, and refine your theories. Never drink your own Kool-Aid and always evaluate how new facts impact case theories.

By the time discovery commences, you may already have an opinion on a motion to dismiss, the briefs supporting the motion, and an answer to the complaint. Though facts may be in dispute, the parties have laid out their legal positions.

The plaintiff will generally have the following discovery goals:

- Gather evidence that meets the claim's elements and gather facts that most closely align with fact patterns established by existing cases.

- Gather evidence that rebuts, undermines, or eliminates defenses. Also gather evidence that can be used to attack the credibility of defense witnesses.

- Fully explore the defendant's view of the facts and its parameters, lock in the facts, and eliminate the introduction of surprise facts.

- Gather evidence needed for experts to render their opinions.

From the defendant's position, the goals are as follows:

- Develop information that could potentially knock out the case without addressing the merits. Look for affirmative defenses including statute of limitations, statute of repose, and laches, to name a few.

- Develop information that undermines case elements. Think about causation, standard of care, duty, and breach of duty. If damages are an element of the claim, secure information as to the damages.[110]

- Develop evidence that reduces or undermines the award of damages, even if your case is lost on liability.

- Gather evidence needed for experts to render their opinions.

Both parties should focus on gathering facts relevant not only for trial, but for other litigation phases that might be outcome determinative:

- Class certification
- Summary judgment

---

110. In some states, damages are an element of the tort of fraud. *See, e.g.*, UWork.com, Inc. v. Paragon Techs., Inc., 740 S.E.2d 887, 898 (Ga. Ct. App. 2013); Robinson Helicopter Co. v. Dana Corp., 102 P.3d 268, 274 (Cal. 2004); Wolford v. Children's Home Soc'y, 17 F. Supp. 2d 577, 584 (S.D. W. Va. 1998).

- Motions in limine

- *Daubert* motions

Evidence gathered through discovery can be used in all the above motions. Each of these motions requires a briefing and—most likely—a hearing. The hearing may be an oral argument, or it may be an evidentiary hearing where witnesses are called. Hence, any discovery plan must contemplate gathering evidence to use in motions.

In the early stage of litigation, after a decision on the motion to dismiss, parties convey to the court their positions regarding discovery period length. Remember that fact discovery precedes expert discovery. Your fact discovery plan must account for any information experts need to render opinions.

Think and rethink how you will use discovery devices: document requests, interrogatories, requests for admission, requests for mental and physical and examination, and requests to inspect property. To make these devices work most efficiently, consider the order in which to use them and what prefatory discovery is necessary.

Consider a medical malpractice case. The defense attorney will undoubtedly request an independent medical or psychiatric examination. The defense will retain a doctor to conduct that examination. What documents or information will that doctor need to conduct the examination and render an opinion?

Think about whether you are missing anything. When devising a discovery plan in technical cases, work with a non-testifying expert to help formulate interrogatories and requests for admission.

When developing discovery plans, be mindful of the rules of evidence. Verify that the evidence gathered is admissible and anticipate possible objections to its introduction. Contemplate the grounds on which you can prevail over those objections. The key evidentiary rules are: FRE 401 on relevancy, FRE 403 on excluding relevant evidence, FRE 801 on hearsay, FRE 803 on hearsay exceptions, and FRE 901-902 on authentication.

As you gather information throughout the discovery process, you should be thinking about evidence that is relevant to attacking the credibility of witnesses. FRE 608 and FRE 609 are the rules that lay the framework for what information will be admissible at trial. Can you find a witness who will testify that another witness has untruthful character? If so, that evidence will be admissible to impeach the witness' credibility under FRE 608(a). Has the witness committed any non-conviction acts that would demonstrate untruthful character? If so, that evidence will be admissible to impeach a witness under 608(b). Lastly, you should be looking for any evidence of prior criminal convictions to impeach a witness pursuant to 609. Understanding the Federal Rules of Evidence will help you to craft your discovery requests.

8.13   Producing the Discovery Information

Documents produced in discovery, whether in hard copy or electronic form, are labeled by number. This number is called a Bates number. The word "Bates" originated from the name of the device used to stamp numbers on hard copies. The device dates back over 100 years. The number changes after each stamp. Bates numbers begin with a three-letter acronym identifying the party producing documents for the case. For example, if the Department of Justice brings an action and produces documents, it might choose to produce documents beginning with the initials "DOJ."

For parties producing hard copies, bates numbering devices still exist and can be used to number documents. In addition, copy vendors offer labeling services for a price; software programs also exist for electronic labeling of documents printed in-house. Bates label privileged documents so that Bates numbers can be referenced on the privilege log.

Electronic documents should also have a Bates label. Discovery vendors provide this service or parties can use labeling software.

Always review documents before producing them. Identifying privileged documents and determining which documents will be used against the client at trial, in motions, and at depositions provides a better understanding of the case.

8.14   Discovery Review

After using all the discovery arrows in your quiver, you will have collected documents, taken depositions, launched interrogatories, and made requests for admission. If the case merits a medical exam or inspection of property, you have done that as well.

Thorough document review is a challenge and requires immersing yourself in the documents. Get in the trenches, read documents, reconstruct events, analyze witness personalities, and always match facts to the law. Put the case puzzle together.

In big cases, banks of firm lawyers work out of "war rooms" where they divide document review by "Bates ranges." Firms have strategies to ensure that most—if not all—documents get reviewed. In a class action, or in a series of actions consolidated through multidistrict litigation, lead counsel may divide document review among participating firms. Counsel participating in the review often have remote access to a database maintained by a vendor. Software enables documents to be marked with notes and labeled as "hot." The term hot generally refers to documents providing direct evidence in a case. However, many cases strictly rely on circumstantial evidence. For those cases, attorneys may label circumstantial documents as hot.

Most document review platforms have word search capability. When developing a narrative and a theory of the case, search by names, document custodian, words, or word combinations. Regardless of search methods, production is often repetitive. Searches may generate singular emails, parts of email chains, or different fragments of an email chain (depending on whether individuals were added to or removed from the email transmission).

As you go through discovery, create mechanisms that allow you to locate documents when needed. Here are some helpful tools:

- Create binders for hot documents and continually update the binders. (The same applies for electronic documents—create and update folders containing hot documents.)

- Create timelines reciting facts. Cite the supporting documents by Bates number.

- Draft your opening narrative. Cite documents by Bates number and cite deposition testimony by page and line.

- Review the complaint, match your allegations to what you learned in discovery, and determine which issues are undisputed.

As your case theory and potential grounds for summary judgment become clear, keep a chart of documents, interrogatory responses, or deposition testimony that support each element of your summary judgment argument. This will help you to identify gaps that you might need to fill in subsequent depositions or requests for admission. This can also be useful for trial if the matter is not resolved during summary judgment.

CHAPTER NINE

DEPOSITIONS

9.1   Introduction

You have interviewed your client, talked to witnesses, secured documents in discovery, and perhaps received answers to interrogatories and responses to requests for admission. You know something about the case, and you may have an overall sense of the underlying facts and even reasoned theories as to the claims. Still, you are curious about the authors of emails, documents, letters, and the "verifiers" of the interrogatories. There are words and phrases in documents that are confusing or raise issues. In sum, you are just plain curious and want answers from live witnesses.

With most cases being resolved before trial, depositions may be your only opportunity to ask live questions and directly confront the opposing party or third-party witnesses. In the past, taking a deposition was the only pretrial mechanism to obtain spontaneous responses from a witness. But with the advent of emails, texting, social media, cellphone photos and videos, we now have real-time remarks—often unedited—from witnesses. We may even have video recordings of events, which in the past could only be described by witnesses. Since attorneys now have access to more information when entering a deposition, today's depositions may sometimes be less about discovering information and more about authenticating information and testing theories.

For many years, trial attorneys have been taught to begin their depositions with background questions focusing, perhaps, on a witness's education and work history. Today, that same information may be easily available on LinkedIn, Facebook, or through Google searches. These questions may be less about getting new information and more about testing how witnesses respond to questions.

Despite the availability of information on social media and the internet, depositions remain an extremely important component of gathering new information during the pretrial process. Depositions are conducted of the following people:

- Parties

- Third parties

- Employees of parties

- Representatives designated by corporations, associations, or entities

- Fact witnesses

- Expert witnesses

Depositions serve the following functions:

- Learning facts

- Identifying witnesses and documents

- Authenticating documents

- Securing facts that will support the admissibility of evidence

- Testing theories

- Exploring grounds for resolution

- Driving settlement

Depositions allow attorneys to secure information that can be used for the following purposes:

- Motions to compel the production of documents

- Motions in limine

- Summary judgment motions

- *Daubert* motions

- Impeachment of a witness at trial

- As admissions at trial or at summary judgment

- Providing testimony at trial where the witness is not available

- Providing testimony at trial where the parties have agreed to substitute deposition testimony for live witnesses

9.2   Getting the Deposition Process Started

Generally, depositions should be taken after documents are secured through document production. Litigation is always nuanced, and there are always exceptions to general schools of thought, as noted below.

Whether to take depositions after serving interrogatories and requests for admission is a strategy call. Sometimes, interrogatories and requests for admission help the opponent better prepare for a deposition; other times these discovery avenues lock witnesses into positions that will be the subject of deposition questioning. Below are the exceptions to these general notions of timing.

First, a deposition informs you how a party stores, retrieves and destroys documents. This is especially true in a dispute about whether a party has documents or can produce them in an economically efficient manner. More specifically, the "proportionality" analysis in Federal Rule of Civil Procedure (FRCP) 26(b)(1) creates potential for disputes over the burden of production, driving the type of factfinding well suited for depositions.[1] The proportionality factors laid in FRCP 26(b)(1)—including the burden or expense of discovery—provide a rough deposition outline for a deposition to determine whether a document request is proportional to the needs of a case. Hence, depositions allow an attorney to obtain necessary information to negotiate the resolution of disputes involving the production of documents or they can provide the necessary evidence to support a motion to compel.

Think of this example: the defendant claims that a particular document request is overburdensome because it will necessitate producing one million documents, which will, according to the defendant, take two years to gather at a cost of $500,000. A deposition of the document's custodian may: 1) determine whether these representations are true; and 2) gather facts or lock in testimony supporting a motion to compel or, alternatively, a negotiated compromise of the discovery dispute.

Aside from disputes involving document production or the proper scope of discovery, you may take depositions in a litigation where you are concerned that the witness may die or leave the country. You can even take your own party's deposition to preserve testimony for trial. A classic example would be a toxic torts case where the plaintiff has a terminal disease and may die before trial.[2] Of course, FRCP 27 provides for "depositions to perpetuate testimony" and the rule outlines limited circumstances where a witness's deposition may be taken even before the commencement of the action. FRCP 27 is intended to preserve testimony that may be lost before "events have ripened to a point where a suit may be commenced" or "while the appellate process" is running its course.[3]

---

1. FED. R. CIV. P. 26(b)(1) ("Unless otherwise limited by court order, the scope of discovery is as follows: Parties may obtain discovery regarding any nonprivileged matter that is relevant to any party's claim or defense and proportional to the needs of the case, considering the importance of the issues at stake in the action, the amount in controversy, the parties relative access to relevant information, the parties' resources, the importance of the discovery in resolving the issues, and whether the burden or expense of the proposed discovery outweighs its likely benefit. Information within the scope of discovery need not be admissible in evidence to be discoverable.").
2. In the movie, "The Rainmaker", the plaintiff—who ultimately died before trial—had his deposition taken early in the litigation.
3. *See, e.g.*, Jay E. Grenig, *Taking or Using Depositions Before Action of Pending Appeal in Federal Court*, 27 AM. J. TRIAL ADVOC. 451 (2004).

Another exception to the "general timing rule" may occur where the plaintiff is seeking injunctive relief and must prepare for an expedited hearing on a preliminary injunction. These situations can arise in labor disputes including those involving breach of contract and injunctions to regulate picketing.[4] Civil rights disputes, including cases under the Fair Housing Act, may also involve injunctive relief; taking depositions early in the litigation process may be necessary to prepare for a hearing on injunctive relief.

Finally, depending on how early a party seeks to begin depositions, leave of court may be required. FRCP 30(a)(2) provides the following:

> **(2) *With Leave.*** A party must obtain leave of court, and the court must grant leave to the extent consistent with Rule 26(b)(1) and (2):
>
> **(A)** if the parties have not stipulated to the deposition and:
>
> **(i)** the deposition would result in more than 10 depositions being taken under this rule or Rule 31 by the plaintiffs, or by the defendants, or by the third-party defendants;
>
> **(ii)** the deponent has already been deposed in the case; or
>
> **(iii)** the party seeks to take the deposition before the time specified in Rule 26(d), unless the party certifies in the notice, with supporting facts, that the deponent is expected to leave the United States and be unavailable for examination in this country after that time; or
>
> **(B)** if the deponent is confined in prison.

9.2.1　The Notice

Depositions of parties are initiated by "notice." When seeking a deposition from a nonparty, you must issue a subpoena to bring the entity or person under the jurisdiction of the court.[5] You may ask a deponent to produce documents at the time of taking the deposition. You may, instead, secure documents through a request, or "subpoena duces tecum," issued well in advance of the deposition. This will allow time to review the documents before the deposition is taken.

FRCP 30(b)(1) provides for "notice." The rule reads as follows:

---

4. *See, e.g.,* United Steelworkers v. Blaw-Knox Foundry & Mill Mach., Inc., 319 F. Supp. 636 (W.D. Pa. 1970) (involving a union's suit to enjoin unsafe working conditions). *See generally,* Boys Mkts., Inc. v. Retail Clerk's Union, 398 U.S. 235 (1970) (sustaining the right to enjoin breach of a collective bargaining agreement so as to preserve the viability of the contractual obligation to arbitrate).

5. Fed. R. Civ. P. 30 advisory committee's note to 1971 amendment. ("Under the rules, a subpoena rather than a notice of examination is served on a non-party to compel attendance at the taking of a deposition"). *See also* Fed. R. Civ. P. 45 (a)(1)(B). *But see* Fed. R. Civ. P. 45(c)(1) (limiting the burden a subpoena can place on a party).

Notice in General. A party who wants to depose a person by oral questions must give reasonable written notice to every other party. The notice must state the time and place of the deposition and, if known, the deponent's name and address. If the name is unknown, the notice must provide a general description sufficient to identify the person or the particular class or group to which the person belongs.

A typical notice looks like this:

**UNITED STATES DISTRICT COURT
FOR THE NORTHEN DISTRICT OF NITA**

NOTICE OF DEPOSITION

[CASE CAPTION]

    To: **[Name]
[Address]**

Please take notice that, pursuant to Rule 30 of the Federal Rules of Civil Procedure, the undersigned will take the deposition upon oral examination of **[name]**. The deposition will begin at **[time]** on **[day], [date], [year]** at the office of Attorney **[name], [address]**. Said deposition shall continue from day-to-day until completion, shall be recorded by sound or stenographic means and shall be before a Notary Public or other individual qualified to administer oaths.

This ___ day of _____, ___. _____

                                     _____

                                     [Name]
                                     Attorney at Law
                                     [Address]

While the rules outline the process, there are common practices that lawyers follow as a matter of professionalism. As we have tried to make clear throughout this book, the word "professionalism" is not just about etiquette. Professionalism is an unwritten code of conduct that makes the practice of law more pleasant while creating efficiencies that inure to the benefit of counsel and their clients.

First, when seeking to take a deposition, email or call opposing counsel to set dates that correspond to witness availability. Confer with your opposing counsel to establish a global case deposition schedule and block out dates, pending consultation with witnesses to determine their availability. Once the dates are confirmed, transmit formal deposition notices to lock in the schedule.

In some instances, you may just transmit a notice of deposition to opposing counsel expecting to negotiate over the date. While this method may not engender an amiable relationship with opposing counsel, it may be necessary where the court has imposed a very short discovery period. In this case, make a record to demonstrate to the court, if necessary, that you at least attempted to make progress on discovery. Under these circumstances, consider drafting a letter of enclosure that looks something like this:

Law Offices of Ramirez & Verosky

Dear Counsel,

I am enclosing the Notice of Deposition of Babke Bernstein for 10:00 AM on August 2 at the offices of Piper & Bingo. While we are on a tight schedule to meet the court's deadlines in this case, we fully understand that there may be a need to adjust the date of this deposition if the proposed date is not convenient for you or Ms. Bernstein. I look forward to your prompt response either confirming the date for deposition or proposing alternatives.

Sincerely,

Milo Fordestein

Alternatively, transmit a letter to opposing counsel setting forth the list of witnesses that you seek to depose, along with proposed deposition dates. Once you both agree to the timing and location, send a confirmatory notice.

Where the witness is a third party, the process for securing a deposition is more complicated because you must issue a subpoena for the deposition. In federal court, an attorney can issue a deposition subpoena to any witness who is within the jurisdiction of the court.[6] It is the subpoena that invokes the authority of the court to compel a witness to be present at a specific time and place for deposition. For federal cases, if the witness is outside the jurisdiction of the local federal court, a subpoena may be issued from the federal court with personal jurisdiction over the witness. The subpoena must be signed by an attorney licensed to practice in that local federal court.[7]

If a witness refuses to honor the subpoena, file a motion to enforce the subpoena and secure a court order compelling a witness to sit for deposition. File the motion in the court issuing the subpoena. For witnesses in "foreign jurisdictions," motions to compel enforcement of a subpoena must be made in that "foreign" federal court.[8] If a witness refuses to honor a subpoena issued by the court where the action is pending, file a motion to compel the pending action. If the subpoena was issued out of a foreign jurisdiction, the court may require the opening of a "miscellaneous case" file and assign the motion to a judge for ruling.

In cases pending in state court, the process for deposing nonparty witnesses is similar; a subpoena must be issued to compel testimony. Where the nonparty witness lives outside the jurisdiction of the state court, the home court must issue a "letter rogatory"—a request for assistance from the foreign court.[9] The request asks the foreign court to issue a subpoena requiring an individual or entity within its jurisdiction to appear and present testimony. If the witness in the foreign jurisdiction fails to honor the subpoena issued by that jurisdiction, you must file a motion to compel enforcement of the subpoena in the issuing court. While each court has its own processes for addressing these matters, generally a "miscellaneous case file" must be opened and then the motion to compel will be directed to a judge for entry or denial of a proposed order compelling attendance at a deposition.

In both federal and state court, nonparties have the right to file a motion to quash the subpoena or for protective order. Quashing the subpoena would mean there is no requirement that the subpoenaed party even sit for the deposition. A motion for protective order may be filed to refine the topics of inquiry, limit the length of the deposition, prevent the deposition from going forward on the noticed day, or prevent inquiry into privileged areas.

---

6. FED. R. CIV. P. 45(a)(3) ("An attorney also may issue and sign a subpoena if the attorney is authorized to practice in the issuing court").
7. FED. R. CIV. P. 45(f). *See also* Prac. L. Litig. with David J. Lender, Jared R. Friedmann, *Subpoenas: Enforcing a Subpoena (Federal)*, PRAC. LAW PRAC. NOTE, https://us.practicallaw.thomsonreuters.com/0-503-1893 (Resource ID W-012-4100).
8. FED. R. CIV. P. 28(b).
9. FED. R. CIV. P. 28 advisory committee's note to 1946 amendment. ("In a case in which the foreign country will compel a witness to attend or testify in aid of a letter rogatory but not in aid of a commission, a letter rogatory may be preferred on the ground that it is less expensive to execute, even if there is plainly no need for compulsive process.").

9.2.2 *How Many Depositions Do I Get and How Long is Each Deposition?*

The Federal Rules of Civil Procedure limit the number of depositions. Each side is entitled up to ten depositions. This generally includes one FCRP 30(b)(6)—organization designee—deposition per case; the defendant may produce several witnesses responsive to each FRCP 30(b)(6) notice. Depending on the requirements of the case, and/or any agreement of the parties, the judge may allow more depositions to be taken.

FRCP 30 limits each deposition to seven hours of actual deposition time. Ask the court reporter or the videographer to keep track of the actual deposition time as the seven-hour limit includes only the time spent "on the record." Restroom breaks, client conference breaks, lunch breaks, and other breaks do not count toward the seven-hour limit.

In contrast to federal courts, state court procedures may vary on the allotted number of depositions and the time limits for each deposition.[10] In both federal and state courts, the parties may also agree to a case management order allowing for more or fewer depositions than provided for in the rules. Further, the parties may agree to extend or decrease the time allotted by the rules for each deposition.

In addition, many courts are amenable to counting expert depositions—which are generally taken at the end of fact discovery—separately from depositions of "fact witnesses." Therefore, plan your discovery, determine what evidence you need to move the case through summary judgment and trial, and establish a schedule for fact and expert discovery.

9.2.3 *Location and Method of Recording*

The notice of deposition should note the site for the deposition and the method by which the deposition will be recorded.[11] FRCP 30(b)(3) states that "[t]he party who notices the deposition must state in the notice the method for recording the testimony." The noticing party can choose audio, audiovisual, or stenographic recording of the deposition. Many parties choose both audiovisual and a stenographic record. While it seems apparent, at the very least, a stenographic record is essential. Transcripts are often used in motions and of course can be read from or shown to the judge or jury at trial.

---

10. *See* N.Y. Comp. Codes R. & Regs. tit. 22, § 202.70 ("[D]epositions shall be limited to 7 hours per deponent."); N.Y. C.P.L.R. 3113(b) ("The deposition shall be taken continuously and without unreasonable adjournment."); Cal. Civ. Proc. § 2025.290(a) (providing for a seven hour time limit in California, similar to FRCP, but allows attorneys to agree to go longer); Tex. R. Civ. P. 199 ("No side may examine or cross-examine an individual witness for more than six hours. Breaks during depositions do not count against this limitation.").
11. Fed. R. Civ. P. 30.

The site for the deposition is generally negotiated between counsel. Counsel may notice a deposition for their office, the office of the court reporter, the office of the opposing counsel, or at some neutral location. Where depositions are taken at out-of-town locations, it is not uncommon to arrange to take the deposition at the office of the court reporter, at a hotel conference room, or at the offices of a friendly counsel. In the era of remote or temporary workspaces, a good fallback for the attorney who does not have a conference room is to hold the deposition at the offices of the court reporter. With prior permission, public libraries, local court houses, and even city halls can serve as reasonable venues.[12]

Selection of a deposition venue involves the following considerations:

- The comfort of your client or the deponent.

- The location of the deponent.

- Whether the venue is large enough to accommodate a videographer.

- Whether the venue has copying capability if exhibits need to be copied.

- Whether the venue has conference rooms for side bar meetings with your client or co-counsel.

- Whether the venue can accommodate individuals with disabilities.

9.2.4 When to Consider Video Depositions

While all depositions are transcribed by a court reporter, video may be important for several reasons. First, video shows things that will not come across on a paper transcript. Long pauses before answering questions, rolling eyes, sighs, and signals to counsel will come across on a video. Videos also record the voice tone of the witness and the tone of counsel as they interject objections. If you believe that opposing counsel is going to be difficult, video can moderate the conduct of obstreperous counsel. Although the internet is filled with examples of lawyers acting inappropriately while being video recorded, they are less likely to do so because video documents their behavior in a way that a transcript cannot.[13]

---

12. One of the authors of this book once deposed a witness in the town hall for Metropolis, Illinois. The deposition had been scheduled for the local library. The parties arrived for their deposition only to find the library closed for the day. They walked two blocks to the town hall and secured permission to take the deposition in the city council meeting room.

13. Staci Zaretsky, *America's Richest Lawyer Is An Inappropriate SOB Who Loves To Drop F-Bombs,* Above The Law (Dec. 19, 2014), https://abovethelaw.com/2014/12/americas-richest-lawyer-is-an-inappropriate-sob-who-loves-to-drop-f-bombs.

If a deposing lawyer anticipates misconduct by an opposing lawyer, then videotaping the deposition may thwart the misbehavior. In most instances, the presence of the camera seems to have a leveling influence and encourage proper behavior by not only opposing lawyers but by deposing lawyers and deponents as well. Not always, but sometimes.

—Michael Flynn, Professor of Law, Nova Southeast University, Shepard Broad College of Law

Videos can sometimes be shown in court just as a deposition may be shown or read in court. Video of an opposing party or an agent of an opposing party satisfy the hearsay exception in the same way as a written statement.[14] Keep in mind that some judges may prefer live testimony if the witness is available. Even under these circumstances, the video may always be used for impeachment purposes. Videos can be bolted into power point presentations used at mediation or during oral arguments.

Videography is an additional cost and budgetary considerations will factor into whether to video record a deposition. Hence, you may decide to video record only a few depositions, or determine that based on the size of the case and its budget, videography is not a consideration.

9.3 Discovery in an Age of Isolation: Depositions and Other Tactics

The COVID-19 quarantine of 2020 required practitioners to acquaint themselves with the practice of remote depositions. Indeed, humans have a way of adapting to impediments. Sometimes the changes they make are so beneficial that they continue in place even after the impediment is abated.[15]

The practice of law, and particularly advocacy, is all about human interaction, and the quarantine imposed by the coronavirus posed an impediment to the practice. Litigators were faced with the task of keeping their cases on schedule during pretrial processes demanding close contact in at least the form of depositions.

When it came to depositions, trial lawyers did not need to entirely reinvent the wheel as most state and federal court rules[16] allow for remote depositions, though some states require that the court reporter and the deponent be at the same location.

---

14. *See* Fed. R. Evid. 801(d)(2).
15. *See* Reuben Guttman & Traci Buschner, *Discovery in an Age of Isolation*, in Remote Advocacy: A Guide to Survive and Thrive 25-29 (Nat'l Inst. of Trial Advoc., 2020).
16. Fed. R. Civ. P. 30(b)(4) ("*By Remote Means.* The parties may stipulate—or the court may on motion order—that a deposition be taken by telephone or other remote means. For the purpose of this rule and Rules 28(a), 37(a)(2), and 37(b)(1), the deposition takes place where the deponent answers the questions.").

National Institute for Trial Advocacy

This requirement is implicit in the federal rules as well, but the parties may stipulate otherwise.[17]

The party noticing[18] the deposition generally may determine the deposition's location,[19] but if there is a dispute about holding a remote deposition,[20] courts have held that leave for remote depositions should be liberally granted upon a showing of good cause.[21] Obviously, the social distancing guidance and "stay at home" orders issued by state and local governments during the Coronavirus quarantine supported holding remote depositions.

Responding to the challenges posed by the quarantine, court reporting firms developed remote deposition offerings, refined their software and remote recording techniques, and engaged in educational outreach with the bar. Reporting firms seized on the quarantine to market remote depositions that allow for the parties to connect both video and audio from their home or laptop computers. Many of these court reporting firms offer training sessions to teach counsel to use the technology. Those training sessions address technology and logistics issues, including the availability of "real-time" reporting and the introduction of exhibits.

The most essential requirement for a remote deposition is that counsel for both sides, the court reporter, and the witness see the exhibits on their individual computer displays as they are introduced. This can be accomplished in a number of ways. Court reporters can receive PDF exhibits in advance and call them up as requested. This has the advantage of limiting screen sharing only to the court reporter and reducing confusion, but questioning counsel must be certain of the order in which they want to introduce exhibits, otherwise there may be confusion when Exhibit Y is introduced before Exhibit B. Alternatively, documents can be scanned and sent to the court reporter prior to the deposition and during breaks in the deposition. This way, the questioner is not locked into a pre-determined order for questions or exhibits. Unfortunately, this process can slow down the deposition, particularly when the case is document heavy. If this process is too complicated or deposing counsel lacks the resources to transmit the exhibits electronically, exhibits can be sent to the

---

17. Fed. R. Civ. P. 29(a), 30(b)(5)(A) (allowing a deposition to be taken "before any person" without court approval, if the parties stipulate).
18. Remember that your deposition notice must indicate that the deposition will be conducted remotely. Fed. R. Civ. P. 30(b)(3).
19. Carrico v. Samsung Elecs. Co., Ltd., Case No. 15-cv-02087-DMR, 2016 U.S. Dist. LEXIS 44841, 2016 WL 1265854 at *1 (N.D. Cal. Apr. 1, 2016).
20. There is "no general policy presuming remote depositions to be the norm," under the federal rules. *See* Kean v. Three Rivers Reg'l Libr. Sys., 321 F.R.D. 448, 453-454 (S.D. Ga. 2017).
21. Id. (citing Guillen v. Bank of Am. Corp., No.10-CV-05825EJD (PSG), 2011 U.S. Dist. LEXIS 97966, 2011 WL 3939690, at *1 (N.D. Cal. Aug. 31, 2011)) (desire to save money on depositions is good cause for remote deposition); Lopez v. CIT Bank, N.A., No. 15-CV-00759BLF (HRL), 2015 U.S. Dist. LEXIS 176575, 2015 WL 10374104, at *2 (N.D. Cal. Dec. 18, 2015). See also Brown v. Carr, 253 F.R.D. 410, 412-413 (S.D. Tex. 2008) (allowing inmate to attend depositions in his civil rights case by video-teleconference).

court reporter by overnight delivery. Here there is no need to assign exhibit numbers ahead of time. Counsel can simply identify the documents by Bates label and ask the court report to affix an exhibit label to the proposed exhibit.

In addition to the logistics of document handling, you will need to consider the audiovisual equipment and software for the deposition. While audio/video products like Zoom may be one route to taking a remote deposition, consult the court reporting service to make sure they are using a secure link or program. This is especially necessary if the deposition will cover HIPAA-protected information or information encompassed by a confidentiality agreement.

Before selecting a court reporter, have a checklist of questions, which may include the following:

- What, if any, software will I need on my end?

- What program will the court reporter be using?

- Is the program HIPAA compliant?

- How does that program allow me to introduce exhibits and make sure all counsel have access to them?

- Will I have a real-time transcript and how will that appear on my screen?

- Will I have the ability to get a quality video record of the deposition?

- How will the court reporter deal with glitches, including loss of internet access?

- How can the parties and the deponent make the court reporter's job less difficult?

How you take and defend a remote deposition will require a bit of alteration from usual practices. Starting with what we call the "admonitions," consider what additional instructions you may need to give the witness:

- "We are taking this deposition remotely; in the event someone loses an internet connection, we have exchanged emails and phone numbers so that we can address the problem."

- "The answers you give here under oath must be your answers and not those given to you, even in the form of hints, from those outside the view of the camera or by email. Do you understand this?"

In terms of preliminary questions, you may want to ask whether the witness is alone—and if not, who else is in the room? And you may want to ask whether the witness has a cell phone or access to emails during the course of the deposition.

The process of remote depositions—as a regular practice as opposed to an exception—is really a new playing field for counsel and the courts. Think about meeting and conferring with opposing counsel to establish the rules for remote depositions.[22] You will want clear rules not just for the parties but also for third parties who will testify under subpoena. The areas to discuss at a meet and confer may include:

- Administering the oath, if there is no existing rule.

- Precluding witnesses from receiving emails or other messaging during the deposition.

- Precluding counsel from sending their client emails while the witness is on the record.

If you are on a short discovery deadline or simply looking to keep your cases moving, start taking remote depositions with witnesses who will be the least confrontational. These may include deponents who will simply authenticate exhibits, confirm facts that are otherwise hard to dispute, or are perhaps sympathetic to your client's case. Once you get comfortable with the technology and the process, you can decide whether to take remote depositions of the tougher witnesses.

One added benefit to taking a remote deposition is that your experts, your client, or other attorneys working on the case will be able to assist in providing real-time feedback to the attorney taking the deposition, via email or text, without the added expense of travel. While the witness should not be prompted by outside parties, nothing prohibits questioning counsel from receiving questions and recommendations. Use that resource to make sure you gather all the facts from the deponent. Request that these additional colleagues be included on the deposition call, but muted and without video so that they are not a distraction. The conference program may even have a chat function that allows you to receive questions and comments on the same screen, cutting down on the number of distractions to your questioning.

Defending a remote deposition has its own challenges. During a period of social distancing or quarantine, you probably cannot sit face-to-face with your client to prepare for deposition. Again, make use of the technology available. FaceTime, Zoom, Microsoft Teams and Skype are very accessible, allow for counsel to communicate with clients, and have the additional benefit of letting you prepare your client to appear comfortable during the remote deposition. In fact, even if you are able to meet in person with your client or witness, if the deposition will be remote, you should include remote practice.

Naturally, deposition preparation involves some document review. Transmit those documents to the client in advance by email, overnight delivery, or through a

---

22. For examples of rules governing remote depositions, *see* United States ex rel. Wollman v. Mass. Gen. Hosp., Inc., No. 1:15-CV-11890-ADB (D. Mass. Aug. 10, 2020).

file hosting service like Dropbox. Again, prepare the client or witness so that they are comfortable viewing the document through screen share and are aware that just because the document appears on their screen doesn't mean they can move or manipulate it—because who of us hasn't tried to scroll down a screen-shared document more than once?

In some instances, your witness may need to mark up an exhibit. The remote process allows for this to be done. A document shared in Zoom can be annotated by the witness, and the annotated version saved as a screen shot. If your client or witness will need to do this, practice this skill before the deposition.

In addition to the logistical and technological side of prepping the client, think about the particular guidance you will need to give because the deposition will be taken remotely. Explain that it is improper for you to communicate by email with the client during depositions. Explain that the client should be listening and watching for you in the event of an objection based on privilege. Explain any rules the court may have imposed for remote depositions.

By the time this book is released, the coronavirus quarantine will have forced counsel and the courts to gain proficiency in remote depositions. New skills and rules will continue to evolve and require counsel to continue learning. On the upside, this technology can save travel time and costs, lending major efficiencies to the pretrial process.[23] Expect to see fewer coast-to-coast excursions to take depositions and the ability to retain a single court reporter for an entire case. Remote depositions were no doubt an immediate fix to an impediment, but they are also the future of the practice.

9.4   Preparing for the Deposition

Curiosity is the best instinct to follow when preparing for a deposition. If you are not curious about your deponent's personality, how their brain stores and retrieves information, and what they know—or do not know—about the facts of the case, you are probably not prepared to take the deposition. The purpose of a deposition is to gather information and to test your theories of the case.

You are looking for evidence that will support or rebut elements of the claims. You are looking for evidence that can help you better understand the context for factual allegations. You are curious about what the witness will say in response to questions that lay out your theories of the case.

---

23. For information on the use of courtroom videoconferencing, the concerns it raises, a discussion of possible solutions, and predictions on the future of videoconferencing see Daniel Devoe and Sarita Frattaroli, *Videoconferencing in the Courtroom: Benefits, Concerns, and How to Move Forward*, Soc. L. Libr., http://socialaw.com/docs/default-source/judge-william-g.-young/judging-in-the-american-legal-system/04devoe-sarita-paper.pdf.

Assuming you are indeed curious, there is a step-by-step approach to preparation. First, isolate and review documents mentioning the deponent. These documents may include emails or memos that the deponent generated or received. Look at personnel files, letters of appointment, meeting attendance records, photographs, videos, and audio recordings of the witness.

Isolate documents that the deponent might know about. Perhaps there is a photo of a meeting; you can show the photo to the deponent and ask them to identify—by name—the individuals at the meeting. Or perhaps the deponent's company issued a contract to a particular vendor. You can show the deponent the contract and ask what, if any, role the deponent had in issuing the contract.

Review documents that can be used to prompt an answer or open an area of inquiry. Such exhibits are called *catalyst documents* and may even include documents that the witness has never seen. Typically, catalyst documents—ones the witness has never seen or may not have familiarity with—include standards, or other statements that are most likely admissible under FRE 201.[24] Consider the following example which shows how a document—never seen by the witness—can be used in a deposition.

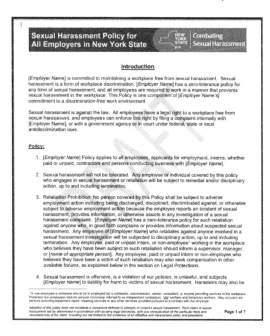

Q: Sir, can you please look at exhibit 1, which is a policy on sexual harassment published by the State of New York?

A: I've never seen this document and know nothing about it.

Q: I would just like to ask you whether you agree with the position of the State of New York that "touching, pinching, patting, grabbing, or brushing against another employee's body" constitutes sexual harassment.

A: Yes. I agree.

Also review—and consider using as deposition exhibits—the answers to interrogatories, responses to requests for admission, document requests and responses, and the complaint and answer. For example, mark the complaint as an exhibit,

---

24. Fed. R. Evid. 201.

direct the witness to particular allegations, and pose questions. Mark interrogatory answers and responses to request for admission as exhibits and pose questions about the responses. You can even ask questions included in the interrogatories to test whether the witness will provide a different answer.

Exhibits can help focus you.

—Roy Hewitt, President, CDI Image, Former Army JAG Officer

Second, once you review the documents, go back and outline the areas that you want to cover in the deposition. At this point, you need not write out questions except for some limited exceptions. For example, if you want to phrase a particular question with absolute precision, write out that specific question. Likewise, you may want to elicit testimony that establishes the necessary evidentiary foundation to ensure that a document, such as a business record, will be admissible at a later point. This may include eliciting testimony to establish exceptions to the hearsay rule, including the elements for a business record. The elements of this business record exception are laid out in FRE 803(6), which provides a ready-made outline for the proper questions necessary to create a record that a document meets the exception.

> **(6)** *Records of a Regularly Conducted Activity.* A record of an act, event, condition, opinion, or diagnosis if:
>
> **(A)** the record was made at or near the time by—or from information transmitted by—someone with knowledge;
>
> **(B)** the record was kept in the course of a regularly conducted activity of a business, organization, occupation, or calling, whether or not for profit;
>
> **(C)** making the record was a regular practice of that activity;
>
> **(D)** all these conditions are shown by the testimony of the custodian or another qualified witness, or by a certification that complies with Rule 902(11) or (12) or with a statute permitting certification; and
>
> **(E)** the opponent does not show that the source of information or the method or circumstances of preparation indicate a lack of trustworthiness.

Third, cull out the most important documents. Go back to your list and do a second "cut" to determine which documents will help you cover the areas you established in your deposition outline. Make copies of the documents that you will want to use as exhibits at the deposition: one copy for yourself, a copy for the witness, and copies for each attorney who will attend the deposition. Clip your copy to the other copies and put it in a numbered folder. Create an index of all of your exhibit folders.

On your copy of an exhibit, take a marker and highlight the word or phrases that you want to ask about. You can also write questions in the margin of your copy. Here is how it works at a deposition:

> Q: Please look at Exhibit 1, the letter you sent to Secretary Kessler on December 14, YR-6. The first sentence of the second paragraph refers to the helicopters being, "flight-ready." Can you tell me what you meant when you used the phrase, "flight-ready"?

Here is the questioner's marked-up exhibit, and how you can use it:[25]

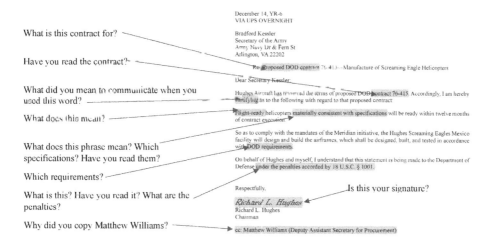

Fourth, now that you have prepared your exhibits, go back and make notations on your outline that reference the exhibits by the index number you have given them.

A typical Deposition Document Index looks like this:

Deposition Document Index

Deposition Exhibit #	Description	Issue	Pg. No.
15	Meeting Attendance Sheet	Jones attended the meeting	23
17	Jones meeting notes	Meeting notes confirming Jones' presence	31
19	Text message from Smith	Text Smith sent Howard during meeting	64

---

25. Paul J. Zwier et al., United States ex rel, Rodriguez v. Hughes, et al.: Motions, Relators Materials (Nat'l Inst. of Trial Advoc., 1st ed. 2016) (exhibit comes from the NITA case file).

This system of preparation is designed to get you to think about the documents, the facts, and your theories of the case. Use the preparation process to learn the case, contemplate the facts, and rethink theories. Use the documents to focus your questions and the documents will be catalysts to prompt answers to questions.

9.4.1 *The Special Role of Documents at Depositions*

Depositions serve many important roles. Chief among them are authentication, encouraging reluctant witnesses to talk, controlling witness evasiveness, testing theories, testing the candor of the witness, and stimulating memory.

9.4.1.1 Authentication

Just as in trials, documents play an important role in depositions. First, documents are used as deposition exhibits in order to authenticate them. The rules for authentication are set forth in FRE 901 and 902 and in analogous state court evidentiary rules. Authentication simply means establishing that the document is what it purports to be. For example, if you are deposing Witness X and believe that you have a copy of an email sent by Witness X to Witness Y, you need Witness X to testify that the document is indeed a copy of an email they sent to Witness Y. Why must this be done? You do not want to find yourself amidst the summary judgment process or at trial only to learn that your opponent contends that the email is a fake.

Where the witness "seemingly" transmitted, received, or signed the document, a good place to start is by asking the witness: "is that your name [or signature] at the top [or bottom] of the page?" Once the witness is locked into admitting that they signed the document or received the document (as in an email), it will be hard for the witness to testify that the document is anything other than what it purports to be. Hence the follow-up question might simply be, "having just testified that you signed this document, what is it?"

If one were to think of three questions that outline the authentication process, those questions would be as follows: 1) can you identify—or recognize—this document?; 2) how can you identify the document?; 3) what is it?

9.4.1.2 Encouraging the Reluctant Witness to Talk

We use exhibits at depositions as catalysts to get a reluctant witness to talk. Exhibits are like truth serums. When confronted with a writing, witnesses are disinclined to fabricate facts and less likely to testify that they have no memory.

We also introduce exhibits to question witnesses on document ambiguities to secure explanation or elaboration. Suppose, for example, a document has the following passage: "please make payment when it is **possible** for you to make the payment." A natural question might be: "when you used the word "**possible**" what did you mean to communicate?"

Ask witnesses about specific words or phrases in a document as a technique or "catalyst" to get the witness to talk. If a witness wrote a word in a document, asking the witness to explain why they selected the word forces the witness—from a psychological perspective—to directly confront a decision they made. A witness might be thinking, "gee I used this word; I will look stupid if I cannot explain why I used it."

9.4.1.3 Controlling Witness Evasiveness

When deposing or interviewing a witness, anticipate that the witness has been coached or prepared. As a starting point, assume that every witness will be told by their attorney not to volunteer information. This means that if you ask a witness, "do you know the time," a prepared witness will simply say, "yes," rather than providing the time. An attorney trained in taking depositions will ask the follow-up question: "what time is it?" One who is not trained may be thrown off track.

With this in mind, and moving to a broader proposition, the truthfulness of any witnesses can be gauged on a spectrum. On one side of the spectrum is a fraction of all witnesses who will be compulsive truth-tellers, and on the other side of the spectrum is a fraction of all witnesses who are compulsive liars.

WITNESS PSYCHOLOGY

COMPULSIVE LIARS   COMPULSIVE TRUTH-TELLERS

Most witnesses—the people in the middle—will follow their counsel's instruction not to volunteer information. These witnesses will look for a plausible basis for evasion but will also have a hard time lying under oath. If they are shown a document reminding them that they do know the answer, they will be confronted with a dilemma. They will know that testifying to no recollection of an event is a lie.

Use documents to prevent a witness from being evasive. A witness asked about the events at a specific meeting may answer, "I don't have a specific recollection of that meeting." A witness shown the attendance list for a meeting or notes of the meeting will find it harder to be evasive. You have educated them that they do know the answer and any response to the contrary is a lie.

This is particularly true where the document establishes that the witness attended a meeting or an event but claims no recollection of what happened. At this point, the witness who answers that they do not remember may feel like they have crossed a line between being evasive and lying.

Keep in mind that many witnesses legitimately do not remember certain events. Documents are important because they jog recollections and prompt complete or more accurate testimony from witnesses who are not trying to be evasive.

9.4.1.4 Admitting to Standards

Documents can prompt the witness to admit to a standard of care or the existence of a duty. The concept of standards of care and duty often come into play in civil litigation. Breach of a standard or duty are often elements that must be proven under varying common-law theories. The breach of a standard or a duty can also be used to demonstrate intent or reckless disregard which may be necessary in order to pierce certain qualified immunities that may be defenses in, for example, defamation cases.[26]

Consider, for example, a malpractice case where the plaintiff claims that his injuries—a severed artery—were caused because the surgeon was conducting two surgeries at the same time. The line of questioning might be as follows:

> Q: Please look at the policy of the American Surgery Association, Exhibit 11, which says, "where a surgeon engages in overlapping surgeries, they should be present for any key and critical parts of each surgery." Do you agree with this statement?
>
> A: Yes

This scenario uses a document—one the witness may not have even seen—to secure the admission of a standard. Even if the witness answers, "no," that answer may be useful because the plaintiff can—pursuant to FRE 201 Judicial Notice of

---

26. *See, e.g.*, New York Times v. Sullivan, 376 U.S. 254 (1964).

Adjudicative Facts—introduce the standard into evidence and argue the inference that because the doctor did not agree with the standard, they ignored it.

Of course, at the deposition, a "no" answer opens the door to asking "why"; the document becomes a catalyst to prompt more inquiry eliciting additional testimony.

Why use documents to establish a duty or standard? Consider this line of testimony:

> Q: Would you agree that it is not safe to talk on your phone while you are driving?
>
> A: It is a complicated question; it depends on the circumstances.

Now try it this way:

> Q: I am showing you Exhibit 14—guidance from the American Car Association—which states: "It is not safe to use your cell phone while driving because doing so may lead to accidents." Do you agree with the position of the American Car Association?
>
> A: Yes.

Use such documents to present the defendant with a respected authority and pit the defendant against the authority. The defendant, confronted with the authority, may appreciate that an answer inconsistent with the authority's position may not appear credible or honest. Such authoritative documents preclude an evasive response and prompt the commonsense answer. Of course, if the witness defies the logic of the American Car Association, they will have to live with testimony that is simply not credible.

9.4.1.5 Testing the Candor of the Witness

We have discussed ways that documents can be used to test the candor of a witness. So far, our use of documents has involved the process of marking them as exhibits, showing them to the witness, and posing questions. There are, however, occasions where your use of documents will not involve their introduction as an exhibit.

Consider the situation where the witness, Aaron Verosky, is the head of Human Resources for a large meat packing company called Good Eats Beef. Good Eats Beef has been sued for violations of the Federal Fair Labor Standards Act (FLSA)[27] because it does not pay workers for time spent donning and doffing safety equipment. Good Eats Beef has been served with interrogatories which seek information about compliance with labor laws and U.S. Department of Labor regulations. Good Eats Beef provided detailed answers to the interrogatories and the answers

---

27. *See* 29 U.S.C. § 201-219.

were verified by Mr. Verosky. At his deposition, Mr. Verosky claims lack of familiarity with labor laws and regulations.

Not showing the witness the interrogatories, you cite, as questions, the very interrogatories that prompted the answers that Mr. Verosky verified. If he claims an inability to answer the questions, you have not only dented the credibility of the witness but also of Good Eats Beef, which tendered the interrogatory answers to the plaintiff.

By way of yet another example, suppose you have numerous documents showing a close relationship between the plaintiff and a witness who has provided supporting testimony. The documents include a wedding invitation, receipts from golf outings and joint family vacations. Consider not showing the witness the documents but simply asking about their relationship with the plaintiff. Depending on the answer, consider saving the documents for impeachment at trial.

9.4.2 Witness Operating Systems and How Their Brain Stores and Retrieves Information

Sometimes witnesses are evasive or plain liars. But more often than one might assume, they do not provide the expected answer because the interrogator has not cracked their operating system, which—among other things—involves how a witness stores and retrieves information. Indeed, all humans have processes by which they store and retrieve information. We store information by time sequence, topic area, time of year, or relationships, to name a few.

If—out of the blue—you ask a witness about their first day of college, they can readily follow counsel's advice about not volunteering information as the response might easily be, "I don't have a specific recollection of that day." On the other hand, if you take the witness back in time with a sequence of testimony leading up to their selection of a college, the college visit and interview, and who drove the witness to college for freshman orientation, you will place the witness into that time frame. A witness who is not inclined to lie will be confronted with the realization that they do indeed know the answer to the question. Hence, to say "I do not recall" would be a lie.

But it really is not just a matter of evasion. Humans, by nature, observe events every day. They lack the random-access memory to store each event, and so they encapsulate events with labels. Sometimes events may be mislabeled; therefore, taking the witness back in time to unpack the events leading to the conclusion can be a valuable exercise because sometimes the conclusion is just wrong. Consider this line of questioning:

Q: Tell me about last Friday.

A: It was a wonderful day.

Now, try unpacking the events by taking the witness back in time to Friday.

Q: Focusing in on last Friday, just five days ago, tell me about your day starting with the first thing you did when you woke up.

A: I got dressed for a funeral.[28]

Another consideration is that not everyone attaches the same meaning to specific words.

Sometimes it is important to make the witness define his or her use of specific words. Here are some examples:

Example 1

A: He was brilliant.

Q: When you use the word "brilliant" what do you mean to communicate?

A: He met expectations?

Example 2

A: It was really dark out?

Q: When you use the phrase "really dark" what did you mean to communicate?

A: It was still light enough to read but if it got any darker, I would need a flashlight.

The above lines of questioning not only show the need to question the witness about their definition of words and phrases, they also demonstrate how listening to an answer and using the witness's own words in a follow-up question can be a mechanism to prompt testimony.

9.5 Deposition Flow

While all discovery depositions are different, a simple way to outline deposition flow is as follows:

1) Off the record:

a) Introductions

b) Seating of the lawyers, court reporter, and witness

2) On the record:

------

28. Throughout this book, including this chapter about the deposition process and the chapters on case preparation, we discuss eliciting facts and unpacking conclusions.

a) Administering the oath

b) Explaining the ground rules and process for depositions

c) Asking the admonitions to eliminate excuses

3) Background

4) Fact gathering

5) Theory testing

6) Admission seeking

9.5.1   Introductions

The deposition process actually begins before anyone goes on the record and the witness is sworn. The seating of parties and the court reporter, the placement of the videographer, and the exchange of courtesy introductions are events that set the tone for the proceeding.

Where does the court reporter sit? The court reporter sits wherever is most comfortable for the court reporter. The court reporter will want to hear the witness, have enough room for hand movements on the keyboard, and be placed with consideration for the receipt of exhibits from counsel which the court reporter will mark before they are handed to the witness.

If there is a videographer, they will sit at the end of the conference table or in such a place as to secure a head-on image of the deponent. The videographer will want to capture an image of the deponent from hands—turning the pages of exhibits—to the top of the deponent's head. Absent agreement otherwise, deposition videos are taken of the witness and not the lawyers.

Counsel for the deponent will want to sit next to their client. The deposing counsel will sit next to the court reporter or at least close enough to hand the court reporter exhibits to be marked. All exhibits are marked by the court reporter before they are handed to the witness. Counsel may pre-mark exhibits, but because exhibits may be used out of order—or not at all—due to the flow of the deposition, pre-marking may lead to exhibits out of sequence. This may later create confusion as to whether an exhibit was lost.

A typical deposition seating chart will look like this:

All present, including the deponent, will typically exchange courtesies before anyone goes on the record. These courtesies can—in a subtle way—set the tone for the proceeding: "I hope you found our office easily." "Can I get you a cup of coffee?" "Do you need a place to hang your coat?" "Can I show you a room you can use if you need to make phone calls?" Such statements communicate cordiality or, as attorneys might say, "professionalism." Litigation is rife with conflict; professionalism can ease the tension. Opposing counsel may have warned the witness that you are "evil;" cordiality disarms the deponent, and perhaps—in the long run—causes the deponent to be less evasive or obstinate.

9.5.2   On the Record: Oath, Ground Rules, and Admonitions

If you are taking the deposition, make sure the witness is sworn in before statements are placed on the record. The court reporter will do this; you just need to say, "please swear in the witness."

If the court or the procedural rules imposes time limits on the deposition, ask the court reporter or the videographer to keep track of the time. During the course of your deposition, you may want to ask the court reporter for the "elapsed time," so you can pace your examination to cover all of the topic areas within your outline.

9.5.2.1 Ground Rules

Next, establish the ground rules for the deposition. Some attorneys begin a deposition by saying something like: "the usual stipulations apply." While this sounds impressive, it is not; there are no usual stipulations. Depositions are governed by the Rules of Civil Procedure, i.e., FRCP 30, and any special rules imposed by the court or by case management agreements or orders. Agreeing to "the usual stipulations" only creates confusion as to the obligations, if any, of the parties.

In establishing ground rules, you have two goals: 1) eliminate the potential for the witness to testify at trial and explain away damaging deposition testimony; and 2) establish rapport with the witness. Your range of ground rules may include the following:

- I want you to know that although we are not in a court of law today, the testimony you are providing will be given as if it were in a court of law and indeed this testimony may be used at trial.

- If there is any question that I ask that you do not understand, please let me know and I will be pleased to rephrase my question.

- Please state your answer orally. A nod of the head will not work because the court reporter can only take down the words that come from your mouth.

Keep in mind that the ground rules you establish can be used to your detriment. Sometimes, attorneys say, "if you need a break to use the rest room, let me know." Unfortunately, deponents and their counsel can use this instruction as an excuse to take a "strategic break" to disrupt the flow of the deposition or to take a witness aside for coaching purposes. If you resist a request to take a break, opposing counsel may say, "but you promised my client that he could take a break whenever he needs one." This opens the door to argument between counsel, which does no more than distract from the purpose of the deposition—securing testimony.

Over time, attorneys have developed other instructions or introductory questions that have become popular. The examples below are variations of the types that routinely appear in deposition transcripts:

- Are you on any medication which can interfere with your ability to provide truthful testimony today?

- Can you do your best to provide me with the most truthful and complete testimony today?

These questions have drawbacks. First, asking a witness whether they are on medication sets a tone for the deposition that may promote obstruction and not candor. The question is simply antagonistic. Moreover, if the witness says, "yes, I am taking mind-altering medications," are you really prepared to stop the deposition and choose another date? What if you traveled across the country to take the deposition?

Suppose the witness is taking drugs that might impact their memory and they answer in the negative. And suppose the witness changes their testimony at trial and claims that the inconsistency is attributable to mind altering medication taken contemporaneously with the deposition. You show the witness their deposition testimony where you asked, "Are you on any medication which can interfere with your ability to provide truthful testimony?" The witness responds, "I did not read the medication's label. I did not know what the drug could do. It impacted my cognition so much that my answer even to that question was inaccurate." What then?

To the extent that there is concern about a witness who takes medication or imbibes on alcohol, you may be able to learn about the problem from medical records or witness interviews. The way to deal with the problem is to ask questions that establish reasonable cognition. These questions can be asked at convenient times during the course of the deposition. Consider the following:

Q: How did you get to the deposition?

A: I drove.

Q: Are you going back to work after the deposition?

A: Yes.

If the witness claims at trial that his cognition was impaired during the deposition, at least you can remind them that it could not have been impaired enough to prevent them from driving to the deposition or going to work.

Second, asking whether a witness can provide the most truthful and complete testimony can cause the witness to place an excuse in the record including, "well I was so nervous that I did not sleep much last night and so I am not at my best." The lesson? Avoid preliminary questions that create a record that can be used against you at trial.

There is a lot of "boiler plate" deposition guidance and questioning offered in deposition instruction and guidebooks. Consider whether such boiler plate questions or admonitions, really serve a function or, perhaps, whether they can be detrimental to your purpose.

9.5.2.2   Background

Once you work through your introductory ground rules, begin the deposition with simple background instructions and questions. Your goals are as follows:

- Get the witness to talk; establish a rhythm of response to your questions.

- Learn how the witness has been coached; will the witness evade even softball questions, e.g., work history and education?

- Determine whether opposing counsel will be obstructionist.

- Secure background information that will allow you to better read the witness and evaluate the witness's abilities.

Examples of introductory instructions:

1) Please state your name and spell it for the court reporter.

2) Please give me a thumbnail sketch of your educational background.

3) Please give me a thumbnail sketch of your work history up through your current place of employment.

You may want to probe into subtopic areas including areas of study, skills, certifications, and specific job responsibilities. Some of this information may later be relevant for the core part of your case, or perhaps for impeachment. Probing into subtopics is what depositions are all about; you start with broad instructions or questions that lay out the terrain. Looking at the terrain, you will see a list of subtopics for further inquiry. The question pattern looks like this:

Q: Please provide me with a thumbnail sketch of your educational background.

A: I graduated from Maxwell Scherzer High School; I have a BA from Yale and a PhD in economics from Harvard.

Going forward, the witness has opened the door to three areas of enquiry:

- The high school experience

- The Yale college experience

- The Harvard graduate school experience

Even at this more granular level, lists can be elicited that provide further areas of inquiry. For example, ask about the witness's college major and have them list required courses for the major.

A word of caution: do not get so enamored with granularity that you waste time. Unless there is a particular reason to get granular with the introductory questioning, it is simply not productive once you have a feel for the witness, their background, and how they are responding to your questions.

9.5.3 Fact Gathering

In the fact-gathering phase of the deposition, you will acquire the core facts to support your theory of the case. You are—as is always the case in discovery—looking for admissible evidence, or for information that may lead you to admissible evidence.

Your search for admissible evidence should be guided by FRE 401, which states:

Evidence is relevant if:

(a) It has a tendency to make a fact more or less probable than it would be without the evidence;

(b) The fact is of consequence in determining the action.

In sum, look for facts you can piece together in a summary judgment brief or at trial. These facts are little pieces of a jigsaw puzzle; pieced together in the right way, they present the complete picture of your case. Sometimes an individual fact or series of facts allow you to argue an inference. What does it mean to argue an inference? If a grain of sand was found in the witness's pocket, you may argue the inference that the witness was at the beach.

Your predeposition outline establishes the topic areas for fact collection. Each topic area is a box filled with information; scour the box clean of all facts like a dog licking a plate of food; no scrap left behind.

When exploring a topic area and gathering new information, begin with open ended questions to get the lay of the land. Words like who, what, when, list, where, why, and describe, are going to be useful. They encourage the witness to talk and help you gather new information. Once you get the lay of the land, ask questions that seek more granular information. Once again, for each topic area, start with broad questions that elicit a series of facts or the lay of the land. Then inquire about particular parts of the terrain.

For those who take depositions, and do it well, the process is intuitive. Teachers of deposition practice have struggled with analogies that can best explain the technique which, with experience, will become second nature.

Consider the board game, "Battleship."

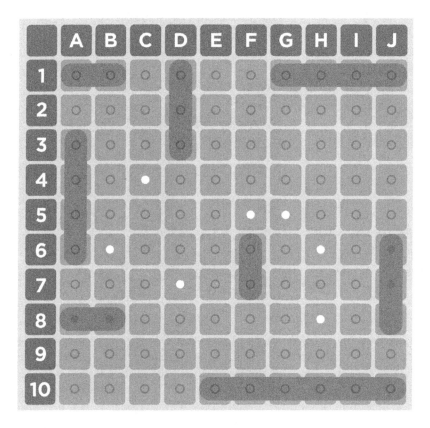

The game involves two players; each places their battleships on a field of play with their locations delineated by coordinates unknown to the other side. In Battleship, a player takes a turn by guessing the coordinates of the opponent's ship locations. A player asks, for example, "do you have a ship at A6?" and the opposing player answers either "hit" or "miss." A game of Battleship lasts for some time because discovering the battleships is based on random guesses with targeted shots. Of course, if the rules permitted, a player could simply ask, "please tell me the coordinates of all your battleships."

While Battleship does not permit this type of question, the rules of depositions are to the contrary. If Battleship played out like a deposition, the questioning would look like this:

Q: Please list the coordinates of all of your battleships.

A: A6, B9, C10, D11, F12, H14.

Q: Have you listed all of your battleships?

A: Yes.

Q: Can you tell me the tonnage of each of the ships you have just listed?

The goal is to get a list, confirm that it is a complete list, and formulate more granular questions for each component on the list. Of course, for each component, you can ask questions that elicit more lists:

Q: For the battleship at A6, identify the names of every officer on the ship.

The Battleship analogy demonstrates the futility of starting off the process with closed-ended, pointed questions that can only result in not securing the totality of information available. To make the point even clearer, if depositions were taken under the rules of Battleship, the questioning might look like this:

Q: Was Adam Jones at the meeting?

A: No.

Q: Was Sam Stuart at the meeting?

A: No.

In depositions, the technique is:

Q: Please list the names of everyone who attended the meeting.

A: Paul, Jon, Abe, and Alice.

Q: Is that the totality of attendees?

A: Yes.

The instruction "please list the names of everyone who attended the meeting" is almost the same as asking for the coordinates of all battleships. The alternative is to randomly ask the deponent about the presence of specific individuals. That approach is inefficient; you may not know all of the names to ask about, or you may forget to ask about the presence of certain individuals.

After acquiring any list, decide what subtopics are worth exploring in more detail. Again, visualize each area of inquiry as boxes of facts; your goal is to make sure that you empty each box of at least all the information that is relevant to your case. As the above example illustrates, you want to know everything about the meeting and everything each person did at the meeting.

Drill down with questions about subtopics. As you work through the subtopics, your questions usually become more focused and narrow, or granular. You are trying to accomplish several things while clearing out that topic box.

- Getting more detail

- Exhausting a witness's knowledge of the topic

- Filling in gaps of information

When securing information about the lay of the land or getting a list, close the loop by asking, "is that all?' This may prompt the witness to add to the list—moreover, at trial, the question hedges against the witness coming up with more expansive testimony, including identifying witnesses who were not mentioned at the deposition. If, at trial, the witness provides a more expansive list, and names, for example, witnesses not mentioned at deposition, you can use your deposition record to impeach by omission (which we discuss later in this chapter).

9.5.3.1   Elicit Facts

When taking depositions, elicit facts as opposed to conclusions. Facts are the building blocks for cases. Conclusions are how we remember a series of facts. Consider this example:

Q: Do you like Coke?

A: It's ok.

The word "like" is a conclusion. Attorneys coach witnesses to evade questions asking for conclusions. They have a harder time when it comes to questions that elicit pure facts:

Q: How many cans of Coke are in your refrigerator?

A: Twenty.

Q: How much money have you spent on Coke in the last month?

A: At least $500.

Why do witnesses have a harder time being evasive when asked to elicit facts? Conclusions allow for a fudge-factor. They are closer to opinion than fact. At least, this is how many witnesses think about questions that seek conclusions. Hence, they are more comfortable being evasive. Questions seeking to elicit facts are more likely to put a relatively honest witness in an integrity dilemma if they know the answer. The witness will be confronted with the realization that evasion is tantamount to a lie, or close to lying. Consider, again, that most witnesses are neither compulsive liars nor compulsive truth-tellers. Also consider, that all witnesses swear to tell the truth and in an age of twenty-four-hour television news, fully appreciate the consequences of perjury.

9.5.4 *Admission Seeking and Theory Testing*

Towards the end of the deposition you have collected lots of new facts and have confirmed many facts that you already knew. You have gathered "admissions" throughout the deposition. Admissions are simply a fact that you want to prove that comes out of the mouth of the deponent and either helps support your theory or weakens the opponent's theory.

Depos flow—I used to say the depo moves from Oprah to O'Reilly, nice and easy at the beginning and the haymakers at the end, but not so they notice the change in tone.

—William Elward, Senior Instructor,
Loyola University of Chicago School of Law

Sometimes you will want to make a conscious choice to get admissions. While admission seeking, you are usually at the granular level of a topic area and using leading questions that are short, declarative statements the witness must confirm or deny. For example, in a car accident case you may believe that the defendant was on the phone when the accident happened, making it more likely that the defendant was distracted. You could ask the following questions:

Example 1

> Q: You were in a car accident?
>
> A: Yes.
>
> Q: You were the driver?
>
> A: Yes.
>
> Q: The accident occurred at 2:52 in the afternoon?
>
> A: Yes.
>
> Q: You placed a call from your mobile number at 2:50?
>
> A: Yes.
>
> Q: You were on that call for ten minutes?
>
> A: Yes.

At this stage, an option is to assemble the facts you have established and believe to be true and see how the deponent handles the conclusions that you want him to accept or admit to. This is called theory testing. It works like this:

> Q: You testified that you were on your cell phone at the time of the accident?
>
> A: Yes.
>
> Q: You testified earlier today that you agreed with the American Car Association guidance that driving while talking on a cell phone is dangerous?
>
> A: Yes.
>
> Q: You would then agree that by driving while talking on a cell phone, you created a danger?
>
> A: I suppose so.

The art of theory testing is to gauge how much the deponent will concede or admit. Would this deponent admit that the accident was caused by cell phone usage? Probably not. Yet, the answer above comes very close to that admission and can be the basis to argue the inference at trial.

Example 2

> Q: Now you acknowledge that your car and Mr. Jones' car collided?
>
> A: Yes.
>
> Q: And prior to the accident you used your cell phone?
>
> A: Yes.
>
> Q: And prior to the police arriving you put the cell phone in your glove compartment?
>
> A: Yes.
>
> Q: You were on the phone at the time of the accident, and you did not want the police to ask you about your phone, so you hid it?
>
> A: Absolutely not.

In the first example, the core facts are laid out in such a way that the deponent cannot do anything but confirm the theory. In the second example, the theory was tested, but probably not confirmed. Yet, the deposing attorney gets the benefit of seeing the witness's reaction and testing whether the reaction is genuine. This is valuable to counsel because they have tested—prior to trial—the defendant's response to a particular theory. Counsel will have sufficient time prior to trial to determine how or if the theory can be used.

We do theory testing in depositions for two reasons. First, we do so to secure clear admissions that we can use in summary judgment motions or at trial. Here we are looking for the precise sound bite that will fit into the anticipated argument. Second, we are looking to see how witnesses will react when they are asked to admit to a conclusion premised on a set of undisputed facts that have been elicited earlier in the deposition or through discovery.

You are not always going to be successful at securing your anticipated admission or proving a theory, and that is OK. The deposition is the place where you want to figure out what does and does not work so that you can be better prepared to handle the other stages of the case, especially the trial.

9.6   Deposing an Organization

You may need information from an organization, including a partnership, association, governmental agency, or corporation, but you do not know who within the organization to notice or to subpoena. FRCP 30(b)(6) and its state court analogue(s) is a useful tool in these situations. The rule provides:

> (6) *Notice or Subpoena Directed to an Organization.* In its notice or subpoena, a party may name as the deponent a public or private corporation, a partnership, an association, a governmental agency, or other entity and must describe with reasonable particularity the matters for examination. The named organization must then designate one or more officers, directors, or managing agents, or designate other persons who consent to testify on its behalf; and it may set out the matters on which each person designated will testify. A subpoena must advise a nonparty organization of its duty to make this designation. The persons designated must testify about information known or reasonably available to the organization. This paragraph (6) does not preclude a deposition by any other procedure allowed by these rules.

An FRCP 30(b)(6) notice shifts the burden, requiring the organization to appoint an individual or individuals to testify on its behalf. The attorney defending the deposition will typically work with the organization to find an individual or individuals who are capable of providing testimony responsive to the notice. In most cases, the organization selects a person who already knows the information or at least has knowledge of most of the information or the topic area. An effort must be made to arm the "organizational designee" with information sufficient to respond to the designated areas of inquiry. Because the testimony of these individuals will be binding on the organization as a statement of party opponent under FRE 801(d)(2), FRCP 30(b)(6) notices should be taken very seriously.

The form of the notice is not complicated. The noticing party will send a notice that reads something like: "Pursuant to FRCP 30(b)(6), plaintiff requests that defendant [or third party] produce for deposition the individual or individuals who can provide testimony on the following topic areas." The notice then lists the topic areas. The noticing party must "designate with reasonable particularity the matters on which examination is requested."[29]

Generally, a court will allow no more than one deposition of each organization. Hence, the notice should contain all of the anticipated topic areas.

9.6.1 *Document Custodian Deposition*

Where there is a dispute regarding document production, sometimes a deposition can be useful to secure the information necessary to negotiate an agreement on the scope of the production. Typically, in large cases, there are issues with regard to how documents are stored, the volume of the documents, and the cost of retrieval. Even after documents are produced, it may be necessary to make sure that entity producing the documents interpreted the request in the way you intended, and that no documents were intentionally or inadvertently withheld.

If the dispute about production impedes any documents from being tendered, the parties may informally agree to a single deposition of the person who can explain the holdup, which may include cost issues. Such depositions, occurring before document production, are taken in furtherance of an effort to break any deadlock holding up production, or to secure information in support of a motion to compel.

A party may also seek this information through a "designation" bolted into the notice of deposition under FRCP 30(b)(6). The designation will look something like:

1) Defendant's (or plaintiff or third party) policies or protocols regarding document retention and destruction.

2) The manner in which defendant (or plaintiff or third party) stores and/or retrieves documents sought pursuant to the document request attached hereto as Exhibit A.

3) The efforts made to search for and produce documents sought pursuant to the document request attached hereto as Exhibit A.

Where the deponent withholds documents pursuant to a claim of privilege, engineer a designation to determine whether the individuals listed on a privilege log[30] are indeed attorneys or individuals within the organization who warrant a claim of privilege. A designation along these lines might read as follows:

---

29. Fed. R. Evid. 30(b)(6).
30. A privilege log is a document indexing privileged documents, typically with an explanation about why the documents are privileged. *See* Cavallaro v. United States, 284 F.3d 236, 244 (1st Cir. 2002).

National Institute for Trial Advocacy

A) The place of employment of any individual listed on the privilege log attached hereto as Exhibit B.

9.7 Representing the Deponent

There are five types of deponents: 1) individual deponents who are your client, 2) deponents who work for your client which is an organization, 3) third-party deponents, 4) organizational designees, and 5) experts. Each type of deponent poses different challenges to representation.

9.7.1 What is Your Relationship to the Deponent?

If your client is an organization, you may be called upon to represent specific employees when the organization is involved in litigation. At the time you are retained, anticipate the employees within the organization who will be deposed and begin the process of interviewing them to see what they know. Collecting information[31] will help you and the witness prepare for the deposition.

Ascertain whether representing employees of the organization presents any conflicts of interest. You may be in a situation in which the organization is a defendant and the employee is a whistleblower. Or the organization may be a defendant with a claim against an employee. Where there is a conflict, consider securing separate counsel for the employee. You will still appear at the deposition to assert objections as to the form of the question and to interpose objections that protect privileges that belong to the corporation. For example, the employee deponent may be asked questions about their communications with the organization's counsel. Even though you are not the employee's personal attorney at the deposition, you may assert the attorney-client privilege—which belongs to your client—by objecting and issuing an instruction not to answer.[32] Even if the deponent does not follow your direction, your client will not have voluntarily waived the privilege.

---

31. The situation where a corporate employee is being interviewed by the attorney representing the corporation raises special attorney-client issues. These interviews are termed as "Upjohn Warnings." Such interviews are commonplace in most internal investigations carried out for the purpose of providing legal advice to a corporation. In *Upjohn v. United States*, the Supreme Court provided important guidance to all attorneys who find themselves interviewing corporate employees. Upjohn Co. v. United States, 449 U.S. 383 (1981). The purpose of the Upjohn Warnings is to make sure that the individual employee being interviewed understands that the attorney-client privilege, as commonly understood, does not apply to their interview with an attorney representing the corporation. Making sure that the employee being interviewed is aware of this fact is a necessity that establishes the ethical character of the attorney's actions while also preserving the corporation's legal ability to control and use the statements by the employee in the manner best suited to its legitimate interests.
32. However, the line between privileged information and nonprivileged information is blurry with 30(b)(6) witnesses because "it is most likely that the lawyer was the source of the information which was provided to the 30(b)(6) witness so that he could answer the questions on behalf of the corporation and bind the corporation to those answers." Fid. Mgmt. & Rsch. Co. v. Actuate Corp., 275 F.R.D. 63, 64 (D. Mass. 2011).

Third-party deponents pose yet another set of issues. If the third-party deponent retains the attorney, the substance of communications between the deponent and the attorney are privileged. This assumes that the communications occurred prior to the start of the deposition; communications during a break in the deposition—other than for the purpose of discussing a privilege issue—may be subject to questioning.

On the other hand, suppose the attorney is preparing a third-party deponent whom the attorney does not represent? Consider this example: you represent a company, and a supplier—who is friendly to the company—is being deposed. You spend an hour talking to the supplier about the deposition, yet because you are not counsel to the supplier, your communications are not encompassed by the attorney-client privilege. Forming an attorney-client relationship may be an option to protect the privilege, but doing so adds responsibilities for you, raises potential conflict of interest concerns, and may allow your opponent at trial to deem the witness an adverse witness and proceed under FRE 611(c) with a cross-examination as opposed to a direct examination.

Organizational designees create yet another set of issues. Defending an FRCP 30(b)(6) deposition starts with a response to the notice. Raise any objections now; otherwise they will potentially be waived. Additionally, because the stakes are high, some FRCP 30(b)(6) requests may merit a motion for protective order to narrow the scope of the inquiry or bar inquiry into attorney-client privileged matters.

Finally, defending expert depositions raises questions about the scope of what, if any, communications between the expert and the counsel can be explored. Questions about facts or information provided to the expert by counsel and relied upon to form the opinion are fair game. Whether questions can be posed about general communications with counsel is a greyer area. In federal court, communications with experts are subject to more liberal protection,[33] while state courts—depending on the jurisdiction—may give deposing counsel latitude to question experts about their communications with counsel.

9.7.2 *Where to Begin*

Representation always starts with deposition preparation. Where the deponent is your individual client, the deposition preparation process begins the moment you first meet with your client to prepare the case. This is true without regard to whether your client is the plaintiff or the defendant. Explain the litigation process, letting the client know that there will be a point in time where they will have to testify, either in deposition, at trial, or both. Your continued interactions with the

---

33. Sara Lee Corp. v. Kraft Foods, Inc., 273 F.R.D. 416 (N.D. Ill. 2011).

client will be with an eye toward that testimony, and your final deposition preparation session or meeting may be a short refresher session.

Preparation should be thorough and relentless. Anticipate what the other side will cover so there are no bad surprises. Engage in practice questioning using different styles—the hostile cross, the friendly banter, etc. I know I've done my job prepping a witness when they tell me after the depo that the prep was harder than the depo itself.

—Michael Williams, Partner, Bienert Katzman Littrell Williams LLP

The most important instruction to give any witness is to tell the truth. In preparing a witness, a lot of words maybe transmitted between you and the soon-to-be deponent, and continued reminders about the importance of telling the truth is critical.

It is perfectly appropriate to suggest that a witness listen to the question and divulge no more than is asked. It is also perfectly appropriate to suggest that a witness may ask for a clarification if they do not understand a question.

If your witness is the plaintiff, you may want to review the complaint paragraph by paragraph. Assume that a plaintiff will always be asked about the complaint and therefore it is a good practice to have your client review the complaint before it is actually filed. The same can be said of answers to interrogatories. The witness may be asked questions about interrogatories or interrogatory answers, requests for production of documents, requests for admission, and documents that reference the witness. Review all of these documents with the would be deponent prior to the deposition.

Preparation can also involve role-play. In asking the witness about the facts, remember the technique of unpacking conclusions. A witness may be inclined to render specific answers based on conclusions that are not based on facts. Role-playing is one method of getting the witness to avoid testifying to conclusions that have no factual support.

9.7.3 Defending at the Deposition

In defending a deposition, an attorney is not a potted plant. Attorneys can interpose objections to the form of the question, objections based on attorney-client privilege or other privileges where applicable, and they can do a redirect at the end of the deposition.

The following is a chart outlining potential objections:

Objections During the Deposition

Valid Objections	Source/Example
Privilege	FRCP 26(b); FRCP 30(c)(2)
	Hickman v. Taylor, 329 U.S. 495, 507-08 (1947)
Form of the Question	FRCP 32(d)(3)
Compound; misleading; ambiguous; argumentative; prejudicial; abusive; leading; repetitious; calls for a legal conclusion, speculation, improper opinion, or narrative; asked and answered	*Order of United Commercial Travelers v. Tripp*, 63 F.2d 37, 39-40 (10th Cir. 1933) (interpreting *Howard v. Stillwell & Bierce Mfg. Co.*, 139 U.S. 199, 11 S. Ct. 500 (1891))
	Batelli v. Kagan & Gaines Co., 236 F2d 167 (9th Cir. Cal. 1956)
Bad Faith/Harassment	FRCP 30(b); FRCP 30(d); FRCP 31(d)
	Hickman v. Taylor, 329 U.S. 495, 507-08 (1947)
Witness Competency, Relevancy, or Materiality	FRCP 32(d)
If curable at the time of deposition, they must be objected to at the time of deposition, or the objection is waived.	*Shutte v. Thompson*, 82 U.S. 151, 160 (1872)
	Detective Comics, Inc. v. Fawcett Publs., Inc., 4 F.R.D. 237 (S.D.N.Y. 1944)

Procedural Objections to Depositions

Valid Objections	Source/Example
Error/Irregularity of Deposition Notice	FRCP 32(d)
Untimely or improper notice	Trade Dev. Bank v. Continental Ins. Co., 469 F.2d 35 (2d Cir. N.Y. 1972).
	Wong Ho v. Dulles, 261 F.2d 456 (9th Cir. Cal. 1958)
Qualifications of Officer Taking the Deposition	FRCP 32(d)

When interposing an objection to form, merely say "objection" and provide enough information to key the opposing counsel into the problem with the question, so that they are on notice of the problem in order to rephrase the question. Speeches—or speaking objections—are not necessary and are frowned upon by the courts.

The attorney-client privilege precludes inquiry into the substance of a communication. The deposing counsel is, however, permitted to seek information to determine whether there is indeed a privilege and, if so, whether it has been waived. For example, these types of questions are permissible:

> Q: Without telling me the substance of the communications, can you tell me the identity of the individuals who were present when you met with counsel?

> Q: Without telling me the substance of the communications with counsel, what, if any, other individuals did you disclose those communications to?

If testimony is sought about the substance of a privileged communication, your objection is "objection, attorney-client privilege." Once you make the objection, instruct the witness not to answer the question. The opposing attorney may ask: "are you going to follow you counsel's instruction?" The opposing counsel may also ask, "If a court compels you to come back and answer the question, can you provide the answer?"

9.8   Obstreperous Counsel and Other Issues

During the course of your practice, you will at some point come across obstreperous counsel. They are individuals who disrupt the deposition through the following techniques:

- Making long speaking objections;

- Making comments that coach the witness;

- Taking breaks to coach a witness; and

- Making statements on the record that mischaracterize the conduct of the opposing counsel.

The classic techniques used by obstreperous counsel include the following:

- After a question is posed, the defending counsel will state, "if you know," which keys the witness into saying, "I don't";

- Stating an objection and providing a paragraph of more explanation as to the impropriety of the question and using words and phrases that coach the witness;

- Stating on the record, "stop waiving your hands and yelling at my client," when the opposing counsel is doing no such thing; and

- Holding the arm of the deponent as a signal not to answer the question.

Dealing with obstreperous counsel is more an art than a science. The most important guidance is not to engage. Once an argument begins on the record, it will be difficult for a judge to ascertain who started it. It is also important to understand that an obstreperous counsel wants the opposition to feel that they did something wrong. Lines such as, "if you knew the local practice here" are common parlance of obstreperous counsel.

If you do not engage an obstreperous counsel, most of the time the bad behavior will cease. If the behavior continues, relief in form of a motion "regulating the conduct of depositions" may be in order.

Of course, while judges increasingly expect parties to solve their own procedural conflicts, there is no shortage of case law regarding discovery disputes of all kinds, including deposition conduct.[34] One seminal and oft-cited case on the subject is *Hall v. Clifton Precision, a Division of Litton Systems Inc.*[35] A twenty-three-year-old decision by Judge Robert Gawthrop of the Eastern District of Pennsylvania involved two issues: "(1) to what extent a lawyer may confer with a client, off the record and outside earshot of the other lawyers, during a deposition of the client, and (2) does a lawyer have right to inspect, before the deposition of a client begins, all documents which opposing counsel intends to show the client during the deposition, so that lawyer can review them with the client before the deposition?"[36]

---

34. In addition to counsel conduct, the courts do provide guidance on witness conduct. In re Shorenstein Hays-Nederlander Theatres L.L.C. Appeals, 213 A.3d 39, 69-78 (Del. 2019) (holding lawyers are responsible for a client's obstructionist behavior and agreeing with the trial court's award of attorney fees and costs to the defendant after a plaintiff member witness engaged in bad faith deposition conduct). "[W]e write to remind counsel that they have a responsibility to intercede and not sit idly by as their client engages in abusive deposition misconduct. Depositions are court proceedings, and counsel defending the deposition have an obligation to prevent their deponent from impeding or frustrating a fair examination. Although counsel can be caught off guard by a client's unexpected, sanctionable outburst, that is not what happened here.... Here, Hays's counsel made no apparent effort to curb her misconduct.... Perhaps this episode can be used positively as a lesson to those training new lawyers on deposition skills. Lawyers have an obligation to ensure that their clients do not undermine the integrity of the deposition proceedings by engaging in bad faith litigation tactics; they cannot simply sit and passively observe as their client persists in such conduct. Given the restrictions on conferring with a client during deposition proceedings, these points obviously should be addressed beforehand in the deposition preparation."
35. Hall v. Clifton Precision, 150 F.R.D. 525 (E.D. Pa. 1993).
36. *Id.* at 526.

Noting that, at the time, "[t]he significance of depositions has grown geometrically over time to the point where their pervasiveness now dwarfs both the time spent and the facts learned at the actual trial" and that "[t]he pretrial tail now wags the trial dog," Judge Gawthrop entered the following nine-point order to prevent what he called "abuse" of the deposition process.[37] That order is instructive, and provides language that could be bolted into virtually any pretrial order:

1) At the beginning of the deposition, deposing counsel shall instruct the witness to ask deposing counsel, rather than the witness's own counsel, for clarifications, definitions or explanations of any words, questions or documents presented during the course of the deposition. The witness shall abide by these instructions.

2) All objections, except those which would be waived if not made at the deposition under Federal Rules of Civil Procedure 32(d)(3)(B), and those necessary to assert a privilege, to enforce a limitation on evidence directed by the court, or to present a motion pursuant to Federal Rules of Civil Procedure 30(d), shall be preserved. Therefore, those objections need not and shall not be made during the course of depositions.

3) Counsel shall not direct or request that a witness not answer a question, unless that counsel has objected to the question on the ground that the answer is protected by a privilege or a limitation on evidence directed by the court.

4) Counsel shall not make objections or statements which might suggest an answer to a witness. Counsels' statements when making objections should be succinct and verbally economical, stating the basis of the objection and nothing more.

5) Counsel and their witness-clients shall not engage in private, off-the-record conferences during depositions or during breaks or recesses, except for the purpose of deciding whether to assert a privilege.

6) Any conferences which occur pursuant to, or in violation of, guideline (5) are a proper subject for inquiry by deposing counsel to ascertain whether there has been any witness-coaching and, if so, what.

7) Any conferences which occur pursuant to, or in violation of, guideline (5) shall be noted on the record by the counsel who participated in the conference. The purpose and outcome of the conference shall also be noted on the record.

8) Deposing counsel shall provide to the witness's counsel a copy of all documents shown to the witness during the deposition. The copies shall

---

37. *Id.* at 531.

be provided either before the deposition begins or contemporaneously with the showing of each document to the witness. The witness and the witness's counsel do not have the right to discuss documents privately before the witness answers questions about them.

9) Depositions shall otherwise be conducted in compliance with the opinion which accompanies this order.[38]

9.9 Impeachment Considerations

A discussion of depositions is not complete without mention of creating a record for impeachment at trial. A deposition transcript can be used at trial to impeach a witness through a prior inconsistent statement. To understand the role that depositions play, it is important to understand the process of impeachment at trial through prior inconsistent statement. The process is governed by the "Three C's": confirm, credit, and confront. Imagine a scenario in which the witness testified at deposition that, "when I went through the intersection the light was red." At trial, however, the witness testifies that the light was green.

On cross-examination, first *confirm* what you heard on direct with the following sequence:

Q: Sir, did I just hear you tell the jurors that when you went through the intersection the light was green?

A: Yes.

Next *credit* the prior deposition testimony with questions along these lines:

Q: Sir, you remember coming to my office back in June and giving a deposition?

A: Yes.

Q: And at the time you took an oath and swore to tell the truth?

A: Yes.

Q: And you did tell the truth at your deposition?

Confront the witness with the deposition transcript and read the following sequence:

Q: When you went through the intersection, what color was the light?

---

38. *Id.* at 531–32.

A: Red.

Ask one final question:

Q: Did I read the words correctly?

A: Yes.

The first lesson here is to make sure that the questions and answers at depositions are clear enough so that they can be used for impeachment at trial. While the above example is straightforward, there is a second variation, which is called "impeachment by omission." Note the following scenario in which the witness at deposition gives the following testimony:

Q: Who was at the meeting on the 19th of June?

A: Joe and Mike.

Q: Was that all?

A·   Yes

Now at trial, the witness testifies as follows:

Q: Tell me what happened at the meeting on the 19th of June?

A: Barbara dominated the meeting with her talk.

The inconsistency is the testimony about the presence and conduct of Barbara, who was not mentioned during the deposition. The same "Three C's" process is used for impeachment, but it works only if the testimony secured at the deposition was so sufficiently clear as to eliminate the presence of any other person at the meeting. This is called "closing the loop" and it is done to set up impeachment by omission.

Q: Did you see any dents or scratches on his car?

A: No.

Q: Did you ever hear any other driver honk at him?

A: No.

Q: So why do you say that Fred is a bad driver?

A: That is just what people say about him.

Q: But you cannot point to any specific facts that support a statement that he is a bad driver.

A: I guess not.

The above is a classic example of a witness who reached a conclusion that is not supported by the facts. The line of questioning is designed to unpack the facts and determine whether the conclusion is actually supported by the facts.

9.10   Expert Depositions

There are numerous reasons to depose an expert including:

- Securing testimony to support a motion to exclude the expert or limit the scope of his or her opinion.

- Securing testimony that can be used to attack the bias or credibility of the expert.

- Securing testimony to show where the expert may actually agree with your theory of the case.

- Confirming that the opinions offered in the expert's report are the totality of his or her opinions.

- Confirming the facts that form the basis of the expert's opinion.

The starting point for preparing for an expert deposition is the expert report. FRCP 26(a)(2)(B) outlines the scope of an expert report:

(a) Required Disclosures.

(B) *Proceedings Exempt from Initial Disclosure.* The following proceedings are exempt from initial disclosure:

(i) an action for review on an administrative record;

(ii) a forfeiture action in rem arising from a federal statute;

(iii) a petition for habeas corpus or any other proceeding to challenge a criminal conviction or sentence;

(iv) an action brought without an attorney by a person in the custody of the United States, a state, or a state subdivision;

(v) an action to enforce or quash an administrative summons or subpoena;

(vi) an action by the United States to recover benefit payments;

(vii) an action by the United States to collect on a student loan guaranteed by the United States;

(viii) a proceeding ancillary to a proceeding in another court; and

(ix) an action to enforce an arbitration award.

In addition to the requirements of FCP 26, FRE 702 governs testimony by expert witnesses.

Rule 702. Testimony by Expert Witnesses

Primary tabs

A witness who is qualified as an expert by knowledge, skill, experience, training, or education may testify in the form of an opinion or otherwise if:

(a) the expert's scientific, technical, or other specialized knowledge will help the trier of fact to understand the evidence or to determine a fact in issue;

(b) the testimony is based on sufficient facts or data;

(c) the testimony is the product of reliable principles and methods; and

(d) the expert has reliably applied the principles and methods to the facts of the case.

The requirements of both FRCP 26 and 702 outline the requirements that must be met by an expert. Pursuant to the Supreme Court's decision in *Daubert v. Merrell Dow Pharmaceuticals, Inc.*,[39] the trial court judge is the gatekeeper for determining whether an expert will be allowed to testify at trial; the judge also has the ability to limit the scope of the testimony.

A deposition of an expert will necessarily drill down on requirements of both the procedural rule and the evidentiary rule. Be prepared to test the expert on how their opinion may change depending on the facts. In expert depositions, hypotheticals are perfectly reasonable.

Where the area of testimony is highly technical, consider working with a nontestifying expert who can help formulate a line of inquiry.

---

39. Daubert v. Merrell Dow Pharms., Inc., 509 U.S. 579 (1993).

CHAPTER TEN

MOTION PRACTICE AND APPEARING IN COURT

10.1   Introduction

Motions move cases. They draw the court's attention to and invoke rulings on substantive and procedural matters. Challenges to personal jurisdiction, substantive jurisdiction, standing, and the sufficiency of the complaint are all made by motion. Motions also secure summary judgment, certify and decertify class actions, preclude evidence, limit the scope of discovery, and compel discovery. The bottom line is if you need the court's help or its ruling on a matter, do it by motion. There are many types of motions in your toolbox.

Not all motions are contentious; indeed, some are consensual. Seek the opposition's view of your request for relief prior to filing the motion seeking a court ruling. Local court rules, or a specific judge's rules, may require a meet-and-confer with the opposition prior to filing. Motions resolved by consent include: 1) motions for extended time to answer a complaint or file a dispositive motion, 2) motions to alter a scheduling order, 3) motions to extend the page limit on briefs, 4) motions to enter into a jointly agreed-upon upon confidentiality order, and 5) motions for leave to file an amended complaint or add parties.

There is no dearth of motions that are opposed—including motions to dismiss, motions for summary judgment, motions to certify a class, motions to strike experts, motions to preclude evidence, and motions to bar discovery.

10.2   The Cheat Chart on Twelve Common Motions

As a general rule, motions that dispose of the case—dispositive motions—do not require consent. Nondispositive motions do require consent. Consent simply means that the moving party reached out to the opposition to determine whether the motion is opposed.

As a case progresses, the parties will likely deal with the following types of motions:

Motion to dismiss	Non-consensual
Motions to extend time to file a brief or answer	Often consensual
Motions to extend the page limit in briefs	Consensual
Motions to file information under seal	Consensual
Motions to admit counsel pro hac vice	Often consensual
Motion to appoint class counsel	Sometimes non-consensual
Motion for class certification	Non-consensual
Motion to compel discovery or for protective order	Non-consensual
Motion for summary judgment	Non-consensual
Motions in limine	Non-consensual
Daubert motions	Non-consensual
Motion for entry of a scheduling order	Often consensual

10.3 When to Go to the Judge

Judges are in the business of resolving controversy. Their time is valuable; they prefer parties work out their differences collectively, especially matters governing the progression of a case. Naturally, courts recognize that parties are unable to work out differences on dispositive motions; but on procedural matters, they require parties to meet and confer, then state in the motion that such efforts were made.

Cases are riddled with imperfections: technical derelictions as to service of process, discovery obligations, or the use of evidence in motions that is technically not authentic. Before bringing an issue to a judge for dispute resolution, decide whether the dereliction impacts the outcome of the case. Suppose a defendant wrote ten emails to colleagues discussing a detailed scheme to commit consumer fraud. From deposition testimony, you discover that defendant told an eleventh colleague about his scheme via email but the email was not produced in discovery. You met and conferred with opposing counsel and opposing counsel did not agree to produce the email in question. In determining whether to file a motion to compel, consider the following:

- Is this just an effort to secure cumulative evidence or might something new be learned?

- Does raising this issue to the court offer an opportunity to educate the court on the evidence being secured during litigation?

- Will the judge look at the request and say, "You already have the admissions you need; why is this necessary?"

The bottom line: invoke the court's decision-making authority strategically, sensitive to the court's limited time. Will this email materially increase your chances to prevail on summary judgment or at trial? Will you even use the email? Is it worth pressing the matter? Does your opposition's reluctance to produce indicate its utility at trial?

Judges also prefer that parties work out their differences on process matters, including time to respond to a pleading and the page limits of a brief. Though the court may take exception to such "joint" motions and deny them, it does not mean the parties should not try to present a united front to the court.

10.4   General Motion Practice Rules (FRCP 5–11)

The basic sources for motions are the Federal Rules of Civil Procedure (FRCP) and the Federal Rules of Evidence (FRE). Those who think the FRCP govern what happens before trial and the FRE govern the trial, are mistaken. During the pretrial stage of the litigation, you must read and interpret both sets of rules in tandem, not in isolation. Matters governing the reasonable scope of discovery, summary judgment, motions in limine, and *Daubert* motions all require analysis of the procedural and evidentiary rules. For example, even in applying FRCP 9(b) to fraud pleadings in fraud cases, plaintiffs might consider reminding the court that at trial cases can be made on circumstantial evidence, as FRE 401 makes no distinction between circumstantial and direct evidence. FRCP 9(b) states pleadings alleging fraud or mistake require particularity of allegations. This may confuse some litigants into believing they need to allege direct evidence. Yet, when FRCP 9(b) is read in context with FRE 401, it is clear that requiring a pleading standard more stringent than the evidentiary standard was not intended.

"Motions, particularly in limine motions, are indispensable. They should be used to highlight critical issues, educate the court, and shape the parameters of a trial through the exclusion or admission of particular evidence."

—Mike Beckwith, Asst. U.S. Attorney, E.D. California

Every rule is there for a purpose and provides an opportunity for creative lawyers to move a court by motion to alter the proceedings in a case. Take, for example, FRCP 1. Few law professors focus on this rule and it probably never appears as a final exam question. For this very reason, and because of its importance, we will mention this rule frequently throughout this book. FRCP 1 states:

> These rules govern the procedure in all civil actions and proceedings in the United States district courts, except as stated in Rule 81. They should be construed, administered, and employed by the court and

the parties to secure the just, speedy, and inexpensive determination of every action and proceeding.[1]

FRCP 1 is the context for every motion interpreting the rules. It is the answer to defense lawyers who want to complicate, extend, and drain the plaintiff's resources. It is also the answer for plaintiffs who want to engage in attenuated discovery that may be useless at trial. For those plaintiffs who know the rules of evidence, the rebuttal may be easy. Responses should demonstrate why a pretrial motion will have material importance to a trial of a case.

Aside from context, FRCP 1 also enables judges to creatively structure case proceedings with an eye toward justice, speed, and economy. Suppose a complaint has twenty-five counts, but all counts depend on the defendant engaging in one discrete action. FRCP 1 allows any party to file a motion requesting the court to enter a scheduling order requiring expedited discovery and a summary judgment briefing on the discrete issue. The assumption is that early resolution of that issue would eliminate expense and prompt early disposition.

Read the rules carefully. Rules provide courts latitude to enter orders creating efficiencies. More importantly, they provide opportunities for parties to think creatively and use motion practice to advance litigation efficiencies. For example, FRCP 23 governs class action conduct. Section (d) allows for creative litigation tactics:

(d) Conducting the Action.

(1) *In General.* In conducting an action under this rule, the court may issue orders that:

(A) determine the course of proceedings or prescribe measures to prevent undue repetition or complication in presenting evidence or argument;

(B) require—to protect class members and fairly conduct the action—giving appropriate notice to some or all class members of:

(i) any step in the action;

(ii) the proposed extent of the judgment; or

(iii) the members' opportunity to signify whether they consider the representation fair and adequate, to intervene and present claims or defenses, or to otherwise come into the action;

(C) impose conditions on the representative parties or on intervenors;

---

1. Fed. R. Civ. P. 1.

(D) require that the pleadings be amended to eliminate allegations about representation of absent persons and that the action proceed accordingly; or

(E) deal with similar procedural matters.

(2) *Combining and Amending Orders.* An order under Rule 23(d)(1) may be altered or amended from time to time and may be combined with an order under Rule 16.[2]

Some motions flow intuitively from the rules, such as motions to dismiss and motions for summary judgment. Other motions not specifically delineated by the rules are based on applying a commonsense approach to guiding litigation in a speedy and efficient manner. Consider motions for expedited discovery. In a damages case, where the conduct already occurred, seeking expedited discovery is generally without basis. When the plaintiff seeks injunctive relief, a judge may find expedited discovery reasonable, particularly if it is tailored. Perhaps the plaintiff files a combined motion for a temporary restraining order (TRO) and the limited expedited discovery needed for preliminary injunction hearings. Plaintiffs should demonstrate that their proposal streamlines litigation. For example, the plaintiff may propose combining the preliminary injunction hearing with a hearing on the merits, so litigation culminates in one hearing.

The overriding rule for motions is: be reasonable. In addition, consider these guidelines:

> Don't drink your own Kool-Aid.

> Think about how opposing counsel will view and respond to the proposed relief.

> Think about how the judge will view the motion.

> Be the judge's problem solver; make their life easier, and earn credibility with the judge and your opposition.

---

2. Fed. R. Civ. P. 23(d).

10.5   Starting the Process

There are two kinds of motions: dispositive and nondispositive. Dispositive motions dispose of the case; nondispositive ones do not. Most judges, and sometimes local rules, require meet-and-confer dialogues between opposing counsel prior to filing nondispositive motions. Meet-and-confers are not pro-forma; take them seriously. They provide opportunities to eliminate undisputed issues, agree on a common course of action, and learn the other side's position regarding the requested relief. While emotion and instinct may counsel an aggressive stance, remember that you *will* have a relationship with your opponent throughout the course of the litigation—you get to decide its tone. Being firm, yet cordial, will result in a different relationship than being rude or aggressive. Meet-and-confer dialogues, like all contacts with opposing counsel, the court, clients, and the outside world, are a place where reputations develop. Be an honest broker and a person who keeps their word. A number of professional conduct rules involve the requisite honesty lawyers must demonstrate in their communications.[3]

There are three possible outcomes of meet-and-confer dialogues. First, the parties may agree that the motion is unopposed or should be jointly filed. Typically, parties negotiate a proposed scheduling or confidentiality order and then file a joint motion seeking its entry. Parties may negotiate a class action settlement and then file a joint motion asking the court to approve the settlement. Motions to extend time to answer a complaint, file a brief, or extend the page limit on briefings are often unopposed. The motion's caption should clearly identify the motion as jointly filed or unopposed. Doing so sends the judge a signal that "this is an easy one to deal with."

The second possible meet-and-confer outcome is that the moving party, after hearing the opposing argument, decides the relief sought is an overreach. The moving party will seek more modest relief, and though still opposed, the relief sought is more likely to be secured. The third possible outcome is the parties do not reach an agreement and the moving party files a motion seeking full relief.

10.5.1   *The Mechanics of a Motion*

While courts typically have their own styles and requirements for filing motions, there are generally three written components needed to initiate a motion:

- the motion itself;
- a proposed order attached to the motion;
- a brief or memorandum of points and authorities in support of the motion.

---

3. *See, e.g.*, MODEL RULES OF PRO. CONDUCT r. 1.2, 1.4, 3.3, 3.4, 4.1, 7.1, 7.2, 8.4 (AM. BAR ASS'N 2020).

Always check the local rules and determine the precise requirements. For example, does the court require that counsel attach a declaration or affidavit to the motion stating that a meet-and-confer conference occurred, but that the parties were unable to resolve the matters in dispute? Does the court allow the parties to combine the motion and the brief into a single document? If there are exhibits supporting the motion, must they be attached to the motion or the brief? While these matters seem like technicalities, judges and their courtroom staff handle many cases, and rules are written to facilitate efficiency. Therefore, strict compliance with the rules is crucial.

Never underestimate the persuasive value of a pretrial brief. It educates the Court on key factual arguments and demonstrates the level of counsel's preparation. You get bonus points if that brief is short and concise.

—Justin Victor, Of Counsel, Greenberg Traurig LLP

When writing motions, set forth in numbered paragraphs the relief sought, the basis of the relief, and the specific form of the relief, i.e.: 1) plaintiff seeks an order compelling interrogatory answers; 2) these reasons merit an order; and 3) what the order or form of relief will look like. Unless the court's rules specify otherwise, attach a proposed order to the motion. The brief or memorandum of points and authorities provides legal support for the relief sought, and often times, more detailed facts.

Support the motion with declarations, affidavits, deposition testimony, or other evidence. Depending on the local rules, these items may be attached as exhibits to the motion or the brief. Whatever route is taken, always make things as simple as possible for the judge. Make the brief and the motion self-contained so neither the judge nor his clerks have to revisit either document to fully understand the argument. Repetition is not generally a problem.

Guidelines for motion drafting vary depending on the type of motion, but the above recitation provides the general framework. If you are served with a motion, your response opposing it will be a "brief in opposition to motion" or "memorandum of points and authorities in opposition to motion." Just like a motion, this brief should cite cases and, when asserting facts, support them with evidence in the form of declarations, affidavits, deposition testimony, or other documents.

Although this book is about pretrial procedure, we continually stress the importance of being conversant with the rules of evidence. Exhibits to briefs should meet evidentiary standards for relevance, hearsay, and authenticity. An appreciation of the evidentiary rules can also broaden considerations of which, otherwise public, documents could have evidentiary value in a case.[4]

---

4. *See* Fed. R. Evid. 201.

The brief supporting the motion, or the motion (if a stand-alone document), is generally formatted as follows:

- Introduction: Assume the court or court clerk will get no further than the introduction. Encapsulate what is being sought, the legal basis for why it is sought, and the practical reason for why the relief should be granted.

- Facts: Include information about the process of the case and its underlying merits. For motions to dismiss, stick to the factual allegations, which are presumed true for the purposes of the motion. For other motions, cite to the record evidence.

- Law: Look for cases with similar facts, in the same jurisdiction, and work from there.

- Conclusion: Summarize the relief sought.

10.5.2   *Who Decides Motions?*

The key to advocacy is knowing your audience.[5] Think about who will decide your motion and their previous rulings on similar issues. Consider whether your request will be viewed as reasonable or an overreach.

Who actually decides the motion? Many state court systems assign one judge to hear the merits of a case and assign other judges to hear procedural motions associated with the case. Some courts assign judges to hear specific motions and a different judge to try the case after the motions are decided.

In federal court, judges sometimes decide all procedural and substantive motions on their own. Other times they assign motions, both procedural and substantive, to a magistrate judge to review the papers, hear argument, and issue a ruling that may be appealed to the district court judge. Depending on the judge, the matter is decided on the papers or the judge hears oral argument.

Why is this information important? If a case has one judge assigned to hear motions and decide matters on the merits, they will, after a while, be familiar with the case and the papers will not need to rehash the background. If each motion is heard by a different judge, background is important, but keep in mind that motions judges are busy and often doing triage.

---

5. *See* Reuben Guttman, *Advocacy Is a Two-Way Street*, The Glob. Legal Post (Apr. 27, 2015), https://www.globallegalpost.com/blogs/commentary/advocacy-is-a-two-way-street-7932750/ ("What you may think is the right message, or form of message to deliver to the decision maker, may not necessarily be the one that resonates. What you may think is the right style may not be appropriate for a particular audience. This is just something to think about; communication is a two-way street.").

10.6   The Motion Itself

Take the following into consideration when motion drafting. We use the word "consideration" because law is both dynamic and somewhat creative. Hard and fast rules tend to ignore that fact, preventing lawyer innovation. In *Muller v. Oregon*, then-lawyer Louis Brandeis drafted what became known as the "Brandeis Brief."[6] The case challenged a state law restricting the number of hours women can work. Josephine Goldmark, an advocacy group research director, and Brandeis, a subsequent appointee to the Supreme Court, wrote a 100-page-plus opposition brief integrating scientific and social science arguments.

Don't be boring. In the criminal context it is many times easier than in the civil as it is difficult not to be a snore in a 100-page motion to compel source code in an Intellectual property dispute. Mix up your writing. Use techniques like alliteration—despondent defendant downed drink after drink; metaphor—despondent defendant fell into a well of depression; or both— like a hapless cruise ship passenger who slips off the deck during a storm, the despondent defendant fell into a depression as deep as the ocean.

—David Wiechert, Principal Partner, Wiechert Munk & Goldstein P.C.

Creativity and trying new approaches is reasonable, but keep in mind the audience and the dignity of the courtroom process.[7] Creativity can mean using analogies or references to books and movies. While analogies are powerful, exercise caution because they can also be a turn off and backfire. Read judicial opinions and the arguments of respected lawyers; they provide excellent guidance and illustration. For example, there is no shortage of references to *My Cousin Vinny* (Twentieth Century Fox 1992), a film beloved by appellate judges throughout the country:

- "In 1992, Vincent Gambini taught a master class in cross-examination. Trial counsel for the National Labor Relations Board and the National Union of Healthcare Workers apparently paid attention."[8] *Chief Judge Merrick Garland, D.C. Circuit*

- "Even popular culture recognizes the importance of cross-examination. See . . . My Cousin Vinny (demonstrating that cross-examination can both undermine and establish the credibility of witnesses)."[9] *Judge Amul Thapar, Sixth Circuit*

- "Defense counsel's obstinate behavior and the court's exasperation with it may be reminiscent for some of the contentious interplay between the fictional characters of Vincent LaGuardia Gambini and Judge Chamberlain

---

6. Muller v. Oregon, 208 U.S. 412 (1908).
7. *See* Guttman, *supra* note 5.
8. Novato Healthcare Ctr. v. NLRB, 916 F.3d 1095, 1098 (D.C. Cir. 2019).
9. Doe v. Baum, 903 F.3d 575, 593 n.1 (6th Cir. 2018) (citation omitted).

Haller in the film 'My Cousin Vinnie.' [sic] On three separate occasions during trial, Judge Haller held Vinnie [sic] in contempt and, each time, made him spend the overnight recess in jail. However, unlike defense counsel here, Vinnie, [sic] a New York lawyer struggling to adapt to the rural-Alabama trial setting, found that the accommodations in jail offered the best night's sleep he could find away from the Big Apple. Upon his return to the courtroom, a revitalized Vinnie [sic] dismantled the credibility of the State's circumstantial case and cleared the names of the 'two yutes' he represented. (And again we see that life follows art)."[10] *Judge William Bauer, Seventh Circuit*

- "To use the apt metaphor coined by Vincent Gambini (one that seems only fitting given the facts of this particular case), a plaintiff may satisfy her burden by building a wall out of individual evidentiary bricks."[11] *Judge Peter Hall, Second Circuit*

- In the dissent, Judge Debra Ann Livingston countered, "The majority invokes the film *My Cousin Vinny* in its discussion of the role of circumstantial evidence in Title VII cases. The film might be more aptly cited for the proposition that some individuals, such as Mona Lisa Vito, Vinny Gambini's fiancée who gained expertise in automotives and auto mechanics working in her father's garage, are well qualified despite a lack of formal credentials."[12] *Judge Debra Ann Livingston, Second Circuit*

Sometimes Simple Makes Sense[13]

SOURCE	REFERENCE	CASE
Dr. Seuss, *One Fish Two Fish Red Fish Blue Fish* (1960)	"As the plurality must acknowledge, the ordinary meaning of 'tangible object' is 'a discrete thing that possesses physical form.' Ante, at 1081 (punctuation and citation omitted). A fish is, of course, a discrete thing that possesses physical form. See generally Dr. Seuss, One Fish Two Fish Red Fish Blue Fish (1960). So the ordinary meaning of the term 'tangible object' in § 1519, as no one here disputes, covers fish (including too-small red grouper)."	*Yates v. United States*, 574 U.S. 528, 553–55 (2015) (Kagan, J., dissenting).
Shel Silverstein, *Where the Sidewalk Ends: The Poems & Drawings of Shel Silverstein* (1974)	"At its core, this case arises from a disagreement about where the sidewalk ends. However, unlike the Shel Silverstein poem, there is no grass growing soft and white, sun burning crimson bright, or peppermint wind."	*Clarke v. Phelan*, No. CV 16-25217-CIV, 2017 U.S. Dist. LEXIS 159513, 2017 WL 4326522, at *1 (S.D. Fla. Sept. 28, 2017) (Scola, J.).

(continued)

---

10. Sutherland v. Gaetz, 581 F.3d 614, 618 n.1 (7th Cir. 2009).
11. Walsh v. N.Y.C Hous. Auth., 828 F.3d 70, 76 (2d Cir. 2016).
12. *Id.* at 91 n.19 (Livingston, J., dissenting) (citation omitted).
13. For more judicial references to popular culture, see Appendix A.

SOURCE	REFERENCE	CASE
Robert Louis Stevenson, *Strange Case of Dr. Jekyll and Mr. Hyde* **(1886)**	"In oral argument before this court, defendant's counsel, ably suggested that to severely punish the defendant for acts which he alleged were committed in a drug-and-alcohol-crazed state of mind would be tantamount to punishing Robert Louis Stevenson's character Dr. Jekyll for the crimes of Mr. Hyde. Of course, counsel's reference was to Stevenson's tale of the Strange Case of Dr. Jekyll and Mr. Hyde. Jekyll, however, freely admitted that he was Hyde, a figure for whom he held no conscious repugnance. Jekyll delighted in his ability to shed his goodness and he reveled in the pure evil that was Henry Hyde. His ability to 'plod in the public eye with a load of genial respectability, and in a moment, like a schoolboy, (to) strip off these lendings and spring headlong into the sea of liberty' constituted an impenetrable mantle and enabled him to laugh at suspicion even though his glance at the mirror reflected only one person. As in Stevenson's fictional tale, the instant defendant cannot say that a person other than himself committed the instant offenses simply because he had ingested drugs and liquor prior to committing the crimes. Defendant pleaded guilty here and does not contend that he lacked the mental state necessary for a finding of guilt. Just as Jekyll was truly Hyde, so also is the defendant the true offender here. As much as our law would prefer to penalize the evil in man for the crimes men commit, we must content ourselves with imposing punishment on those men in whom the evil lurks."	*People v. Green,* 371 N.E.2d 356, 358 (Ill. App. Ct. 1977) (Reardon, J.) (citation omitted).
Charles Dickens, *Bleak House* **(1891)**	"This 'suit has, in course of time, become so complicated, that ... no two ... lawyers can talk about it for five minutes, without coming to a total disagreement as to all the premises. Innumerable children have been born into the cause: innumerable young people have married into it;' and, sadly, the original parties 'have died out of it.' A 'long procession of [judges] has come in and gone out' during that time, and still the suit 'drags its weary length before the Court.' Those words were not written about this case, see C. Dickens, Bleak House, in 1 Works of Charles Dickens 4–5 (1891), but they could have been."	*Stern v. Marshall,* 564 U.S. 462, 468–69 (2011) (Roberts, C.J.).

(*continued*)

SOURCE	REFERENCE	CASE
Bob Dylan, "Like a Rolling Stone" (1965)	"The absence of any right to the substantive recovery means that respondents cannot benefit from the judgment they seek and thus lack Article III standing. 'When you got nothing, you got nothing to lose."[14]	*Sprint Commc'ns Co. v. APCC Servs., Inc.,* 554 U.S. 269, 301 (2008) (Roberts, C.J. dissenting).
John Lennon, "Imagine" (1971)	"The meaning conveyed by a monument is generally not a simple one....What, for example, is 'the message' of the Greco–Roman mosaic of the word "Imagine" that was donated to New York City's Central Park in memory of John Lennon? Some observers may 'imagine' the musical contributions that John Lennon would have made if he had not been killed. Others may think of the lyrics of the Lennon song that obviously inspired the mosaic and may 'imagine' a world without religion, countries, possessions, greed, or hunger."[15]	*Pleasant Grove City v. Summum,* 555 U.S. 460, 474–75, 475 n.2 (2009) (Alito, J.) (citation omitted).
***The Shawshank Redemption* (1994)**	"It is undisputed that an inmate could hide contraband in or under a Kufi.[16] As the witnesses repeatedly testified, contraband can be hidden anywhere by inmates."	*Ali v. Stephens,* 69 F. Supp. 3d 633, 645, 645 n.5 (E.D. Tex. 2014) (Hawthorn, J.).

10.6.1   *The Initial Motions*

When a complaint is filed, the defense has two options. The first option is to answer the complaint, but doing so concedes personal jurisdiction, proper venue (whether grounds exist for the court to hear this case), and subject matter jurisdiction (for the time being). Remember: subject matter jurisdiction cannot be waived in federal court. Answering immediately also forecloses the defense's opportunity to assert a cause of action against the plaintiff. An answer starts the clock on a process that takes the case through discovery, summary judgment, motions in limine, and trial.

The second option is to respond by motion. The most common motions occur under FRCP 12(b), which outlines several different possibilities.

---

14. Bob Dylan, *Like A Rolling Stone,* on Highway 61 Revisited (Columbia Records 1965).
15. "The lyrics are as follows: 'Imagine there's no heaven [i]t's easy if you try. No hell below us [a]bove us only sky. Imagine all the people [l]iving for today ... Imagine there's no countries [i]t isn't hard to do. Nothing to kill or die for [a]nd no religion too. Imagine all the people [l]iving life in peace ... You may say I'm a dreamer [b]ut I'm not the only one I hope someday you'll join us [a]nd the world will be as one. Imagine no possessions I wonder if you can. No need for greed or hunger [a] brotherhood of man. Imagine all the people [s]haring all the world ...You may say I'm a dreamer [b]ut I'm not the only one. I hope someday you'll join us [a]nd the world will live as one.' J. Lennon, Imagine, on Imagine (Apple Records 1971)."
16. "Although fictional, the court is reminded that, in The Shawshank Redemption, Andy Dufresne was able to secrete a rock hammer in his Bible, which he used to dig a tunnel out of prison to effect his escape."

(B) How to Present Defenses. Every defense to a claim for relief in any pleading must be asserted in the responsive pleading if one is required. But a party may assert the following defenses by motion:

(1) lack of subject-matter jurisdiction;

(2) lack of personal jurisdiction;

(3) improper venue;

(4) insufficient process;

(5) insufficient service of process;

(6) failure to state a claim upon which relief can be granted; and

(7) failure to join a party under Rule 19.[17]

Motions asserting any of these defenses must be made before pleading, if a responsive pleading is allowed. If a pleading sets out a claim for relief that does not require a responsive pleading, the opposing party may assert any defense to that claim at trial. A defense or objection is not waived by joining it with one or more other defenses or objections in a responsive pleading or in a motion.

Subject matter jurisdiction—whether the court has the power or authority to hear the case—presents some of the most interesting challenges. In federal court these challenges may come up under the U.S. Constitution Article III. Constitutional challenges include lack of diversity jurisdiction, federal question jurisdiction, and no injury in fact (making the case not ripe or moot). Standing and subject matter jurisdiction challenges occur because a plaintiff lacks standing under the statute. A classic example is a plaintiff, who pleads antitrust injury under the Sherman Act,[18] but is not directly injured by the alleged conduct. Similar standing problems may occur, for example, under the Racketeer Influenced and Corrupt Organizations Act (RICO) statute.[19]

The court considers facts outside the four corners of the pleading only in limited circumstances. Under the federal pleading standards, when a judge evaluates a motion to dismiss for failure to state a claim, the court strips out the complaint's conclusory allegations and judges the allegations' sufficiency based on the facts alleged.[20] However, there is an exception to this rule. The court may consider

---

17. FED. R. CIV. P. 12(b).
18. Sherman Antitrust Act, 15 U.S.C. §§ 1-38.
19. Racketeer Influenced and Corrupt Organizations Act (RICO), 18 U.S.C. ch. 96 §§ 1961-1968. *See* Holmes v. Securities Investor Protection Corp., 503 U.S. 258, 268-69 (1992) ("[A] plaintiff who complain[s] of harm flowing merely from the misfortunes visited upon a third person by the defendant's acts . . . generally . . . stand[s] at too remote a distance to recover.").
20. *See, e.g.*, Ashcroft v. Iqbal, 556 U.S. 662 (2009); Bell Atl. Corp. v. Twombly, 550 U.S. 544 (2007). *See also* United States v. Gen. Hosp. Corp., 394 F. Supp. 3d 174, 188–89 (D. Mass. 2019) (denying a motion to dismiss stating, "Wollman has pled facts that, taken as true, show

documents incorporated in the complaint by reference.[21] Common examples of evidence incorporated by reference are contracts, employment termination letters, and workplace rules. To use documents referenced in the complaint, attach the document to the motion or opposition to the motion. When citing to the document, point to local case law permitting use of the complaint documents incorporated by reference. When the authenticity of the document is in question, consider drafting a declaration or affidavit authenticating the evidence and referencing the evidentiary rules governing authentication.[22]

In subject matter jurisdiction challenges, you may present evidence outside the scope of the pleadings. Some parties even argue that discovery is necessary to rule on the jurisdiction issue.[23] Discovery under these circumstances only occurs on rare occasions. Declarations, or affidavits, are often used when the matter involves a plaintiff's "injury in fact."

Declarations or affidavits are necessary in motions attacking personal jurisdiction and insufficient service. The plaintiff may provide declarations or affidavits from the process server and defense counsel may have the client attest to matters of jurisdiction and the insufficiency of process. For example, a client can provide an affidavit or declaration, which documents their lack of contacts with the jurisdiction. An attorney can, for example, provide an affidavit or declaration detailing what efforts were made to effect service of process.

10.6.2 Discovery Motions

Discovery motions generally seek to accomplish the following:

- Require the production of documents or testimony.

---

that the example claims at issue were false. She has documented more than ten pairs or trios of surgeries that were carried out in violation of the rules governing concurrent or overlapping surgeries . . . that the surgeons involved failed to designate a qualified teaching physician . . . that these practices resulted in unnecessarily prolonged anesthesia, that MGH used a relatively non-descript informed consent form and routinely took other affirmative steps to conceal the practice of concurrent and overlapping surgeries from patients . . . and that surgeons falsified or failed to keep accurate records to conceal their practices. Finally, Wollman's assertions imply that Defendants falsely certified compliance with the applicable regulations and billing rules when they submitted claims to Medicare and Medicaid. Taken as true, these allegations show that Defendants violated the billing rules . . . and submitted claims to Medicare and Medicaid that falsely asserted that the services provided complied with applicable regulations and rules." (citations omitted)).

21. FED. R. CIV. P. 10.
22. In federal court, the applicable evidentiary rules are FED. R. EVID. 901, 902.
23. *See* Oil, Chem. & Atomic Workers Int'l Union, AFL-CIO v. Pena, 18 F. Supp. 2d 6, 16-18 (D.D.C. 1998), *aff'd sub nom.* Oil, Chem. & Atomic Workers Int'l Union, AFL-CIO v. Richardson, 214 F.3d 1379, 1383 (D.C. Cir. 2000).

- Establish parameters about the production of documents, testimony, responses to requests for admission or interrogatories, or other discovery matters.

- Compel the production of documents, responses to requests for admission or interrogatories, or other discovery matters.

Federal Rule of Civil Procedure 26(b) addresses both the scope and restrictions on discovery.[24] This rule is the basis for a myriad of motions in discovery disputes. Remember that judges detest discovery disputes. Disputes are a distraction unless they involve matters material to the ultimate resolution of the case. Attempt resolving these differences before seeking court intervention. If resolution is unfeasible, seek the court's intervention judiciously, especially during the course of a litigation. Where time and circumstance permit, use your motion to compel discovery to aggregate all disputes in one motion rather than seeking relief in a piecemeal fashion. Cumulative motions are efficient and provide the court with a more complete picture of the litigation.

When determining whether to file a motion to compel discovery, carefully consider why the information is necessary. Not only will the judge ask this question, they will also think about the burden of producing documents and the potential privileges involved in document production, answers to interrogatories, and deposition questions.[25] Before deciding to oppose discovery, the opposing party must assess whether the fight is necessary or whether it is best to reserve battle for more important issues.

After a judge hears their position, litigants sometimes mistakenly assume those arguments automatically bode well for the case, that the court will undoubtedly loathe the other side, or that their discovery dispute may spur settlement. Discovery disputes are analogous to fights on an elementary school playground where the teacher wants to quickly resolve the dispute without finding fault. Does the comment, "I don't care who started it" sound familiar?

10.6.3 Class Certification Motions

Class action suits entail one plaintiff bringing a cause of action on behalf of other, similarly situated individuals or parties. Class actions create efficiencies in the

---

24. *See* Fed R. Civ. P. 26(b).
25. United States v. Town of Irmo, No. 3:18-CV-03106-JMC, 2020 WL 1025686, at *5 (D.S.C. Mar. 3, 2020) (granting in part plaintiff's motion to compel involving the scope of discovery, inadequate privilege logs, and the defendant's failure to provide ESI in native format because the defendant asserted only "a 'blanket objection' to a request for the production of documents" without explaining "how that production constitutes a negative impact" and further stating that "'an evasive or incomplete disclosure, answer, or response' to a discovery request is 'treated as a failure to disclose, answer, or respond.' Parties are prohibited from 'assert[ing] conclusory, boilerplate objections that fail to explain the precise grounds that make the request objectionable.'" (citations omitted)).

litigation process, so courts do not have to deal with numerous parties whose claims arise out of common sets of fact and law. Cases proceed as class actions when class representatives' claims are typical of the other class members' claims, ensuring that class representatives adequately represent the class.[26]

A party files what is known as a putative class action. The complaint must establish why the case qualifies as a class action and define the class encompassed by the complaint. It must also seek either certification as a claim for predominantly injunctive relief—where class members may not opt out—or a claim for damages—where class members may opt out. This is the distinction between an FRCP 23(b)(2) class and FRCP(b)(3) class. In a case involving injunctive relief it is virtually impossible to issue equitable relief that leaves out specific members of a class. Hence, an FRCP 23(b)(2) class does not have the opt out issues that apply to an FRCP 23(b)(3) class. One of the practical consequences of this distinction is that a defendant may condition a settlement agreement upon a certain percentage of the class participating in the settlement and thus not opting out to pursue their own individual relief.

The court independently determines: 1) whether the litigation should proceed as a class action; and 2) who shall be class counsel. These two questions are not mere formalities. Oftentimes, a wrongful act impacting numerous parties causes more than one class action complaint to be filed. Under these circumstances, courts may consolidate the complaints and, by motion practice, determine who should be class counsel. When negotiations determine class counsel, a motion must be filed with the court seeking approval on the agreed-upon proposal.

Whether a matter proceeds as a class action may require discovery to establish if the claim meets class action requirements.[27] Class certification will involve motions practice and generally a hearing. The motions will require the introduction of facts through affidavits, declarations, deposition testimony, and other evidence. Often, class certification—particularly in cases involving securities fraud and employment discrimination—will involve expert testimony. The expert testimony may range from an array of issues that address FRCP 23 requirements.

The class certification motion presents the facts and legal standards and applies the law to the facts. Introduce your evidence as exhibits attached to the motion or brief. In the motion or brief, refer specifically to relevant portions of the exhibit by Bates number, page, or line.

Although class certification is a procedural device, remember that certification decisions can be dispositive as a practical matter. Imagine a claim on behalf of 25,000 class members, each of whom has $5,000 in damages. If the class is certified, the case's aggregate value is $125,000,000. If not certified, the case is merely a claim for $5,000, and perhaps not worth the transaction's cost of litigation.

---

26. Fed. R. Civ. P. 23.
27. Rather than cite the requirements, see Fed. R. Civ. P. 23(a), (b).

10.6.3.1 Motions to Consolidate for Pretrial Purposes

The types of claims easily suited to class action treatment include securities fraud claims, antitrust law violations, and discrimination claims where injunctive relief is the predominant form of relief sought. Claims involving defective products or drugs, where the harm may be individualized and the latency periods vary, are unfit for class treatment. [28] Historically, these claims, categorized as "mass torts," consolidate hundreds or even thousands of cases for pretrial purposes, then get transferred back to their original forum for trial.

In the federal court system, a judicial panel on multidistrict litigation entertains motions to consolidate cases for pretrial purposes and transfer those cases to a single venue. Approximately half of all pending federal court cases were consolidated in front of a single judge for pretrial purposes.[29] Defendants often want claims consolidated because it creates litigation efficiencies with document production, interrogatory answers, and depositions. In addition, judges presiding over cases for pretrial purposes can issue dispositive orders ending the litigation or eliminating claims. The consolidation process sets cases on a path for possible global resolution. Once consolidated, the presiding judge appoints a "steering" or "coordinating" committee. A judge may also appoint a "liaison counsel" responsible for communicating with attorneys whose clients' cases were consolidated. Appointment of counsel is handled by motion. Once cases are placed in the Multidistrict Litigation (MDL) process, parties may pick bellwether cases for trial. The merits of the cases can then be determined, with both sides positioned to negotiate a global settlement available to those plaintiffs uninterested in risking further litigation once the case is reassigned a venue for trial.

In contrast to class action-governed, specific procedural rules, the process that applies to an MDL panel-transferred case is at the discretion of the transferee judge. In the federal court system, judges can seek guidance from the *Manual on Complex Litigation*, published by the Federal Judicial Center. Unfortunately, their manual was last updated in 2004.[30]

Many criticize the MDL process for its lack of transparency and its denial of individual claimants selecting their own lawyer to navigate the pretrial process. Additionally, once consolidated, the likelihood of a case being returned for trial is less than 4 percent.[31] When a case is returned for trial, it may be handed to an attorney working off record evidence developed by other counsel. This can steepen

---

28. *See* Amchem Prods., Inc., v. Windsor, 521 U.S. 591, 622-29 (1997); Ortiz v. Fibreboard Corp., 527 U.S. 815 (1999).

29. *See* James M. Beck, *The Need for Real MDL Rules Will Only Grow More Acute*, Drug & Device L. Blog (April 15, 2009), https://www.druganddevicelawblog.com/2019/04/the-need-for-real-mdl-rules-will-only-grow-more-acute.html#.

30. Manual for Complex Litigation (4th ed. 2004).

31. U.S. Jud. Panel on Multidistrict Litig., Calendar Year Statistics (2018).

trial counsel's learning curve considerably, creating a dynamic where the client has little choice but to accept a global settlement. Hence, while a motion to consolidate may appear procedural, it can have a substantive impact on the case.

10.6.4 *Motions for Summary Judgment*

There are two motions that can be directly dispositive of a case: the motion to dismiss and the motion for summary judgment. While motions for class certification, *Daubert* motions, and motions in limine can undermine a case or make it not worth litigating, motions to dismiss and summary judgment motions directly challenge the case itself.

Approach drafting your dispositive motion by asking yourself "What would the judge need to rule from the bench?" What I mean by that is include all the facts, findings, and legal conclusions for me to rule in your favor in one document. It makes my job easier when, in one motion, you make the yellow brick road clear and give me all the bricks! (obligatory Kansas reference added for emphasis).

—*Judge Amy Hanley, District Court Judge, Douglas County, KS*

A motion for summary judgment generally occurs at the close of discovery, when either party can show "that there is no genuine dispute as to any material fact and the movant is entitled to judgment as a matter of law."[32] The summary judgment option is open to any party, but the defense most often moves for summary judgment. A party can also move for partial summary judgment to decide a particular issue in the case.[33] Sometimes, summary judgment for certain issues can dispose of the entire case. The statute of limitations, statutes of repose, causation, reliance, materiality, and contributory negligence are all discrete matters involving the application of law to fact. When the facts are undisputed, the law may be decisive. For example, imagine a fraud case, with a three-year statute of limitations that runs from the date the plaintiff knew, or should have known, they were defrauded. At the plaintiff's deposition, the following testimony was taken:

> Q: When did you first realize you were injured as a result of what you say was "defendant's pattern of false statements?"
>
> A: About four years ago.

---

32. Fed. R. Civ. P. 56.
33. For example, if there is no genuine issue of material fact concerning liability in a car crash personal injury case, the court may grant summary judgment on liability. Then, the only question remaining for the jury would be damages or any defenses.

Q: And is that when you knew that defendant had—as you allege in your complaint—"defrauded" you?

A: Yes.

The above deposition testimony is exactly the type of evidence that allows a defendant to seek summary judgment based on a statute of limitations defense. Understanding summary judgment requirements can guide discovery. When parties seek summary judgment during discovery, they are trying to lock in admissions or evidence that cannot be disputed. Meanwhile, parties who fear summary judgment look for evidence that creates a dispute of fact, allowing the case to move past summary judgment and on to trial.

As previously stated, summary judgment is granted when the movant is entitled to judgment as a matter of law because there is no genuine dispute of material fact.[34] In 1986, the Supreme Court decided three cases: *Anderson v. Liberty Lobby, Inc.,*[35] *Celotex Corp. v. Catrett,*[36] and *Matsushita Electrical Industrial Co. v. Zenith Radio Corp.*[37] These cases make up the "Summary Judgment Trilogy" and set the standard for summary judgment as discussed in Chapter One. While these cases provide the framework, it is important to analyze the law of each circuit and jurisdiction.

Motions are both fact and exhibit intensive. Therefore, when filing for summary judgment, pay attention to local court rules and judge's rules governing motion format and presentment. As a general proposition, your summary judgment motion must have a "statement of undisputed material facts." While some facts may be in dispute, those facts material to resolving the motion are arguably not in dispute. For example, a summary judgment motion based on the statute of limitations in a fraud case can concede disagreement on facts governing the alleged fraudulent representations. But because the plaintiff knew, or should have known, that they potentially had a fraud claim more than four years ago, outside the statute of limitations, the facts material to the statute of limitations question are arguably not in dispute.

The statement of undisputed facts can be a separate document referenced in the motion or the brief. The statement should recite the undisputed facts paragraph-by-paragraph, with citations to an appendix containing the record evidence. The record evidence may include emails, deposition transcripts, photographs, or even flash drives containing electronic data. The evidence in the appendix must be admissible and authentic.[38] Prior to summary judgment, the parties should meet

---

34. Fed R. Civ. P. 56.
35. Anderson v. Liberty Lobby, Inc., 477 U.S. 242 (1986).
36. Celotex Corp. v. Catrett, 477 U.S. 317 (1986).
37. Matsushita Elec. Indus. Co. v. Zenith Radio Corp., 477 U.S. 317 (1986).
38. The Federal Rules of Evidence apply to summary judgment motions, so parties should be mindful of hearsay.

and confer to resolve, by agreement, authentication matters and other evidentiary challenges. Some evidence may be self-authenticating.[39] Other evidence may be authenticated through deposition testimony, declaration, or affidavit.

Those opposing a motion for summary judgment generally enter a counterstatement into the record. The counterstatement responds to the statement of undisputed material facts and adds a "statement of disputed material facts." The counterstatement should reference record evidence identifying a dispute of material fact and indicate what the opposing party believes is material evidence in dispute.

Do not neglect to argue the law as well as the facts. For example, in our fraud case, the moving party may present statutes or case law demonstrating the statute of limitations for fraud cases is three years and runs from the date the plaintiff knew, or should have known, the facts needed to file a complaint. The opposing party may argue the statute of limitations is actually five years, not three years, because a different state law applies, or the statute was tolled.

Whether preparing a motion for summary judgment or opposing such motions, do not overlook the preliminary question: who bears the burden in such motions? There may be overall burdens associated with establishing no disputes of material fact and smaller burdens such as the burden to produce or disclose evidence. Hence, it is essential that counsel bore into the process of how the court evaluates summary judgment motions while using the briefing and oral argument to remind the court of the burdens. In drafting a motion for summary judgment, encapsulate the argument in the simplest terms. Complexity is an invitation to kick the can down the road to trial.

10.6.5 *Daubert Motions*

In *Daubert v. Merrell Dow Pharmaceuticals, Inc.*,[40] the Supreme Court designated trial court judges as the "gatekeeper" of whether an expert should be heard, excluded, or partially excluded. Many states have followed *Daubert*, applying its logic to state court proceedings.

> Authoritative opinions in 27 states either formally adopt *Daubert* or cite it while taking a similar approach that directs judges to assess reliability by reference to appropriate factors: Alabama, Alaska, Arkansas, Colorado, Connecticut, Delaware, Hawaii, Kentucky, Louisiana, Massachusetts, Michigan (statute covering suits for injury or death), Montana, Nebraska, New Hampshire, New Jersey, New Mexico, North Carolina, Ohio, Oklahoma, Oregon, Rhode Island, South Dakota, Tennessee, Texas, Vermont, West Virginia, and Wyoming.[41]

---

39. FED. R. EVID. 902.
40. Daubert v. Merrell Dow Pharm., Inc., 509 U.S. 579 (1993).
41. CHRISTOPHER B. MUELLER & LAIRD C. KIRKPATRICK, FEDERAL EVIDENCE § 7:10 (4th ed. 2020).

One mechanism to dismantle an opponent's case is excluding expert testimony. Similarly, a ruling that permits testimony may drive settlement talks if the testimony increases a party's chance of success in front of a jury. When contemplating and preparing a motion to exclude expert testimony, consider both the procedural and evidentiary rules. FRCP 26(a)(2) provides:

(2) Disclosure of Expert Testimony.

(A) In General. In addition to the disclosures required by Rule 26(a)(1), a party must disclose to the other parties the identity of any witness it may use at trial to present evidence under Federal Rule of Evidence 702, 703, or 705.

(B) Witnesses Who Must Provide a Written Report. Unless otherwise stipulated or ordered by the court, this disclosure must be accompanied by a written report—prepared and signed by the witness—if the witness is one retained or specially employed to provide expert testimony in the case or one whose duties as the party's employee regularly involve giving expert testimony. The report must contain:

(i) a complete statement of all opinions the witness will express and the basis and reasons for them;

(ii) the facts or data considered by the witness in forming them;

(iii) any exhibits that will be used to summarize or support them;

(iv) the witness's qualifications, including a list of all publications authored in the previous 10 years;

(v) a list of all other cases in which, during the previous 4 years, the witness testified as an expert at trial or by deposition; and

(vi) a statement of the compensation to be paid for the study and testimony in the case.[42]

This procedural rule specifically references FRE 702, 703, and 705. Therefore, read the procedural and evidentiary rules in context when formulating a motion to exclude an expert. Such motions can seek exclusion based on noncompliance with the procedural rule or its evidentiary counterpart. FRE 702 states:

Rule 702. Testimony by Expert Witnesses

A witness who is qualified as an expert by knowledge, skill, experience, training, or education may testify in the form of an opinion or otherwise if:

---

42. Fed. R. Civ. P. 26(a)(2).

(a) the expert's scientific, technical, or other specialized knowledge will help the trier of fact to understand the evidence or to determine a fact in issue;

(b) the testimony is based on sufficient facts or data;

(c) the testimony is the product of reliable principles and methods; and

(d) the expert has reliably applied the principles and methods to the facts of the case.[43]

Daubert motions address the issues outlined in FRE 702 (a)–(d) and rely on the expert's report and deposition, opposing expert testimony, learned treatises, or other evidence explicating admissibility issues.

10.6.6 *Motions in Limine*

Motions in limine pursue judgments about the admissibility of evidence. A motion seeking to admit evidence may be referred to as a reverse motion in limine. As a technical matter, a motion in limine can also bar certain evidence in summary judgment motions. During the summary judgment stage, evidentiary challenges are generally submitted in pleadings supporting or opposing the motion. When a brief in support of or opposing summary judgment has a page limit, consider filing an independent motion in limine. If granted, it allows additional pages to brief the matter and highlight the importance of evidence preclusion requests.

Preparing a motion in limine or an opposition to the motion in limine requires an understanding of the Federal Rules of Evidence. Several potential bases for excluding evidence are available:

- Relevance—the evidence does not have any tendency to make a "fact" more or less probable than it would be without the evidence (and the fact at issue is of consequence in determining the action).[44]

- The evidence is relevant but should be excluded because "its probative value is substantially outweighed by a danger of one or more of the following: unfair prejudice, confusing the issues, misleading the jury, undue delay, wasting time, or needlessly presenting cumulative evidence."[45]

- The evidence is hearsay and not otherwise subject to one of the exceptions.[46]

---

43. Fed. R. Evid. 702.
44. *See* Fed. R. Evid. 401.
45. Fed. R. Evid. 403.
46. *See* Fed. R. Evid. 801, 802, 803, 804, 805, 807.

- The evidence is not authentic.[47]

- The evidence is privileged.[48]

The above objections would not preclude a review of the documents for discovery purposes, except if a document is privileged. If a party learns the opposing party has privileged documents or information, they must immediately address the issue; otherwise, there is a risk that the privilege will be waived. Consider the following hypothetical:

> A former director, Jane James of the Big Z Company, was subpoenaed to testify in an MDL proceeding where Big Z was sued for negligence and strict liability stemming from its sales of a blood thinner that caused patients to bleed uncontrollably. Big Z's lawyers advised board members on Big Z's litigation strategy, what directors may say about the litigation, and the findings of an internal investigation conducted by the lawyers.

In this scenario, Big Z's counsel is concerned Director James will be asked to divulge her communications with Big Z attorneys. If Director James answers questions about communications with counsel— without an objection and an instruction not to answer—the corporation will no doubt waive the privilege. Part of the deposition preparation must involve understanding what questions will necessarily trigger attorney client privilege responses. The lawyer and their deponent will be able to anticipate the questions and objections and instructions not to answer will be timely asserted.

Alternatively, the attorney defending the deposition may seek a meet and confer meeting with opposing counsel to establish some ground rules, which would preclude questioning on communications that may breach the privilege. If the deposition really only involves a few such communications, counsel can easily deal with this matter on a question-by-question basis. The key, however, is to keep in mind that privileges can be waived.

Be aware that litigation is fluid. The law changes constantly. Technology changes the context by which law is applied. The court system, and the rule of law, struggles to keep up with the changes. Motions practice—as a whole—is the place where lawyers need to be creative and use common sense. The goal is to move the case to resolution as efficiently as possible.

---

47. *See* Fed. R. Evid. 901, 902.
48. *See* Fed. R. Evid. 501.

CHAPTER ELEVEN

SETTLEMENT AND ALTERNATIVE DISPUTE RESOLUTION

11.1 Litigation as a Path to Resolution

Litigation risks complete strangers—either a judge or jury—deciding the outcome of a case. This "Solomon-like" threat can create an opportunity for the litigants to reach agreement and impose their own terms of resolution. The litigation process is itself no small element in triggering this settlement dynamic—discovery brings transparency to claims, facts and defenses; litigation brings parties together at depositions and court appearances. It's a logical step to extend this to settlement meetings.

The only way to effectively settle a case is to be ready to litigate it. You need to know all the facts and the law inside and out to effectively negotiate. Think of the settlement like an abbreviated trial. Your opposing counsel is not a neutral juror, but it's still your goal to move the needle. You must convince the opposing party that the risks of trial outweigh the benefits of settling, and to do that you must preview how convincing your trial presentation would be if settlement fails.

—Professor Veronica Finkelstein,
Drexel University Thomas R. Kline School of Law

Emerging facts, time delays, changes in a party's personal needs, and mounting litigation costs also force parties to reassess their legal positions. Along the way, decisions on procedural motions may tip the balance of power, compelling parties to reexamine their chances of victory.

The litigation process not only provides counsel with new information regarding the case's strengths and weaknesses, it provides a reality check for clients who—sometimes despite their counsel's advice—do not fully appreciate their legal position. Tough questions at a deposition can be another important reality check built into the litigation process. Clients confronted with direct questions, posed in harsh terms, are forced to think about their case's strengths and weaknesses, as well as whether any unfavorable or embarrassing information might come out during the litigation.

Settlement is possible at any point in litigation; however, "settlement windows" typically occur either prior to an activity or phase of litigation that requires expending significant time and resources, or after pivotal case rulings. The classic settlement windows are:

- Prior to filing a complaint

- After receipt of a complaint

- Before and after a decision on a motion to dismiss

- Before a large expenditure of time and money in discovery

- Before or after summary judgment motions are filed and decided

- Before and after *Daubert* motions or motions in limine are filed and decided

- Pretrial

- After jury selection

- At the conclusion of the plaintiff's case

- At the conclusion of the trial but before the judge's ruling or jury's verdict

At each settlement window, parties must decide whether to hold or fold. Advancing to the next stage of litigation involves additional costs and court rulings or fact development through discovery that may impact the odds of a successful outcome. Be aware of these variables and the potential implications and communicate this information to your client. Because clients make the ultimate decision regarding settlement, lawyers must inform clients of case developments and provide necessary insight on strategy.

Judges often require parties to address settlement matters early in the litigation. FRCP 26(f) provides for early discussion about the potential for resolution; scheduling orders governing case progression may require the more formal mediation process to reach a final resolution. Judges may inquire about settlement prospects at scheduling conferences and sometimes mandate mediation after deciding a dispositive motion to sustain or clarify the claims.[1]

Judges may either order mediation or assign a magistrate to facilitate settlement discussions. Mediation and private arbitration are types of alternative dispute resolution (ADR). Mediation is much different from arbitration. In mediation, the parties collaborate with a neutral to facilitate agreement. In arbitration, a neutral

---

1. *See, e.g.,* United States *ex rel.* Brown v. Celgene Corp., 226 F. Supp 3d. 1032 (C.D. Cal. 2016) (denying in part motion for summary judgment and ordering mediation).

presides over a court-like, yet private, proceeding and renders a decision to be imposed on the parties. Arbitrator decisions are binding and rarely overturned by courts unless the arbitrator's ruling was a result of fraud.[2]

11.2 Settlement Theory and Strategy

Your first look at a dispute may reveal only the areas where the parties are far apart. The key to settlement is to focus on where you agree and then iron out the differences. This strategy works particularly well where the case involves prophylactic or injunctive relief. But the strategy can still be effective when the case is about monetary damages. The key to this strategy is to forget that it is a lawsuit—which by nature implicates ill will or animosity—and think of it as a business problem. Consider plaintiffs who buy a defective refrigerator. They sue for the cost of a new refrigerator and for damages attributable to spoiled food. The commonality between the parties is that litigation costs will exceed the recovery. The case needs to be settled.

I'm reluctant to settle with someone who is eager to settle, there's something I don't know, they're not telling me, or I can get more if I say no. Now of course sometimes I'm as eager as they are to be done with the case, but often someone who is eager can give you more.

—William Elward, Senior Instructor,
Loyola University of Chicago School of Law

When filing a lawsuit or defending a case, assess where the litigation may lead your client. Will this case be trimmed down or decided by motions at some point in the litigation? Will the mere filing of a complaint provoke a settlement dialogue, or will the defendant dig in their heels and fight? Perhaps the most important questions are: What does the client really want from the case? Is it achievable? What is the best approach for achieving the desired result? Clients often modify their

---

2. *See* Dominion Video Satellite, Inc. v. Echostar Satellite L.L.C., 430 F.3d 1269, 1275 (10th Cir. 2005) ("Judicial review of arbitration panel decisions is extremely limited; indeed, it has been described as among the narrowest known to law. Under § 10 of the Federal Arbitration Act, a court may vacate an arbitration award in certain instances of fraud or corruption, arbitrator misconduct, or where the arbitrators exceeded their powers, or so imperfectly executed them that a mutual, final, definite award upon the subject matter submitted was not made. In addition, we have acknowledged a judicially-created basis for vacating an award when the arbitrators acted in manifest disregard of the law. This standard requires a finding that the panel's decision exhibits willful inattentiveness to the governing law. Merely erroneous interpretations or applications of law are not reversible. Put another way, we require more than error or misunderstanding of the law[.][A] finding of manifest disregard means the record will show the arbitrators knew the law and explicitly disregarded it. Finally, we review a district court's factual findings in confirming the award for clear error and its legal conclusions de novo."(citations omitted) (quotations omitted)).

expectations during the lengthy litigation process, so check in with clients periodically about settlement.

At some point during the litigation, your view of the case's merits is likely to differ from your client's. Attorneys must often act as intermediaries, negotiating with both the client and the opposition. This truism applies to both plaintiff and defense counsel. This dynamic differs depending on whether the client is an individual or entity. If the client is an entity, which form? Entities range from publicly traded corporations to nonprofit membership organizations. Each has its own governance and constituency groups that potentially weigh in on the settlement process. There may be a board of directors, ownership blocks, a general counsel, and a chief executive officer. Every group or person may have an opinion on settlement, sometimes even a stake in the game depending on whether the litigation benefits them personally or is a detriment to them. Consider, for example, a partnership sued over the alleged malfeasance of one partner. The alleged wrongdoer may have an interest in resolving the case while their partners are reluctant to reach into their pockets and make the plaintiff whole for someone else's wrongdoing.

Another settlement factor is insurance coverage. When dealing with insured claims, a third-party assumes the risk and may be better suited to make dispassionate decisions relating to case resolution.[3]

11.2.1   Understanding Your Opponent's Decision-Making Process

Consider both your client's and the opposing party's "politics" and decision-making process. Individual plaintiffs suing a corporate defendant should put themselves in the defense counsel's posture and ask, "what is the end game and how does that impact the corporation?" Suppose an individual sues a large chemical company, claiming its laundry detergent caused cancer. On the surface, the case involves one victim, medical costs, money for pain and suffering, and potential punitive damages. However, to the corporation there is another factor; the case is really about the integrity of a billion-dollar-a-year product. If the defendant knew of the detergent's safety issues and did not disclose it, they could be implicated in securities law violations. Individual directors may be similarly exposed under state corporate laws for breach of fiduciary duty. The corporation or its corporate officials might even be subject to criminal liability. Such claims are not one-off events. The mere filing of a complaint, and the subsequent publicity, might compel others to file suit (and possibly be rolled into a multi-district litigation proceeding). For the individual plaintiff with discrete damages, what does this scenario communicate? Does the best settlement window occur pre-litigation? Each case presents its own unique

---

3. The question of whether a party is insured for the claim also depends on the type of claim. Negligence claims are more likely to be insured, while intentional torts and breach of contract are less likely to have coverage.

facts and politics. Over the course of the litigation, be sensitive to the nuances and carefully consider all resolution possibilities.

11.2.2 *The Impact of Role on Settlement*

Always consider the settlement process within the context of the litigation process and your role as plaintiff or defense counsel. Opposing counsel each contemplate the "end game" from different perspectives. Plaintiff's counsel focuses on quick and efficient case movement, beyond motions practice, and on to trial. Plaintiff's counsel must prepare clients for a range of possibilities: document production, deposition testimony, answering interrogatories, court appearances, and trial testimony. Although very few cases are actually litigated to trial, clients should assume their case will continue and require their participation throughout all litigation phases. No attorney wants to be confronted by an apathetic client no longer willing to participate in the process. Client accusations such as, "you told me this case would settle and that I would never have to testify," suggest counsel failed to properly communicate with the client throughout the course of the case.

Similar to a plaintiff counsel developing litigation goals and strategies, a defense counsel investigates ways to eliminate the litigation and whittle down claims. In the case of a corporate defendant, defense counsel also monitors settlement—the dollar amount required to make the case "go away" versus litigation costs, and how settlement could injure the client's brand and reputation, exposing the client to other legal claims, including criminal liability.

Both plaintiff and defense counsel should remind clients that opportunities to resolve the case will arise. Those opportunities are tempered by the framing of the case and windows of opportunity that exist at certain decision points. As discussed in Chapter Seven, certain claims, by their very nature, can polarize the parties and thus eliminate some settlement windows. A defendant facing a fraud or discrimination claim may wish to defend their position by putting enough on the public record to demonstrate a viable defense. The desire to mount an aggressive defense may be emotional, not economic, if the defendant feels their character has been questioned. And yet, depending on the defendant, claims that inflame others and lead to a robust battle may also inspire quick settlement.

As also discussed in Chapter Seven, the theory selection lawyers engage in at the beginning of a case can impact the potential for resolution. The term "theory selection" refers to the choice to sue for breach of contract, fraud, or both. Should the complaint be pleaded with facts sufficient to move the case forward to discovery? Or, should the complaint be laden with potentially inflammatory facts that polarize the parties and likely eliminate settlement windows? This discussion is not meant to counsel against aggressive litigation, only to state that attorneys must forecast the impact of any litigation strategy and juxtapose that strategy against the client's goals.

11.3 The Client

Personalizing a case is one of the biggest mistakes attorneys make. As the attorney, you are neither the plaintiff nor the defendant. You are an advocate with an obligation to represent the client "zealously and diligently within the bounds of the law."[4] At the end of the day, however, it is the client's case. Attorneys can investigate, cull out and present the best facts, and explain damaging facts, but an attorney cannot fabricate or conceal facts. There is no shame in losing a case when an attorney did all they could for the client. There is, however, shame in winning a case by violating the ethical constrains that bind counsel.

Attorneys wanting to secure and maintain good client relationships may easily share in their client's woes. They may be tempted to suggest the court treated both the attorney and the client poorly, and complain that the defendant (or the plaintiff) is the evil empire. This is a bad dynamic.

Zealous and diligent representation requires an attorney to remain objective when evaluating the likelihood of success and managing client expectations. For example, a wrongful discharge client believes they are entitled to millions of dollars in damages. However, if the client secured a new and higher paying job within days of termination, the attorney should advise the client their new job's salary may mitigate damages, eliminating any potential for a windfall recovery. Before communicating your opinion to the client, take the time to review the facts and the law with them. Do so without first rendering your opinion. Let the client come to their own conclusion. Often, they will reach the same conclusion you reached.

Another factor that will influence how you discuss settlement with your client is the type of client you have. Is your client an individual or a company? If the client is a company, are you dealing with an in-house lawyer or a businessperson as your primary contact? If it is a lawyer, are they familiar with litigation or does their practice involve other aspects of the law, such as deal-making or patent prosecution? Is your client a first-time litigant, entirely unfamiliar with litigation, or are they a seasoned veteran who has been involved in litigation before? Each of these answers will help determine the amount of detail you need to share with your client. While most clients expect you to prepare a budget for any litigation, an in-house lawyer who manages litigation on a regular basis is likely to be aware of the general categories of expense and can roughly estimate the cost of litigation. However, a client unfamiliar with litigation will require more information from you. For example, you will need to discuss the costs of litigation generally, including electronic discovery, expert witness fees, travel for depositions if witnesses are out of the area, court reporter fees, and any other costs that might not be obvious to someone who hasn't

---

4. *See, e.g.,* D.C. Rules of Pro. Conduct, r. 1.3. The word "zealously" has over the years been qualified in many jurisdictions to prevent encouragement of counsel from crossing the bounds of ethical conduct.

been involved in a lawsuit before. This information is a critical component in settlement assessments because most clients will want to balance the cost of litigation against the potential for recovery or liability.

11.3.1 *Managing Client Expectations*

Though lawyers often bargain with opposing counsel, they sometimes must also bargain with their own clients. The bargaining process begins with managing expectations. Once the lawyer-client relationship is established, provide a realistic assessment of the case's merits. Throughout litigation, candidly communicate possibilities, outcomes, and consequences. For example, if the case survives a motion to dismiss, reassure the client by stating, "this is good for us, we are where we need to be. But remember, there is a lot of work ahead and the defendant can still eliminate or whittle down our claims."

Use measured and thoughtful words to simultaneously deliver a comforting and encouraging message and provide a realistic assessment. Some clients gravitate to the "cheerleader" attorney, but they quickly tire of the cheerleader upon realizing how misleading and/or unhelpful the cheerleading is to overall strategy calls.

When an attorney properly manages client expectations, the "client-bargaining-phase" of the settlement process either runs more smoothly or can be eliminated. Managing expectations is a balance between listening, crediting a client's position, and giving the client enough feedback to make a reasoned choice. Consider this dialogue:

> Client: I was terminated from my job and would like to sue my employer for one million dollars.
>
> Lawyer: What have you been doing since you lost your job?
>
> Client: I have not done anything. My hope is that I can get the money from my former employer and start my own company.
>
> Lawyer: How much did you make in your job?
>
> Client: $25,000 a year.
>
> Lawyer: Being terminated is awful. You must feel terrible. However, we will need to discuss the litigation process and the remedies for wrongful termination.

Absent egregious circumstances, the client in the above scenario appears to have unrealistic expectations for what litigation can achieve. Moreover, the client was not really seeking to be made whole, but envisioned litigation as a way to finance a business venture completely unrelated to the cause of action. Analogous situations are red flags that may justify declining the representation. Underlying motivations are sometimes hard to detect or do not emerge until late in the representation—continue scrutinizing client motives that may impact settlement objectives throughout the litigation.

The lawyer also credited the client's emotion by saying, "you must feel terrible." You cannot begin managing expectations unless you credit the client's feelings or emotions.[5] That feeling or emotion may very well be rationally based, but that does not mean the client's desired legal remedy necessarily follows.

Use your initial interview to help your client understand that legal advice is neither an evaluation of morality nor justification of the client's pain or emotions. Legal advice simply concerns whether a remedy in a court of law is achievable. Remind them that just because something may seem wrong or unethical, it is not necessarily illegal and there may not be a legal remedy. Clarify the distinctions. If unclear, clients may disregard legal advice because they believe their lawyer is insensitive to their emotional issues.

When an attorney cautions that a settlement offer may fall short of the client's expectations, clients may instinctively assume the attorney lost faith in the client's position. This may stem from situations where the client misrepresented facts to the attorney or was not entirely forthcoming with information. Clients are generally reluctant to disclose bad facts or the full story until they have developed trust in their attorney over a period of time. Keeping the client informed of the litigation's progress helps manage expectations as the client discovers the pitfalls of litigation along with the lawyer. If, for example, discovery reveals bad facts your client knew but did not disclose in the hopes that they would not be discovered, you must communicate that new information has come to light and explain how this new information may impact the case. Use such damaging revelations to "shake the tree" and see if any other information falls out. This information may be good or bad—sometimes an embarrassing revelation leads to helpful new facts, now that the details the client hoped to have omitted are known. In any event, point out that if *this* fact came to light, any other secrets they are keeping likely will as well.

11.3.2 *Litigation Risks*

Litigation risk is frequently cited as the reason a party wants to settle. Litigation risk can be fundamentally distilled down to the element of the unknown. It is the risk of what might happen at trial. It may be that new documents or information damaging to your case come to light right before—or worse, at—trial. It may be that your key witness does not testify well. It may be that the judge or jury simply prefers the evidence of the other side's witnesses to yours. There is also the possibility that the jury or judge simply gets it wrong; it does happen.

---

5. This technique is called empathetic understanding and is discussed in section 3.6.2.2.

National Institute for Trial Advocacy

Technical requirements, such as more stringent burdens of proof (e.g., fraud cases) are also factors to consider when evaluating litigation risk. Will the judge or jury be persuaded enough by the evidence to meet that higher burden? Another possibility is a defense lawyer in a medical malpractice case facing a sympathetic plaintiff who sustained real injury. The plaintiff's injury may prompt a jury award of damages even if the defendant's liability is questionable. Sometimes jurors feel compelled to provide an award to a plaintiff out of compassion rather than a fair review of the evidence presented.

Parties need to contemplate the unknown and factor it into their decision-making process when considering whether to file or settle proceedings. For the plaintiff, this usually involves figuring out how much they are prepared to "discount" their claim in exchange for eliminating the risk of losing at trial. For a defendant, it means determining out how much they are willing to spend in settlement to avoid that risk.

The issues discussed here may be intuitive to a lawyer, but not necessarily to a client. Client communication is crucial, from initial agreement to the representation throughout the litigation process. There should be no surprises. Direct and candid dialogue will enable thoughtful analysis when settlement windows open.

11.4   Discussing Settlement with the Court

Rule 16 of the Federal Rules of Civil Procedure (FRCP) specifically mentions and contemplates settlement as part of the litigation process.[6] Accordingly, every status conference with the judge may be an opportunity to discuss settlement options. Let your client know the issue may come up any time you are before the judge. As already mentioned, managing expectations is critical. Explain to the client that cases generally settle, though not always, so the judge will be interested to know whether there have been settlement negotiations or whether there is a realistic possibility of settlement.

Status conferences take place throughout the course of the litigation, but the most likely times for a judge to inquire about settlement are: 1) after the first dispositive pleadings, such as a motion to dismiss; 2) after summary judgment; and 3) at pretrial conferences. Learn the judge's style as it relates to settlement. Do they try to pressure parties into settling? If so, what strategy do they use? Do they refer cases for mediation or separate settlement discussions with a magistrate judge? Do they suggest that they may rule a certain way on dispositive motions that are pending or on critical pieces of evidence to send a message to one party that their case may not

---

6. *See* Fed. R. Civ. P. 16(a) ("In any action, the court may order the attorneys and any unrepresented parties to appear for one or more pretrial conferences for such purposes as:…(5) facilitating settlement.").

be as strong as they think? Some judges may even suggest a dollar amount at which they think the case should settle.

Use this information about the judge's approach as a catalyst to get what you want. If your opponent has an unrealistic view of their case, encourage settlement discussions with the judge. Think about what arrows you have in your quiver to push settlement. Do you have a number that you want to put out there? If you think your number is fair and reasonable, letting the judge know that your client is interested in settling but the opponent is the one who seems to overestimate their chances of success may result in the judge applying pressure on the opponent. Or are you going to use this as an opportunity to lock into a process, such as mediation? The judge may welcome suggested solutions about a process for getting to resolution.

The judge can also help when your client is the one being unrealistic. If you have a client who, despite your counsel, seems extremely confident in their chances of success and refuses to consider reasonable settlement offers, bring them to a conference with the judge. Many judges who plan to raise the issue of settlement will require a client representative to attend. It can be helpful for the client to hear an assessment of their chances directly from the judge. As discussed in more detail later in this chapter, mediation can also be an effective tool to persuade a recalcitrant client that settlement is the best option.

Some judges do not like to pressure the parties to settle early in the litigation. In that case, parties may first hear about settlement at the pretrial conference or while preparing a pretrial order in advance of the conference.

FRCP 16 also indicates that settlement may be the subject of a pretrial conference:

> (C) Attendance and Matters for Consideration at a Pretrial Conference.
>
> **(2)** *Matters for Consideration.* At any pretrial conference, the court may consider and take appropriate action on the following matters:
>
> **(I)** settling the case and using special procedures to assist in resolving the dispute when authorized by statute or local rule;

Implicit in FRCP 16(c)(2)(i)'s "special procedures" are mediation, arbitration, or resolving the case by agreeing which facts are, and which facts are not, in dispute, bifurcating damages from the liability litigation, or agreeing to a bench trial or a trial before a magistrate as opposed to a judge.

11.4.1 *Mediation: Process and Preparation*

Mediation contemplates opposing parties' different and, sometimes, unrealistic expectations for case resolution. The mediator creates processes that function both as "client reality checks" and mechanisms to bridge differences between opposing parties. A neutral third party, the mediator, assists opposing parties to communicate with each other in hopes of reaching a resolution that is agreeable to everyone. Mediators can help generate options that will move the parties towards settlement by focusing on the interests of each party. This can be particularly helpful in cases where communication between the parties has broken down.

The mediator can be a tool for an attorney in the bargaining process with their own client. As previously stated, if the attorney properly communicates with the client throughout the litigation process, the mediator can reassure the client that the ultimate deal is reasoned and a good one weighed against litigation risk. If your client maintains an unrealistic view of the litigation despite your counseling, the mediator can help persuade the client that the ultimate deal is a good one by providing an independent third-party perspective that is consistent with the counseling you have offered.

At the end of the day, settlement is about making the best deal, under the best circumstances, even if painful or imperfect. Parties are willing to compromise but may want assurances they are not capitulating or being "pushovers." Mediators can provide such positive reinforcement, which may be particularly important for corporate clients with various levels of leadership or ownership that must be assuaged.

Don't expect to convince anyone at a mediation to settle or increase their authority more than 20 percent. The convincing must be done long before you get there, through depositions, assembling the best experts, a good strong demand letter, laying everything out. We have no good information that we withhold. We want them to have everything we have that helps. Pick a very high number to get their reserves up. Always ask for at least twice what you really want so they can bully you down.

—Philip Freidin, Founding Partner, Freidin Brown PA

Courts may require private mediators or appoint a magistrate to conduct the proceeding. If the court does not appoint a magistrate to preside over settlement discussions, the parties must find their own mediator. How does one find an appropriate mediator? Existing resources to help attorneys track down mediators include organizations such as the American Arbitration Association (AAA)[7] or the JAMS Foundation[8] (mediator directories). Another approach is to review settled cases involving similar issues and try to identify the mediator used. Search for colleagues, such as retired judges or esteemed members of the bar, who may have transitioned into the field of mediation. Keep a contact list of mediators you have worked with or that others recommend. Approach other members at bar functions or solicit

---

7. Am. Arb. Ass'n., https://www.adr.org.
8. JAMS, https://www.jamsadr.com/jamsfoundation.

feedback on legal listservs to continually expand the list. For cases involving technical or scientific issues, it is important to pursue mediators with relevant background
or training so they may quickly grasp the technical side of the case.

Consider these factors when compiling your list of mediators:

- Does the mediator have expertise or familiarity with the area of law governing the dispute?

- Does the mediator have the gravitas to be convincing?

- Is the mediator someone your client will listen to?

- Is the mediator respected by or known to the court?

- Has the mediator resolved similar disputes?

- Is the mediator available during the needed time frame?

- Is the mediator within your price range?

- Is the mediator potentially biased?

- What are the mediator's rules?

The mediator's level of expertise in the pertinent subject matter or legal area is
important. You want them to "get it" and reduce the case to the key issues. A lack of
knowledge also lessens the mediator's persuasiveness. A client may dismiss a mediator's guidance if the client feels the mediator does not understand the issues or
their business. In addition, mediators with a steep learning curve are costly because
they bill for each hour of preparation and for each day of mediation. If they have
to familiarize themselves with an industry or basic foundational information on
the area of law, this could substantially increase the cost of the mediation. Cost
consideration is not a minor issue. Depending on the mediator, costs range anywhere from hundreds to thousands of dollars a day. Mediators not only charge for
their time but may also bill for an assistant's time. Gather this information upfront.
Fortunately, parties generally split mediation costs on a 50/50 basis. Payment of
outstanding mediation costs can be a sweetener added into any settlement.

The matter of "gravitas" is critical. If your opponent is a large corporation, you
want a mediator whose opinion will be respected by the corporation's general counsel and other decision makers including the CEO and the board of directors.

Mediators who know, or are known to the court, can offer feedback regarding
how specific judges may rule on critical and unresolved matters. Retired judges
serving as mediators often have a good perspective. Advice from an individual with
gravitas may factor into resolution where a party is looking for insight on how their
case will play out if settlement is not reached. For example, a corporate general

counsel not only wants the best deal for their client, but also the support to rec-ommend settlement to the company and perhaps even its board of directors. The ability to say, "we went to mediation with a retired judge who sat on the bench with the very judge who presides over the case and who opined that this case would not be dismissed on a summary judgment," may be an important factor in settlement.

When assessing potential mediators, ferret out possible biases. Does a mediator have a reputation for favoring plaintiffs or defendants, or individuals over corporate parties? Does a mediator have close ties to your opponent's law firm, such as being a former partner there? As noted previously, it can be important to find a mediator with knowledge of the particular industry or area of law at issue in the litigation. However, be sure to understand where this familiarity comes from. For instance, in a labor and employment case, if the mediator has lots of experience with labor law, that might be perceived as a plus. If that experience comes from being part of labor unions and representing labor unions, however, that experience actually might be detrimental to a corporate client. Even though the mediator would have a clear understanding of the issues in the case, they may be predisposed to credit the employee's version of the case.

Generally, opposing counsel exchange names of mediators they would find acceptable. The parties might exchange lists of three or five mediators, with the hope that there would be at least one name common to both lists. Ultimately you will be most successful agreeing on a mediator if you identify someone who can objectively assess the case without any preconceived biases for either side.

Once selected, the mediator will require the parties to sign an agreement stating expectations for the parties, addressing matters of confidentiality or privilege, and specifying mediation costs. The mediator will also request each party consult their calendar and reserve a date and time for mediation. Scheduling a mediation typ-ically requires either a half day or full day to meet with the mediator. Parties can either attend a live, in-person meeting or, to save time and costs, participate using a videoconference platform, such as Zoom.

The mediator should require the presence of the principals, the respective cli-ents, or those with authority to resolve the case. When decisionmakers are not at the negotiating table, mediations are an expensive and unproductive process. Of course, for the experienced mediator, the decisionmaker's presence is a requisite stressed from the onset.

Be aware of confidentiality rules when utilizing a mediator. While several states have enacted the Uniform Mediation Act, which establishes a confidentiality privi-lege for mediation communications to the extent agreed upon by the parties, it may be preempted by local statutes governing mediation which vary by jurisdiction.[9]

---

9. UNIF. MEDIATION ACT, § 8 (UNIF. L. COMM'N 2003) ("…mediation communications are confidential to the extent agreed by the parties or provided by other law or rule of [the] State.").

Depending on the circumstances, you may want the mediator to suggest that parties execute broader confidentiality restraints than those accorded by state statute and court rules.

The mediation process varies depending on the size and type of case. The following is a basic outline of what one can expect:

- The mediator may ask for pre-mediation submissions including, a position statement, a copy of the complaint and answer, and any opinions issued by the court.

- The mediator may require—as part of the pre-mediation submission—the parties provide written answers to specific questions about the case.

- The mediator will discuss which submissions are for the mediator's eyes only and which may be shared with opposing counsel.

- The mediator may ask the parties to sign confidentiality agreements.

- The mediation may begin with each party making short statements outlining their position and the opportunity to respond to the other party's position.

- The mediator will put the parties in different rooms and begin the process of shuttle diplomacy.

- Plaintiffs should expect the mediator to begin the process with you making a demand that the mediator relays to the other side.

- As the mediator relays counteroffers and counter-demands, expect discussion surrounding the specific portions of the case including facts, theories, and points of law.

Attorneys and clients generally enter mediation having evaluated their litigation risk and have a vision of their case's value. This means:

- They have a value for the case if certain claims are eliminated, motions in limine are granted, or if the evidence does not pan out as the client anticipated at the beginning of the case.

- They have a notion for what the defendant will pay to avoid trial.

- They have a sense of what the case expenses will be if the matter is not resolved.

Make this evaluation as objective as possible. Notwithstanding an effort to make a candid assessment of litigation risk, parties—particularly clients—enter mediation expecting results that may or may not be realistic. Clients often ask, "doesn't the mediator see how bad the other side is?" The mediation process injects the parties a dose of reality. Although they assess each side's obstacles in their litigation journey, the mediator's job is bringing the parties to a resolution, not deciding which party is "right." Mediators view settlement as a success. Noted Miami trial lawyer Phillip Freidin calls it "losing the dream." Parties often enter into mediation with "dream" expectations; mediation readjusts their settlement objectives. This realignment may occur several times during a mediation. Veterans of mediation or settlement negotiations maintain that a good settlement is one where each side walks away unhappy: each party compromising on what they really wanted and neither party completely happy with the result.

Mediation preparation begins with client preparation. Clients should know what to expect. Explain that experienced mediators engage in shuttle diplomacy, directing parties to consider their own litigation risk. In simple terms, mediators separate the parties into different rooms and "beat up on them," challenging their assumptions, pointing out bad facts and bad law, and highlighting law or facts detrimental to their case. Clients may become emotional during this process. Warn your client that negative remarks may be made about their case. Advise your client that mediation is an opportunity to preview case problems so they may later assess and address the detriments.

While clients and/or principals are required to attend mediation, the role they play at the mediation can vary. They can be listeners and make settlement decisions or take a more active role, discussing facts and areas of damage. Moreover, a client may remain silent during any face-to-face meetings with the opposing party but may share information in "sidebar" discussions with the mediator. There is value in this approach because the mediator is able to receive sufficient information to bargain with the opposition, but the opposition will not have an opportunity to preview a cross-examination. Discuss these strategies in advance and come to an agreement with your client about what level of participation they will have.

When preparing the pre-mediation submission, think carefully about the most important pieces of information and law that you want the mediator to know. Rarely will you include all the evidence that you would present in a trial; instead, determine your key themes and the evidence or law that supports them. Highlight key weaknesses in the opponent's case, particularly if the opponent does not view them as problematic. The mediator's assessment of this information will confirm either your opinion or that of your opponent. Keep in mind, however, that in conveying information potentially driving settlement, you are also telegraphing case strategy that will help the opposition prepare for trial if the matter is not resolved. For these reasons, there may be value in holding back information and relaying it to the mediator in person, perhaps even in confidence. Some mediators request a submission that is only for them and will not be shared with the opposing party. Think carefully about what information you will include in each submission. If there is no mediator-only submission, consider waiting until the mediation to privately share certain information with the mediator rather than including it in your submission.

If the mediator allows for opening statements, think of the presentation as both an opening and closing for a trial. The same skills governing advocacy are important in mediation. Keep it simple and factual. Timelines, witness lists, and key documents are good tools for bringing a mediator up to speed. Lay out the facts, discuss the legal theories, and apply the law. When using PowerPoint presentations in your opening statement, incorporate and highlight key exhibits as well as quotes from important case opinions, language from statutes, or jury instructions that will guide fact analysis. As with all advocacy, facts and law are more convincing than conclusions and hyperbole. Be methodical and professional. Your opponent will be judging your case, your client, and your ability to make the case. As noted above, this will serve as a preview of your case to your opponent; the impact can be positive (inducing settlement) or negative (helping your opponent prepare for trial if the mediation is unsuccessful).

If the parties agree to a settlement at mediation, it will be "papered." This involves a number of steps. First, do not leave the mediation without a basic outline of their agreement. This will help to avoid a situation where there was not a true "meeting of the minds." Mediators can draft a summary of what the parties assented to or create a checklist of agreed-upon terms. The final agreement will follow. The mediator may stay involved, tweaking the language relevant to the agreement's non-monetary terms. Typical non-monetary terms including the following:

- The covered conduct: By settling the case, the plaintiff receives some form of relief in exchange for a release. What is the release's scope? Is the defendant seeking a release from conduct not alleged in the complaint? Is the plaintiff concerned about such an expansive release to conclude the deal?

- Who is bound: Does the agreement release only the defendant, or does it also release agents, successors, and assigns? If there is an injunction or requirement that specific steps be taken per the settlement agreement, who ensures compliance?

- When will the agreement be effective? If there is money to be paid, when will it be paid and to what account? Is payment by check or wire transfer? If the agreement requires specific actions like rehiring an employee, what is the timing for those events?

- Will the agreement be confidential? Can tax preparers view the confidential agreement if necessary? What are the consequences if there is a breach of confidentiality? Is the settlement void or will there be liquidated damages set forth in the agreement?

- How will the parties characterize their relationship going forward? Will there be a statement or press release? Are the parties restricted in what they can say about each other? Will there be an agreed-upon statement that the parties use to respond to media inquiries about the case?

- <u>What law will govern interpretation of the settlement agreement?</u> This is an issue often left until the last minute when parties have not fully researched the impact of the decision.

- <u>How will the agreement be enforced?</u> Will there be another mediation, or perhaps an arbitration, or will the parties be forced to seek relief in the courts?

If the parties do not agree to a full settlement, there are still options short of taking the entire case to trial. Sometimes you can take issues out of the litigation. The parties may agree on certain facts or what specifically is in dispute about a certain claim. While this is often limited to non-dispositive issues, it can still be helpful to narrow the remaining issues for trial.

Another option is to engage in mediation arbitration, which is basically an agreement by the parties that whatever claims are not resolved by mediation will be resolved by binding arbitration. This may put additional pressure on the parties to settle at mediation because arbitration may be able to occur earlier than a scheduled trial and because, in addition to the costs of preparing a case for and presenting a case at arbitration, the parties also have to pay the arbitrator, which can considerably increase the cost.

11.4.2 *Settling Without a Mediator*

Mediators destigmatize the initial outreach for settlement, which may be perceived as a sign of weakness and complicate the process. However, parties often settle cases without a mediator. In fact, for cases that are simple disputes, resolution is a matter of reasoned business judgment. These situations occur when the case itself may be easy, but the litigation costs and fees are disproportionate to the value of the case.

Consider a case where the plaintiff purchased a defective generator and sues the defendant for $10,000, the generator's purchase price. Perhaps all the plaintiff wants is a replacement generator and only filed the lawsuit because the defendant refused to respond to emails proposing this resolution.

Once filed, plaintiff's counsel might tell defense counsel, "we will spend a lot of money on a case where a defective product just needs a replacement . . . . any thoughts about how to make this go away?"

The above scenario presents a narrative suitable for resolution without a third party. Suppose, instead, a more complicated matter such as a wrongful discharge employment case. Plaintiff's counsel must pick the right moment, either when the complaint is sustained on a motion to dismiss or after the first deposition, to ask defense counsel, "where are we going with this case?" This simple phraseology does not indicate desperation and sets the tone for opposing counsel to discuss solutions that make business sense for both sides.

When trying to settle a case, avoid hyperbole, threats, or polarizing language. Any potential settlement requires that opposing counsel talk, share information, and not feel uncomfortable. In the discussion between or among opposing counsel, one can refer to damaging documents or testimony, but couch such comments in the least offensive way. For example, you might tell the opposing counsel, "this has nothing to do with you of course, but John Smith's testimony on pages 44–47 will support our statute of limitations defense."

Oftentimes, attorneys in settlement negotiations support their positions by making comments like, "the jury will hate your client" or "the judge is never going to allow that expert witness to testify." By nature, lawyers have their own views about what decisionmakers will opt to do. Stating how the evidence will be viewed—in conclusory terms—is often not convincing. Instead of saying "the jury will hate your client," it may be better to say, "the jury will hear that your client has a fraud conviction." Rather than "the judge is never going to allow that witness to testify," simply point opposing counsel to an opinion authored by the judge supporting said conclusion.

Parties in mediation need to trust the mediator. If there is no mediator, opposing counsel are serving in that role and it falls upon them to trust each other. Lawyers will undoubtedly begin discussions with a level of distrust. However, as negotiations progress, they begin to trust each other, and reach a settlement. Here is how the dynamic works:

> Plaintiff Counsel: We have exchanged proposals back and forth. Now, we can keep doing that or I can be candid and say that if you propose a settlement of $125,000, my client will give you a complete release.

> Defense Counsel: Can we get it done for $120,000?

> Plaintiff Counsel: I will recommend that to the client.

> Defense Counsel: Let's talk tomorrow.

The above example illustrates the types of exchanges in which experienced counsel routinely engage. Settlements occur when business judgments and discussions, rather than emotionally charged arguments, are made. This exchange could easily be two businessmen negotiating a product's cost as opposed to opposing counsel trying to settle a lawsuit.

11.5   Other Settlement Approaches

11.5.1   *Bellwether Trials*

Specific case types might lend themselves to other creative settlement approaches. In multi-district litigation or other mass tort actions, the parties may decide to try some "bellwether" cases to help value the claims for settlement purposes or to answer causation or liability issues common to a group of claimants. Typically, the court selects a case or cases from a pool of cases that each side proposes. In order for this approach to be successful, the cases' facts generally should be typical and representative of other cases in the broader litigation. The outcome of these bellwether trials sets the stage for settlement negotiations.

11.5.2   *Summary Jury Trials*

Summary jury trials are increasingly being used in civil litigation in the United States as a tool to advance settlement negotiations. Summary jury trials take place after discovery has been substantially completed and pending motions are resolved. Each side offers abbreviated case presentations to a mock, six-member jury (drawn from a pool of real jurors), the party representatives, and a presiding judge or magistrate. The mock jury renders an advisory verdict. The rules of summary jury trials vary from state to state[10] and even from judge to judge, but generally, the evidence presented is extremely limited, with most trials taking place in a single day. This can make them an attractive option for cases where a trial on the merits may take substantial time. After the verdict, the parties and their attorneys may have the opportunity to discuss the verdict with the jurors. Then they are required to, once again, try to settle the case before proceeding to trial.

Summary jury trials can be an effective tool in driving settlement because hearing a judgment rendered by an "actual" jury will result in one party or the other becoming more amenable to settlement. This can be particularly applicable in cases where one of the parties has an unrealistic view of their case. Another potential benefit is that it can provide a party with their "day in court," if that is a motivating factor preventing settlement.

A major criticism of summary jury trials is that the result is often one party wins, and the other party loses. This can actually make the winning party even less likely

---

10. For example, in Texas summary jury trials are defined by the statutes: "(a) A summary jury trial is a forum for early case evaluation and development of realistic settlement negotiations. (b) Each party and counsel for the party present the position of the party before a panel of jurors. (c) The number of jurors on the panel is six unless the parties agree otherwise. (d) The panel may issue an advisory opinion regarding the liability or damages of the parties or both. (e) The advisory opinion is not binding on the parties." TEX. CIV. PRAC. & REMEDIES CODE § 154.026. In Michigan, summary jury trials are binding on the parties. *See* Authorization of Pilot Project, 2015 Mich. LEXIS 586 (2015) (extended to March 25, 2020).

to settle and force the parties further away from settlement. Therefore, be selective in the cases for which you use this approach. For example, a summary jury trial may provide little to no value in a case that is likely to hinge on issues of law because the jury is the arbiter of facts and not law.

11.5.3 *Early Neutral Evaluation*

Unlike summary jury trials, which take place well into the litigation process, early neutral evaluation (ENE) typically takes place soon after a case is filed. In ENE, the parties submit their case to a neutral evaluator, usually an attorney, through a confidential evaluation session. This can be written comments or an in-person meeting. The neutral evaluator considers each side's position and provides a balanced and unbiased evaluation of the case, including the likely outcome at trial. This evaluation is designed to help the parties form a more objective assessment of their positions and inspire the parties to explore settlement.

The primary benefit of ENE is that it occurs early in the process before the parties have incurred significant expenses. The main limitation of ENE is that the assessment is based on incomplete information. Sometimes the information provided in discovery can completely change the trajectory of a case. The neutral evaluator in ENE does not have the benefit of knowing all the facts, so the evaluation of the case is limited.

CHAPTER TWELVE

PUBLIC INTEREST AND LITIGATION: REPRESENTING THE LITTLE GUY

12.1 Introduction

Law students agonize over what employment prospects will be available upon graduation. Law school placement deans and admissions officers assuage their concerns, and make efforts to recruit new students, by pointing to post-graduation employment statistics.

The truth is that attorneys with litigation skills are always employed. The worst that can be said about their plight is a nonexistent client base. But again, in truth there are plenty of clients to be had. From landlord-tenant and wage-and-hour cases to discrimination cases, there is no shortage of people who need lawyers. And, with laptop computers, online research, electronic document storage, electronic filing, and even remote depositions and court hearings, there is a world of opportunity for solo practitioners, small firms, or those that want to represent the voiceless. More so than ever before, the public interest world is a boundless world of opportunity for lawyers; below are just some examples:

Issue	Type of Case
Race, gender, and national origin discrimination cases	Civil Rights
Age discrimination cases	Civil Rights
Religious discrimination cases	Civil Rights
Wage-and-hour cases	Employment
Wrongful termination of employment cases	Employment
Landlord tenant matters	Contracts and Torts
Immigration cases	Immigration
Consumer litigation	Contracts and Torts
Personal injury litigation	Tort
Constitutional torts	Civil Rights

(continued)

Issue	Type of Case
Prisoners' rights cases	Civil Rights
Whistleblower cases	Employment, Civil Rights, Products Liability, Contracts
Investor arbitrations	Fraud, Contract, Torts

There are more cases than attorneys to handle them. Some cases are too small for big law firms charging high hourly rates or for well-heeled plaintiff contingency firms thriving on high-dollar recovery cases. And some cases present conflicts of interest for big firms that might otherwise dabble in pro bono efforts.

For lawyers just starting out, the opportunities are vast. Seek out cases that no one will take, cases that would likely go without representation but for lawyers eager to get their feet wet. Myriad cases are absent a home and some of those cases may have a major impact on the rule of law. The history of civil litigation is replete with examples of precedent-setting cases taken on by less-experienced counsel—lawyers motivated by fear of failure and driven by the passion to make a difference. Plaintiff counsel in *Loving v. Virginia*,[1] the landmark case challenging a Virginia law prohibiting interracial marriages, were only in their 30s when they argued before the Supreme Court.

Some of these cases, especially those brought under statutes with fee and cost-shifting provisions, can be quite lucrative. Older civil rights statutes, such as the post–Civil War reconstruction statutes, contained fee-shifting provisions.[2] Fee-shifting provisions are found in many consequential statutes:

- Title VII of the Civil Rights Act of 1964 (covering employment discrimination)

- Fair Labor Standards Act (FLSA) (covering minimum wages and overtime)

- Federal Fair Housing Act (FHA)

- The post–Civil War Civil Rights Law 42 U.S.C. §§ 1981 and 1983

- Almost all federal environmental laws

- Age Discrimination in Employment Act (ADEA)

---

1. Loving v. Virginia, 388 U.S. 1 (1967).
2. *See* 42 U.S.C. § 1988 (providing potential attorney's fees for § 1981, 1982, 1983, 1985, and 1986).

- Americans with Disabilities Act (ADA)

- Equal Pay Act

- False Claims Act (FCA)

- Employee Retirement Income and Security Act (ERISA)

- Federal antitrust laws

Moreover, in many class action suits allowing recovery of damages, the "common fund doctrine" permits counsel to be paid out of the common fund created to compensate the class.[3] This means that attorneys who recover money in class actions can also recover their fees and costs. In many instances, they can recover a multiplier of their actual rate. Courts determine compensation by looking at the hours worked, a data point known as "lodestar," and the recovery or benefit for the class.

Even attorneys not litigating a statutory cause of action with a fee-shifting provision may enter into a common-law contingency fee agreement, compensating the attorney with a percentage of the recovery. This occurs in negligence, intentional tort, and breach of contract cases. Attorneys use contingency agreements in everything from medical malpractice cases to collections matters. Contingency agreements allow those with limited financial resources to have their day in court.

Finally, some clients and counsel prefer blended agreements where the attorney takes a lower hourly rate in exchange for a bonus based on recovery. The bonus is calculated as a percentage of the recovery, but at a lower percentage rate than if the case were litigated on a straight contingency.

If you choose to represent the voiceless in public interest litigation, understand the various compensation arrangements. Just because litigation is in the public interest, does not mean it is unprofitable; lawyers are entitled to compensation.

If you are uncomfortable plunging straight into courtroom litigation, consider the extensive list of matters subject to mandatory arbitration. Arbitration proceedings, even small proceedings, offer tremendous opportunities for newly minted members of the bar.[4] In arbitration, the evidentiary rules are more relaxed, the proceedings less formal, and ultimately less intimidating. The process favors the

---

3. *See, e.g.,* John Leubsdorf, *The Contingency Factor in Attorney Fee Awards,* 90 YALE L.J. 473, 476 (1981).
4. Bender v. A.G. Edwards & Sons, Inc., 971 F.2d 698, 699 (11th Cir. 1992) ("Since Gilmer v. Interstate/Johnson Lane Corp., it is clear that Title VII claims are subject to compulsory arbitration." (citation omitted)).

actual hearing of evidence by a factfinder as opposed to dismissal through the pre-trial process.[5] Although compulsory arbitration is not good for the American legal tradition, it does present opportunities for many lawyers.[6]

Contracts govern whether a case is subject to mandatory arbitration.[7] The types of agreements that may contain mandatory arbitration clauses include:

- Employment agreements

- Labor contracts

- Agreements for the sale of goods

- Agreements covering the purchase and sale of securities

- Agreements with banks and other financial institutions

Well-heeled companies often include compulsory arbitration clauses in a variety of contracts, from consumer agreements to employment agreements. They assume that these agreements deter experienced lawyers from taking minor cases or because these agreements compel adjudication in a private forum without the public scrutiny that can generate press coverage. The point is that large players enforce arbitration perhaps because they believe fewer people will be able to find

---

5. Martens v. Smith Barney, Inc., 181 F.R.D. 243, 252, 255-56 (S.D.N.Y. 1998) (holding that an employee cannot be "compelled to arbitrate claims they did not agree to arbitrate" and that Title VII claims can only be arbitrated in an arbitral forum that does not subvert the Title VII statutory scheme by meeting "certain standards of procedural fairness," not imposing "financial burdens on plaintiff access to the arbitral forum," and allowing "remedies central to the statutory scheme"). Relevant procedural fairness standards include forum neutrality, unbiased arbitrators, discovery, and relaxed evidentiary rules. *Id.* at 255. Examples of financial burdens include expensive filing fees and fee-shifting agreements requiring plaintiffs to pay a portion of the arbitrator's fee. *Id.* at 256. "Remedies central to Title VII's statutory scheme" refers to those remedies available if adjudicated in court: attorney fees, equitable remedies, and monetary damages. *Id.*
6. Arbitration agreements are successfully used in collective bargaining agreements to efficiently resolve workplace disputes. But those agreements are the result of arms-length bargaining. Unfortunately, arbitration clauses are bolted into a myriad of other contracts from employment agreements to credit card agreements. These disputes are resolved absent transparency and decisions or opinions with precedential value, elements that would be present if the cases were litigated in court. This means that many discrimination cases, for example, are resolved absent the transparency that is necessary to eradicate such practices.
7. *E.g.,* Am. Express Co. v. Italian Colors Rest., 570 U.S. 228, 233-39 (2013) (holding federal courts cannot invalidate a class action arbitration waiver where arbitration would cost plaintiffs more than potential recovery). Justice Scalia, writing for the majority, stated the text of the Federal Arbitration Act "reflects the overarching principle that arbitration is a matter of contract. And consistent with that text, courts must 'rigorously enforce' arbitration agreements according to their terms, including terms that 'specify with whom [the parties] choose to arbitrate their disputes, and 'the rules under which that arbitration will be conducted.'" *Id.* at 233 (emphasis omitted)(citations omitted).

---

counsel to take on such cases. This is why taking on arbitrations can be a public interest endeavor.

Even smaller arbitration cases present opportunities for a new lawyer. They can also be the foundation of business models for firms or groups of lawyers choosing to practice; for example, litigating employment arbitrations or arbitrations with securities brokers/dealers.

If you are conducting an arbitration required by contract, the contract may specify the process for arbitration or it may say "arbitrate pursuant to the rules of the American Arbitration Association." The Association's rules specify the process for moving a case to arbitration and securing an arbitrator.

Once selected, the arbitrator typically schedules a phone conference to discuss pretrial matters including discovery and hearing dates. Arbitrations are entirely about actual adjudications. Motions to dismiss, motions for summary judgment, and *Daubert* motions are rare. Because there is no jury, the rules restricting evidence are not as stringent.

While an arbitrator's decisions can be challenged in court, the grounds to overturn those decisions are often limited. Lawyers pursuing arbitrations generally have the mind-set: "If I can secure quick and cheap relief, great. But I am not going to make adjudicating the matter at hand a lifetime occupation."

12.2 Professionalism and the Public Interest Lawyer

Those involved in public interest law believe in the cause for which they litigate. They observe housing discrimination and seek out cases to eradicate the blight of discrimination. They observe polluters and want to represent aggrieved clients by bringing cases that result in a healthier environment. Public interest lawyers are passionate about their causes. That passion energizes these lawyers and drives their accomplishment. And yet, even a public interest lawyer, should not let passion or emotion cloud their objectivity or cause them to personalize the litigation. Personalizing the litigation can manifest in painting the opposition's advocate as the enemy, spewing hyperbole that obscures the facts, or taking ethical shortcuts because you believe your goal is honorable.

When George Barrett, one of the nation's great civil rights attorneys and a Nashville legend, died in 2014, the Nashville power elite and civil rights community emerged to pay their respects. An obituary for Barrett noted the following:

> Perhaps the elegance of George Barrett was his ability to advocate for change while maintaining the deepest respect from those who enforced the status quo. He once told the *Vanderbilt Alumni Magazine* "either you can be a lawyer or a demonstrator, but you can't do both.

> I was glad to manage protest routes and get Vietnam demonstrators out of jail, but I won't march with you. I think a lawyer has to decide."[8]

These lines, this simple message, are important words of wisdom for those holding themselves out as public interest lawyers.

Barrett understood that public interest work often involves challenging the status quo. Cases should focus on the controversy over an unfair or immoral practice, not on the lawyers defending the practice. The advocate for change must convince custodians of the status quo that change is in order. The advocate for change must shed any perception that they are radical. Expanding a dispute to levy attacks on defense counsel is contrary to the primary objective: change. Barrett appreciated all these elements and taught others their value.

Public interest advocates become an easy mark for criticism because their cases raise questions of ethics, integrity, and morality. Some defense lawyers detract attention from the substance of the case by focusing attention on plaintiff counsel's conduct. In public interest matters, professionalism is not solely about who can deliver a dynamic message that resonates, it is also about safeguarding that messenger from personal attacks that can derail a case.

The American Bar Association's Model Rules of Professional Conduct 2.1 delineates a lawyer's role as an advisor:

> In representing a client, a lawyer shall exercise independent professional judgment and render candid advice. In rendering advice, a lawyer may refer not only to law but to other considerations such as moral, economic, social and political factors, that may be relevant to the client's situation.[9]

Client education and control are also essential. Your client may feel they are a "victim of the system," or have been unjustly dealt with by government or the rule of law. Perhaps this is true. Yet, the client must appreciate your position as a member of the bar and an officer of the court. For you to do your job, you cannot let the client compromise your obligations to the tribunal and your commitment to professionalism. "Professionalism" allows even parties diametrically opposed to each other to cooperate and resolve a dispute. In the public interest realm, the attorney-client relationship only works if the client respects their lawyer's obligations and understands that according such respect is a critical part of achieving their goals in a court of law. What does this mean in real terms? The client allows counsel to grant extensions, if appropriate, and does not pressure counsel to file motions designed solely to harass. When documents are tendered in discovery on a confidential basis,

---

8. Reuben Guttman, *Profiles in Justice: A Distinguished Lawyer and Friend*, The Glob. Legal Post (Sept. 11, 2014), https://m.globallegalpost.com/blogs/commentary/profiles-in-justice-a-distinguished-lawyer-and-friend-31240996/.
9. Model Rules of Pro. Conduct r. 2.1 (Am. Bar Ass'n 2020).

the client honors confidentiality orders. For court appearances, the client is clothed in a manner that respects the solemnity of the proceeding. During depositions or trial testimony, the client is respectful of opposing counsel and the court. For the most part, these are not genuine concerns. Yet it is important that counsel fully grasps client objectives and proclivities, properly educates the client, and possibly refrains from engagement if the client does not respect the counsel's obligations.

12.3   Representing the Little Guy

You file your complaint and then receive a letter from a big firm advising you to drop the lawsuit or they will move to dismiss and seek sanctions. The firm offers to discuss the matter by phone; you accept the invitation. They say you are a young lawyer with a bright future and your client's sexual harassment allegation besmirches the reputation of a pillar of the local community. They claim to like you and do not want to cause you harm, "but will do what is necessary" because they too have ethical obligations. After the call ends, you stare at the ceiling wondering if everything you have worked for is going down the drain.

The key is not to panic and not to give in; the key is to think like a lawyer. Tell your opposition that you appreciate the phone call but request they send the relevant evidence and legal authority supporting their position. They may respond with, "we are not going to do your homework for you." Such a response often indicates their position might be mere posture, an effort to scare off a young lawyer. However, if they send you the cases and relevant evidence, study the materials. Discuss them with your client. Maybe even consult others in the bar or a former law school professor. If the materials demonstrate your client's case is meritless, discuss this with your client because the case may need to be voluntarily dismissed. On the other hand, after reading the materials you may discover that the cited cases do not support the defendant's propositions. If the defendant's position is without merit, then threats to move for dismissal and seek sanctions is also without merit.

One can avoid this situation by sending the opposition a demand letter in advance of filing the suit. Lay out the claims and the facts and give them an opportunity to meet with you and your client to convince you the case is without merit. Demand letters used in this way can be a useful part of due diligence. You might even learn something that will strengthen your case by allowing you to anticipate a defense and plead accordingly.

After filing the suit, a motion to dismiss arrives. The motion's final page indicates it is the work of multiple lawyers. You are concerned that you will be outmaneuvered, out-staffed, and are not up to the task. Take a deep breath. You care about this client and their case. You have passion and even some fear of failure or fear of inadequacy. These are positive things. The fear and passion make you work harder. Read the motion, make a binder of the cited cases, and begin to distinguish them. As previously mentioned, you may find that some cases do not support the propositions for which they were presented. Move through this process methodically. Every glitch you discover in your opponent's argument will bolster your confidence. Bear in mind that this process is not easy; your opposition will make arguments requiring contemplation. The process will keep you up at night. It is a process akin to solving a puzzle; it is painstaking; it is simply what the practice of law is all about.

Until his passing, George Spiegel was one of the nation's leading public interest energy lawyers. Spiegel went to Amherst College and graduated from Harvard Law School. A brilliant lawyer who could have had his pick of virtually any large corporate firm, Spiegel instead dedicated his career to public interest law. Spiegel often spoke about representing the "little guy" as he called it. Spiegel told young lawyers, engaged in their first battle against big law, "File a piece of paper; any paper. The other guy will come back with a big brief that cites lots of cases. Just read the cases, distinguish them, often they won't apply; you will find that the other side has done the research work for you."[10] Spiegel's comments, although a bit tongue and cheek, are apt. His advice is that lawyers need not be intimidated by a large pleading, particularly one that cites a lot of cases.

Similarly, imagine you arrive in court and your opponent appears with several lawyers. Once your case is called, the opposition exchanges pleasantries with the judge. The judge may respond by saying, "Mr. Smith, it is nice to see you in my court room again." You feel diminished or sense that justice will not be dealt even-handedly. There is no question that justice is imperfect. Judges are human, they have predilections and biases. Your job is to remain professional, listen carefully, identify the judge's concerns, and respond accordingly. If it is your first time in front of the judge, remember you are building rapport, building credibility. Do not be intimidated by opposing counsel and the minions seated at the defense table or packed in the gallery. Only one attorney speaks at a time. Neither firm size nor views from high-rise office windows impact the quality of words spoken in court.

Inoculate yourself against the above situation by learning as much as possible about your judge and your opposition beforehand. You may discover opposing

---

10. Author Reuben Guttman had the privilege of collaborating on many cases with the late George Spiegel. Spiegel, a founding partner of Spiegel & McDiarmid, spent his forty-plus years as a lawyer pursuing public interest causes. He litigated consumer rights and anti-competition actions, challenging private utility companies' efforts to deny public utility systems access to local marketplaces. Spiegel argued throughout the federal court system. Most notably, in 1971, the United States Supreme Court ruled in favor of Spiegel's client, a municipal utilities department (The Court reversed and remanded a Fifth Circuit decision relating to a private utility imposing standby charges. The Court determined the Court of Appeals overstepped its role because in the Federal Power Act, Congress delegated judgment of cost, compensation, and reimbursement issues to the Federal Power Commission). *See* Obituary, *George Spiegel Dies at 78*, Wash. Post, https://www.washingtonpost.com/archive/local/1997/10/26/george-spiegel-dies-at-78/9642b8a8-af02-46ae-85fe-d658a461d580/ (last visited October 8, 2020); *See also* Gainesville Utils. Dep't. v. Fla. Power Corp., 402 U.S. 515 (1971).

counsel appears frequently in front of the judge or that opposing counsel is a well-known, respected member of the bar. This information can guide how to present yourself in court. Yet, whatever your opponent's reputation, competence, or esteem, the case is not about the lawyers. The case is about the facts and the law; it is about a dispute between clients. Remember that you are an advocate for one side and not personally a party to the dispute.

12.4 Matching the Big Guy's Resources

Your document requests result in the production of hundreds of thousands of documents. You fret because you lack the ability to review each of these documents before depositions begin, let alone before the trial. Relax. You do not need to read every document. Your goal is to collect the evidence necessary to prove your case and rebut the defenses. Even if you were to review 100,000 documents, how many would actually be used as deposition or trial exhibits? How many documents would never be introduced at trial because they would be cumulative or confuse the jurors? This does not mean reviewing all documents has no value. It simply means that if you are low on resources, do what is feasible under the circumstances. Remember to keep your client informed, be clear about what you can and cannot do.

As discovery progresses, you strongly believe your opponent is withholding documents. Perhaps you learn, through a document custodian's deposition, that the defendant did not search all the relevant files for documents. This is bothersome because such conduct is fundamentally wrong, if not unethical. However, do you actually need the documents to prove your case, or do you just want to engage in battle because it is fashionable or something you think every lawyer should do? If you appear in court and the judge asks, "why are these documents so essential to your case," what will you say? The point is to pick your battles. Your opposition wants to delay the case and run up the transaction costs; motions practice is a defendant's friend. File strategic motions that will make a difference in the case. Use the judge's valuable time for the disputes that count. The judge will appreciate you doing so.

Dick Harpootlian, a well-known South Carolina trial lawyer with a national reputation, says it best: "As a plaintiff's lawyer, your goal in litigation is to get from A to Z without touching the twenty-four letters in between." By that, Harpootlian means you need to do what is necessary to get to trial and win while avoiding endeavors that do not help the cause.[11]

---

11. Author Reuben Guttman had the privilege of co-counseling cases with Dick Harpootlian, a practitioner and South Carolina State Senator. Harpootlian has a quick wit as evidenced by this online profile containing tips for trial lawyers. *See* Reuben Guttman, *Profiles in Justice: A 'One of a Kind' Trial Lawyer*, THE GLOB. LEGAL POST (Nov. 11, 2013), https://www.globallegalpost.com/blogs/commentary/profiles-in-justice-a-one-of-a-kind-trial-lawyer-837156/.

When you get a case requiring extra resources or expertise, there is nothing wrong with bringing in counsel to assist you. Assembling coalitions to litigate cases is the new normal. When taking the coalition route, have an agreement up front specifying how fees and costs will be divided. The client must agree to the participation of additional counsel and the client must be apprised of how counsel will be compensated. Doing so is an ethical obligation.[12]

If assembling a team of attorneys for a case, apportion work responsibilities and create systems so that documents can be shared and analyzed. Consider that even if the case is not a large class action, or a high damage personal injury matter, you can still solicit help from other members of the bar willing to joint venture all or parts of a case.

12.5 "I Am Not Up to the Task"

You just passed the bar. A client comes to you saying that they lost their job because of their race. Their company was bought out and the buyer is eliminating Hispanic employees. At first, the new supervisor ignored the client. The supervisor then began assigning onerous tasks, piling on more work. Unable to meet these demands, your client was disciplined and ultimately terminated from employment. Now your client has no job, no money to pay a more experienced lawyer an hourly rate, and the firms that work on contingency think his case is too small. You are the lawyer of last resort. Unfortunately, you lack the necessary experience for the case. You have never been to court on your own, never drafted a complaint, or taken a deposition. You feel an ethical obligation to tell the client you cannot accept the case. On the other hand, you are the client's only option and you could use the work, as well as the experience.

Great legal rulings, those that markedly altered the rule of law, result from lawyers placed in this exact position. Make certain the client fully understands your background; do not misrepresent your qualifications or skills. Be honest with the client. If they decide to hire you with full knowledge of your background, you will begin the relationship on honest footing.

12.6 Publicity and the Public Interest Lawyer

Litigation is a catalyst for change, not just in the courtroom but also in the court of public opinion. It can spur legislation and compel officials to regulate or enforce existing law. Our cars, food, housing, and clothing are safer because litigation exposed improprieties and propelled government action.

---

12. Model Rules of Pro. Conduct r. 1.1 cmt. 6-7, 1.2, 1.5(e) (Am. Bar Ass'n 2020).

The press is a consideration in litigation; it is especially a consideration in public interest litigation, which is often targeted to change practices that are both accepted and pervasive. The ABA Model Rule of Professional Conduct 3.6 specifically addresses trial publicity. Rather than paraphrase it, below is the rule quoted in totality:

Rule 3.6: Trial Publicity

(a) A lawyer who is participating or has participated in the investigation or litigation of a matter shall not make an extrajudicial statement that the lawyer knows or reasonably should know will be disseminated by means of public communication and will have a substantial likelihood of materially prejudicing an adjudicative proceeding in the matter.

(b) Notwithstanding paragraph (a), a lawyer may state:

(1) the claim, offense or defense involved and, except when prohibited by law, the identity of the persons involved;

(2) information contained in a public record;

(3) that an investigation of a matter is in progress;

(4) the scheduling or result of any step-in litigation;

(5) a request for assistance in obtaining evidence and information necessary thereto;

(6) a warning of danger concerning the behavior of a person involved, when there is reason to believe that there exists the likelihood of substantial harm to an individual or to the public interest; and

(7) in a criminal case, in addition to subparagraphs (1) through (6):

(i) the identity, residence, occupation and family status of the accused;

(ii) if the accused has not been apprehended, information necessary to aid in apprehension of that person;

(iii) the fact, time and place of arrest; and

(iv) the identity of investigating and arresting officers or agencies and the length of the investigation.

(c) Notwithstanding paragraph (a), a lawyer may make a statement that a reasonable lawyer would believe is required to protect a client from the substantial undue prejudicial effect of recent publicity not initiated by the lawyer or the lawyer's client. A statement made pursuant to this paragraph shall be limited to such information as is necessary to mitigate the recent adverse publicity.

(d) No lawyer associated in a firm or government agency with a lawyer subject to paragraph (a) shall make a statement prohibited by paragraph (a).[13]

The principal messages are: 1) when talking to the press, stick to the public record; and 2) be most cautious when communications are immediately prior to jury selection, especially when the jurors are impaneled and not sequestered. What does "sticking to the public record" mean? It means limiting your comments to the four corners of filed court documents and quoting from them.

Of course, sometimes publicity is truly necessary for the case. With class actions, a press interview can communicate to class members information about a filed complaint or events that transpired during a hearing. Communication with the press is also a means of informing the community-at-large of their existing rights.

The ultimate arbiter of whether press comments run astray is the presiding judge. Investigate whether the judge has established their own rules governing press coverage. Talk to those familiar with the judge, get opinions on how the court may react to press coverage. Consider the ethical rules and the rules imposed by a particular judge. But remember that talking to the press—within the confines of the rules—is what lawyers do; the rule of law is built on an open court system, oversight by a free press, and scrutiny by an informed citizenry.

12.7 Whistleblowers and the Public Interest

A discussion of public interest law is not complete without mentioning "whistleblowers." Perhaps the best way to describe whistleblowers is to say that they are individuals who challenge the status quo.

Whistleblowers are important to our rule of law and enforcing compliance with existing statutes and regulations. Today, whistleblowers enjoy statutory and common-law protections.[14] Many state and federal statutes, which present substantive obligations and proscriptions, provide separate rights of action for those who blow the whistle on noncompliance. Aside from the statutory protections, many states carved out bodies of common-law protections for individuals taking affirmative steps to report those violating laws and recognized standards.[15] And there is

---

13. MODEL RULES OF PRO. CONDUCT r. 3.6 (AM. BAR ASS'N 2020).

14. *See generally,* WHISTLEBLOWER LS., www.whistleblowerlaws.com (last visited October 8, 2020) (providing a broad discussion of whistleblower protections, frequently asked questions, and the types of fraud for which whistleblowers may file suit).

15. Pierce v. Ortho Pharm. Corp., 417 A.2d 505, 512 (1980) ("We hold that an employee has a cause of action for wrongful discharge when the discharge is contrary to a clear mandate of public policy. The sources of public policy include legislation; administrative rules, regulations or decisions; and judicial decisions. In certain instances, a professional code of ethics may contain an expression of public policy."); House v. Carter-Wallace, Inc., 232 N.J. Super. 42, 48-49 (App. Div. 1989) ("[N]o New Jersey case has recognized a claim for wrongful discharge based solely upon an

a body of law that provides redress, under a theory of constructive discharge, for employees who leave a workplace because they do not want to partake in wrongdoing or because harassment has made the environment untenable.[16] Below is a list of some of those statutes:

Whistleblower Retaliation Statutes

Statute	Legal Citation	Statute of Limitations	Intake Agency or Judicial Forum
Age Discrimination in Employment Act (ADEA)	29 U.S.C. § 623(d)	180–300 days	EEOC/state employment discrimination agency; private cause of action in federal court
Americans with Disabilities Act (ADA)	42 U.S.C. § 12203(a) 29 C.F.R. Part 1640	180–300 days	EEOC/state employment discrimination agency; private cause of action in federal court
Civil Rights Act of 1964 ("Title VII")	42 U.S.C. § 2000e-3(a)	180–300 days	EEOC/state employment discrimination agency; private cause of action in federal court
Clayton Act (antitrust)	15 U.S.C. § 2087	180 days	DOL
Clean Air Act	42 U.S.C. § 7622 29 C.F.R. Part 24	30 days	DOL/OSHA
Comprehensive Environmental Response, Compensation and Liability Act ("Super Fund")	42 U.S.C. § 9610 29 C.F.R. Part 24	30 days	DOL/OSHA

(*continued*)

---

employee's internal complaints about a corporate decision, where the employee has failed to bring the alleged violation of public policy to any governmental or other outside authority or to take other effective action in opposition to the policy . . . a mere difference of professional opinion between an employee and those with decision making power in a corporation is not a sufficient basis to establish a wrongful discharge." (citations omitted)).

16. *See, e.g.*, National Labor Relations Act § 8(a)(3), 29 U.S.C. § 158(a)(4); Civil Rights Act of 1964 § 704(a), 42 U.S.C. § 2000(e)-3(a); Age Discrimination in Employment Act of 1967 § 4(d), 29 U.S.C. § 623(d); Americans with Disabilities Act of 1990 § 503(a), 42 U.S.C. § 12203(a); Employee Retirement Income Security Act of 1974 § 510, 29 U.S.C. § 1140.

Statute	Legal Citation	Statute of Limitations	Intake Agency or Judicial Forum
Employee Retirement Income Security Act (ERISA)	29 U.S.C. § 1132(a), 1140	Earlier of 6 years after (a) the date of the last action which constituted a part of the breach or violation or (b) in the case of an omission, the latest date on which the fiduciary duty could have cured the breach or violation or 3 years after the earliest date on which the plaintiff had actual knowledge of the breach or violation	Federal District Court
Energy Reorganization Act	42 U.S.C. § 5851 29 C.F.R. Part 24	180 days	DOL/OSHA
Fair Labor Standards Act (wage & hour, child labor, minimum wage, overtime)	29 U.S.C. § 215(a)(3) 29 C.F.R. Part 783	2 years; 3 years if willful violation	DOL, Federal District Court, or state court
False Claims Act	31 U.S.C. § 3730(h)	See most applicable state law for statute of limitations	Federal District Court
Family and Medical Leave Act ["FMLA"]	29 U.S.C. § 2615	2 years; 3 years if willful violation	DOL, Federal District Court, or state court
National Labor Relations Act	29 U.S.C. § 158(a)(4)	6 months	NLRB
Occupational Safety and Health Act	29 U.S.C. § 660(c) 29 C.F.R. Part 1977 ("Part 11(c)")	30 days	DOL/OSHA-no private cause of action
Safe Drinking Water Act	42 U.S.C. § 300j-9	30 days	DOL/OSHA
Sarbanes Oxley Act	18 U.S.C. § 1514A	180 days	DOL/OSHA
Solid Waste Disposal Act	42 U.S.C. § 6971 29 C.F.R. Part 24	30 days	DOL/OSHA
Toxic Substances Control Act	15 U.S.C. § 2622 29 C.F.R. Part 24	30 days	DOL/OSHA

In addition to the above, False Claims Acts at both the federal and state levels provide whistleblowers with bounties if they bring litigation that recovers money for the government. False Claims Act cases can offer exciting opportunities for public interest work in coordination with state and federal civil prosecutors.

12.8   The Myriad of Opportunities

There is—in sum—few things more exciting than bringing cases that have broad sweeping impact. This is what public interest litigation is all about. It is quintessentially American; it is our legal tradition. It is what lawyers do and it is how the court system makes laws that have broad sweeping impact with, at times, more immediacy than the legislative process.

APPENDIX A: *SOMETIMES SIMPLE MAKES SENSE* QUOTATIONS

Sometimes Simple Makes Sense

Source	Reference	Case
Dr. Seuss, *The Lorax* (1971)	"We trust the United States Forest Service to 'speak for the trees, for the trees have no tongues.' Dr. Seuss, *The Lorax* (1971). A thorough review of the record leads to the necessary conclusion that the Forest Service abdicated its responsibility to preserve national forest resources."	*Cowpasture River Pres. Ass'n v. Forest Serv.*, 911 F.3d 150, 183 (4th Cir. 2018) (Thacker, J.).
Dr. Seuss, *Horton Hatches the Egg* (1940)	"Ironically, the defendants' prior motion for summary judgment was, in many ways, merely a motion for reconsideration of this court's post-*Markman* hearing claim construction order. Thus, this present motion for reconsideration is essentially the defendants' effort to take a third bite out of the *Markman* apple. The court finds that the defendants' present motion requires little analysis and the court's view of it can best be summed up with the slightly modified words of Dr. Seuss: "I meant what I said, and I said what I meant. [The court's] faithful [to its prior decisions] one hundred percent."	*Hydro-Thermal Corp. v. Pro Sonix, LLC*, No. 07-C-918, 2010 U.S. Dist. LEXIS 34729, 2010 WL 1441239, at *1 (E.D. Wis. Apr. 8, 2010) (Goodstein, J.) (citations omitted).
Dr. Seuss, *Horton Hatches the Egg* (1940)	"By referring Plaintiff to the *Bridgewater* opinion, and ordering that Plaintiff, in its response to the motion to compel, fully meet its burden to support its claims of privilege, I went out of my way to remind Plaintiff that it would not be enough for Plaintiff to simply *claim* privilege, but that it would have to prove that each email met all the elements of each privilege claimed."[1]	*Campero USA Corp. v. ADS Foodservice, LLC*, 916 F. Supp. 2d 1284, 1288, 1288 n.2 (S.D. Fla. 2012) (McAliley, J.).
Dr. Seuss, *Horton Hatches the Egg* (1940)	"There is no principled way to reconcile these conflicts without assuming that in enacting the Whistleblower Law, the Oregon Legislature—unlike Dr. Seuss's Horton the Elephant[2]—did not say what it meant and did not mean what it said."	*Draper v. Astoria Sch. Dist.* No. 1C, 995 F. Supp. 1122, 1140, 1140 n.13 (D. Or. 1998) (Stewart, J.)

(continued)

Source	Reference	Case
Dr. Seuss, *Horton Hatches the Egg* (1940)	"Where the Legislature 'meant what [it] said and said what [it] meant,' we must be true to the statute's intent. See Dr. Seuss, *Horton Hatches the Egg* passim (1940)."	*Burlington Elec. Dep't v. Vermont Dep't of Taxes*, 576 A.2d 450, 452–53 (Vt. 1990) (Allen, C.J.).
Dr. Seuss, *Horton Hatches the Egg* (1940)	"[W]e believe that the supreme court, like Dr. Seuss's Horton the elephant, meant what it said and said what it meant—rule 1.442(c) applies in all cases where proposals for settlement are authorized by Florida law, without an exception for claims against litigants relating to property they own as tenants by the entirety."	*Graham v. Peter K. Yeskel 1996 Irrevocable Tr.*, 928 So. 2d 371, 373 (Fla. Dist. Ct. App. 2006) (Gross, J.) (footnote omitted).
Dr. Seuss, *Horton Hears a Who* (1954)	"I respectfully dissent. A person is a person is a person ..., and an illegal sale is an illegal sale is an illegal sale ..."	*Koehnen v. Dufuor*, 590 N.W.2d 107, 113 (Minn. 1999) (Page, J., dissenting).
Dr. Seuss, *Yertle the Turtle and Other Stories* (1950)	"'Silence,' the King of the Turtles barked back, 'I'm king, and you're only a turtle named Mack.' Those in authority do not readily accept public criticism by their subordinates. They are particularly sensitive when employee censure brings their governance into public disrepute. Hence, employee comment about a superior is likely to lead to consideration of drastic retaliation, including instant dismissal."	*Davis v. Williams*, 598 F.2d 916, 917–18 (5th Cir. 1979) (Rubin, J.) (footnote omitted).
Dr. Seuss, *Yertle the Turtle and Other Stories* (1950)	"Dr. Seuss' rhyming narrative about Yertle, The Turtle, concludes: 'And the turtles, of course... All the turtles are free [a]s turtles and, maybe, all creatures should be.' We do not extend the doctrine of protected activity so far as to suggest that all public employees are free to say and do whatever they choose. Boundaries for conduct may be set by regulations that provide ascertainable standards and are sufficiently limited so they do not chill the exercise of first amendment rights."	*Davis v. Williams*, 598 F.2d 916, 922 n.8 (5th Cir. 1979) (Rubin, J.) (citation omitted).

(continued)

Source	Reference	Case
Dr. Seuss, *The Sneetches and Other Stories* 26 (1961)	"We agree that the bankruptcy court construed section 525(a) too narrowly. We are therefore faced with a conflict between Bankruptcy Code sections 525(a) and 365 reminiscent of Dr. Seuss's intractable North Going and South–Going Zax. And it happened that both of them came to a place. Where they bumped. There they stood. Foot to foot. Face to face."	*In re Stoltz*, 315 F.3d 80, 84 (2d Cir. 2002) (Parker, J.).
Dr. Seuss, *The 500 Hats of Bartholomew Cubbins* (1938)	"Once we reversed the original judgment incorporating the first jury's verdict and our mandate issued, the first verdict became null and void in its entirety. The district court could no more reinstate the damages portion of the first verdict than it could substitute the second jury's award with a larger sum pulled out of a magically appearing hat. See Dr. Seuss, *The 500 Hats of Bartholomew Cubbins* (1938)."	*Wheeler v. John Deere Co.*, 935 F.2d 1090, 1096 (10th Cir. 1991) (Baldock, J.).
Dr. Seuss, *The 500 Hats of Bartholomew Cubbins* (1938)	"Moreover, in AS 09.17.020(f)—a provision that appears shortly before subsection .020(j)—the tort reform act already imposes an express cap on punitive damages; to read subsection (j) as placing a second cap on top of the first cap thus carries us into a Seussian realm.[3]"	*Evans ex rel. Kutch v. State*, 56 P.3d 1046, 1077, 1077 n.44 (Alaska 2002) (Bryner, J., dissenting) (footnote omitted).
Dr. Seuss, *The 500 Hats of Bartholomew Cubbins* (1938)	"This system allowed the broker to factor into the transaction how much would be paid to the broker by the lender for placing the loan. Unless you are Bartholomew Cubbins,[4] wearing more than one hat will surely lead to trouble."	*Raiolo v. B.A.C Home Loans*, No. 024567/09, 2010 N.Y. Misc. LEXIS 5760, 2010 WL 4868144, at *3, *3 n.6 (City Civ. Ct. Nov. 8, 2010) (Straniere, J.).
Shel Silverstein, *The Giving Tree* (1964)	"Much like the lock in *Wolverton*, a reasonable factfinder could conclude that the trees had inherent value."[5]	*Frango v. Commonwealth*, 782 S.E.2d 175, 180, 180 n.5 (Va. Ct. App. 2016) (Russell, J.).

(continued)

Source	Reference	Case
Shel Silverstein, "Sarah Cynthia Sylvia Stout Would Not Take the Garbage Out" from *Where the Sidewalk Ends: The Poems & Drawings of Shel Silverstein* (1974)	"Like Shel Silverstein's proverbial Sarah Cynthia Sylvia Stout, the petitioner in this case, Robert S. Cunningham, would not take the garbage out. So, reminiscent of Sarah's daddy who, in the famous poem would scream and shout, Cunningham's homeowner's association did the modern equivalent. It instituted litigation."	Fountain Valley Chateau Blanc Homeowner's Assn. v. Dep't of Veterans Affs., 79 Cal. Rptr. 2d 248, 250 (Ct. App. 1998) (Sills, J.).
Shel Silverstein, "Helping" from *Where the Sidewalk Ends: The Poems & Drawings of Shel Silverstein* (1974)	"Berninger is a would-be edge provider working on new technology that he believes could provide much enhanced telephone service—but *only* if he could be assured that 'latency, jitter, and packet loss in the transmission of a communication will [not] threaten voice quality and destroy the value proposition of a high-definition service.' He is ready to pay for the assurance of high-quality service, and asserts that the Commission's ban on paid prioritization will obstruct successful commercial development of his innovation. Berninger appears to be exactly the sort of small, innovative edge provider that the Commission claims its Order is designed to assist. In the words of Shel Silverstein's children's song, 'Some kind of help is the kind of help we all can do without.'"	*U.S. Telecom Ass'n v. Fed. Commc'ns Comm'n*, 825 F.3d 674, 757 (D.C. Cir. 2016) (Williams, J., concurring in part and dissenting in part) (citation omitted).
Robert Louis Stevenson, *The Master of Ballantrae* (1889)	"The crux of plaintiff's claim, as noted earlier in this decision, was his belief that his long-standing and substantial investment of time and energy somehow ripened into at least a life estate, if not outright title by adverse possession, or that he owned the Cottage because of his desire to preserve it for the enjoyment of future generations. This brings to mind a quotation from Robert Louis Stevenson, 'Let any man speak long enough, he will get believers.'"	*Delahant v. Stevenson Soc. of Am., Inc.*, No. 000455–08, 2008 N.Y. Misc. LEXIS 5162, 2008 WL 4096449, at *6 (Essex Cnty. Ct. Sept. 5, 2008) (Richards, J.) (citation omitted).

(continued)

Source	Reference	Case
Robert Louis Stevenson, "A Letter to a Young Gentleman Who Proposes to Embrace the Career of Art," in *The Lantern Bearers and Other Essays* (Treglown Ed. 1988)	"I concur separately in the judgment of the majority because I believe the opinion and the syllabus should be confined to the issue presented in the case—the test for determining the civil liability of children (and their parents) arising from their conduct while at play—and because I would hold that minors engaged in recreational or unorganized sports activities are liable only for their intentional acts. The prospect of judging the conduct of children while at casual play on a scale of negligence should cause us to ask ourselves what has changed since Robert Louis Stevenson observed in 1888 that '[y]outh is wholly experimental.'"	*Marchetti v. Kalish,* 559 N.E.2d 699, 704 (Ohio 1990) (Moyer, C.J., concurring).
Robert Louis Stevenson, *Strange Case of Dr. Jekyll and Mr. Hyde* (1886)	"The record before this Court reads like the *Strange Case of Dr Jekyll and Mr Hyde*. Defendant, young Jaier (or Mr. Sharpe), stands before this Court at age seventeen, facing charges including Attempted Robbery First Degree, Possession of a Firearm During the Commission of a Felony ('PFDCF'), Carrying a Concealed Deadly Weapon and Possession, Purchase, Own or Control of a Firearm (Handgun) by a Prohibited Juvenile." "As stated, the underlying charges relate to an attempted robbery. However, the State portrays Defendant as a violent and dangerous individual. It asks the Court to consider that, although not charged, Mr. Sharpe has been a person of interest in violent and deadly gang-related feuds that have plagued the City of Wilmington. In wild *Jekyll/Hyde* contrast, representatives from YRS—as well as the only expert that testified in this case—present a different picture of Jaier.	*State v. Sharpe,* No. 1904007802, 2020 Del. Super. LEXIS 19, 2020 WL 119647, at *1–2 (Jan. 10, 2020) (Medinilla, J.) (footnotes omitted).

(continued)

Source	Reference	Case
	He has excelled while in custody. Commended for achieving highest 'Goldshirt' status for behavior while detained, not only do they recommend his return to the Family Court, they stress that Jaier can be rehabilitated through higher Level IV or V treatment and programming through YRS that he has yet to receive. Imploring the Court is also Jaier's strongest advocate—his Mother—a mother of six who holds down two jobs and clearly loves her son. Maternally, she further suggests that because she is an 'activist with the kids,' her willingness to allow people to flow in and out of her home has caused her son to find himself caught in the cross hairs of Wilmington Police investigations. In this *Jekyll/Hyde* quandary, the defense argues that to place Defendant in an adult facility would undoubtedly lead to the demise of young promising Jaier, while the State counters that failure to keep him monitored in this Court serves only to strengthen the more violent and dangerous Mr. Sharpe as he transitions into adulthood."	
Robert Louis Stevenson, *Kidnapped* (1886)	"This, and similar testimony given by the defendant, is the proof of a trade or sale, as distinguished from a letting, to which the trial court adverts in its memorandum; but, frankly, we are not at all impressed with its reliability. It reminds us of a conversation from Robert Louis Stevenson's 'Kidnapped,' between Allan Breck and David Balfour: 'Can you swear that you don't know him, Allan?' asked David, referring to the Appin murderer. 'Not yet,' replied Allan; 'but I've a grand memory for forgetting, David.'"	*Berghuis v. Schultz*, 137 N.W. 201, 204 (Minn. 1912) (Brown, J.).

(continued)

Source	Reference	Case
Robert Louis Stevenson, *Treasure Island* (1883)	"This case is a question of title or right to possession of certain lost treasure, between the finder thereof and the owner of the land upon which it was found. Lost and found articles are always interesting from the human standpoint. The greatest Teacher ever to live on this earth illustrated his teachings with the parables of the lost pearl, the lost sheep, the lost coin, and the lost boy. The discovery of the key to the location of lost or hidden treasure has been of fascinating interest to author and reader alike. When Robert Louis Stevenson wrote his immortal 'Treasure Island,' he enveloped it with the most appealing and alluring quality of treasure trove. 'Fifteen men on a dead man's chest, Yo-ho-ho and a bottle of rum,' brings again to our minds Captain Bill and a certain 'seafaring man with one leg.' Buried gold has been the theme of writers and has given to their writings an entrancing interest, whether the reader be the growing boy or the sedate and settled old man."	*Groover v. Tippins*, 179 S.E. 634, 634–35 (Ga. Ct. App. 1935) (Guerry, J.).
Robert Louis Stevenson, *Virginibus Puerisque* (1881)	"Robert Louis Stevenson's description of marriage as 'a field of battle'[6] aptly describes the contractual 'marriage' between the parties in this case, who have twice appeared to be headed for 'divorce,' only to reconcile at the last moment. They have returned to this court now for the third time, and it appears that this time the breakup is final."	*U.S. Network Servs., Inc. v. Frontier Commc'ns of W., Inc.*, 115 F. Supp. 2d 353, 354, 354 n.1 (W.D.N.Y. 2000) (Larimer, J.).
Robert Louis Stevenson, *Prince Otto* (1885)	"Some strand of our own misdoing is involved in every quarrel."	*Borders v. Rippey*, 184 F. Supp. 402, 404 (N.D. Tex. 1960) (Davidson, J.).
Bob Dylan, "Subterranean Homesick Blues" (1965)	"[C]ourts have often eschewed the need for expert testimony when matters are within common knowledge and experience."[7]	*L.A. Unified Sch. Dist. v. Superior Ct.*, 175 Cal. Rptr. 3d 90, 107, 107 n.16 (Ct. App. 2014) (Kussman, J.).

(continued)

Source	Reference	Case
Bob Dylan, "It Ain't Me, Babe" (1964)	"Rather than provide any documentation to support his contention such as showing that his vehicles were elsewhere at those times and places, claimant offers the Bob Dylan 'It Ain't Me, Babe' plea."	*Kinkopf v. Triborough Bridge & Tunnel Auth.*, 764 N.Y.S.2d 549, 558 (City Civ. Ct. 2003) (Straniere, J.).
Bob Dylan, "The Times They Are A-Changin'" (1964)	"The Civil Rights Act of 1964 was the culmination of decades of debate and political maneuvering over various civil rights proposals. In the end, it took three momentous events to finally propel the bill to the top of the agenda of Congress and the Administration. The first was the August 1963 march on Washington during which Dr. Martin Luther King, Jr., gave his famous 'I have a dream' speech. The second was the September 1963 bombing of a black church in Birmingham, Alabama, in which four little girls were killed. The third was the assassination of President Kennedy, whose support for the bill carried even more weight in Congress and with the public after his untimely death. It was in this time that Bob Dylan warned, 'Come Senators, Congressmen, please heed the call. Don't stand in the doorway, don't block up the hall.'"	*Erickson v. Bartell Drug Co.*, 141 F. Supp. 2d 1266, 1269 n.4 (W.D. Wash. 2001) (Lasnik, J.).
Bob Dylan, "Like a Rolling Stone" (1965)	"The closest [the plaintiffs] have come to asserting a concrete interest in the grizzly are expressions of members' desires to observe wildlife generally. . . . [A]t one point…the plaintiffs asserted that there was 'no evidence that grizzly bear habitat exists in the Decision Area.' Plaintiffs cannot claim an injury to their grizzly-viewing interests if they do not think there are grizzlies in the area to begin with. 'If you've got nothing, you've got nothing to lose.'"	*Mountain States Legal Found. v. Glickman*, 92 F.3d 1228, 1236–37 (D.C. Cir. 1996) (Williams, J.) (citations omitted).
Bob Dylan, "Gotta Serve Somebody" (1979)	"So, for the reasons outlined above, the Undersigned is not going to adopt Procaps' rule, which would, in effect, require me to maneuver through a thorny thicket of legal arguments to reach a destination which facially appears inconsistent with well-established (and frequently quoted) Eleventh Circuit law."[8]	*Procaps S.A. v. Patheon Inc.*, 141 F. Supp. 3d 1246, 1286, 1286 n.27 (S.D. Fla. 2015) (Goodman, J.).

(continued)

Source	Reference	Case
Bob Dylan, "The Times They Are A-Changin'" (1964)	"The Court's implication, *ante*, at 2629, that where electronic privacy is concerned we should decide less than we otherwise would (that is, less than the principle of law necessary to resolve the case and guide private action)—or that we should hedge our bets by concocting case-specific standards or issuing opaque opinions—is in my view indefensible. The-times-they-are-a-changin' is a feeble excuse for disregard of duty."	Justice Antonin Scalia, who was ever the literalist, skimmed the title off an early Dylan song without attribution, mocking the majority's ducking an issue by rationalizing about the rapidly changing nature of technology: *City of Ontario v. Quon*, 560 U.S. 746, 768 (2010) (Scalia, J., concurring).
The *Shawshank Redemption* (1994)	"If Corrections refused to release him, he could challenge that failure, likely (and ironically) in a habeas proceeding. He could not decline the award, thereby staying in prison, even if he wanted to do so."[9]	*Bowling v. White*, 480 S.W.3d 911, 917, 917 n.6 (Ky. 2015) (Noble, J.).
The *Shawshank Redemption* (1994)	"These various definitions of "escape" consider only the prisoner's departure from custody, not the responses of the prison officials. Indeed, to suggest that an inmate escapes when prison officials learn he is missing simply defies our understanding of an escape as well as common sense."[10]	*United States v. Novak*, 284 F.3d 986, 989, 989 n.4 (9th Cir. 2002) (Trott, J.).
The *Shawshank Redemption* (1994)	"Benji Stout is no Edmond Dantès, who famously escaped from prison by cutting open a body bag with an improvised knife and hiding in the bag, to be flung unknowingly into the sea by gravediggers. Nor is he Andy Dufresne, who slowly chiseled his way to freedom and destroyed a sewer pipe in effectuating his escape. *See The* Shawshank Redemption (Castle Rock Entertainment 1994). I would have no quarrel with the conclusion that either of their escapes would be a 'crime of violence' for our purposes today."	*United States v. Stout*, 706 F.3d 704, 710 (6th Cir. 2013) (Donald, J., dissenting) (citation omitted).

(continued)

Source	Reference	Case
The Shawshank Redemption (1994)	"It is not uncommon at the end of a story for the protagonist to ride off into the sunset or drive off into the distance after the main conflict of the story has been resolved. To name just a few, the following films include such endings: Little Miss Sunshine (2006), Good Will Hunting (1997), The Shawshank Redemption (1994), Indiana Jones and the Last Crusade (1989), and The Graduate (1967)."	*Kightlinger v. White,* No. B210802, 2009 Cal. App. Unpub. LEXIS 9345, 2009 WL 4022193, at *6 (Nov. 23, 2009) (Chaney, J.).
The Shawshank Redemption (1994)	"Plaintiff depicts his years in the Clements Unit as a cross between the *Shawshank Redemption* and Franz Kafka's *The Castle.* He is sexually abused. He reports the abuse to a deaf and inimical prison bureaucracy. Prison bureaucrats retaliate with ever-increasing abuse that they either directly cause or allow to take place. Plaintiff becomes so desperate to escape the 'psychological and emotional torture' that he repeatedly mutilates himself and escapes from a prison van. He petitions the federal courts for relief only to be shut down and forced to shuttle from prison to prison eighteen times in a furtive search of safety. Scarred, scared, and adrift in existential crisis, he is driven to petition the Court for an order of euthanasia."	*Kidd v. Dir. of Fed. Bureau of Prisons,* No. 2:19-CV-113-Z, 2020 U.S. Dist. LEXIS 26488, 2020 WL 759298, at *4 (N.D. Tex. Feb. 14, 2020) (Kacsmaryk, J.).
The Shawshank Redemption (1994)	"In closing argument, defense counsel described defendant as a man 'on the brink' after his release from prison, likely suffering from paranoia and delusions, not knowing where he would get his next meal or sleep at night. 'He found his world collapsing in upon him, and ... did the only thing ... he could think of to bring order and a semblance of control back in his life.	*People v. Bordelon,* 77 Cal. Rptr. 3d 14, 21 (Cal. Ct. App. 2008) (Marchiano, J.).

(continued)

National Institute for Trial Advocacy

Source	Reference	Case
	He got himself arrested so that he could go back behind those prison walls....' Counsel concluded his argument with a reference to the inmate in the movie 'The Shawshank Redemption' who could not cope with life outside of prison after his release and hanged himself."	

1. "The words of Horton the Elephant come to mind: 'I meant what I said, and I said what I meant. An elephant's faithful one-hundred percent!'"

2. "I meant what I said and I said what I meant... An elephant's faithful One Hundred per cent!"

3. "See DR. SEUSS, THE 500 HATS OF BARTHOLOMEW CUBBINS."

4. "Bartholomew Cubbins is the lead character in the Dr. Seuss story, 'The 500 Hats of Bartholomew Cubbins.'"

5. "'Although individuals may value trees differently, it is indisputable that people enjoy trees for a multitude of reasons. Trees provide shade, habitats for animals, and convert carbon dioxide into oxygen. Some people simply enjoy looking at trees. Trees and their wood are used for many purposes. The beauty and uses of trees have inspired works of literature.' *See e.g.,* Joyce Kilmer, "Trees," (1913) *reprinted in Trees and Other Poems* 19 (George H. Doran Co. 1914) (extolling the beauty and virtues of trees); Shel Silverstein, *The Giving Tree* (Harper & Row 1964) (cataloguing the many uses of a tree and its products)."

6. "'Marriage is like life in this—that it is a field of battle, and not a bed of roses.' *Virginibus Puerisque,* I, ch. 1 (1881)."

7. "Both federal and California state courts have explained the essence of this rule by citing singer-songwriter Bob Dylan: 'You don't need a weatherman to know which way the wind blows.'"

8. "Iconic singer/songwriter Bob Dylan musically discussed this type of situation in his 'Gotta Serve Somebody' song . . . . The following lyrics, which place an individual's status in the universe in context, could easily apply to the legal universe—i.e., a federal magistrate judge handling a case by consent who is asked to disregard language which the binding appellate court has often used and which has not been expressly reversed: 'You may be a state trooper, you might be a young Turk / You may be the head of some big TV network / You may be rich or poor, you may be blind or lame / You may be living in another country under another name / But you're gonna have to serve somebody, yes you are.'"

9. "Though at first it seems absurd to think that a prisoner would want to stay in prison, it is not difficult to imagine reasons why a long-serving inmate would want exactly that. Long-serving prisoners may become 'institutionalized,' in the sense of becoming comfortable only in an institutional setting, and they often have limited opportunities and face substantial challenges upon release that can be so overwhelming as to make continued incarceration a preferred outcome. Though the most prominent examples may be fictional, *see The Shawshank Redemption* (Castle Rock Entertainment 1994) (portraying two characters, Brooks and Red, who contemplate breaking parole to be sent back to prison 'where things make sense' and they 'won't have to be afraid all the time'), there have been real-life instances."

10. "For example, Andy Dufresne escaped from Shawshank Prison when, just after 'lights out,' he disappeared into a tunnel hidden behind a poster of lusty Raquel Welch. That prison officials did not discover Andy's absence until the next morning, by which time he was well on his way to Zihuatenejo, did not change the fact that he had escaped the previous evening. The Shawshank Redemption (1994)."

APPENDIX B: SAMPLE REQUEST FOR PRODUCTION

UNITED STATES DISTRICT COURT
FOR THE DISTRICT OF X

Plaintiff A
 	
    Plaintiffs,
 	
    v.
 	
Defendant X
 	
    Defendants.

Civil Action: 12-34567-X

PLAINTIFF'S FIFTH SET OF
REQUESTS FOR PRODUCTION TO DEFENDANTS

Plaintiff, by and through her undersigned counsel and pursuant to Rules 26 and 34 of the Federal Rules of Civil Procedure, hereby requests that Defendants ("Defendants," or "you") respond to the following requests for production within thirty (30) days after service.

INSTRUCTIONS
The following instructions shall apply to the document requests contained herein.

1. Except as provided below, you should produce the original of each document described below or, if the original is not in your custody, a copy thereof, and, in any event, all non-identical copies which differ from the original or from the other copies produced for any reason, including, but not limited to, the making of notes thereon.

2. Any document in its native format should include any and all of the document's associated meta-data (embedded digital data), embedded

attachments, hyperlinks and any and all other files or other digital objects (such as attachments and header data in the case of email or related usage logs from a file management system) or links (such as addresses), associated to that document.

3. Documents should be produced in standard load files in ".dat" or ".csv" form. Standard metadata fields in the respective load files should include fields such as, but not limited to, "Begdoc, Enddoc, Begatt, Endatt, Family Range, To, From, Cc, Bcc, Subject, Author, Date Sent, Date Received, Date Modified, Company, Application Type, MD5Hash, Custodian, Page Count, Header, Original File Name." A document link should also be provided with all native files in the respective ".dat" load file.

4. Image load files should be in "opt" or "lfp" format. Images should be provided as single page "tiffs" or "PDFs," with extracted text (OCR) on the document level as a text file.

5. These requests relate to all documents that are in your possession, custody or control or in the possession, custody or control of your predecessors, successors, parents, subsidiaries, divisions, or affiliates, or any of your respective directors, officers, managing agents, employees, attorneys, accountants, or other representatives.

6. If production of a document is withheld pursuant to a claim of privilege, as to each such withheld document state the following information:

a. The privilege claimed;

b. A precise statement of the facts upon which said claim of privilege is based;

c. The following information describing each purportedly privileged document: (i) its nature, e.g., agreement, letter, memorandum etc.; (ii) the date it was prepared; (iii) the date it bears; (iv) the date it was sent; (v) the date it was received; (vi) the identity of the person who prepared it; (vii) the identity of the person who sent it; (viii) the identity of each person to whom it was sent or to whom it was intended to be sent, including all addressees that received copies and all recipients of copies; (ix) a statement as to whom each identified person represented or purported to represent at all relevant times; and

d.   A precise description of the place where each copy of that document is kept, including the title and description of the file in which said document is found and the digital location of such file, including the exact file name, file path, and network address.

7. Whenever a document is not produced in full or is produced in redacted form, so indicate on the document and state with particularity the reason or reasons it is not being produced in full and describe to the best of your knowledge, information and belief, and with as much particularity as possible, those portions of the document that are not being produced.

8. If a document responsive to these requests was at any time in your possession, custody or control, but now is no longer available for production, state the following information as to each such document:

a.   Whether the document is missing or lost;

b.   Whether it has been destroyed;

c.   Whether the document has been transferred or delivered to another person or entity and, if so, at whose request and to whom it was transferred;

d.   Whether the document has been disposed of otherwise; and

3.   A precise statement of the circumstances surrounding the disposition of the document and the date of the document's disposition.

DEFINITIONS

Unless a specific definition is provided below, the words and phrases contained in this subpoena should be given either their ordinary, dictionary, common sense definition. Objections on account of vagueness should specifically explain why you believe the request is vague and should state your understanding of the information being sought along with a response consistent with your understanding. Additionally, the following definitions shall apply:

1. As used in these requests, "person" shall include natural persons, proprietorships, corporations, public corporations, municipal corporations, state governments, local governments, governmental agencies, political subdivisions, partnerships, groups, associations or other business or public organizations.

2. To "identify" a document means to state the date of the document, its author, each person to whom the document or any copy thereof was sent, and every person having custody of the document or a copy thereof. Where the name or identity of a natural person is requested, please state the individual's full name, home and business addresses, home and business telephone numbers, and email address(es). Where the name or identity of an organization is requested, please state the organization's full name, business address and business telephone number.

3. The term "and" shall include the term "or."

4. The term "or" shall include the term "and."

5. The terms "relating to," "with respect to," and "refer to" shall mean embodying, containing, comprising, indicating, concerning, referring, identifying, describing, discussing, involving, evidencing, or otherwise pertaining to.

6. Unless specifically stated to the contrary, all words and phrases utilized here shall be given their ordinary, dictionary, and common-sense definitions. Additionally, unless another meaning is obvious from the context, the terms used here shall have the same meaning as they have in the Complaint in this action.

7. "Communications" means the transmittal of oral or written information, facts, or ideas, including, without limitation, communications in the form of any discussion, conversation, inquiry, negotiation, agreement, understanding, meeting, telephone conversation, letter, correspondence, note, memorandum, e-mail, text message, instant message, telegram, advertisement, or other form of exchange of words, whether oral or written.

8. "Documents" or "document" shall have the broadest meaning permitted under Rules 26 and 34 of the Federal Rules of Civil Procedure